D0459592

The Videomaker Guide to Video Production
Fourth Edition

The Videomaker Guide to Video Production
Fourth Edition

From the Editors of Videomaker Magazine

Introduction by Matt York, Publisher/Editor

Preface by John Burkhart, Editor in Chief

Editorial Staff
Jennifer O'Rourke—Managing Editor
Mark Montgomery—Technical Editor
Charles Fulton—Associate Editor

AMSTERDAM • BOSTON • HEIDELBERG • LONDON • NEW YORK • OXFORD
PARIS • SAN DIEGO • SAN FRANCISCO • SINGAPORE • SYDNEY • TOKYO
Focal Press is an imprint of Elsevier

Acquisitions Editors: Elinor Actipis, Cara Anderson
Publishing Services Manager: George Morrison
Project Manager: Kathryn Liston
Assistant Editor: Robin Weston
Marketing Managers: Marcel Koppes, Becky Pease

Focal Press is an imprint of Elsevier
30 Corporate Drive, Suite 400, Burlington, MA 01803, USA
Linacre House, Jordan Hill, Oxford OX2 8DP, UK

 Recognizing the importance of preserving what has been written, Elsevier prints
its books on acid-free paper whenever possible.

Library of Congress Cataloging-in-Publication Data
Application submitted

British Library Cataloguing-in-Publication Data
A catalogue record for this book is available from the British Library.

ISBN: 978-0-240-80968-7

For information on all Focal Press publications
visit our website at www.books.elsevier.com

07 08 09 10 11 12   10 9 8 7 6 5 4 3 2 1

Printed in the United States of America

This book is dedicated to Thomas Jefferson for his commitment to pluralism, diversity and community. He would be happy to see readers of this book exercising freedom of the electronic press.

Civil liberty functions today in a changing technological context. For five hundred years a struggle was fought, and in a few countries won, for the right of people to speak and print freely, unlicensed, uncensored and uncontrolled. But new technologies of electronic communication may now relegate old and freed media such as pamphlets, platforms and periodicals to a corner of the public forum. Electronic modes of communication that enjoy lesser rights are moving to center stage.

Ithiel de Sola Pool
Technologies of Freedom
(Harvard University Press, 1983)

Contents

Preface

There has never been a better time to be an independent video producer.

The once formidable barriers to video production have been falling one by one, and for the last 20 years, Videomaker Magazine has been chronicling that fall, and doing our best to hasten it.

The first barrier was the cost of the equipment. Million-dollar edit suites and camcorders costing over $100,000 used to rule the television landscape. Now you can get much better images and polished productions from a $1,000 consumer camcorder and a laptop.

The second barrier was training. Because of the expense of the equipment, access used to be limited to a technical elite, and an apprenticeship was the only way to learn the trade. However, as prices fell, the demand for knowledge on production and editing techniques began to grow. That's where Videomaker Magazine came in, and by extension, the book you're holding in your hands now.

The third barrier, I'm excited to say, is in the middle of falling right now. That barrier is distribution. For a long time you could create a compelling video program, but getting it out in front of a sizeable audience was a frustrating and difficult process, ruled by the soul-crushing broadcast distribution system. Now, however, with recent advances in the speed of the Internet and the rise of video sharing sites, you have an equal platform on which to compete with the majors.

There has never been a better time to be an independent video producer.

You have access to:

1. Affordable equipment

2. This book

3. Audiences by the millions worldwide.

Now get out there and make something!

John Burkhart
Editor-in-Chief
Videomaker Magazine

Introduction:
If You Are New to Making Video: Welcome!

Matt York
Publisher/Editor of Videomaker Magazine

The craft of making video is an enjoyable one. Whether video production is for you a pastime, a part-time moneymaker or a full-time occupation, I am certain that you will enjoy the experience of creating video. There are many facets to video production. Each brings its own pleasures and frustrations, and each will stretch your abilities, both technical and artistic.

Video is a wonderful communication medium that enables us to express ourselves in ways unlike other media. Television is pervasive in our society today. The chance to utilize the same medium that the great TV and film producers have used to reach the masses is an incredible privilege. Video is powerful. Video is the closest thing to being there. For conveying information, there is no medium that compares with video. It overwhelms the senses by delivering rich moving images and high-fidelity sound. Having grown up with TV, many of us lack the appreciation for its power. Compared with radio or print, television profoundly enhances the message being conveyed. For example,

reading about a battlefield in war can be less powerful than hearing a live radio report from a journalist with sounds of gunfire, tanks, rockets, incoming artillery fire and the emotions from an anguished reporter's voice. Neither compares with video shot on a battlefield.

It is amazing that you can walk into a retail store, make a few purchases in a few minutes and walk out with all of the essential tools for producing video. For less than $1,500, you can buy a DV camcorder and a personal computer and suddenly, you have the capacity to create video that rivals that of a television station. The image and sound quality of a DV camcorder is better than broadcast television as viewed on an average TV. The transitions and special effects, available with any low-cost video editing software package, exceed the extravagance of those used on the nightly news.

These days, more and more people are watching high definition TV and video-sharing sites like YouTube. If you want to make a video for an HDTV audience, you might need to invest something more like $2,300. However, if you want to share your videos on the Internet, all you need is a webcam and you can upload directly to one of the many video-sharing sites. Realistically, if you are reading this you have a greater commitment to excellent video, which requires a camcorder and video editing. While many of the videos on these video-sharing sites are of low quality, there are plenty of people uploading and sharing some wonderfully produced videos. Video sharing is a wonderful new way to reach anyone on the planet who has an Internet connection.

There was a time when any message conveyed on a TV screen was perceived as far more credible than if it were conveyed by other media (i.e., print or audio cassette). While that may no longer be as true, video messages are still more convincing to many people.

Once a highly complex pursuit, video-editing is now just another software application on a personal computer. We all realize that simply using video editing software doesn't make someone a good TV producer any more than using Microsoft Word makes one a good writer. However, the ability to edit video in your own home or office is so convenient that it enables more people to spend more time developing their skills.

One of the most rewarding experiences in video production is getting an audience to understand your vision. The time between the initial manifestation of your vision and the first screening of the video may be just a few days or several years, but there is no more satisfying (or nerve-wracking) feeling than witnessing an audience's first reaction to your work.

PART I
Video Gear

A guide to essential equipment: what to buy, how it works.

1
Camera Buttons and Controls

Robert G. Nulph, Ph.D.

It's easy for first-time camcorder owners to be intimidated by all of the buttons and controls that seem to sprout from every recess and surface of a new camcorder. Believe me, if you don't know how to focus, adjust your iris or when to select a different shutter speed, you are not alone. In this column, we will give all you beginners an overview of the various buttons, controls, dials and knobs common to camcorders.

Power, Eject and Record Buttons

Somewhere on the camcorder, there is a power switch. This switch often includes a save, standby or neutral position so that the camera goes into a power save mode when not recording, to preserve battery life. If your camcorder goes into the standby or save mode, simply push the standby button to power it back up. Power switches sometimes have a "lock" feature that prevents you from turning the camera on accidentally. To disengage this lock, press in the power switch to move it. The power switch might also be part of the switch that changes the mode of the camcorder from camera to playback VCR.

The eject button is also a standard feature on all camcorders. This button, often colored blue, can be found most anywhere on the camcorder. Usually they are located on the side, top or bottom of the camcorder near the tape door. By pressing this button, you can eject your tape or open the tape door so that you can insert your tape into the tape carriage. On many camcorders, the door opens and the tape carriage then pops or slides out. If this is the case with your camcorder, when loading the tape into the camcorder, slide your tape into the carriage, then let the camcorder pull the tape inside before closing the outside door. This allows you to make sure that the camcorder firmly seats the tape into its internal mechanism.

All camcorders have a record button, of course. This button is usually red and is located where your thumb sits when holding the camcorder in your right hand. Some camcorders also have a record button on top or in the front for easier access when using the camera with a tripod. The record button starts and stops recording while in camera mode. On some cameras, the record button also acts as a record/pause button when your camcorder is in the VCR mode.

Focus

The buttons, knobs or dials that control the lens and the picture are perhaps the most important controls on the camera. As a beginner, you may tend to let the camera do the work in Auto mode. However, as you get used to your camcorder and do more shooting, you may want to switch it to manual so that you can take greater control of your focus.

The focus button or dial is usually located on or near the lens but, on some camcorders, it is on the side of the casing. By setting the camera for automatic focus, you let your camera do the focusing, sending out an infrared beam, computing the distance and setting the lens. This sounds great, but in practice, there are many problems with it. Anything that moves across the lens will cause it to change focus and, even though your subject may not change position, the camera is constantly checking the focus and changing it. This constant check and rechecking of the focus causes your picture to drift in and out of focus and is a major drain on your battery.

If you are not comfortable focusing manually, let the camera focus automatically, then switch to manual. This effectively locks the focus until you change it again. Some camcorders allow you to hold the manual focus button down so that the camera focuses using its auto function. Then, when you release the button the camera enters the manual focus again so that it won't auto-fluctuate (see Figure 1-1).

Zoom

The zoom control is usually a couple of buttons, a slider or a rocker switch on top of the camera. These buttons have the letters

Figure 1-1 One good way to use the focus controls (if you aren't confident doing it yourself) is to let the camera automatically focus and then switch the focus to manual (i.e., lock the focus).

W for Wide (zoom out) and T for Telephoto (zoom in). You can also think of these as aWay and Towards. These buttons change the focal length of the optical system, which controls how close or far away your subject looks. The zoom can be a very helpful feature, but be careful not to overuse it. Its primary use should be in setting the image size before you begin recording; try not to zoom during recording. Recorded zooms often don't look very good unless your camcorder has a variable speed zoom and you practice using it a lot.

Iris (Aperture)

Some camcorders have an iris or aperture control dial (see Figure 1-2). The iris controls the amount of light that enters the camera. By turning the dial, you can make the image brighter or darker. Aperture is measured in f-stops (e.g., f/1.8–f/16), with larger numbers indicating smaller openings. Some camcorders do not have explicit iris controls and instead adjust the overall exposure through some combination of iris and electronic amplification (gain).

Figure 1-2 *The iris controls the amount of light that enters the camera. By turning the dial, you can make the image brighter or darker.*

Figure 1-3 *Stop Motion—Fundamentally, shutter speed controls the amount of light that is coming into the camera.*

Manual aperture control can be handy when your subject is standing against a bright background. The camera automatically reads the scene as being bright, so it closes the iris, making your subject very dark. By turning the iris control dial, you can make your subject brighter (with the background likely becoming overexposed). Many cameras have an explicit backlight button that may help you do this semi-automatically. You can avoid using the backlight button if you watch your backgrounds and change your shooting location. Always try to place your subject so that the background is a little darker than the subject. You can usually make your subject brighter by turning him or her so he or she almost faces the sun. You can also reduce the brightness of the background by zooming in on your subject.

Shutter Speed

Fundamentally, shutter speed controls the amount of light coming into the camera, with faster shutter speeds letting in less light (see Figure 1-3). Faster speeds also decrease the amount of blur for fast moving subjects. This comes in very handy when you slow the video down in your editor. Without the shutter speed control, the slowed-down video would show blurred motion. By increasing the shutter speed, the motion will be crystal clear, even if the image is paused.

The one problem with higher shutter speeds is that it decreases the amount of light that enters the lens. If shooting outdoors at midday, this is not much of a problem, as the sun provides a lot of light. Indoors, however, you will have to add light if you want to use the high-speed shutter function.

White Balance

The white balance button is a necessary feature on a camcorder. This button sets the electronics of the camera so that they see colors accurately (see Figure 1-4). Surprisingly perhaps, different kinds of light sources (fluorescent, the sun, incandescent bulbs) produce slightly different colors of light. To use the white balance button, point your camera at a white piece of paper or cloth after you set up your shot. Press the white balance button and you'll see an icon in the viewfinder blink off and on. When the camera is white balanced, it will stop blinking. Make sure you white balance every time you change position or light sources. Watch out for a subtle, periodic cycling of automatic white balance under fluorescent lights, especially when using slower shutter speeds.

VCR Controls

Most camcorders have basic VCR controls built into them. These controls

Figure 1-4 *The white balance button is a necessary feature on a camcorder. This button sets the electronics of the camera so that they see colors accurately.*

Figure 1-5 *Record Review—You might also find a record review button that you can press to check what you just recorded. When you press this button, the camcorder rewinds the tape and plays back your last few seconds of footage.*

include Rewind, Fast Forward, Play, Pause and Stop. You might also find a record review button that you can press to check what you just recorded (see Figure 1-5). When you press this button, the camcorder rewinds the tape and plays back your last few seconds of footage. The camera does not have to be in the VCR setting to do this, making it a very handy function.

Clicking Off

We've covered the most common camcorder buttons, but your camcorder may have a few more buttons. Read over your manual and experiment using the different settings. If you've had your camcorder for a while, but have only shot in Auto mode, it may be time to take more control of your camcorder. Have fun and enjoy making videos.

Sidebar 1

Direct Focus

On still cameras, the focus ring is often mechanical, and a turn actuates a direct change in the position of the optics. On almost all camcorders, the focus ring is not mechanical. Instead, the movement of the focus ring by your hand translates into an electronic signal that then translates into the movement of the lens. This makes the focus ring seem mushy and unresponsive to changes.

Sidebar 2

Menus

Camera designers are faced with a dilemma: too many buttons can be baffling, yet too few restrict a videographer's freedom. Design engineers have attempted to solve this issue by putting the most commonly used controls on the body of the camera and placing seldom-used items in electronic menus. More advanced cameras tend to have more buttons, while simpler point-and-shoot models tend to have more menus. If your camera doesn't have a button that is listed in this article, check the on-screen menu.

2
HDV = High Def Value

Paul M. J. Suchecki

If you're eager to leap into High Definition production, but prefer to limit your six-figure purchases to real estate, then HDV is for you. In the same way that miniDV revolutionized standard definition shooting, the not quite three-year-old HDV format is doing the same for Hi Def. Affordable HDV is available today, but myriad variations can confound a buyer.

At first glance, you might suspect that the video princes have sidestepped their usual format wars. HDV was created by a partnership of Canon, Sharp, Sony and JVC. Much is in common. HDV records in MPEG-2 on miniDV cassettes. The aspect ratio is wide screen 16:9, while the output is 1080i (1080 pixels horizontally scanned interlace) or 720p (720 pixels scanned progressively). The tape run time for HDV is the same as for miniDV so your 63-minute cassette will last more than an hour. Since the top throughput of HDV tops out at the same data rate of DV tape, video can be readily loaded to an edit system in real time via FireWire.

However, there are differences: HDV1 from JVC records at 19 megabits per second

in MPEG-2 with a resolution of 1280 × 720 pixels (progressive). HDV2 from Sony and Canon records in MPEG-2 at 25 megabits per second with a resolution of 1920 pixels by 1080 (interlaced). If you shoot JVC's HDV1, you won't be able to transfer through FireWire from a Sony HDV2 deck or camcorder. Sony's HDV doesn't play back on JVC either. Canon adds to the compatibility issues with an "F" setting on its camcorders that won't play back on either a JVC or Sony deck. In practical terms this means that you'll either be digitizing directly from your camcorder or committing to HDV1 or HDV2 for your complete production and post chain.

Camcorder Overview

Professional HDV camcorders are now available from Canon, JVC and Sony. Let's break down what they share and how they differ beginning with 3 1/3″ CCDs. These are much smaller than 2/3″ professional Betacam or HDCam camcorders. 2/3″ HDV is coming but for now the smaller chips common in all these cameras present a challenge.

The shorter focal lengths of HDV give greater depth of field, which helps ease the critical focus issues with shooting in High Def. It's an asset for run and gun ENG-style shooting. However, some videographers are going to be using HDV for digital cinematography. Since much of the "film look" is due to a shallow depth of field, you'll need to pick up a set of neutral density filters to cut down on light, thus opening your iris to greater isolate your subject against soft focused backgrounds. This is where a matte box proves handy, giving you a choice of options like gradients to take down the exposure of the sky. Another way to emulate film is to use a prime lens, which is usually sharper than a zoom. For this, you'll need a camera that offers interchangeable lenses (Canon and JVC at present).

There is less tolerance for bad focus because the HD image is noticeably sharper. All the top end HDV cameras offer both electronic viewfinders and external LCD's, but they go further offering peaking enhancement in black and white viewfinder mode so that in-focus elements are tinged with color. Sony allows a camera operator to temporarily double the center of the image for a focus check.

HD cameras allow you to monitor with standard definition field monitors. However, for critical applications such as an ultimate transfer to film, get a portable HD monitor. Very good LCD options are available.

Shoulder-mounted cameras are easier to handle during extensive handheld shooting. When possible get a camcorder with XLR inputs for your mics. Most HDV camcorders will allow the user to shoot in NTSC DV as well as HDV. Sony's HVR-Z1U also plays back in DVCAM, 1080 50i and PAL. The Canon can record to PAL with an optional upgrade.

The Hornet's Nest of 24P

"Film look" is a combination of lighting, low depth of field, wide exposure latitude,

camera moves defined by prime lenses and finally 24 progressive frames. Sony uses a CineFrame mode that replicates the look of film with a 3:2 conversion of internal 1080i that works by throwing away a field of data. Canon has a simulated progressive capture mode that's designated "F." It works by interlaced scanning twice in the time of a normal field. Compared to true progressive, this process does create some artifacts. JVC's HDV-1 actually uses genuine 720 24p recording making it the far better camera to use if film is the ultimate destination for your show. You can export directly to a film-style edit system without converting the frame rate.

MPEG-2 Compression

DV and HDV compress images very differently. In DV, like HDCam and Digital Betacam, the videocompression is purely *intraframe*, comparing and compressing within each individual image. It's the same kind of compression most photos used on the Internet (e.g., JPEG). Each frame is compressed independently. Since HDV is MPEG-2, it uses both *intraframe* and *interframe* compression. Interframe compression happens in what is called a GOP or group of pictures, made up of I, B and P frames. The I frame is encoded independently. The next frame to be encoded is a P or predictive frame, which anticipates changes in the video discarding redundant information. Between the I and P frames, B or bi-directional frames fill in, looking both backwards and forwards. It's played back I–BB-P BB P etc., with the next I frame determined by the size of your GOP. Since most video has redundancy across frames, the method works well until there is a lot of change. While shooting HDV be wary of rapid camera motion like fast pans, which can overwhelm the compression process.

Sony also recommends using its better quality HDV vs. DV tape. If you're unlucky enough to have a dropout on a recorded I frame, you have no backup immediately

fore and aft. The glitch will affect everything in your GOP.

Editing

Editing HDV footage is more problematic
than cutting DV. Since each DV frame is
compressed independently, the footage
can be cut at any frame without affecting those next to it. In HDV, the I frame,
the only truly intact frame, is typically
recorded once every half second or less.
The rest are extrapolated across the GOP.
Any transition while editing, even a simple cut, requires an entire decompression
and then recompression of every frame in
the GOP.

Non-linear HDV editing demands a lot
of processing power to extract and then
reconstruct an image at a transition. MPEG
hardware encoding is usually cleaner and
faster than software only, so consider
investing in a dedicated HDV encoding
board. Some will also give you real time
playback on a monitor. No matter what

edit system you choose, you'd be wise to
get as much RAM and the fastest CPU's
you can afford. The good news is that the
file sizes will be as manageable as working in DV, so you don't have to buy the
gig a minute of storage that uncompressed
standard definition editing requires.

Compression issues are exacerbated
if you are shooting in simulated 24P. If
you've ever cut film that was telecined,
you've seen the field complications that
arise from a 3/2 pulldown. Both Sony
and Canon's HDV cameras do a reverse
2/3 which requires even more sophisticated processing with MPEG-2 during
editing. These HDV modes can produce
unintended motion artifacts. Some videographers planning to finish on film have
opted for shooting in PAL mode at 25 fps.
They find the 4% speed difference less
objectionable than the processing errors
caused by pseudo 24P.

Choose your HDV package based on
your specific shooting needs. Each one has
its tradeoffs.

Sidebar 1

The Natives and the Non-Natives

Different editing programs handle the long GOP MPEG-2 file format of HDV in different ways.
The two main workflows today consist of native and non-native HDV editing.

Native brings the long GOP *I*, *B* and *P* frames into the editing program unchanged. At this
point, to cut in between most frames, a conversion process would have to take place. Some
time after the cut and before output to tape, the GOP would have to be reconstructed (rendered). Though there is slight degradation of the image, proponents of native editing believe
this to be the cleanest, not to mention quickest way to edit HDV footage. Only those GOPs that
are altered need to be reconstructed at output.

Non-native HDV editing usually involves the use of an intermediary. The long GOP must be
converted, or transcoded, into a group of *I* frames. Though a time-consuming render is necessary when capturing footage and putting back out to tape, there is no interruption to the editing work flow during cutting as all the frames are now all *I* frames, just as if it was DV footage.
Some of the drawbacks here include the need for more hard drive space as the conversion
from long GOP could take up to four times the space, generation loss on conversion and longer
render time when capturing and outputting.

Of course, both camps claim their process produces both a better workflow and a better out-
putted image.

Sidebar 2

HDV Glossary

16 × 9 aspect ratio is the ratio of the width to height of an image.

Depth of field is the front to back area of apparent focus in a shot. It is affected by focal length of the lens, iris size and camera to subject distance.

Intraframe compression is a technique that compresses the video by removing redundancy from individual video images.

Interframe compression is a technique that achieves compression of a video file by eliminating redundant data between successive compressed frames. In a shot sequence of a red balloon sailing across a blue sky, for example, most of the image stays the same and is redundant from frame to frame.

- MPEG-2 refers to an interframe and intraframe compression scheme instituted by the Motion Picture Experts Group. It differs from other MPEG compressions in that it is used to encode audio and video for broadcast signals. DVD uses MPEG-2 compression.

- Interlace Scanning (i) Picture a Venetian blind representing scan lines. The odd lines, like the slats of a blind, are all scanned in one field. The even are scanned next. Put together they make up one complete frame of video.

- Progressive Scanning (p) This is a scanning method where the lines are scanned in numerical sequence from top to bottom. This action in video more closely simulates how film records information.

- Megabits per second (Mbps) a number representing the amount of digital data moved through a single point within a second of time.

3
How DV Works:
Inside the Technology

Bill Fisher

Ladies and gentlemen, step right up! Inside this tent you'll have a remarkable opportunity to get closer than ever before to digital video, otherwise known as DV. I'll give each of you an unusual close-up look at the mechanics of DV, at the various DV formats on the market and at the reasons DV can do so much, so well. So follow me into the tent of wonders!

Look—the journey is already beginning. We're now shrinking, small enough to penetrate the inner workings of a DV camcorder. Let's enter through the lens housing and start exploring.

Light, Sound and Current

As we move through the zoom lens, note that at this point, digital video is a lot like analog video. Light and sound enter the camera through a lens and microphone and then a computer transforms the real world into electronic signals.

Digital and analog part ways fairly soon, however. The tiny silicon charge-coupled device (CCD) at the end of the lens barrel uses hundreds of thousands of pixels to make DV look incredibly sharp and clean, with around 500 lines of potential resolution (or more, in three-chip pro cameras).

From Analog to Digital

Next we come to the circuit boards, which do an enormous amount of the work of making your DV footage look and sound fantastic. The software coding and computer components contained in the boards produce a digital replica of each moment of video and audio in the analog-to-digital conversion process. There is also circuitry that works in reverse, for playback on your television. It's the "digital" part of DV that puts this technology head and shoulders above consumer analog video formats. Digital video is pure data, not analog signals, allowing pristine and endlessly repeatable transmission of high-resolution data through an all-digital pathway.

Doing the Math

All consumer digital video formats (Mini DV, Digital8, DVCAM and DVCPro) utilize the same basic data format and data rate (25 Mbps) to encode and decode 30 fps NTSC video data.

- *Sampling* DV encoding hardware samples each frame of video for luminance (brightness) and chrominance (color) information. It uses 4:1:1 (Y:U:V or YUV) sampling for this operation (see Figure 3-1). The hardware scans each line of every 720×480 video frame, taking four pixel samples of luma information (Y) for every one pixel sample it takes of chroma information (U and V). That cuts down on extra data and also provides the right mix of luma and chroma detail to satisfy our eyes, which are more sensitive to brightness (luma) than color (chroma).

- *Compression* The DV brain then mathematically compresses each resampled frame of video to speed throughput and save storage space on tapes and hard drives. This is accomplished with a 5:1 DCT (discrete cosine transform) mathematical algorithm that discards as much unnecessary image information as possible while retaining much of the quality of the original image.

- *Audio* A separate sampling process takes the audio signal (after pre-amplification) and turns it into data as well. An audio sample rate of 48 kHz (with a 16-bit depth per sample) produces a single track of high-fidelity digital stereo audio (2 channels). Alternately, a 32 kHz sample rate with a 12-bit depth yields two stereo tracks (4 channels total), one of which can be used for voiceover narration.

- *Vital data* All of this pristine but compressed digital information is bundled with additional vital pieces of generated data. This information includes time code, time/date information and digital pilot tone signals to replace the conventional control track of analog video, which the DV format lacks.

- *Error correction* Also added to the data mix are error correction bits. Digital video data travels in tiny packets and the DV hardware adds unique codes that verify and correct corrupted data bits.

Express Delivery

The whole package is finally bundled in data packets compliant with the DV standard. Every one of these packets—each the size of a single DV track—contains four independent regions: a subcode sector for time code and other data, a video sector, an audio sector and a sector for insert editing and track data (see Figure 3-2). These packets move at a rate of 25 Mbps (megabits per second), which translates to

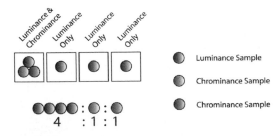

Figure 3-1 *4:1:1 Sampling—DV Encoding hardware samples each frame of video for luminance (brightness) and chrominance (color) information taking four pixel samples of luma information (Y) for every one pixel sample it takes of chroma information (U and V).*

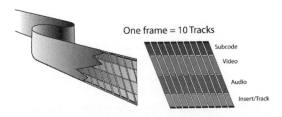

Figure 3-2 *10 Tracks, 1 Frame—Each frame of DV video is made up of 10 tracks, each of which is divided into four subsections.*

roughly 3.5 MB of disk storage space per second of DV video.

Where the Action Is

We've seen the brains, but now we've come to the brawn—the spinning drums that record data onto the tape and read it off. The drum that houses the heads is a polished metal cylinder that's angled in the cassette compartment and rotates at a very high rate. Rollers hold the tape against the drum's grooved surface, where a number of electromagnetic heads make slanted swipes across the surface of the tape, recording tracks of data that correspond exactly to the DV packets described above.

Everything about this system is microscopic and its measurements are in microns, or thousandths of a millimeter. In fact, the record heads are so small, the tracks are so narrow and the data they contain is so densely packed, that a minute of digital video—about 200 MB of information—occupies less than two meters of tape. Put another way, a DV cassette can hold about 13 GB of digital information.

The Skinny on Digital Formats

Everything up to this point is common to the 25 Mbps Mini DV (DV25), Digital8, DVCAM and DVCPro formats. When it comes to recording to tape, however, manufacturers have developed several different ways to store the data.

Mini DV tape comes in a 55 mm wide plastic cassette to fit consumer camcorders.

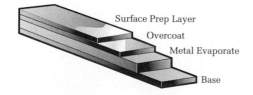

Figure 3-3 Physical Format—Metal Evaporated (ME) Mini DV tapes have a number of physical layers protecting the important data layer.

The tape itself is 6.35 mm wide and is coated with metal that was deposited using an evaporated processing technique (ME) (see Figure 3-3). It moves at a rate of about 19 mm per second, with a track width of 10 microns. The typical 60-minute Mini DV cassette is about 70 m long and stores around 13 GB of data. The closely related standard DV tape (designed for use in VTRs) is the same tape format, but comes in a cassette that's twice as big and holds as much as 180 minutes of tape.

DVCAM (Sony) and DVCPro (Panasonic) formats are modified DV25 for the professional market. They use a wider track pitch for greater reliability and move the tape past the heads much faster. Both formats offer as much as three hours of running time on a single cassette.

The DVCPro format has several other pro-level features. DVCPro tapes use a metal particulate (MP) process instead of ME. Unlike Mini DV and DVCAM, DVCPro can use optional linear tracks at the top and bottom edges of the DV tape to record analog time code and audio information.

The Digital8 format also has idiosyncrasies. Larger than Mini DV tape, Digital8 records onto 8 mm and Hi8 tape. The key difference is that in a Digital8 camcorder, the tape moves twice as fast as in its analog relatives, and the signal is digital. The Digital8 format is backward-compatible with the analog 8mm format. That's a big plus if you have a closetful of legacy 8 mm gear and tapes (see Figure 3-4).

Decks

Most of what you've seen here applies to digital VTRs as well. Decks use the same processing system as camcorders to understand analog and digital signals. Where decks differ from, and usually outshine, camcorders is their mechanical robustness and their multiple digital and analog input/output capabilities. These units also offer format cross-compatibility: many DV, DVCAM and DVCPro decks can play back all of the different tape formats.

25 Mbps DV Tape Formats			
Tape	Pitch (microns)	Tape Speed (in mm/sec)	Cassette Dimensions (mm)
MiniDV	10	18	66 × 48 × 12
DVCam	15	28	66 × 48 × 12
Digital8	16	29	95 × 63 × 15
DVCPRO	18	34	98 × 65 × 15

Figure 3-4 *All consumer digital video formats utilize the same basic data format and data rate (25 Mbs) to encode and decode 30 fps NTSC video data.*

Output and Beyond

We conclude our tour at the camcorder's FireWire connection. And that's appropriate, because FireWire is a big part of DV's success. FireWire is a data transfer protocol like USB or Ethernet. FireWire moves dense packets of data at extremely high rates, and that makes it perfect for moving DV data between camcorder and computer. The DV/FireWire one-two punch has created a real revolution in consumer video, enabling all-digital desktop video production.

Parting Advice

As you leave this tent of wonders, make sure to remember that all DV equipment, from the most economical camcorder to the most elaborate high-end VTR, makes use of basically the same computational brain. And as for the many differences, don't worry about the underlying technology. Whether your DV comes in the form of a pro camera with a giant lens, a portable deck with an LCD screen or a palm-size camcorder for travel, there's a digital heart in all of these devices.

Sidebar 1

Standards

FireWire, like DV, is an international standard (IEEE-1394) that technology manufacturers have agreed to abide by in the interest of compatibility. But that doesn't mean that everyone agrees on what to call the standard. Apple Computer, which played a large role in developing the technology, named it FireWire and Sony dubbed their version i.LINK.

Sidebar 2

Longevity

Anyone who's used analog formats has seen dropouts and other signs of signal loss resulting from faults on the magnetic tape or from recording problems. When it comes to longevity, expect analog tapes to last at best 15 years before they start to degrade. Error correction built in to DV eliminates many dropouts, but what about longevity? Since DV tapes use magnetic material to record data, you'll see gradual deterioration of these signals, too, though error correction can make up for some loss. Fortunately, it's easy to make perfect backup clones of DV tapes via FireWire.

4
Dissecting a Digital Camcorder

Scott Anderson

Dooley may be a little crusty, but he's the kind of guy you can trust with your camcorder. So when mine broke, he was the man to fix it. This was the perfect chance to learn the inside story about this amazing piece of technology, from the moment that the light hits the lens to the final TV output (see Figure 4-1).

"There's a lot of technology crammed into this little thing," said Dooley, who actually seemed to glow when he talked tech. "It has lenses, motors, gyros, microphones, a clock, a tape deck, a computer and a TV. Not to mention a dozen input and output jacks. It's a robot-operated entertainment center in the palm of your hand. So, how did you break it?" he asked.

"I didn't break it; it just stopped working," I said, somewhat defensively.

"Well, let's crack 'er open," Dooley replied. "And don't worry, I won't hurt your baby. Now hand me that tool kit."

I passed him a large kit containing everything from a basic screwdriver to a space-age remote control. In a few seconds he had the back off the camcorder and was pulling its guts out.

"Here's where it all starts," he said, holding up my precious zoom lens. "The lens is one of the most important, and expensive, parts of the camcorder. No amount of electronic wizardry can make up for a crummy lens."

He pointed at two small gray cylinders alongside the lenses. "See these? These are little motors to control the autofocus and the zoom," he said. "Essentially, this is a sophisticated robot eye that responds to what the camcorder brain tells it to do (see Figure 4-2). Yours has an optical stabilizer built into the lens; a squishy prism that uses a tiny gyroscope to keep the image steady."

"What's that?" I asked, pointing to a chip the size of a postage stamp on a tiny circuit board.

Shaking Hands with My CCD

"That's the CCD," he said, "a chip that converts light to electricity. These things

15

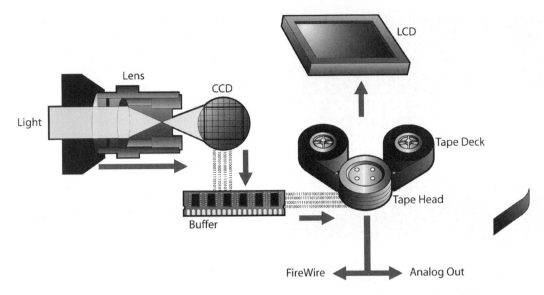

Figure 4-1 *Video Out—This greatly simplified diagram may give you some idea of the complexity of getting a picture from the world at large to a place where we can see and edit it.*

Figure 4-2 *The Lens—More than just glass for concentrating light, modern camcorder lenses have complex servos and gears for zooming and focusing.*

have been around for almost 25 years, but they keep getting better. It's a grid of tiny light sensors that engineers call photo-sites and computer folks call pixels. The new ones are more sensitive for low-light situations and have more pixels for higher resolution. The more light that hits a photo site, the greater the voltage output."

"But won't that just give you black and white? How do they see in color?" I asked.

"Well, there are basically two ways, but they both work by splitting the light into red, green and blue," Dooley said. "One technique uses prisms to split up the light and send it to three different CCDs. That's hot stuff, but expensive and bulky. Your camcorder just has one CCD, and it puts different-colored filters over the pixels," he said, handing me a diagram of a colored grid (see Figure 4-3).

"But this thing is mostly green," I replied. "Won't everyone come out looking seasick?"

"Actually, the eye sees better in the green part of the spectrum, so that grid works great. But if you think about it, this technique cuts into your resolution. You need to combine three mono-colored pix-els to get one colored pixel. Software helps to smooth things out, but the more pixels you can get in your CCD, the better your final resolution. Typically, a camcorder has 300,000 to 500,000 pixels, but some new ones have a megapixel (1 million pix-els). You could shoot HDTV with that kind of resolution."

"I want one!"

"Save your money, bud," Dooley growled. "Most megapixel CCDs are just for still images and HD cams ain't cheap. Now pay attention. These CCDs are scanned just like a TV, pixel by pixel, row after row. The

Figure 4-3 *The Retina—The CCD records the light that is focused by the lens in discrete pixels.*

output creates a varying voltage that travels through an analog-to-digital converter. Can you guess what that does?"

"Converts analog to digital?" I asked with a smirk.

"You're smarter than you look, pal. That digital signal gets stored in what they call a memory buffer, which is really just like computer RAM," Dooley said. "Once you have it in the buffer, you can use all kinds of software tricks on it. Some camcorders even throw in digital special effects, but I see yours doesn't."

"Naw, I like to do my effects on the computer," I said.

"Your camcorder uses optical stabilization, but some camcorders also use this buffer to stabilize the image," he said. "The software finds a feature and tries to keep it nailed down. If the camera shakes, the software electronically moves the image in the

opposite direction to cancel the motion. That uses up some pixels around the border though, which dings your resolution a bit. The image is also used to determine exposure. There are at least two ways to do that. One electronically changes the amount of time that the CCD is allowed to gather light. The other way is to control a physical iris with another tiny motor.

"Your camcorder also uses this digital image to focus," he continued. "It has software that checks on the contrast of the image and controls the focusing motors. As long as the contrast increases, it will keep shifting the focus. But as soon as the contrast starts to go down, it knows it just passed the sweet spot, and it backs up a notch for perfect focus. There are other focusing methods; the most common uses an infrared beam. It just measures how long it takes light to bounce off your subject and then calculates the distance from that. It works just fine, but other infrared sources can fool it, like candles or fires.

"Finally," he went on to say, "another software program compresses the image by a factor of five before it gets saved to tape."

The Tape Deck

Dooley reached into the camcorder and pulled out the tape deck. I fervently hoped he knew how to put that thing back.

"That brings us to the tape deck part of the camcorder," he said. "Here, tiny write heads spinning at high speed lay down the digitized image track, along with the captured audio. The heads are little electromagnets, and as the pixels are read out of the buffer, the signal magnetizes the tape (see Figure 4-4).

"That's really the end of the camcorder story," Dooley said, "except for how you get the video out again. For that, you need to read the tape back. This is just like the write process in reverse. The tape goes by the read head and every little magnetic spot on the tape converts back into bits of data. This is digital data, which is very robust stuff. Since a bit of data is binary—on or off—it's difficult to swamp

Figure 4-4 The Head—The play/record head spins at a high rate of speed and is divided into a number of horizontal tracks.

Figure 4-5 In and Out—The interface between the analog world and the camcorder is most often bi-directional on many modern DV camcorders.

it with noise. Even if noise does manage to destroy a bit, there are extra bits reserved for error correction, which means that you can count on a reliable, 100-percent perfect recording and playback. It is this fact that makes digital so remarkable. No matter how many times you copy it, there is no generation loss like there is with analog video.

"On the way out, the video image is again stored in the buffer. Now, you can run it into a computer with a FireWire connection and edit it if you want. But if you just want to display it on a TV, you need to convert the digital image back to analog, the only thing a typical TV can handle (see Figure 4-5). What do you suppose they use for that, my friend?"

"A digital to analog converter?" I proposed.

"Right again, genius. That same circuit can also send a signal to the LCD viewfinder on your camcorder. It's interesting that although both CCDs and LCDs come from the computer world, they are both usually wired for analog inputs and outputs. So, your digital camcorder is really a hybrid, with a lot of conversion going on between the analog and digital worlds.

"Pretty soon, you can expect a fully digital signal path, which will give even better results. In the end, you'll still need to convert to analog for standard viewing, but soon, even the TVs will be digital."

Dooley surveyed the entrails of my camcorder strewn across the table. "Well, that about sums it up," he said. "Except for one thing. Your camcorder has something you don't see very often."

Dooley held up the tape unit. "This thing seems to have a toaster in it. Or at least someone must have thought so. Otherwise, why would there be a piece of bread in the cassette holder?"

"What?" I yelped. "No way, unless the twins got into it…"

"You should keep your kids away from this thing, Anderson. Hand me the tweezers."

Dooley fiddled around a bit and then triumphantly plucked out a hardened chunk of bread squished into the shape of a DV tape. "It should work a whole lot better now," he said.

Sidebar 1

Quality Issues

The Lens

Lens Quality: This is the most important part of your camcorder and usually the most expensive. It doesn't matter how many lines of resolution you have if the image is out of focus. Premium optical coatings do a better job of preventing color fringing and reflections.

Zoom: An important aspect of a lens is its zoom capacity. Modern optics are computer-designed and incredibly complex. Keep in mind that big zoom ranges may sacrifice optical quality and speed, and long zoom settings will require a tripod or an image stabilizer.

Stabilizer: Optical stabilizers let you use those zoom settings to the max, and they don't sacrifice CCD resolution the way electronic stabilizers might.

Speed: Faster lenses capture more light, so you can take shorter exposures. This is especially important for shooting sports events and low-light situations.

The Microphone

We tend to concentrate on the video parts of a camcorder, but the audio is just as important. Fortunately, audio is much easier and cheaper to deal with. Audio data is just a fraction of the size of the video data.

It's difficult to put a high-quality microphone on such a small object. Nevertheless, camcorder makers have done a decent job within a tight budget and even tighter spaces. If you're looking for better quality, look for an input jack for an external microphone. Then you can hook up whatever you want, including remote mics.

The CCD

There are two things to look for in a CCD: the resolution and the sensitivity. The resolution depends mostly on how many pixels the CCD has, but is reduced somewhat if electronic image stabilizing is used. The more CCD chips you have, the better. For sensitivity, choose a low-lux CCD that can see well even in low light conditions.

Sidebar 2

WARNING! Don't Try This at Home!

The editors of Videomaker do not recommend opening your camcorder's case under any circumstances. Doing so will certainly void your warrantee, and may cause permanent damage to the camera or personal harm to you. We recommend that you always (and only) have your video camera repaired by a trained professional.

5
All about Lenses

Jim Stinson

Without passing through a lens, the light falling on your camcorder's CCD would be as empty of information as a flashlight beam. The camcorder's lens converts incoming light from a gaggle of unreadable rays to an ordered arrangement of visual information—that is, a picture. It's the lens, then, that makes video imaging possible. Without it, your camcorder would record an image of blank white light.

All videos are successions of individual images, each made by forcing light to form a recognizable picture on a flat surface. You can do it with just a tiny hole in the wall of a darkened room, but it's easier to use a lens.

A lens does far more than just render light into coherent images; it also determines the visual characteristics of those images. For this reason, every serious videographer should know how lenses work and how to use them to best advantage.

A Little Background

As long ago as ancient Greece, people noticed that when they put a straight pole into clear water, the part of the pole below the water line seemed to bend. The mathematician Euclid described this effect in 300 BC. But it wasn't until 1621 that the scientist Willebrord Snell developed the mathematics of diffraction. Diffraction is the principle stating the following: when light passes from one medium to another—say from water to air or air to glass—it changes speed. And when light hits a junction between two media at an angle, the change in speed causes a change in direction.

Lenses, which refract light in an orderly way, were perhaps unintended side effects of glass blowing: if you drop a globule of molten glass onto a smooth, plane surface it will naturally cool into a circle that's flat on the bottom and slightly convex on top—an accidental lens. Look through this piece of junk glass and behold: things appear larger.

Now, hold the glass between the sun and a piece of paper and you can set the sheet on fire—but only if the glass-to-paper distance is such that all the sun's rays come together at a single point on the paper.

At some unknown moment somebody thought, "*Hmmn*, if it works with the sun, maybe it'll work with other light sources, too." In a darkened room, this someone held the glass between a piece of paper and an open window. Sure enough, at a certain lens-to-paper distance, a pinpoint of light appeared.

But then a bizarre thing happened. When the experimenter slowly increased the glass-to-paper distance, an actual picture of the window appeared, small, to be sure and upside down, but so detailed that he could see that tree outside, framed in the opening. (You can try this yourself with a magnifying glass.)

Back to the Present

If you've ever seen a cutaway diagram of a modern zoom lens, you have a grasp on how far we've come from that first accidentally dropped blob of glass.

The camcorder zoom may contain a dozen pieces of glass or more. Some of these permit the lens to zoom, some make the lens more compact by "folding" the light rays inside it and some correct inescapable imperfections called lens aberrations.

But since you didn't sign up for an advanced physics seminar here, we'll pretend that the camcorder zoom is a simple, one-element lens. We can do this because the basic idea is exactly the same: when a convex lens refracts light, the light's rays converge at a certain distance behind the lens, forming a coherent image on a plane still farther back.

The plane on which the focused image appears is the *focal plane*, the place where the light rays converge is the *focal point* and the distance from the focal point to the axis of the lens is the *focal length*. *Note*: Contrary to common belief, the focal length is *not* the distance from the lens to the focal plane.

Your camcorder's image-sensing chip sits at the focal plane of the system, behind the actual lens.

Notice also that Figure 5-1 shows an additional measurement: *maximum aperture*, or, in plain language, the lens's ability to collect light. Get comfortable with lens *aperture, focus* and *focal length*, and you've got everything you need to know about camcorder lenses. So let's run through 'em.

Open Wide

The *aperture* of a camera controls how much light enters the lens. In one way, a lens is just like a window: the bigger it is, the more light it admits. But a lens isn't quite as simple as a window, because the amount of light that gets in is also governed by its focal length (the distance from the lens to the focal point).

For this reason, you can easily determine maximum aperture—the ability of a lens to collect light. Use this simple formula: *aperture = focal length divided by lens diameter.*

For example: if a 100mm lens has a diameter of 50mm, then 100 divided by 50 is 2. The lens's maximum aperture is 2, expressed as "f/2." Lens apertures are "f stops."

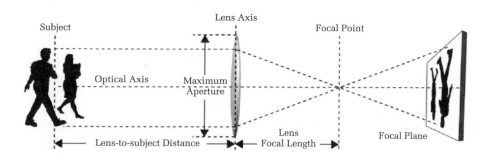

Figure 5-1 *The geometry of a simple lens.*

Since the amount of shooting light varies from dimly lit rooms to bright sunshine, all lenses have mechanical *iris diaphragms* that progressively reduce the aperture in brighter light. Your camcorder's auto exposure system works by using this diaphragm to change the lens's working aperture. In other words, the iris is changing the effective diameter of the lens.

These changes occur in regular increments called "stops," as noted. Each one-stop reduction in aperture size cuts the light intake in half. Most consumer camcorders fail to indicate these f stops. But some units—as well as most familiar single-lens reflex film cameras—indicate f stops by a string of cryptic digits: 1.4, 2, 2.8, 4, 5.6, 8, 11, 16, 22.

Why use these peculiar numbers to label f stops? Simple: long ago, lenses with maximum apertures of f/2 were very common, so f/2 became the starting point. F/1.4 is the square root of f/2; and if you look at the other f stop numbers you'll see that each is a multiple and/or root of another. (Some figures are rounded off: f/11 is not precisely a multiple of f/5.6.)

Just as confusing, these strange numbers appear to work backward. As the f stop number gets bigger, the aperture gets *smaller*. F/22 is the smallest common aperture and f/1.4 (or even 1.2) is the largest.

Why should you care how big the hole is in your camcorder lens? Because the working aperture has important effects on image quality and depth of focus. For critical applications, lenses create better images in the middle of their range of apertures. But for videographers, the crucial concern is the effect of aperture on focus.

Lookin' Sharp!

Before we can explain how aperture affects focus, we need to see what focus is and how the lens does it.

To start with, remember that the focal plane is the *one and only* plane on which the light rays create a sharp (focused) image. If you look at Figure 5-1 again, you'll see that the subject, the lens axis, the focal point and the focal plane are all in a fixed geometrical relationship. That is, you can't change one without affecting the others. You can't move the lens closer to the subject without changing the path of the light rays. And if you do that, you change the position of the focal plane.

In Figure 5-2a, the subject is a long distance from the lens, and its image appears sharply on the focal plane. Since the camcorder's CCD is on that plane, the recorded image is in focus.

Figure 5-2b shows what happens when you move closer to the subject. The geometry of the light rays moves the focal plane forward *away from the CCD*. The result? When the rays do hit the CCD they no longer form a sharp image. You're out of focus.

The solution: change the position of the lens to compensate for the shift in subject distance. As you can see from Figure 5-2c, doing this returns the focal plane to the CCD's position and the image is back in focus again.

This is exactly what happens in your camcorder lens. Lens elements move forward and backward to focus the incoming light on the CCD. Most camcorder zoom lenses feature *internal* focusing: the lenses move inside a fixed-length lens barrel. Most still cameras use *external* focusing: you can actually see the lens grow longer as its front element moves forward for closer focusing.

What's in Focus?

If you adjust the lens to focus on a subject near the camera, then the distant background will often go soft. That's because every lens at every aperture and focusing distance has what's called a certain *depth of field*. Here's how it works. Strictly speaking, the lens focuses perfectly only on one plane at a certain distance from it. Objects receding from that plane—or advancing from it toward the lens—are all technically out of focus.

But in reality, objects up to a certain distance behind or in front of this imaginary

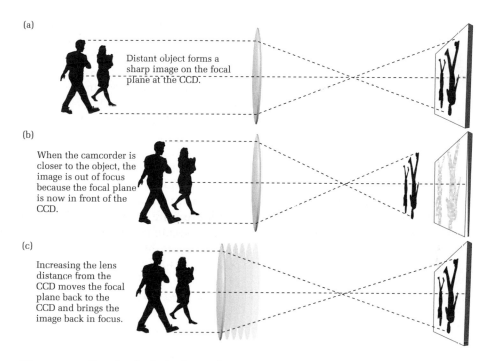

(a)

Distant object forms a sharp image on the focal plane at the CCD.

(b)

When the camcorder is closer to the object, the image is out of focus because the focal plane is now in front of the CCD.

(c)

Increasing the lens distance from the CCD moves the focal plane back to the CCD and brings the image back in focus.

Figure 5-2 *How (and why) a lens's focus is changed.*

plane still appear sharp to the human eye. This sharp territory from in front of the focal distance to behind it is depth of field.

Two factors govern the extent of the depth of field: 1) the focal length of the lens and 2) the working aperture. Since we've already covered aperture, let's see how it affects depth of field.

Each drawing of Figure 5-3 represents a picture made with the same lens, at the same distance from the subjects, and focused on the same person, the woman. The only variable is the aperture. As you can see, the higher the f stop, the greater the depth of field.

In Figure 5-3a, the stop is very high (f/22) and all three subjects are sharp. *In* Figure 5-3b, the aperture widens to the middle of its range (f/5.6). Now the depth of field is more shallow and the man and the tree are at its front and back boundaries. They're starting to lose sharpness.

Open the aperture all the way to f/1.4 (Figure 5-3c) and the depth of field is quite narrow. Though the woman remains sharp, the man and the tree are just blurs. Once

again, the higher (smaller) the f stop, the greater the depth of field, and vice versa.

As noted above, depth of field is also governed by the focal length of the lens. But first, we need to see what that geometrical abstraction *focal length* really means to practical videographers.

The Long and Short of It

The focal length of a lens affects three important aspects of the image: *angle of view, depth of field* and *perspective*.

The angle of view gives the lens its name.

In Figure 5-4, a wide-angle lens (here an angle of 85 degrees) includes a great deal of territory. A normal lens (here 55 degrees) is less inclusive, and a telephoto lens has a very narrow angle of view indeed (here 12 degrees). So, at any distance from the subject matter, the wider the lens angle, the wider the field of view.

Incidentally, the angles selected for Figure 5-4 are only typical examples. Each category—wide, normal and narrow (telephoto)—includes a range of angles.

(a)

f/22

At high (small) lens apertures, depth of field is deep.

(b)

f/5.6

At medium lens apertures, depth of field is reduced. Foreground and background are now slightly soft.

(c)

f/1.4

At low (large) lens apertures, depth of field is quite shallow. Foreground and background are now very soft.

Figure 5-3 *Lens aperture affects the depth of field (all shots made at the same focal length and focused on the woman).*

So while 12 degrees is a narrow angle, 9 degrees is also a narrow angle, though slightly more extreme.

As a videographer, you exploit the differences in lens angle of view all the time. For example: shooting a birthday party you may zoom out to your widest angle, to include more of the scene when the small room won't let you move the camcorder farther back from the action.

Going Soft

Earlier, we noted that lens aperture affects depth of field. Now let's see how lens *focal length* also affects depth of field.

As you can see in Figure 5-5, the wider the angle, the greater the depth of field.

In bright sunshine, a wide-angle lens will hold focus from a couple of feet to the horizon. At the other extreme, in dim light a telephoto lens may render sharp subjects through only a few inches of depth. Notice that we include the light conditions because aperture and focal length working together always govern depth of field. But the rule is, at *any* aperture, the wider the lens angle, the greater the depth of field, at any distance from the subject.

Take special note of that last phrase, *at any distance from the subject.* When some photographers can't get enough depth of field they think, "Hey, no problem: I'll increase my depth of field by going wide-angle."

Wrong! If you widen the angle you *will* increase depth of field, but you also reduce the size of the subject in the frame. To return it to its former size in the wide-angle view, you must move the camera closer. What's wrong with that? There's one last rule of focus we haven't mentioned yet: at *any* focal length (and any aperture too), the closer the lens is to the subject, the less depth of field in the image.

See the problem? Moving closer to compensate for the smaller image effectively wipes out the depth gained from going wide-angle. It's a wash.

We said that widening the angle decreases the subject size, and that leads us to the most dramatic effect that focal length has on the image: *perspective.*

Perspective and Focal Length

Perspective is the depiction of apparent depth—a phantom third dimension in a two-dimensional image.

In the real world, even people with only one functional eye can gauge distance, because the farther away objects are, the smaller they appear. Moreover, they diminish in size at a certain rate because of the geometry of the human optical system.

But other optical systems, such as camcorder lenses, may have very different

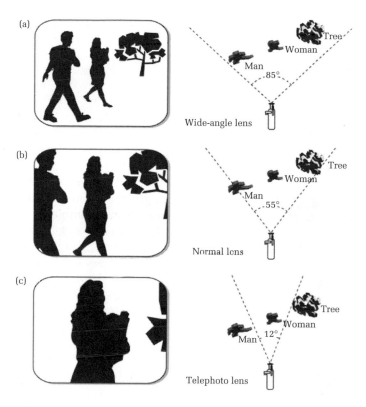

Figure 5-4 *Lens focal length affects angle view (camera is the same distance from subjects in all shots).*

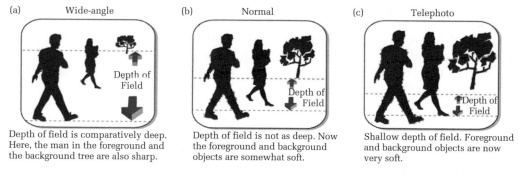

Depth of field is comparatively deep. Here, the man in the foreground and the background tree are also sharp.

Depth of field is not as deep. Now the foreground and background objects are somewhat soft.

Shallow depth of field. Foreground and background objects are now very soft.

Figure 5-5 *Lens focal length affects the depth of field (all shots made at the same aperture and focused on the woman).*

geometries, and objects may shrink much faster or slower than they do in human vision. The perspectives of different lenses depend entirely on their focal lengths.

As you can see, wide-angle lenses exaggerate apparent depth.

Objects shrink quickly as they recede. Normal focal lengths imitate the moderate perspective of human vision (which, of course, is why we call them "normal"). Telephoto lenses reduce apparent depth.

Background objects look much bigger and the space between them and the foreground appears compressed.

As the ground plans beside the drawings in Figure 5-6 show, you have to move the camera in order to achieve these different effects. As you change from wide-angle to telephoto, you must pull back so that the reference figure in the foreground (the man) remains the same size and in the same position in the frame. If you simply

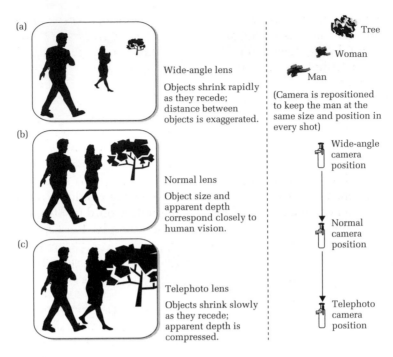

Figure 5-6 *Lens focal length affects relative object size and apparent depth (man, woman and tree are all the same height).*

zoomed in from the first camera position, you would instead get the effect shown in Figure 5-4.

Wide-angle lenses can deliver very dramatic results. People and vehicles moving toward or away from the camera appear to hurtle past. A roundhouse punch swoops toward the lens like an incoming meteor.

But since they exaggerate depth, wide-angle lenses have drawbacks as well. Get too close to people's faces in wide angle and their noses will grow to elephant size.

On the opposite side, telephoto lenses can make great compositions on the screen by stacking up pictorial elements. For instance, if you want to dramatize congestion and pollution, get an extreme telephoto shot of a freeway at rush hour, viewed head-on. Because you're squeezing a mile's worth of cars into 100 yards of apparent depth, you make a bad problem look ten times worse.

Telephoto shots are great for suspense. Near the climax of *Ferris Bueller's Day Off* our hero must make it home through neighborhood backyards before his parents arrive. In one suspenseful telephoto shot, Ferris runs straight toward the camera—and runs, and runs, and runs—without seeming to make any progress. It's the telephoto focal length lens, of course, that compresses the distance he's actually covering.

What's What Here?

So far we've talked about wide-angle, normal and telephoto focal lengths without actually naming any. So what's a wide-angle lens, anyway: 8 mm, 28 mm, 90 mm, 200 mm? The answer: *all of the above*. For a full-size VHS camcorder, wide angle is 8 mm; for a 35 mm still camera it's 28 mm; for a 4 × 5 studio view camera it's 90 mm; and for an 8 × 10 behemoth it's 200 mm. In other words, the perspective delivered by a certain focal length lens depends on the size of the image it creates.

If you draw a picture of it, it looks like another dose of geometry; don't worry, it's really just common sense. The image created by a lens has to fill the camera's frame, right? But the frame is rectangular and the lens is round. That means that the lens diameter must slightly exceed the diagonal of the frame.

Conveniently, lens designers discovered long ago that for any size format, "normal" perspective is produced by a lens focal length slightly greater than the frame diagonal. That's why a 15 mm lens is normal on a camcorder with a half-inch chip, but a 35 mm still camera takes a 50 mm lens instead. (On the larger camera a 15 mm lens would be an ultra-wide.)

What does this mean to you and how do you interpret the lens markings on your camcorder? To understand the answer, you need to know what your camcorder lens is and how it works.

Zoom!

Unless you're using an older style, C-mount lens camera, or a surveillance camera discarded from a convenience store, your camcorder comes with a zoom lens. A zoom lens allows you to shift between focal lengths without changing lenses. In addition, it possesses two critical characteristics:

You can set the zoom lens at any and every focal length between its extremes. That means, if your camcorder lens ranges from 8 to 80 mm, you could, theoretically, set it at a focal length of 43.033 or 78.25 mm.

The zoom lens remains at the same focus throughout its zoom range. Focus on your subject at any focal length and the subject will stay in focus if you zoom in or out. *Note:* some inner focus lenses do not have this capability.

Okay, so your zoom lens is marked, say, 8–80 mm. What does that mean? What's wide-angle, normal and telephoto in that range?

8 mm would be wide-angle, about 15 mm would be normal and 80 mm would be telephoto. But regardless of what's normal for a given lens, the smaller the number (8 mm in this case), the wider the angle. The larger the number (here 80 mm), the tighter the angle.

Today many compact cameras use 1/3-inch CCDs, so their zoom lenses feature shorter focal ranges. In this format, a normal focal length is around 10 mm, a wide-angle setting would be 5 mm, and a strong telephoto would be 50 mm.

For example: the Canon XL1 Mini DV camcorder has a 16:1 zoom that ranges from 5.5–88 mm. By contrast, the Fuji H128SW Hi8 camcorder's 12:1 lens ranges from 4.5–54 mm. Both have 1/3-inch CCDs.

As you can see, knowing what focal lengths mean can affect your choice of camcorder. The Canon offers you a longer telephoto; the Fuji a wider wide-angle. But to interpret the numbers, you have to start with the size of the CCD. 10 mm is a "normal" focal length for a 1/3-inch CCD, while 15 mm is considered normal for a 1/2-inch CCD. Once you figure out your normal focal length, you can roughly calculate wide-angle and telephoto lengths as percentages of normal:

- 35 percent of normal: extreme wide-angle.

- 50 percent of normal: wide-angle.

- 70 percent of normal: mild wide-angle.

- 200 percent of normal: mild telephoto.

- 400 percent of normal: telephoto.

- 500 percent of normal: long telephoto.

As you can see, even the simplest lens on the simplest camcorder is a miracle of modern optical technology. A long, long way from that accidental glop of molten glass.

6

Image Stabilizers:
The Technology That Steadies Your Shots

Robert J. Kerr

If you want steady pictures, use a heavy camera. Unfortunately, today's small format camcorders fly in the face of this general rule of thumb; they're so light, the slightest external vibration can affect the quality of their images.

Enter the image stabilizer. Developed specifically to address this problem, these nifty gadgets now grace many small, lightweight camcorders. In this chapter, we'll examine the types of image stabilization systems and how they work.

A Short Stability History

I suppose that even the cave artists back at the dawn of pre-history had trouble freezing images of fast-moving antelope in their minds before they attempted to draw the beasts accurately on their cave walls. Portrait painters, too, have dealt with the problem of fidgety subjects; perhaps even famed Civil War photographer Matthew Brady cursed the artillery shells shooting past him during his long exposures.

Getting a steady image has been a problem for artists, photographers, cinematographers and videographers for as long as these arts have been practiced.

In the earliest days of photography, the size and weight of the camera and the long exposure time made the tripod *de rigeur*; it was the only way to achieve steady images. As film speed increased, so did portability; cameras such as the hand-held Kodak Brownie brought portable photography to every family. The relatively wide-angle lens further reduced the sensitivity to small camera movements. Still, the motion to depress the shutter trip lever required a steady hand for a steady picture.

That was then, this is now. Today's very fast film and electronic flash make steady still photographs the rule.

On to the silver screen. The first cinematographers also used heavy cameras mounted on tripods. Later, the shoulder supported 16mm cameras also proved heavy enough to provide steady images— if the cinematographer stood still.

Filmmakers got around this limitation by mounting cameras on automobiles and airplanes to capture moving shots. They laid down dolly track, much like train rails, to allow smooth camera movement in action scenes. In the 1970s, Garret Brown invented the Steadicam™, a stabilization device cinematographers on the move used to keep shots steady via an elaborate counterbalance. Again, the success of the Steadicam™ depended on its significant mass.

The story was much the same for early television cameras, whose weight and size also required tripod mounting. Resourceful engineers developed massive camera mounts that panned and tilted effortlessly and glided smoothly across studio floors.

With the late 1970s came the introduction of lightweight battery-operated videotape recorders. Getting steady video pictures with these early models—shoulder-mounted or hand-held—was a problem. A problem aggravated by addition of the zoom lens with its telephoto capability some time later. Various "body brace" mounts appeared on the market for those who wanted to improve the steadiness of their videos, but the light weight of the cameras made them very sensitive to body or other external motion.

The next major coup: the appearance of the solid state electronics color camera for broadcast news gathering. This 25-pound shoulder-mounted camera could be held reasonably steady at moderate focal lengths of the zoom, but required great stamina on the part of the cameraperson. Not to mention that long focal length shots were a real problem.

The Steadicam™ mount developed for the movies could be used for video cameras, but television applications proved infrequent. Advances in solid state electronics made studio cameras smaller and lighter; the addition of housings and heavy zoom lenses kept them heavy enough to provide smooth operation. Enter the 1980s and the rapid growth

of the portable color camera/recorder and camcorder industries. Light weight was a priority; the introduction of the CCD camera chip made video cameras smaller than ever. The palmcorder overtook the steadier, larger shoulder-mounted models; its small size—coupled with a zoom lens—made steady pictures a problem. Fortunately, the same technology also supplied the microcircuit advances needed to provide the solution.

About this time, Garret Brown invented a smaller, lighter version of his Steadicam™ stabilization device. The ever-popular Steadicam JR™ helps to stabilize the images of camcorders weighing less than 5 pounds. It completely isolates the camera from rotational body movements, thanks to a delicate balancing system featuring a low-friction gimbal between the camera and the support handle.

This device, although useful, is not one you'd carry with you on vacation. It will fold to a shoulder mount configuration, but is best applied to specific shooting problems you can plan in advance. When properly deployed, the Steadicam JR™ can yield steady video pictures.

Not too long ago, numerous manufacturers including Panasonic, JVC, Hitachi, Sony and Canon introduced different systems that reduce image jitter problems. Unlike the Steadicam JR™, these systems are integrated into the camcorder itself and do not employ any external hardware.

There are two main image stabilization systems: optical stabilization and electronic stabilization.

The All Electronic System

The electronic system operates by first reducing the area of the CCD chip from which the video image is read (see Figure 6-1). This smaller image then increases in size to fill the whole screen. The exact area scanned then shifts electronically to compensate for unwanted external movement of the camera. Since this system does not actually sense the movement of the camera it must sense camera shake

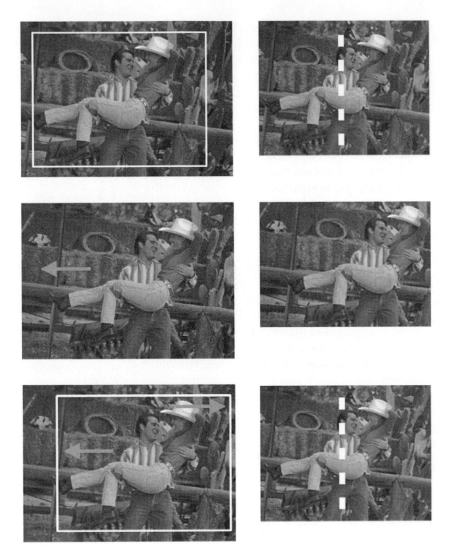

Figure 6-1 *Electronic Image Stabilization.*

from the image only. The trick is to tell camera movement from movement of the subject.

Some manufacturers use a motion detection method based on fuzzy logic. How much to compensate for movement is a decision based on comparing the two images. An image freezes in computer memory and divides into numerous quadrants. A processor compares the differences between the individual quadrants of the frozen image and the current image. If all quadrants change in the same direction, the processor deduces that camera movement caused the differences between the current and stored images. The area of the

CCD being scanned then shifts in the opposite direction to cancel the movement.

Changes in fewer than all quadrants indicate subject rather than camera movement and no compensating action occurs. If quadrant analysis indicates that both the subject and the camera moved, fuzzy logic calculates the image shift needed just to compensate for the camera movement.

One criticism of this system: the loss in image quality brought about by reducing the number of pixels used to create the picture. This loss is noticeable to varying degrees on most camcorders, virtually invisible on others. By the time the video signal goes to the tape and back, especially on standard

8 mm and VHS models, image loss is negligible. Most videographers will find the added stability to be worth the tradeoff.

Optical Image Stabilization

Optical stabilization operates very differently from the electronic system. Instead of sliding an undersized image around the CCD camera chip, the optical system corrects for camera movement before the image reaches the chip. This way, the full resolution of the CCD occurs at all times. The result: no image degradation.

The key optical component is a variable bend prism. As light passes through a prism, it bends in the direction of travel. The amount of bending—known as *refraction*—is a function of the angle at which the light strikes the "in" side of the prism, the relative angle of the "exit" side and the refractive properties of the prism material.

Refraction is what you see when you look at an object at the bottom of a pool or stream. If you look straight down on the object, the light reflected from it passes straight through the surface of the water. No bending or refraction occurs, and you see the object in its actual position. If you view the object in the pool or creek from an angle, thanks to refraction you'll think the object is considerably higher than it really is. If you've ever been spear fishing you'll know what I mean. Try to spear fish from above the water, and you'll have to aim the spear below the spot where you "see" the fish.

Back to the prism. When you think prism, you probably think about how it breaks up light into the color spectrum. Like how raindrops make a rainbow. You see the rainbow because different colors of light bend by differing amounts as they pass through the prism.

Rainbows may be pretty, but they're not so desirable in image stabilization systems; to eliminate any potential rainbow problems manufacturers choose prism materials carefully and restrict the angle of refraction to no more than 1.5 degrees.

The prism used in the optical stabilization system is a unique variable angle

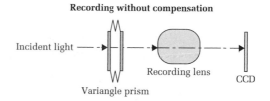

Recording without compensation

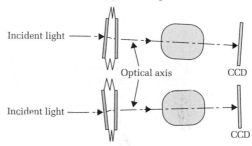

Figure 6-2 *Optical Stabilization System.*

design consisting of two glass plates joined at the circumference by a flexible bellows. A silicone fluid with controlled refractive properties fills the space between the lenses (see Figure 6-2).

When the two plates are parallel, light passes through undisturbed. If, however, the plates contract at any point on the perimeter, the light path bends away from the compressed area. Thus the system can actually *steer* the optical image by manipulating the prism.

The next step: how the system can tell when to perform such steering.

The optical system requires two motion sensors, one for pitch (tilting up and down) and the other for yaw (panning side to side). The sensors amplify and process the motion signals to determine where and how to move the image. The results convert to electric current applied to two drive actuators, one for pitch and one for yaw. These actuators adjust one of the glass plates in the prism relative to the other, directing the image back to its proper position on the CCD sensor.

Field Testing the Two Systems

The easiest way to show how effective these two image stabilization systems are is to test them under adverse conditions. In this case, the test consisted of video recorded on a road of moderate roughness by one camera equipped with electronic image stabilization and then by a second, fitted with optical stabilization.

I did the videotaping from the passenger side of a car, while my business partner drove. We completed one complete trip over the test course for each camcorder. We used a medium telephoto zoom setting to exaggerate the effects of camera motion. Then we brought the tapes back to the studio and compared results.

Both systems provided extraordinary improvement in the stability of the image. With either type of camera, shots of the cars ahead of us stayed steady in the picture—even as the dashboard of the test vehicle shifted up and down at the lower part of the picture. Certainly video from moving vehicles proves much more usable when you engage the image stabilizers.

The optical system makes no use of video information, so it cannot wrongly interpret moving objects as camcorder motion. The same is not true, of course, for the digital system. The question was, how well would its fuzzy logic compensate for an actual moving subject combined with camera pitch and yaw? The answer: fuzzy logic did an excellent job; road images remained steady—even when the car dashboard bounced up and down in the lower part of the picture.

Being almost completely mechanical, the optical system experiences some inevitable delay as its components move and adjust. This makes it somewhat slower to respond to quick jolts, but this does not adversely affect normal operation. A happy by-product of the mechanical system: its remarkable smoothness.

The electronic system is very fast, and tried to compensate for even the most instantaneous bumps in the road. Some image jump occurred, as though the electronics eventually gave up on fixing the jump and instead started fresh with a new image.

An interesting test result with both systems' pan or tilt actions, with the stabilizers engaged, the movement of the image in the viewfinder lagged behind the camera movement, or "floated." The effect is only noticeable when moving the camera while looking in the viewfinder; I didn't notice it when viewing the recorded videotape. This simply tends to demonstrate that two dramatically different approaches provided almost exactly the same satisfactory result.

Cynic that I am, I tend to view a lot of "features" on the higher priced camcorders simply as opportunities for the video department salespersons to move customers to higher priced models.

Not so, however, for the two image stabilizers described here. They work, and prove very useful in many situations, particularly hand-held "shots of opportunity."

Image stabilization is a feature well worth having, particularly on today's small, lightweight camcorders. Use it, and your images will be easier to watch; shoot hand-held telephoto shots without it, and—well, just try it. You'll see what we mean.

7

Solar Panel Imaging: Secrets of the CCD

Loren Alldrin

Buried deep within your camcorder lies a fabulous image sensor that sets it apart from most other image-capturing devices. This image sensor is called a charge-coupled device—that's CCD to you and me.

If you're like most videographers, you probably don't know much about this hidden treasure. And that's a shame. Knowing the hows and whys of CCDs can help make your videography more effective. It can help you differentiate one model from another and decide which camcorder to buy. Moreover, CCD sensors benefit from some of the fastest-advancing technology in camcorders; know the future of sensors and you can peek into the very future of camcorders.

The Short Explanation

Defining the CCD is, uh, simple: a CCD, or interline transfer charge-coupled device, is a tightly packed array of tiny photodiodes consisting of silicon oxide and alternating P and photosensitive N semiconductor

regions on an N-type substrate. Every 1/60th of a second, a transfer pulse triggers a vertical transfer CCD lying between pixel rows to sweep accumulated charges out to the horizontal transfer register (H-CCD) and output amplifier. Newer designs employ an additional P+ embedded photodiode to improve signal-to-noise ratio by controlling irregular dark currents (see Figure 7-1).

Don't worry—that definition went over my head, too. Try this: imagine a huge grid made up of rows of solar panels. Each square-foot panel sits atop a small battery. Only a few inches separate each panel from those to its north and south. About a foot of space lies between one column of panels and the next; within that space you'll find a small pathway running next to each column, as well as along the bottom of the grid. The grid encompasses hundreds of panels in each direction, stretching for about 1/4 of a mile on a side.

When light strikes the panels, they charge their individual batteries. Panels exposed to more light charge faster, while those in the dark build up little or no charge. After

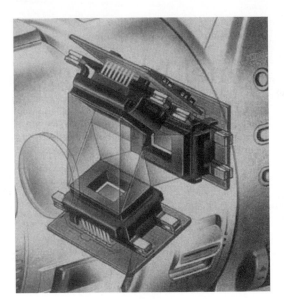

Figure 7-1 *Three-chip designs from Sony and Panasonic use three CCD sensors arrayed around a light-splitting prism.*

a given period of time, tiny trucks drive down between the vertical rows of panels to measure each battery's charge. The trucks then quickly discharge the battery they're measuring and move on to the next panel. When the trucks reach the end of the row, they dump their information onto a conveyor belt. This belt carries the data from the panels back to a central station. It's here that high-paid managers combine the individual measurements, evaluating the electrical output of the grid. Their final report looks a whole lot like a video image.

To relate this rather loose analogy to an actual CCD, first we need to reduce the size of the solar grid by a factor of about 75,000. Most of today's CCDs measure a mere 1/6 inch from corner to corner, though most higher-end camcorders have much larger image sensors.

In our little analogy, solar panels serve as the individual pixels. Today's sensors actually boast hundreds of thousands of these pixels, etched onto the top of a silicon wafer by chemical and photographic processes. The machine tolerances and cleanliness required for making sensors is truly superhuman; most CCDs come from completely automated factories where humans play minor supporting roles. A

tiny speck of dust, harmless enough to us, can actually shut down the CCD manufacturing process.

The batteries represent the buildup of charges in the pixel. Since CCD pixels are photosensitive, they create a charge in proportion to the light striking them. Lots of light makes for a greater charge, while darkness leaves them with little more than the small random charges we call noise. Smaller pixels gather less light and generate weaker charges, a principle manufacturers must address to produce smaller chips and pixels. More on that later.

The trucks mimic the action of the vertical transfer registers, electronic roadways that carry charges out of the active sensing area of the CCD. These registers are necessary because the record electronics do not read charges directly from individual pixels. Instead, charges move en masse down the vertical transfer registers until they reach the edge of the chip.

The conveyor belt is like the horizontal transfer register, which unloads the charges from its vertical counterpart. The horizontal transfer register carries charges off the CCD along the edge of the sensor. Their destination: the amplifiers and specialized circuits that process the signal before recording (see Figure 7-2).

The high-paid managers represent the camcorder's record electronics, processing and modifying signals for recording on magnetic tape. Specialized chips combine color and brightness information into one signal, boost its level and then send it on to the record heads.

Generating a final report on the status of the solar grid could take hours—depending on the speed of the trucks and whether or not those high-paid managers get stuck in an important meeting. In a camcorder, however, videotape records a "final report" from the CCD sensor sixty times per second. If only our government worked that fast.

Sensor Overload

When a solar panel receives too much light, it overcharges its battery. The truck

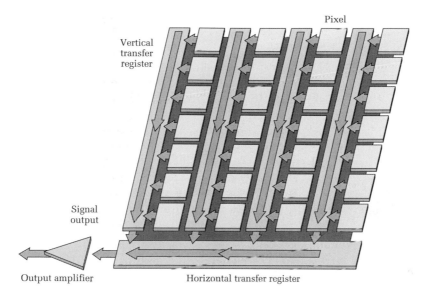

Figure 7-2 *In a standard CCD sensor, pixels feed charges to vertical transfer registers. These in turn feed the horizontal transfer register. From there, signals move through an amplifier to the record electronics.*

tries to read this abnormally high value, only to cook its tiny charge meter in the process. When the truck gets to the bottom of the row, it picks up a new charge meter, but until then severe damage can occur. All the readings it currently holds, as well as all subsequent measurements, are wrong. They all read maximum on the charge meter.

Something similar occurs when a given area of a CCD receives too much light. The vertical transfer register overloads, muddling all the charges for that row. This creates a bright, vertical smear in the image, extending out above and below the offending spot. You've probably seen this before, especially when shooting a bright spot of light against a dark background.

This type of image smear is unique to CCD sensors. Complimentary Metal oxide semiconductor (CMOS) sensors read each pixel directly, doing away with the need for vertical transfer registers and their associated image smearing. CMOS sensors had fallen out of favor with manufacturers, but have recently experienced a renaissance with the advent of HD camcorders. New CCD designs address the bleed problem, resulting in chips less prone to streaking.

Shutter Shenanigans

Although you've heard the term high-speed shutter tossed about, there's actually no such component in the lens/sensor assembly. This term comes from the sensor's ability to mimic the effects of a film camera's fast shutter speed. In a film camera, opening the shutter's blades for a very short period of time exposes the film to a brief snippet of light. Thus a film camera can freeze even the fastest motion.

To understand how this works in a video camera, let's go back to the solar panel scenario. In just minutes, it will be time to measure the grid. But instead of letting the panels finish gathering a complete charge, the trucks sweep through the grid to discharge all the batteries. When the trucks return to collect measurements, the panels have been charging for just a few minutes. Output is lower, but management can still get a picture of the grid's status.

This is what happens with a camcorder's high-speed shutter. No mechanical blade assembly snaps open and shut; instead, the camcorder gives the pixels less time to charge before whisking their signals off to the recorder. If you select an extremely fast shutter speed, say 1/10,000th of a second, the pixels charge up as usual during the first 99 percent of the record cycle. Then, just 1/10,000 of a second before recording, the sensor discharges the pixels. What's recorded on tape is a brief slice of time, representing only the last tiny bit of the record cycle. Since most subjects don't move very far in 1/10,000th of a second, a high-speed shutter freezes the action. Whereas a single frame of an airplane propeller made at 1/60th of a second might show a blur, a single frame of the propeller made at 1/10,000th could show it standing still, each blade distinct.

Two matters to keep in mind when shooting with a high-speed shutter:

1. *Lighting.* Since pixels have so little time to charge, the intensity of the light must be greater to produce a usable image. The higher the shutter speed, the brighter the light required. Shooting at 1/10,000th of a second requires strong daylight. A more conservative setting of 1/2,000th of a second still requires sunlight or strong indoor lighting.

2. *Depth of field.* Because it needs more light, high-speed shutter forces the camcorder's iris to open up. This in turn reduces depth of field, a boon to creative videographers whose camcorders lack manual iris control.

If you want to soften the background behind your subject, reduce your depth of field by increasing shutter speed.

Some camcorders offer a slow-speed shutter, which has the exact opposite properties of high-speed. Slow-speed shutter delivers an image in less light, though much more image smear results. If you're shooting a stationary subject in extremely low light, slow-speed shutter may deliver an improved image. At the very least, you can use it as a unique special effect.

Here's how it works: The trucks servicing our solar array still sweep through the panels to gather readings; they simply don't discharge the batteries completely before reading the charge. This allows the panels to build up a greater charge, boosting the resulting values. Since the batteries retain some residual charge, each reading includes some values from the previous cycles. In the same way, a camcorder in low-speed shutter mode allows the pixels' charge to build up for longer than just one record cycle. It effectively "averages" the light, making fast-moving subjects smear and bleed.

Shrinking CCD Panels

Let's say that the owner of the field that contains the solar array wishes to sell off some of his land, leaving the panels with about 40 percent less area. We can't reduce the number of panels, so there's only one solution—make them smaller. To pack the same number of panels on our now-shrunken plot of land, we must cut them down to just over 7 inches per side. We buy new, smaller trucks and a shorter conveyor belt and fire up the new array. The managers are not happy.

Seems the scaled-down array now puts out about 40 percent less energy. These are lean times, and a cut in output simply won't do. The high-paid managers hire a few high-paid engineering consultants to increase the panels' sensitivity.

There you have it: the plight of the shrinking CCD. Like a tiny solar panel, a pixel's output is a function of its surface area. Shrink the pixel, and its sensitivity suffers. When sensitivity falls, so does the camcorder's low-light performance and resistance to video noise. But manufacturers can't ignore the benefits of smaller sensors—they achieve the same depth of field with smaller lenses. Smaller lenses in turn make for smaller camcorders, and smaller camcorders seem to sell better.

The solution: the microlens. Basically a tiny, translucent bubble formed over each pixel, the microlens gathers incident light that would have otherwise missed the pixel's active sensing area. CCD makers form microlenses into the CCD itself, increasing the effective area of the pixel without actually making it any larger. Thanks to the microlens, 1/3-inch CCDs are now a reality. This microlens technology is so effective, in fact, that a 1/3-inch sensor with micro-lenses may outperform the larger 1/2-inch designs—like realizing even more output from our solar array after placing a glass canopy over each panel.

Another way to offset the effect of smaller pixels is through better amplification. Noise is an enemy to any kind of electrical signal, and smaller signals are the most prone to it. Amplifying a signal just as it leaves the pixel reduces noise and strengthens output. At the time of this writing, manufacturers are experimenting with a new type of CMOS (complementary metal oxide semiconductor) sensor invented by NASA/JPL called the APS CMOS (Active Pixel Sensor) that places an amplifier at each photosite.

These technologies have led to sensors a scant 1/4-inch across—a big step toward the next generation of ultra-compact camcorders.

Smaller or Better

The same technology that allows sensors to shrink allows advances in the other direction as well. If pixels offer improved sensitivity at a smaller size, then CCD makers can pack more pixels on the same size chip. Once manufacturers increase the pixel count of a given sensor, they face a tough decision. They can use the additional pixels for a higher resolution video image, or they can employ them for special image effects at the standard resolution.

Electronic Image Stabilization (EIS) is a good example of such an effect. An increase in pixel count from 410,000 to 470,000 allows the camcorder to use just the central 90 percent of the chip for imaging without resolution loss. Move this region in opposition to the camcorder's movement, and you reduce shake on hand-held shots. Whereas previous EIS schemes resulted in an inevitable loss of resolution, this system shows no noticeable softness of the image.

Color Blind

Some of you may remember from your high school science class that solar panels respond only to the amount of light striking them, not the color of the light. In the same way, CCD pixels are colorblind. So how does a camcorder record a color image?

Camcorders with a single CCD sensor use a mosaic color filter placed over the pixels. Imagine a huge stained-glass window lying over our solar panel array. This window alternates panes of color—either red, green and blue or their complements, yellow, magenta and cyan. Each solar panel sits directly under a colored pane, and responds only to that color of light. When the managers tally up the charges, they make note of each panel's color.

By tracking which pixels see which color, a camcorder extracts both a luminance (brightness and detail) and chrominance (color) signal from a monochrome sensor. Color filters are relatively easy to add to a CCD, though they compromise both color and brightness portions of the video signal. Because there are a limited number of pixels responding to a given color, chrominance has only about 1/4 the resolution of the luminance signal. Placing a colored filter over the pixels also reduces their sensitivity and low-light performance.

There are better, albeit more expensive, ways to coax color information out of monochrome sensors. The best system is the one professional cameras have used for years—three sensors, or chips, with one sensor devoted to each of the three primary colors. Just behind the lens, a precision-made prism splits the incoming light into its red, green and blue components. Some manufacturers use an array of dichroic mirrors to sift the light; these coated mirrors reflect only a certain color, letting the rest pass.

Because there's no color filter clouding the sensors in three-chip designs, resolution does not drop. With a chip "specializing" in each primary color, hues are very accurate and natural. The result: a better picture than a single CCD can deliver.

Future CCDs

The trend toward smaller CCDs will most likely die with current 1/6-inch designs. Sensors of this size will work with incredibly small lenses, making the transport and tape medium itself the biggest obstacles to further camcorder downsizing.

Manufacturers will undoubtedly continue in the other direction, toward larger sensors with increased resolution. Chips with pixel counts measured in the millions allow for special effects and electronic stabilization without resolution loss. The advent of HDTV and the growing popularity of today's 16:9 formats will drive the market toward ultra-high-resolution sensors. HDTV cameras already have 2/3-inch sensors with over two million pixels.

Advances in sensors drive other areas of the video market as well. Camera resolutions are already much greater than those of camcorder transports. As sensors evolve far beyond the recording ability of camcorders, consumers will push for new video signal formats. Sensor evolution shows no sign of slowing. As long as there's a sun in the sky sending light to CCD pixels and solar panels alike, better sensors will be here to capture it. The future of sensors is bright indeed.

8
Sifting the Light:
A Look at Lens Filters

Dave Welton

Did you know that Ansel Adams used a lens filter in virtually all of his photographs? It's true. If lens filters can do wonders for black-and-white photography, just imagine what they can do for your videos.

Lens filters offer a simple way to get better images. These wafers of glass can soften the face of a bride, fake a sunset at high noon or add sparkle to the chrome on a vintage car.

I asked professional videographer Myron "Buzz" Buzzini to help guide us through the world of lens filters. With 30 years of image-gathering experience—in both photography and video—Buzz was the perfect man for the job.

Buzz is a firm believer in the power of lens filters. He first used them with film, but didn't forget their usefulness as he made the transition to video.

On a bright Northern California morning, Buzz visited my office with a big bag of filters. We pointed my camcorder out the window and experimented with each one. In the article that follows, we'll share some of the insights that Buzz and I discussed that morning—insights that could help any videographer in their quest for high-quality images.

What's in a Filter?

According to Buzz, "A lens filter is little more than a piece of glass that attaches to the front of a camcorder's lens." Two basic types of filters are available: round filters that screw onto the front of the lens, and square filters that slide into a special housing attached to the lens.

The round variety is available in many different sizes. Make sure the lens filter you purchase will fit your camcorder's lens—not all camcorders have threads the same size. Generally speaking, palm-sized camcorders have smaller lens thread sizes, and full-sized camcorders have larger sizes.

Common camcorder lens thread sizes include 34, 37, 43, 46, 49, 52, 55 and 72 mm. The thread size is often marked on the front of the lens. If you can't find it there, check the specifications page of your owner's manual; it's typically listed under "lens diameter."

Square filters that slide into a special holder—called a matte box—offer an advantage over the round variety: the filters are all the same size, so only the matte box need be fitted to a particular camcorder lens. This aspect is handy if you have two different camcorders, or even a camcorder and a 35 mm still camera. You simply buy a matte box for each camera, then use the filters with either unit.

Both the matte box and round filter systems allow a videographer to use multiple filters. With the threaded type, you simply screw one filter onto another. With the matte box variety, just slide another square filter into the housing.

Filter Types

With Buzz's help, we'll sort through the different types of lens filters and explore applications for their use. Let's start with basic filters and work our way to the more exotic species.

"If you only have one filter, make sure it's a skylight filter," Buzz says. "And keep it attached to your lens, always."

To the human eye, a skylight filter (also called a haze or UV filter) looks like a clear piece of glass, but don't be fooled. This filter does its magic by reducing the ill effects of both ultraviolet light and atmospheric haze on an image. Equally as important, this filter will protect your expensive camcorder lens from fingerprints, dust, grime and damage. When you buy a new camcorder, get a skylight filter, attach it and leave it attached—permanently.

Neutral density (ND) filters reduce the amount of light that enters a camcorder's lens. They prevent exposure problems in very bright scenes—like a white polar bear on a snow bank on a sunny day, for example. Available in various densities, these filters work like a pair of sunglasses.

"Neutral density filters are great if you want to blur the background of a portrait-type image," says Buzz. To do this, simply focus on your subject with a neutral density filter attached to your camcorder, and—just like magic—the background obscures into a pleasant fuzzy smudge. The filter forces the camcorder to open its iris wider, which reduces the depth of field, leaving the background out of focus. Naturally, this works best when the background is some distance away from the subject.

A polarizing filter eliminates reflections from shiny surfaces like water or glass. These filters rotate in a specially designed housing; the videographer simply looks in the viewfinder and twists the filter until the reflections diminish. It's quite an amazing effect, when you see it for the first time. They really work.

Polarizing filters are also great for darkening the sky while making it appear slightly bluer.

Color correction filters perform the same function as your camcorder's white balance circuits; they correct the color temperature of the incoming light so your colors will look right, indoors and out. Since all camcorders now include white balance circuits, there's not much need for these filters in videography. They're still commonly used in film cameras, though.

Creative uses for colored filters abound. After all, they're available in almost every color of the rainbow. For example, a blue filter helps simulate a moonlit night; a sepia filter adds an old-time, historical look to an image. Have fun, and experiment with plenty of different colors.

Exotic Varieties

The center spot filter is great for portrait shots because it creates a sharp center image surrounded by a soft, fuzzy border. It's perfect for romantic wedding images.

The fog-effect filter creates "mist" where none previously existed. These filters will also enhance the appearance of existing fog. Like many filters, fog filters are available in different grades, or "strengths," that alter the intensity of the effect.

A soft-focus filter gives a soft look to an entire image. They're perfect for facial

Figure 8-1 *Fog Effect Filter.*

Figure 8-2 *Star Effect Filter.*

close-ups because the filter actually blends away tiny lines in the skin. A warm color is sometimes added to soft focus filters to enhance skin tones. This combination can actually make people look better than they do in real life.

Graduated filters are transparent on the bottom and very gradually change to an opaque color on top. A classic application for a graduated filter is enhancing, or outright faking, a sunset. With the camcorder mounted on a tripod and a graduated amber filter attached, carefully frame the image so that the colored portion of the filter overlaps the sky. Since the bottom portion of the filter is clear, the lower portion of the scene is unaffected, while the sunset glows beautifully. If you're using a matte box filter system, it's easy to adjust the filter's effect by simply sliding it up and down within the housing.

A star filter transforms points of light within an image into brilliant star shapes. These filters add glamour and excitement to any scene. Be careful not to overuse this filter; the effect will lose its punch once you've seen it a few times.

Avoiding Grime

After placing an accidental fingerprint on one of Buzz's filters, I decided to ask about cleaning. "Don't use window cleaner!" he quickly said. According to our expert, the chemicals in a typical glass cleaning solution can actually dissolve the coating on a lens or filter. Ouch!

"Also, be sure not to use facial tissue," he added. "Blow off the dust before you begin. You wouldn't want to 'sand' your lens, would you? That's precisely what happens when you use a rough facial tissue on a dusty lens." Special lens tissues and cleaning solutions are available at video and photography stores.

To remove dust from a lens, either use a special brush designed for that purpose, or a blast of air from an aerosol lens cleaner. Buzz makes a final lens cleaning admonition: "Avoid using eyeglass cleaning products because they might be too abrasive—eyeglass lenses are usually tougher than camcorder optics."

Unfortunately, life sometimes throws us challenges—like when your niece graces your lens with a chocolate-coated thumb print. Of course, you don't have any lens cleaning supplies handy. What to do?

Hopefully, you have a skylight filter protecting your lens. If so, simply remove it and continue shooting—this time, out of reach of your niece.

But what if you don't have a skylight filter? In a pinch, Buzz says it's OK to run tap water over a filter to clean it. Use a soft cotton-fiber cloth to dry. Another option is the time-tested technique of breathing on the glass, then wiping with a soft cloth. But limit these emergency procedures to lens filters—not expensive camcorder lenses. You can always buy another lens filter, but replacing the lens on most camcorders is an expensive and complicated proposition.

If you're reading this and simultaneously kicking yourself because you've broken Buzz's cleaning rules for years, hold on before you pitch your expensive optics in the trash heap. Scratched optical coatings are salvageable—it's possible to remove the coating and spray on a new one. This service is available through good video or photography retail outlets and repair facilities.

Filter Care

Most filters come packaged in round plastic cases. These cases are great for protecting filters when they're not on a camcorder. But don't expect a filter to last if you're in the habit of slipping them in your pants pocket or throwing them into a camera bag. They'll become scratched and useless in quick order.

Buzz offers a space-saving alternative for lens filter storage: screw all filters together and put a lens cap on both ends. This protects each filter, and reduces the amount of space they would occupy if each filter was in its own case.

What can you do if you can't unscrew a filter because it's too tight? Use a lens filter wrench. These devices are similar to a jaw-type jar opener, and they have the same purpose—to help loosen stuck threads. Is there a better solution? "Yes. Don't over-tighten the threads, and keep them clean from grime," says Buzz.

Buzz recalls a harrowing experience he had while on a back-country shoot. A couple of filter cases fell out if his shirt pocket, rolled down the hill and vanished into a fast-moving stream. He never saw the cases—or their contents—again. The moral of this story? Always stow your gear safely and securely.

Let's Go Shopping

A quick glance at a deceptively simple filter could give you the mistaken impression that one brand is as good as another. "Not so," says Buzz. He instructs videographers to look for filters that use a threaded metal retaining ring to hold the glass inside the metal housing. The retaining ring holds the glass against a small flange on the other side of the housing. Some filters use a plastic device to hold the glass in place; Buzz doesn't like this type because the plastic often becomes loose with wear.

Avoid filters with housings made entirely of plastic; these housings may not retain their shape. Also, be careful to check the quality of filters pitched as an add-on sale to a camcorder purchase.

Shop for filter housings painted matte black; these help to reduce unwanted reflections. And look for filters that come with storage containers. Shop around—the price can vary widely on the exact same filter.

A wide range of manufacturers offer a countless variety of lens filters. There are literally too many different brands and types to mention here. A quick glance through one company's catalog revealed over 30 different filters available in 14 different sizes—and that's just the screw-in variety.

Generally, the larger the filter, the higher the price.

If you're feeling overwhelmed by the huge selection of lens filters, fear not. Some filter companies have selected a few of their most popular filters and assembled them in pre-packaged kits; these are worth checking out.

One filter manufacturer makes it easy to sample the world of lens filters before you buy. Tiffen makes their Hollywood/FX Demo Kit available on loan from participating dealers. The comprehensive kit has 30 different filters including center spot, polarizing, color-graduated and star filters. Also packaged in the kit is a selection of Tiffen's versatile Pro-Mist and Soft/FX filters that combine a warming filter with fog and soft focus effect. The kit comes with adapter rings to fit popular camcorders: 49, 52, 55, 58, 62, 67 and 72 mm. Call to see if your dealer is participating in this program.

Cokin offers their Optilight filter kit in 37 and 46 mm sizes ($32 regular kit price; $52.99 with polarizing filter). Four different configurations are available to fit your videography needs. All kits include a skylight filter and two other assorted filters which may include neutral density, polarizing, warm color or soft focus filters.

No Free Lunch

So far, all we've talked about are the wonders of lens filters. Is there a downside? Yes.

First off, there's an optical price you pay when using lens filters. Each additional lens distorts the image and reduces the intensity of the light that enters your camcorder. Better filters offer less chance of these ills, but even the best glass distorts the light passing through it a little bit.

While lens filters won't affect the accuracy of a camcorder's external white balance sensor, through-the-lens (TTL) white balance systems may require that you manually adjust the white balance after adding filters (if manual white balance is available). If you don't have a color viewfinder, use a color monitor so you can see the effect of the filter on your image. This is good advice no matter what filter you're using.

The matte box filter system is great, but before you buy, make sure it won't interfere with your automatic focus system. This is more likely to happen with older camcorders without inner focus lenses. You may have to resort to manual focusing.

Ideally, you should use lens accessories that directly fit your camcorder's lens threads. But when that's not possible, a myriad of threaded filters are available to solve the problem. If you must adapt, start with filters that are bigger than your lens. A smaller filter might cause undesirable darkening at the corners of the image (called "vignetting"). This effect is most noticeable when you zoom to a wide-angle setting.

There's no doubt that videographers love their high-tech electronic toys. But don't forget there's a simple way to improve images without circuitry—lens filters.

9
Dissecting a Video Editing Computer

Joe McCleskey

Ever wonder what exactly makes a video editing computer work? Ever want to know what separates the ordinary, game-playing, document-creating PC from the kind that can easily pump out hour-long, professional-looking home videos? No matter if you already own a video editing computer or plan to buy one—it still pays to know exactly what makes this special breed of machine tick. We'll discuss PCs here, since they are much more dissectible than Macs, but the concepts are the same.

In this article, we'll take apart a typical video-editing computer piece by piece, much the same way you might have taken apart a hapless frog in junior high science class. Why? To help you troubleshoot problems, increase performance, and make more informed purchasing decisions.

So without further introduction, let's put on our rubber gloves, grab our scalpels, and get busy.

Software

Editing software is the interface between your ideas and a finished product. Software used in video editing covers a wide range of different types and capabilities, including nonlinear editing, photo and graphics manipulation, audio editing and special effects creation, to name just a few. Once you've got the basic system together, the software provides the means to make your video dreams a reality. It's what you'll spend the most time learning to operate—and the most time blaming when things don't work properly—so don't skimp here; be sure to find the software that works best for your needs.

CPU

The CPU (central processing unit) is the heart of any computer. A computer can really do only two things: 1) perform calculations and 2) move or copy information. The CPU does these things; in essence, it is the computer itself on a single chip. A video editing computer needs the fastest CPU available for rendering. Some use two or more CPUs; video editing machines greatly benefit from an added CPU to share the task of rendering video files, even if the software doesn't explicitly support multiple CPUs.

Motherboard

The motherboard holds the CPU, connecting it to the other parts of the machine. The part of the motherboard that ships info back and forth between the components is called the bus. Video editing machines require motherboards with fast bus speeds in order to handle the immense flow of information that takes place while editing. Faster bus speeds result in faster rendering times. Also located on the motherboard are places to connect peripheral devices—hard drives, video capture cards, FireWire cards and memory. In video editing machines, the motherboard should have a number of open PCI slots for peripheral devices, lots of room to expand RAM, connections for high-speed hard drives and a bus speed of at least 100 MHz.

RAM

RAM (random access memory) is a computer's temporary storage place for information. It's the place where the software stores and moves pieces of information for processing. A video editing computer typically has lots of high-speed RAM available—at least 1 GB for starters, but often several times that. Both speed and quantity of RAM will have an effect on the rendering speed of your computer: the more, and the faster, the better.

Hard Drives

The hard drive of a computer is the place where information gets stored in the long term. (Contrast this with RAM, which stores information only until you turn off the computer). When you capture a clip, it writes onto the hard drive. Note that editing computers should have two hard drives—one for the operating system and software, and another solely for video and audio capture and storage. The separate video/audio drive should be the largest, fastest drive you can afford, should spin at 7,200 RPM and should minimally support a true sustained data transfer rate of at least 5 MB per second in order to handle the rigors of video editing. And always remember: the amount of storage space on the video capture drive directly relates to the length of video clips you can work on at any one time. You can never have too much space and good drives can be found for as little as $0.25 per gigabyte.

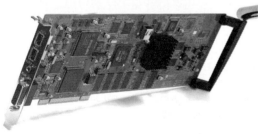

Video Capture/FireWire Card

To edit video on a computer, you need some way to get the video from the camera or VCR onto the hard drive. This is the role of the video capture card (or, more commonly, the FireWire or IEEE 1394 card). A digitizer card can take an ordinary analog video signal and digitize it (change it to a series of ones and zeroes). A FireWire card allows transfer of digital video from a digital camcorder or VCR to the hard drive. Video capture cards vary widely in price and performance, but the only real concern with a FireWire card is whether or not it works and continues working—the resulting video will look exactly the same as it did when you shot it, regardless of the quality of the FireWire card. Some capture cards have special hardware that improves rendering speed and performance during editing.

10
Battery Basics

Michael Fitzer

Does this sound familiar? You're running out of daylight but you only have one more shot to get off before you "call it a day." There are still two ticks left on your camera's battery indicator and then suddenly … everything goes black! A dead battery on your camera and no charged spare in your bag means … no shot. Knowing more about the type of batteries on the market and how they work will allow you to find the right one for your needs and hopefully keep you from missing that golden moment.

What Is This Little Thing?

Everyone knows what a battery is … right? Okay, before reading on, see if you can come up with a definition for the word. You have 10 seconds.

Okay, time's up. Coming up with the correct definition was probably more difficult than you thought, right? Put simply, a battery can be any kind of tool that stores energy for later use. However, in this context, the word battery refers to any electrochemical mechanism that uses two electrodes—an anode and a cathode—connected via an electrolyte, that converts chemical energy into electricity.

Eenie, Meenie, Minie, Moe

There are a number of durable and dependable batteries on the market. As for manufacturers, it's difficult to call one better than another. Canon, Sony, Fuji, Kodak, JVC, Panasonic, Kyocera, they all make quality products. Knowing which type of battery best suits your needs will allow you to make the right choice, at the right price.

When thinking about your next battery purchase, there are three different battery types you will want to consider, NiCd, NiMH, and Li-Ion.

- NiCD—Nickel Cadmium is an older cell technology. However, it has a good weight to energy ratio and a good service lifetime, which makes it a good choice for portable devices. A drawback to the NiCD battery type is it is well known for suffering memory effect. Therefore, it is best to let Nickel Cadmium batteries completely discharge before recharging.

"Memory effect," more accurately described as voltage depression, refers to the understanding that when a battery is not completely discharged between recharging cycles, the battery "remembers" the shortened energy cycle and thus delivers a reduced run time. Voltage depression does not mean your battery has low storage capacity nor will it permanently damage your battery. Fully discharging and then recharging the battery will often correct the problem.

- NiMH—Nickel Metal Hydride is the most common battery type available on today's market. While other cell types are more popular because of their ability to hold a charge, NiMH cells are relatively inexpensive to produce and that low production cost transfers to you, the consumer. While NiMH cell types do experience memory effect, it is not nearly as prevalent in this type as it is in the NiCD batteries. NiMH batteries can also be charged many more times than NiCD batteries.

- Li-Ion—Lithium Ion is one of the most recent advances in battery cell types now on the commercial market. Advances with Li-Ion cell types make these batteries lighter than their counterparts, saving users the physical wear-and-tear of transporting and using heavier battery types. Additionally, the Li-Ion cell type provides more power and suffers no real problems with memory effect. As for price, advanced engineering costs associated with the Li-Ion technology mean a much higher cost for you, the consumer.

When used under normal conditions (i.e., no extreme heat, moisture or excessive physical abuse), any of these cell types will provide you 2 to 3 years of dependable operation.

Smart Batteries

So, you've been out in the field for most of the day. You'd like to continue uninterrupted but are unsure about which one of your batteries has the most charge. In the old days you might swapout batteries on your camera or other portable device, to reveal which one is up to the task. However, many batteries today are now equipped with complex "fuel gauging" technology that allows users to read a built-in lighted meter that indicates how much battery life remains on the current charge.

Batteries that utilize fuel-gauging microprocessor technology are more expensive than those without, but some consider the increased user friendliness worth the extra cost. While they are efficient mechanisms, no battery can hold a charge indefinitely. Just like single use batteries, rechargeable batteries, when left unused for long periods, will de-charge on their own. As previously stated, to avoid problems with voltage depression it is best to de-charge and then recharge or "cycle" your battery. You might think that in order to de-charge the battery you have to use it until it quite simply quits or pay more for a battery charger/de-charger. While those solutions ensure a full de-charge, depending on what you're doing at the time, that former scenario could prove to be rather inconvenient and the latter is more expensive. While it's best to cycle your batteries at least once every month to ensure maximum performance, you do not necessarily have to be using your battery to make sure it de-charges. You can leave it unused for a long period of time and achieve the same results. Just be sure when you store your batteries that they have attained a full charge and keep them in a cool, dry place.

Alternative Fuel "Sell"

With all the talk about new ways to energize the country, the potential doesn't stop at the car in your driveway. Someday very soon you will be able to walk into your local retailer and purchase a handy little fuel cell for your home video camera. In fact, if current research is any indication, fuel cells that use methanol as their primary renewable source of energy could be available for portable consumer devices in a few years.

While these new sources of energy pack up to 60 percent more energy than the most reliable battery on the consumer market, the chance that they'll immediately replace your standard batteries is slim. Nevertheless, the possibilities are very exciting. When the technology finally comes into play you will no longer replace your battery or have to hunt down an A/C outlet to recharge. Instead, your camera (or other portable device) will house a fuel cell capable of accepting a liquid or gaseous "injection" in order to recharge. Whether you're next battery purchase is driven by need, desire or price, there's a battery on the market for you. Just remember, no matter what type you buy, following the rules of good care will ensure you get the best performance out of your battery.

Sidebar

Compact Chargers

If you want to charge your batteries but hate packing and unpacking the standard charging plate and AC adapter cord, a number of manufacturers are making compact wall chargers. There's no cumbersome plate and no long cord to manage. Simply snap your batteries into place, flip up the AC plug and let the action happen.

Conventional AA Approach

Many digital cameras on the market can use the conventional AA-size batteries. While very affordable to stock, the standard alkaline batteries are no match for the video world. A couple of zooms, some recording, a playback and "poof" you're out of juice. But there are some rechargeable AA NiMH cells that do well to serve short-term needs. Just make sure you're packing a quality brand and a darn-good charger.

Michael Fitzer is an Emmy award-winning commercial and documentary writer/producer.

11
Data Storage Devices: Room to Move

Charles Fulton

There are a lot of considerations for storage when you're dealing with video. You need room on a hard drive to capture footage. You need a scratch drive for rendering effects. You need an optical drive for outputting your projects. You might need an archive system too.

With all the need for storage, where do you start? Well, by reading this sentence, you've taken the first step in realizing that storage is a vital part of your video workflow. We'll try to take you through the rest of the way.

On the Inside

Your editing computer has at least one hard drive. This drive is used to boot your computer and also to store your applications. You could capture video to this drive, but the better way is to capture to a different hard drive. (A lot goes on behind the scenes on your computer, all requiring a lot of hard drive writes. These writes accumulate and degrade the performance of the drive for anything else you need

to do with it.) You can add another drive fairly easily if you know what interface your machine uses.

I Need More Space—Quick!

The most common interfaces that data moves through on its way to or from storage media (on the type of computer system most of us use) are ATA, SATA, eSATA, FireWire and USB 2.0. ATA and SATA are internal interfaces. eSATA is an external version of SATA—the primary difference is the use of a different connector that is more tolerant of abuse. All of the speed that SATA offers is duplicated with eSATA.

FireWire and USB 2.0 are popular for their ease of use and portability, though neither has the raw performance of ATA, SATA or eSATA. While FireWire and USB 2.0 are both fast enough to handle DV streams, the performance hit will rear its ugly head when you're rendering effects or your final project. That said, if you find yourself needing more hard drive space right now and there's no eSATA port and you don't have room for another internal drive, it's hard to go wrong with a FireWire or USB 2.0 drive.

There are also some benefits to using a network-attached storage (NAS) device. If you have a gigabit Ethernet switch between this device and the computers you edit with, you can get some remarkably high data transfer rates. The added benefit is that you can access the same files from any computer on your network.

What should you look for on a hard drive? Capacity is the first thing that usually comes to mind, naturally. The sweet spot for price vs. capacity (lowest cost per gigabyte) is moving toward 500 GB drives, now that the big manufacturers are shipping 750 GB and 1 TB drives. You'll also see a reference to cache size—8 MB is most common, but anything above 2 MB is generally fine. Big caches give you a speed advantage for dealing with a lot of small files, not a handful of really big files. Spindle speeds of 7200 rpm are the most common you'll come across, for good reason: they're fast and they're a good value. While you can get 10,000 and 15,000 rpm hard drives, they're pricey and they run hot. But if you need to render something really fast, this is one potential place where you could get a speed advantage. We think the best place to implement a drive with a spindle speed above 7200 rpm is as a scratch drive, though we've seen a few computers that have them installed as boot drives.

Out with It

Once you get your project just the way you want it, you need to output your project. If you're operating in standard def, this means writing a DVD (see the January 2007 issue's DVD Authoring Software Buyer's Guide for more on this). DVD burners have become nearly a commodity item, but there are some differentiating factors. First, check out the software bundle. OEM versions of a popular disc authoring program and a DVD-Video player app are the most common

apps that you'll come across. If the drive includes LightScribe, the ability to burn a label directly to the reverse side of special discs, labelmaking software is generally included as well.

Most drives sold today burn both DVD-R and DVD+R, along with their rewriteable variants. A handful of drives can also handle DVD-RAM as well. CD burning is pretty much a given as well, but a notable drive that lacks CD reading or writing capabilities is Pioneer's BDR-101A Blu-ray burner.

Speaking of Blu-ray, this is the most common HD disc format for burning at the moment. Toshiba, however, has finally announced the first HD DVD burners, the SD-H903A (desktop) and the SD-L902A (mobile). It's worth noting that most disc authoring software titles that are aware of HD burners are aware of Blu-ray drives and not HD DVD at this point, but we'd half-expect some software developers to offer patches to allow burning of formats they don't already support. It's still too early to declare a winner to the format war, but the entrant of an HD burner to the fray certainly makes things more interesting. As magazine editors and as fellow consumers, we just hope the war draws to a conclusion—the sooner, the better.

Not-Too-Cold Storage

Now that you're done with your project, what do you do with the raw footage and all of your project files? If you logged your tapes with your editing software, you won't need to keep the original capture files around, since you can re-capture from tape if necessary. If you'd rather not re-capture, you can burn everything in your project to DVD (you'll probably need several DVDs for bigger projects) or onto Blu-ray or HD DVD. Another option for really big projects or recurring clients would be simply copying all of your project files, including video clips and audio clips, onto to a new hard drive, then removing the hard drive and putting it into a padded box and onto a shelf with a label. This is a somewhat expensive option, but it's an extremely convenient one.

As far as long-term storage of any type of media goes, the maxim "if you're comfortable, it's comfortable" can be safely followed. Avoid wild fluctuations or extremes of temperature and humidity, and keep the dust down if at all possible. The general recommendation is 68 degrees Fahrenheit at 40% relative humidity. There are some good discussions of best practices for archiving your media online—do a little searching and you'll find the information you need.

12
Sound Track: Microphone Types

Robert G. Nulph

Has the selection of microphones offered by your favorite electronics store ever overwhelmed you? Have you stared in awe at the vast array of silver or black, big or small, expensive or cheap microphones available to you? Have you wondered about HiZ versus LowZ, dynamic versus condenser, cardioid versus omnidirectional or shotguns and lavaliers versus handheld and boundary mics? Throughout this chapter, we will take a look at impedance, the two major ways microphones work, microphone pickup patterns and microphone styles. So sit back, relax and proceed through this quick look into the sometimes confusing world of microphone choice.

HiZ and LowZ

Before you choose the style of microphone you'd like to use, you have to know what impedance of microphone is compatible with your camcorder. Your system might require a HiZ microphone input.

Impedance is the resistance to the flow of electrical current in a circuit or element. We measure impedance in ohms, a unit of resistance to current flow. The lower the impedance, the better the microphone or recording device.

Most older consumer camcorders have a high impedance (HiZ) microphone jack meant to be used with high impedance microphones. These microphones range in impedance from 600–1400 ohms. HiZ microphones are very sensitive and require very little amplification, which is why less sophisticated consumer equipment is designed for them. They are, however, susceptible to hum and electronic noise and can be used only with a very short microphone cable.

Low impedance microphones, with an impedance level of 100–600 ohms, have become the norm in video production. Even much of today's consumer equipment now has low impedance inputs to allow you to use professional microphones. Using these professional microphones with low impedance gives you two advantages: (1) They are not as affected by electronic hums and noises that can be caused by fluorescent lighting or electric motors and (2) you can use long cables without worrying about outside interference.

If you buy a microphone and plug its cable into your camcorder and nothing happens, it may be due to an impedance mismatch. If your camcorder requires a HiZ microphone and all you have are professional mics, don't despair. You can purchase an inexpensive LowZ to HiZ transformer. Plug your microphone cable into the transformer and the transformer into your camcorder. You should now be able to use any professional microphone with your system. Now that we've gotten impedance choice out of the way, we can move on to the other mic variables.

Inner Workings

Most microphones fall within one of the two major families: dynamic or capacitor (condenser) microphones. The dynamic microphone has a fixed magnet, a diaphragm that moves when sound hits it, and a coil attached to the diaphragm. When the diaphragm moves, the coil moves, making changes in the magnetic field. These changes generate voltage through the microphone cable to the recorder, amplifier or speakers (see Figure 12-1).

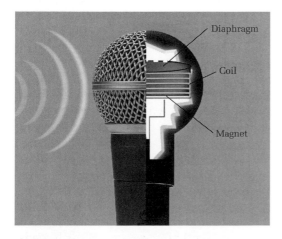

Figure 12-1 *Dynamic Mic—In a dynamic mic, a vibrating diaphram moves a magnet and coil past one another to create an electrical signal.*

The dynamic microphone has a number of attributes that you need to take into account when deciding on the type of microphone you need. This type of microphone is extremely durable. Dynamic mics can tolerate wide temperature ranges and humidity as well as take a great deal of abuse. I have seen them dropped, banged around, used in the dead of winter, in the high heat of a tropical rain forest and even (believe it or not) used as a hammer (not recommended), all without affecting the mic's ability to record high quality audio. Dynamic mics are also fairly inexpensive. Good quality dynamic microphones like the Shure SM58 costs around $200. Lower quality dynamics run as low as $77. Even the extremely good dynamics rarely cost more than $350.

Another attribute of the dynamic mic is its ability to provide a warm, rounded sound for vocals and yet take the abuse of recording high impact sounds such as drums and screaming voices. Many lead singers in rock bands use the handheld dynamic because of its ruggedness and its ability to pick up a wide range of sounds from screams to whispers. However, the dynamic microphone has a less accurate sound reproduction than the condenser.

A final advantage of the dynamic is that it requires no outside power. Plug it into your recorder or sound system and go. No batteries or power supplies needed. In video work, the dynamic microphone is ideal for on-camera interviews, recording very loud sound sources and crawling around the toughest terrain.

The capacitor or condenser microphone uses variations in voltage within a capacitor. The capacitor, which is capable of holding an electrical charge, is made up of two parallel plates, one fixed and one moving, separated by a small space. When sound waves hit the movable plate, it vibrates and causes a change in the amount of voltage held by the capacitor. This change in voltage is sent down the wires to be recorded or amplified through speakers (see Figure 12-2).

The condenser microphone has a number of attributes that are important for the videographer to consider. The condenser mic is not so rugged as the dynamic, and the more expensive models are downright delicate. They range in price from around $100 for a basic condenser to well over $5,000 for a high-end studio mic. Although the condenser is usually more expensive, its frequency response and true sound rendering make it ideal for the videographer seeking the best fidelity.

You will have to consider one other attribute when purchasing a condenser microphone: its need for an additional power source. A battery, or AC power source can provide this additional "phantom" power. If you have a mixing board with phantom power built into the inputs, it will supply power to any mic you plug in. You can purchase a condenser microphone and begin using it right away. However, if you plan to plug a phantom-powered microphone into your camcorder, you'll need to purchase a phantom power unit to supply juice for your mic. Fortunately, most microphones that you would use for field production have a battery space built in. You just have to remember the batteries.

Pickup Patterns

Whether you choose either a dynamic or condenser microphone, you must also decide the best pickup pattern for your production. There are four primary pickup patterns to choose from: omnidirectional, cardioid (or unidirectional), hypercardioid (or shotgun) and bidirectional (see Figure 12-3).

The omnidirectional microphone picks up sound in every direction—front, back and sides (see Figure 12-3a). This microphone is good if the sound source comes from a wide variety of directions and is moving from one side to another in front of the mic.

The cardioid or unidirectional microphone picks up sound primarily in a heart shape from the front of the microphone, including a little from the sides, but does not pick up from the back (see Figure 12-3b). This pickup pattern is excellent for voice mics and miking musical instruments.

The hypercardioid microphone picks up only sound from the front and is very directional (see Figure 12-3c). You must point it at the sound source to get a good pickup. This type of pick-up pattern is excellent for isolating sound sources like bird calls, individual actors talking in a drama, or isolating one voice in a sea of voices.

The bidirectional microphone picks up sound from two distinct sides of the mic (Figure 12-3d). You would use a mic

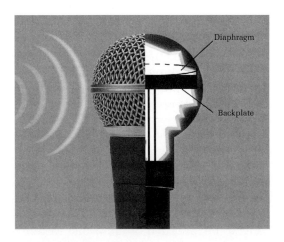

Figure 12-2 *Condenser Mic—A condenser mic uses changes in capacitance in the element to turn sound waves into an electrical signal.*

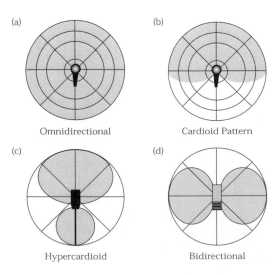

Figure 12-3 *Pick It Up—Microphones come with various pick-up patterns. You need to know how to use the one you have.*

with this pickup pattern primarily to record two voices talking into the same microphone.

You can find all of these pickup patterns in a variety of microphone styles. Some of the more expensive microphones even have switches that enable you to choose multiple patterns from a single mic.

Styles of Microphones

After you make the choice between dynamic and condenser, and select an appropriate pickup pattern, you have to choose what style of microphone to use. This choice is entirely dependent on the type of production you are doing and whether or not you want to see the mic on screen. The major types of microphone styles are: handheld, shotgun, lavalier or lapel mic, boundary or PZM (Pressure Zone Microphone) mic and parabolic mic (Figure 12-4).

The handheld microphone is just that, a microphone that you hold in your hand. This mic is usually flat black or metallic and generally has either an omnidirectional or cardioid pickup pattern. It is ideal for direct addresses to the camera by your talent. It looks good and the talent can handle it quite easily. It is the mic of choice for TV news reporters, singers, politicians and talk-show hosts.

The shotgun microphone is a long slender mic that usually has a hypercardioid or even a supercardioid (extremely focused) pickup pattern. You would primarily use this microphone in field production, mounted on a suspension mount at the end of a long fishpole. The boom operator who manipulates the fishpole keeps the microphone out of the frame about 18″ from the talent's mouth so that they can pick up a consistent voice level. You can use this mic to record sound effects and other sound sources because it picks up sound only from the direction it is pointing, cutting most of the sound from its sides and back.

The lavalier or lapel microphone is a very small microphone that the talent can wear on his or her lapel or someplace near his or her mouth. You can hide these microphones in costumes or weave them into an actor's hair. If you ever get bored during a live play or musical, try to find the mics on the main actors. Costume designers and makeup artists are very ingenious in finding places to hide the mics and power packs. Lavaliere microphones usually have an omnidirectional or cardioid pickup pattern and closely mic a single talent. You can also use the omnidirectional lavalier to mic various acting areas by hiding them in plants, furniture and other set pieces. Just be careful that the talent doesn't touch or bang into their hiding place. You will definitely hear it.

The boundary microphone is a fairly new style of mic that has really made a name for itself lately. This mic is mounted on a flat surface and usually has an omni-directional pickup pattern. These are great for miking conferences where you have a flat table with people sitting all around. You can use them extensively as stage mics (not placed directly on the stage where footfalls would create heavy interference) to enhance theatre sound levels; or use them to record a group of people in a closed environment like a class or seminar.

The parabolic microphone is for long-distance audio pickup. This extremely directional microphone looks like a small handheld satellite dish which reflects all of the sound to a center-mounted microphone. This mic is primarily used to record the sound at sporting events or to pick up the sounds of wild animals. Both this microphone and the shotgun microphone are ideal for picking up middle to high frequency ranges but are not suitable for high quality, total range sound recording.

Microphone Accessories

As with all equipment, once you find the microphone you want to use, you have to accessorize. A friend of mine who runs a recording studio is constantly explaining the need for the strange looking ring with what looks like panty hose stretched over it. This is an extremely important

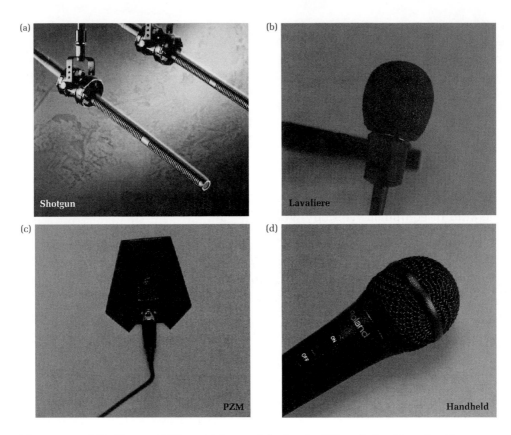

Figure 12-4 *Mic Types—Different mics work better in different shooting situations; you may need more than one in your kit.*

Figure 12-5 *Things That Go Pop—A pop filter reduces the intensity of popping Ps and Bs in narration.*

microphone accessory called a windscreen or more precisely, a pop filter. He places the mesh surface in front of the microphone so that the talents' breath does not pop the microphone when he or she says words with hard "P"s and "B"s (see Figure 12-5).

Windscreens come in a variety of shapes and surfaces. If you ever see a microphone with a gray or other colored foam ball covering its end, you are seeing one type of windscreen. Another popular windscreen used with shotgun microphones is a zeppelin or blimp (these names coming from their resemblance to the early 1900s aircraft). These windscreens completely enclose the microphone and are attached directly to the fishpole or mic stand. If you see someone using a big hairy microphone outdoors, he is using a blimp with a windjammer cover. This cover is extremely effective when you are shooting in windy conditions.

Shock mounts or suspension mounts are another extremely valuable microphone accessory. Suspension mounts prevent sounds traveling through the mic stand or fishpole from being picked up by the microphone. Soft elastic materials like rubber or nylon suspend the mic so that the sounds created by your hands rubbing the fishpole or something hitting the mic stand are not heard. It is extremely important that you use a suspension mount when using a shotgun on a fishpole.

Mic Check

When buying microphones and accessories, the kind of equipment you buy will depend on the type of production you do. Look at your needs and compare them with the instruments described above. There is a microphone designed for every type of production. It is up to you to decide what your production requirements are and the microphone that will best fit your audio needs.

13
Putting Radio to Work: The Low-Down on Wireless Mics

Larry Lemm

A wireless microphone system can be a videographer's best friend or worst enemy. Learn how wireless microphone systems work and you'll be able to choose and use the best system for your needs, so you can get the best audio possible.

The Basics

There are a few different types of wireless microphone system setups. They all require three separate parts to make them all work as one: a microphone, a radio transmitter and a radio receiver (see Figure 13-1).

Some wireless systems have hand-held microphones with built-in transmitters. Others use lavalier microphones with small transmitter packs strapped to a person's belt. These are very popular and provide a discrete method of miking a subject. It is important to note that a moderately priced wireless microphone often won't

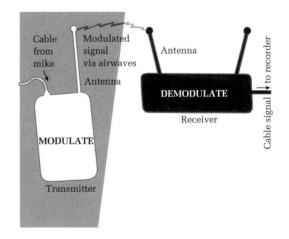

Figure 13-1 *The transmitter modulates the signal coming from the microphone onto a radio frequency carrier wave and transmits it through the air. The receiver demodulates this signal back into a form your camcorder can record.*

have the same frequency response range as a moderately priced wired microphone. Some of the frequency range is sacrificed in the transmission from transmitter to receiver. This signal loss may not be noticed when miking a person speaking, however, because the human voice falls in the middle of the frequency range.

Wireless microphone systems operate in two different radio frequency ranges. These acronyms, also used in TV, will probably seem familiar. The FCC licenses wireless mics to operate between 150 to 216 MHz in the VHF (Very High Frequency) spectrum. It also licenses operation between 400 and 470 MHz and again between 900 and 950 MHz in the UHF (Ultra High Frequency) spectrum. Much lower frequency, and usually much cheaper, mics, operate between 41 and 49 MHz where they are subject to interference from all kinds of other devices.

VHF wireless microphone systems are generally less expensive than UHF systems. Much like VHF TV stations, VHF wireless mics have less range and power than their UHF counterparts.

Your Own Tiny Radio Station

A wireless microphone system's transmitter pack is essentially a tiny radio station. The mic attaches to a tiny transmitter, which has a tiny antenna and a tiny power supply (in the form of a battery). This usually means tiny signal strength too, which is why your signal won't stretch across town like a high-powered radio signal. Instead of calculating your range in miles, the range of the tiny radio station within your wireless mic is measured in feet. And it's usually less than a few hundred feet for VHF and less than 1,000 feet for UHF.

On the other end of this cozy little microphone system is the receiver. It works much like a car radio, except it only tunes into the channels that your transmitter uses. For most videographers, wireless systems that use small battery-powered receivers are often favored over larger table-top systems that cannot attach to a camcorder.

Breaking up Is Easy to Do

Using a wireless microphone system presents some potential dangers. On a

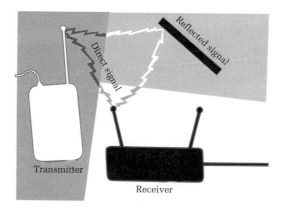

Figure 13-2 *Multipath interference results from the transmitter's signal bouncing off objects in the environment. When a signal and its delayed reflection enter the receiver, they may be recorded at a reduced quality—or may result in no signal getting recorded at all.*

densely populated shoot, where several other videographers are using wireless mics, you may encounter interference with another mic operating on the same radio frequency. With more and more radio devices in use, it's more and more likely for that to happen. Most wireless systems, however, offer a few different channels to work with, so hopefully you'll notice that type of interference before you roll tape.

The next type of interference, multipath interference, is an inherent flaw of using radio frequencies (especially indoors), and often requires wireless microphone manufacturers to double-up on the electronics in a system (see Figure 13-2).

Multipath interference occurs after a transmitter sends out a radio signal. Some of the signal goes directly to the receiver, but other parts of it bounce around and sometimes hit the receiving antenna with just enough delay to cancel out the signal or cause interference. Multipath interference is the reason developers had to come up with diversity and true-diversity wireless systems.

Truly Diverse

What's diversity to a wireless microphone? Well, there are two answers, and

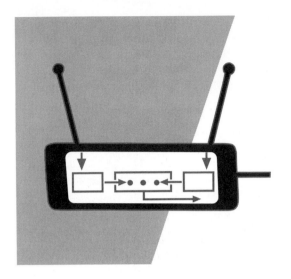

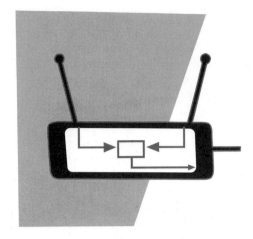

Figure 13-4 *An "ersatz" diversity system has two antennas, but only a single receiver.*

Figure 13-3 *A true diversity receiver contains two antennas, two receivers and a switcher.*

both are aimed at eliminating the effects of multipath interference.

A true diversity system has two antennas, each leading to a separate receiver. A kind of switcher monitors these two for signal strength and makes sure the strongest of the two is sent out to the recorder on a moment-by-moment basis (see Figure 13-3). A good diversity system does this quickly and seamlessly, introducing no static or switching noise into the signal.

On the other hand, we have "ersatz" diversity mics. From the outside these look like the true variety, as their receivers also have two antennas. The difference, however, lies within. If you cracked one open, instead of finding two receivers and a switcher, you'd find that both antenna wires lead to the same receiver (see Figure 13-4). The single receiver receives the signals from both antennas all the time. This type of system is not as effective as the true diversity type at eliminating the effects of multipath interference.

On the Level

The last thing you should understand about a wireless microphone system is the receiver's output. There are three types of outputs: mic level, consumer line level and professional line level.

Small, portable systems that attach onto your camcorder and plug into its microphone jack use mic-level outputs. The output of consumer line-level units, however, measures −10dB and the output of professional line-level receivers measures +4dB. Be sure to add the correct attenuation and adaptation to either of the latter before trying to plug the output into your camcorder's mic jack.

Consider a wireless system that has mic-level inputs that you can strap onto your camcorder and go to town. You may consider a more expensive wireless microphone system, designed with musicians in mind. But you may also need a soundboard to use one of these to get best results. No matter what type of video you make, understanding how wireless mics work will help you be a better shopper and a better video producer.

Sidebar

Wireless Audio Advice

Here are several tips for getting the best sound from any wireless microphone system:

- **Keep it close.** Keep the distance between transmitter and receiver as short as possible. Every wireless system has its limits. The shorter the transmission, the stronger the signal.

- **Don't stray too far.** The goal of a wireless microphone is usually to unhook your talent from cables. You may be able to accomplish this with an extremely short distance between microphone and receiver. Try putting the receiver near the talent, just out of the camera's view, and run a longer cable to the camcorder (wherever it may be).

- **Reposition the receiver.** If you just can't get a clean signal, especially indoors, try moving the receiver. RF signals bounce around in strange ways, and a movement of just three or four feet could make a huge difference.

- **Reorient antennas.** Sometimes, simply cocking an antenna can reduce dropouts (that's why antennas are usually hinged). Try laying the receiver's antenna horizontal instead of vertical, try a 45-degree angle or try spinning the receiver itself 90 degrees.

- **Watch those batteries.** Wireless systems eat batteries quickly, and can get rather flaky as the battery voltage drops. If all else fails, try new batteries.

- **Try a different environment.** If all else fails, you may need to try a completely different shooting location. Some locations are not friendly to wireless systems, while the room down the hall may pose no problems. As a rule, wireless microphones fare better outdoors than in.

14
Monitoring the Monitors

Edward B. Driscoll, Jr.

As recently as ten years ago, choosing a video monitor essentially meant picking some flavor of cathode ray tube technology. But that was before digital TV and, especially, HDTV. The burdens these newer technologies place on monitor design have caused new successors to emerge to challenge the time-tested CRT format, and those successors are making quite a splash.

Since monitors are no longer a one size fits all technology, let's look at some of the decisions involved in choosing a new monitor.

CRT: An Old Standby Soldiers On

"CRT technology is quite mature, is declining in sales, but absolutely is not dead" Chris Pollitt, product marketing manager for PC displays at Philips (www.philipsusa.com) says. But "when you're looking at editing video, one of the things you want is the most accurate color. CRTs, even though it's old technology, still have the highest color gamut, covering pretty much the entire NTSC spectrum, And they don't have any refresh issues: there's never any motion blurring. If you have fast moving objects, a CRT is

more than capable of responding to those. And they're also quite affordable, especially these days."

There are always tradeoffs of course: CRTs have a large desktop footprint, and can generate a fair amount of heat. "But from a color, refresh and cost standpoint, there's absolutely nothing wrong with a good 19 to 22-inch CRT for these types of applications" Pollitt adds.

Plasma and LCD: Thin Profiles Grow in Popularity

When plasma TVs debuted in the mid-1990s, they represented a new archetype in television design: flat, sleek and wide. They could be hung on a wall, like a painting. And just as the first mass-produced TVs of the late 1940s and '50s once did before they were banished to dens and bedrooms, they helped to reintroduce the concept of the TV as the focal point of the upscale living room. And like early TVs they are expensive—a real luxury item.

In recent years though, plasma has had stiff competition in the flatlands battle from LCD monitors. LCD technology actually dates back to the 1970s (remember when digital calculators and watches began to first appear?), although by the mid-1990s, upstart plasma TVs wound up capturing the lion's share of publicity and sex appeal. But because of the popularity of LCDs in the computer monitor industry, an impressive LCD manufacturing infrastructure has been built up, particularly in Asia. Since the start of the 21st century, to maximize investments in that technology, LCD manufacturers have also turned to producing televisions, dramatically lowering their costs in recent years.

Newer Formats Co-Exist Nicely

LCDs fill a niche: plasma TVs cannot be produced in sizes smaller than 32 inches, and most LCDs are smaller than that screen size, so are perfect for desktop computing applications. Pollitt of Philips adds, "tests have shown that an LCD is easier on the eyes than a CRT. It doesn't create as many negative effects over a long period of time," because of the absence of flicker.

Matt Foust, regional sales manager of Princeton Graphics (www.princeton graphics.com) says, "in the past, when the contrast ratios of LCDs were not as good as they are now, there were some color differences" between LCD and CRT. "Nowadays, with contrast ratios going above 500 to 1 and 700 to 1, they're able to change the settings inside the LCD display to avoid that problem. Technology has caught up."

But Foust is quick to mention that older, and even brand-new, but inexpensive LCD displays can have poorer contrast ratios, such as 300 to 1, or 450 to 1, making this a key feature to check when buying, especially if you are using it for editing.

Buying an LCD monitor is becoming increasingly affordable. "Wide panel LCDs have traditionally been very expensive, but there's a lot of good news on that front," notes Pollitt. "There are three sizes that are coming into play at very, very attractive end-user price points. You've got the 23-inch and 24-inch wide displays. These are typically 1,920×1,200, so 2.3 million pixels. So you've got great pixel density and a 16×10 aspect ratio. Those products which were in the $1,500 to $2,000 space, are now in the $900 to $1,200 range."

For those using LCDs as computer monitors, and/or in the video editing workspace, in addition to allowing for viewing of 16×9 HDTV footage without letterboxing, these monitors also make it possible to have multiple documents open side-by-side, making them highly flexible workstations. In the Philips line, these products include the 23-inch 230WP7 (which streets for around $1,200) and a 20-wide 200WB7, streeting for $499.

The CRT technology of standard TVs has worked effectively for over 60 years. But as Douglas Woo, president of Westinghouse Digital Electronics (www.westinghouse digital.com) once told me, "When you move to digital television and high-resolution displays, CRTs, while they can do it, are not going to be the product that carries that burden further into this century." That doesn't mean that a high quality CRT might not still be more than adequate for the task you assign it. It's a safe bet though, that at some point, its successor will be flat and thin.

But will it be LCD or Plasma ... or even a soon to be released technology such as SED (Surface-conduction Electron-emitter Display) pioneered by Canon and Toshiba? Well, that's up to you and the need your new monitor will fill.

15
Screen Time

Charles Fulton

There's nothing like a nice, big display. A big display on your computer means more screen real estate for timelines, preview windows, audio mixers and meters, scopes and more. A big TV lets you sit further back and fills your field of vision with your program. A video projector takes your viewing (whether your source is a computer, a camcorder, a DVD player, a VCR or a satellite receiver) to the next level, allowing you to show your production to hundreds of your closest friends all at once, on the same screen.

Plugging In

You can plug practically any video source into a projector. The vast majority of modern projectors have at least composite, S-Video and VGA inputs; but component video (YPrPb/YCrCb), DVI (with or without High-Bandwidth Digital Content Protection, or HDCP) and HDMI (High-Definition Multimedia Interface) inputs are becoming increasingly available, at ever decreasing price points.

Note, however, that if you intend to tune local off-air broadcasts or cable feeds with your projector, you will need a tuner of some kind, as there are no projectors that we know of that include RF inputs or tuners. A VCR makes a fine tuner for off-air broadcasts or unscrambled cable, but you will need a cable box to tune in scrambled analog cable or any flavor of digital cable. A few companies (notably ADS and Hauppauge) make computer-based TV tuners, and there are a bunch of video cards based on ATI and NVIDIA chipsets that include TV tuners as well.

Going HD

If you've got HDV on your mind, a projector offers a price-competitive way for displaying HDV video, along with pretty much any other kind of HD signal that you want to show. A set of component video inputs on your projector will allow you to view the output from any of today's HDV camcorders. It's possible that future HDV camcorders may add a digital video output such as HDMI or DVI; or that future projectors may be equipped with FireWire inputs and have the appropriate codecs for playing back DV or HDV.

While projectors that can handle 720p video without having to scale the picture are relatively common, unscaled 1,080i is still hard to find at a reasonable price point. On the computer side, 1,024 × 768 is the most common native resolution available; but native 1,280 × 1,024 projectors are becoming common—although they're still a bit on the expensive side.

Bring It with You

Like everything else in the video universe, projectors are continuing to get smaller and lighter. It's not hard to find projectors that can easily fit in a briefcase, for taking your show on the road on a moment's notice, or otherwise traveling light.

One thing to consider, though, is that bulbs are rather pricey and fragile—but thankfully, the life span of bulbs seems to be improving somewhat. You'd probably want to have a spare on hand if you are going on the road, but keep it in somewhere safely padded.

Don't Forget Audio

Projectors' is design, first and foremost, is for video reproduction. Most projectors do have small speakers that are usually acceptable for small boardroom settings, but generally won't satisfy the audio needs for most other applications. If you are presenting the premiere of your latest video, you'll definitely want to make sure you have access to good hardware such as a home surround sound system and a larger venue, or you'll want to make arrangements to rent a sound system.

Big Time

A projector makes a fine addition to the toolkit of any videographer. Like so many other items of technology, we're excited to see where projectors are heading, as prices continue to become more reasonable and projectors become more durable and portable. The continuing adoption of HDTV will certainly help in price decline, and the increased competition in the consumer electronics arena will keep this delivery option interesting.

16
Resolution Lines

Bill Rood

With video equipment manufacturers increasingly engaged in spec wars over lines of resolution it seems appropriate to investigate those figures, what they mean and why they're so often misleading. Knowing how to measure resolution will help you make a smart purchase the next time you look for a camcorder, VCR or monitor.

Much of the confusion centers around the use of the term "lines." Lines of horizontal resolution should not be confused with scan lines. In America, the National Television Standards Committee (or NTSC) television system mandates that the television picture will consist of 525 vertical scan lines, each scanning from left to right on the screen. This fact does not change, no matter how sophisticated the video gear.

So when a manufacturer boasts that a device features "400 lines of resolution," the reference is not to vertical resolution, or the number of scan lines. What's under discussion is horizontal resolution, or, more specifically, horizontal luminance resolution. The chroma resolution in the NTSC system is as little as one tenth that of the luminance, depending on the particular hue. So for our purposes, I'll discuss only luminance resolution.

When a Line Is Not a Line

While the number of scan lines is fixed and can be counted, the number of "lines" in the term "lines of horizontal resolution" is in fact strictly a unit of measurement. There are no actual lines you can count, except with a special test chart (see Figure 16-1). You can put your face right up to the picture tube and see the scan lines, but you can't see lines of resolution.

We should actually refer to horizontal luminance resolution as "video frequency response." It's expressed in megahertz (MHz), usually with a tolerance, just as with audio equipment. Unfortunately, consumer video equipment manufacturers apparently believe this is too complicated for the average consumer to understand, so they use the questionable lines method instead. Measurements stated in lines also sound more impressive than those expressed in megahertz. Three hundred lines sounds better than three-and-a-half megahertz.

So how does this frequency response differ from vertical resolution? You can measure video frequency response by examining just one of the 525 scan lines, provided you are displaying a test signal

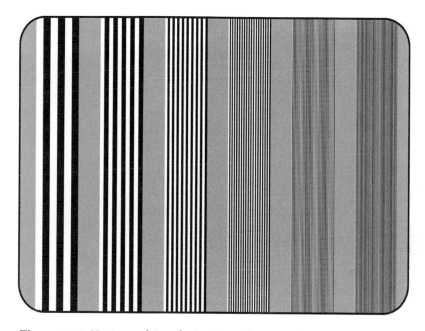

Figure 16-1 *Horizontal Resolution Test Chart.* Credit: Thomas Fjallstam.

of vertical bars. The frequency response of the entire picture should be the same on every line.

As an example, let's examine one scan line of a black-and-white picture. As the scan line traces from left to right, we'd see that the brightness of the line at any given point is a function of the picture content at that point. If the picture consists of a white picket fence against a dark background, the line would start off dim, then brighten as it reproduced one of the pickets. It would go dark as it passed between pickets, then brighten again when it hit the next one. And so on. This sequence would continue until the end of the line.

What happens if we make the pickets on the fence closer together? The line still must switch between light and dark, but faster. In effect, we've upped the frequency of the input signal we're trying to reproduce. At some point, a given piece of gear cannot make the changes fast enough; thus, we arrive at the limits of its resolution. As the pickets got closer, they would begin to appear less bright. Finally, you would no longer distinguish a picket from its neighbor. The black and white pattern will melt into a neutral gray.

Specs Game

So how do we measure video frequency response, or obtain horizontal resolution specifications?

For equipment handling video signals in a purely electronic form, use a test signal known as "multiburst." This signal contains a series of bursts, nothing more than white/black/white transitions. Tiny picket fences, if you will, each higher in frequency than the one previous. When viewed on an oscilloscope, each burst should offer the same amplitude.

If the signal drops off as the frequency rises, you know you're seeing high-frequency response roll-off. The frequency of each burst is fairly standard; usually 0.5 MHz, 1 MHz, 2 MHz, 3 MHz, 3.58 MHz and 4.2 MHz. The beauty of this method is its extreme precision, with no sloppy guesswork.

For devices which pick up or display images, like cameras and monitors, virtually the only way to determine horizontal resolution is to display a special resolution chart (see Figure 16-2). This chart features little wedges: a series of converging black lines on a white background. As the lines

RESOLUTION TEST CHART

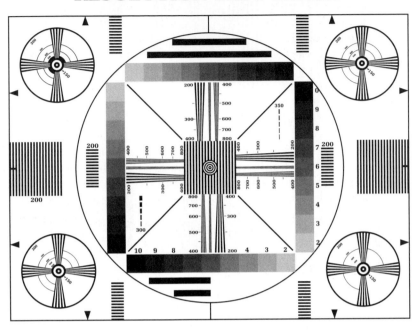

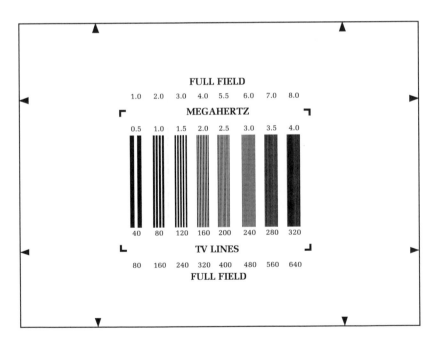

FREQUENCY RESPONSE TEST CHART

Figure 16-2 *Resolution and Frequency Response Test Charts.*
Credit: Earl Talken.

come closer together, you again begin to encounter a point where the change from black to white to black occurs so quickly the lines become indistinct.

Along the outer edge of the wedge at regular intervals are line numbers, reading 200, 250, 300, 350, 400 and so on. This is where "lines of resolution" comes from.

As you might guess, it's a rather inexact method at best; the scale is quite coarse, and open to interpretation as to where exactly the lines blur together. It also doesn't take into account the fact that while black/white/black transitions may be visible, they may appear at a substantially reduced level, indicating high-frequency roll-off.

Unfortunately, this method is used to spec virtually every piece of consumer video gear, be it camera, VCR, disc player or whatever. This means you should take any stated resolution spec with a grain of salt the size of Nebraska. There's much room for error, interpretation and fudging.

Lines to Megahertz

Approximately 80 TV lines equals 1 MHz of video bandwidth. So a piece of equipment rated at 300 lines would feature a video frequency response of roughly 3.75 MHz. This is all well and good, except the 300 lines figure most likely came from observing the wedge pattern, and may be less than accurate. Also, it's impossible to tell by this method if the response is flat at 3.75 MHz, or even if there's any response at all.

With an off-air broadcast, video frequency response cannot rise above 4.2 MHz. Using the above formula, we could then say that TV broadcasts feature 336 lines of resolution. The reason for the limit? The design of the television transmission system from way back when. It places the audio carrier at 4.5 MHz; picture information must vanish by that point.

Most TV broadcasts originate from digital video, stored either on hard drives or from digital videotape, such as D-1. These machines also master virtually everything seen on pre-recorded home video, from VHS, to DVDs. These digital masters are a "full" 480 lines of resolution, or 6 MHz of "flat" video frequency response. Unfortunately, the best resolution figure you can hope to see from broadcast is 360 lines—80 "lines" × 4.5 MHz.

Until all manufacturers come clean and start stating horizontal resolution in terms of megahertz, and within a certain tolerance, we'll never have a reasonable standard with which to compare products.

Until then, read the specs if you will, but don't make judgments based upon them alone.

17
Switch It!

Edward B. Driscoll, Jr.

Choosing a video switcher is a significant decision for most video producers. While a video project's cinematography determines what it looks like, it's the video switcher that gives a multiple camera shoot its overall professional sheen. Video switchers (or video mixers, as they're also known as) are particularly essential for a live production. A talented operator can use a switcher to blend on the fly individual video cameras with dissolves, wipes, and other effects, and frequently—but not always, as we'll discuss in a few moments—the sound as well. For a video director, the switcher is practically like a musical instrument, and shot timing and dissolves are often timed for an almost rhythmic feel that's subliminal, but palpable.

For someone new to this aspect of video production, the switcher's myriad of knobs, faders, T-bars, inputs and outputs can appear overwhelming at first. But each video input has the same controls as all of the others, so there is a great deal of duplication. In other words, once you understand what's going on with one row, you'll understand what goes on with the other rows.

Swiss Army Knives Don't Always Make the Best Weapons

Although a few manufacturers might give you the impression that their switchers can do everything, it's always best to have some idea ahead of time what the main type of production you'll be using the unit for. Some units will be more flexible and allow you to work on different types of projects. Others are more limited, but may be perfectly suited for the type of production you do every week.

Are you going to use the switcher at a live performance on location? Then consider one with its own custom-fitted travel case. Unless the switcher is going to be fitted into a studio control desk and never be transported, buying the case could be well worth the extra cost to protect the delicate circuitry inside. In addition, for those location jobs, you might want to consider a unit like the Datavideo SE-800, which has its own optional small bank of attachable video monitors.

But if you're working in a studio, then external monitors will give you a better idea what the audience is seeing, and small proprietized monitors become less important.

I/O Silver!

Of course, planning your input and output needs ahead of time is necessary. How many cameras will you need to switch? Are you mixing sound as well? All of these questions should be answered up front.

Most switchers will have a mixture of composite and S-video inputs. Higher-end switchers will have bayonet-style BNC inputs. Whether these are worth the price depends again on your use: if you're working in a high-traffic area, a bayonet mount's protection against accidental un-plugging is worth the price.

Not all video switchers are set up to also do audio. Again, ask yourself where the work is going to be done. If you're doing location work, a combined unit may make transport easier. A stand-alone audio mixer will probably have more features, and can provide somewhat better sound quality than combined units. If all-in-one sound and video is valuable to you, make sure the unit has a sufficient quantity of audio inputs and outputs for your needs.

High definition switchers are an even newer beast. Check out a switcher such as Edirol's V-440 HD if high def is definitely a high concept requirement. But be prepared to pay a fair chunk of change as an early adopter.

Check for Effects

Effects are another big consideration. Generally, the greater the cost of the switcher, the greater the number of effects it has built-in, but this isn't always true—with some switchers, you're paying for durability, not a myriad of flashy effects. Typically, video switchers allow for chroma key effects, a variety of wipes and pattern dissolves, and the ability to do titles. Some mixers allow for a variety of chroma colors, others less so. Also, some units feature a beats per minute (or "B.P.M." as all the cool hip-hop guys like to say) display to allow V-Js in clubs to sync-up transitions and effects to the beat of the music that's playing. Others also include a MIDI-input, allowing the switcher's effects to be remote-controlled using MIDI, the common language of electronic musical instruments.

Lower-end machines often lack chroma key, but typically have luminance control, allowing them to at least insert simple titles into a project. These types of low-end mixers also occasionally lack preview outs, but then they typically offer very simple effects, and thus little need to preview.

Focus Enhancement MX-4 is a well-equipped mid-priced switcher capable of producing a myriad of video effects. It includes a T-bar control, which, as we'll discuss in a moment, may or may not be an important feature for your needs.

The T-Bar Debate

Finally, what many consider the most important control on the switcher requires a decision. Although to some it might just be a lever, whether a switcher has a T-bar control or not is often high on many users' list of priorities. Some low-end switchers lack a T-bar, which doesn't mean a T-bar is always what you want. First of all, T-bars are infamous for being bumped if the switcher is in a crowded area. And, some users, especially when they are doing VJ-style productions, prefer the quicker response of a fader, as opposed to the slow, but more precise feel of a T-bar. Obviously, again, it helps to know what types of material the switcher will primarily be used for. Numark's AVM01 streets for less than $1K, and lacks a T-bar, but is an extremely popular switcher with the V-J set.

As a rule, you'll benefit the most having some idea of what most of the projects you'll be using your switcher for entail. But also try to leave some room for expansion. And don't forget to consider the environment that it will be used in, as well. That's a fair amount of decision making that will go into your purchase, but it will pay off with a switcher with features that are built for the long run.

18

Try a Tripod:
Some Valuable Features
in the Three-Legged Race

William Ronat

Few pieces of video support equipment are as useful as the tripod. Simple in concept, elegant in function, the tripod has a long history of bringing needed stability to the world of photography.

In pre-video days, tripods served still and motion picture cameras. As far back as the 1860s, people like Matthew Brady were lugging tripods onto battlefields to help steady huge still camera equipment.

And before tripods became popular for image gathering, they supported the surveyors' levels used to map out the countryside.

Why, you may wonder, a *tri*pod? Why not a monopod, or a quadrapod, or an octopod? This question doesn't require an Einstein to answer. One leg: camera falls down. Two legs: camera falls down. Three legs: camera stands up. Four legs: one more leg than you need.

The triangle is one of the most stable configurations for a support device. Ask a karate expert, or an offensive lineman. Or, for that matter, a tree.

Why a Tripod?

I know what you're thinking. "What do I need with a tripod? It's just one more thing to tote around."

Maybe you're right. If you have a steady hand, and/or a lens stabilizer, you may never encounter a situation requiring a tripod. But if you shoot professional video and work with heavy equipment, you know that working hand-held for any length of time can get darned uncomfortable. Just try holding your hand on top of your head for a couple of hours to simulate the experience.

Aside from avoiding pain, tripods are handy if you want to be in your own shot.

Say you're shooting a news story for a cable access show and you want to do a stand up. This is the shot where you appear on camera, looking solemn, finishing up with, "for Cable Access, this is John Smith, reporting from Bosnia."

Using a tripod, you can stop somebody passing by, make him or her stand in the spot where you'll be standing when you talk to the camera. You can then compose the shot using this surrogate John Smith. Lock down the tripod. Take the passerby's place and say your piece.

Three S Theory

A tripod's purpose can be described in the famous Three S Theory, which I just made up. Tripods keep it *Steady*, keep it *Straight* and keep it *Smooth*.

Put a camera on a tripod and it will be steady. It won't bob, wave or float, assuming it's locked down. It will sit there like a rock until you get ready to move it. That's steady.

Keeping your shot straight is a little trickier. Let's say you've set your camera on the tripod so your shot is looking out across a flat desert. The horizon is that line where the sky meets the earth. In a standard shot, the horizon should be kept parallel to the top and bottom of your frame. Cancel this if you're trying for the Dutch angle so popular in the old Batman TV shows, where everything is tilted. It's possible for a shot to start out looking straight, horizon parallel to the top of the frame. But when you pan, the horizon will start to go downhill.

This happens because your tripod legs stand in such a way the camera isn't level to the horizon. Your tripod is sitting with two legs on either side of the front of the camera; the third leg points behind the camera, and is shorter than the front two legs. Even though your shot looks level when the camera's pointed straight ahead, when you pan, the camera begins to lean in the direction of the third leg.

Or, as I like to put it: look out, the world's tilting.

On the Level

Some tripods come with a leveling bubble, a handy gizmo that is nothing but a bubble floating in liquid.

You position the bubble either inside a circle or between two lines on a tube. By moving the bubble to its correct position your camera becomes perpendicular, relative, I think, to the gravitational pull of the Earth (but don't hold me to this). The result: you can pan your camera 360 degrees, the horizon staying straight in the frame.

You can position the bubble by raising or lowering the tripod legs or by adjusting the tripod's head—if the head attaches to the tripod with a claw ball. The latter allows you to loosen the head and position the leveling bubble without touching the legs. A nice feature.

The last S in the Three S Theory is keep it Smooth. The part of the tripod responsible for this action is the head. Some tripods don't have heads: cameras attach directly to the tripod. But on more sophisticated tripods the camera attaches to a plate, the plate attaches to a head and the head attaches to the tripod.

Using smooth resistance, a head helps make camera movement smoother. This resistance, known as drag, is usually adjustable. With a small amount of drag the camera pans or tilts easily. Add more drag and moving the camera becomes more difficult.

If you don't want the camera to move at all, you engage the locks. There are separate drags and locks for both the pan and tilt functions of the head. If you want a pan but no tilt, you can lock the tilt control and the camera will only pan. And vice versa.

Heads and Legs

Heads come in two flavors: fluid head and friction head.

A friction head creates resistance by pushing metal against metal. A fluid head floats on a bed of oil or some other viscous fluid. Friction heads aren't as smooth as fluid heads, but they're also cheaper, which is the way things usually work in this world.

Tripod legs generally extend by telescoping. This is necessary to position a tripod level on a hill or stairs. With tripods that extend you can get your camera high up in the air, useful when you must ascend to eye-level with NBA players. Some tripods have a center column that cranks even higher.

A word of caution here: if you get up too high, your camera, tripod and everything else can tip over. So put a sandbag in the center of the tripod to make it more stable.

Some tripods allow the legs to straighten out until the head is resting almost on the ground. Good for low shots. Good angle for your remake of *Attack of the Fifty Foot Female Mud Wrestler*, featuring a point of view shot from the terrified town's perspective. Coming soon to a theater near you.

Wheels

With a nice smooth floor you may be interested in tripod dolly wheels.

What's a dolly? That's a movement of the camera and tripod. These moves can take the camera around the subject, or the camera can follow people at the same speed as they move. They require your tripod to have wheels or they require you to place your tripod on a wheeled device. These shots are very pretty, but they're also very difficult. If you don't have a smooth even surface every little dolly bump will translate into a very big video bump.

Wheels are handy, however, as transportation. Just leave your camera, extension cords, a grip bag and a light attached to the tripod and roll on to the next location. Sure beats carrying them.

Another feature you may want is quick release; a plate or shoe attached to the bottom of the camera. The plate fits into the head to secure the camera. But if you

want to go hand-held in a hurry, you flip a switch or push a button to immediately release the camera.

If the head screws into the bottom of the camera, it will obviously take a lot longer to turn, turn, turn the knob to get it off again. Most professional model tripods feature quick release.

The Envelope, Please

Before leaving the subject of tripods, we should explore the Steadicam™. You may say, "Say, that's not a tripod!" And you'd be right. But it performs some of the same jobs, so we'll give it a glance.

The Steadicam JR™ is a system that balances your camera so completely the image seems to float on air. It eliminates shakiness, allowing a camera operator to walk up stairs or run along the ground without applying objectionable jiggle to the image. It's a slick little system, creating videos that look like feature film.

But a Steadicam™ is not the same as a tripod. Although it has a stand, you can't lock it down on a shot. Also, some people think a Steadicam™ is like a gyroscope, forcing your shot to remain horizontal. Wrong. There's a bubble level on the monitor to show the operators when the shot is level, but it's up to the operator to keep it there. My conclusion: Steadicams™ are great tools, but should supplement a tripod, not replace it.

If you're in the market for a tripod, shop around. Try the model before you buy. As you test drive the tripod think about the three Ss: keep it Steady, keep it Straight, keep it Smooth. If you watch your Ss, you should be O.K. And if at first you don't succeed, try another tripod.

PART II
Production Planning

Every minute spent in planning saves ten in execution. Here's help in getting yourself organized.

19
Honing Your Ideas: From Concept to Finished Treatment

Stray Wynn Ponder

If you're like most videographers you probably have more project ideas than you can shake a camcorder at. So with a little talent and the right equipment, you should be able to produce top quality video work, right?

Right. Then why do so many great ideas fizzle out somewhere between that first blinding spark of inspiration and the final credit roll?

The answer is simple: before the lights come up, before the cameras roll, even before you write the script, you must take two essential steps if your video is to find and follow its true course:

Step One: clearly define your concept.

Step Two: write a concise treatment.

A concept nails down your program's primary message, and the manner in which you will deliver it to your primary audience. Later, as you navigate the winding curves of production, you'll think of the concept as your destination. A treatment is a written summary of the video's purpose, storyline and style. It will become your road map. These tools will help you maintain solid and continuous contact with the video's intended direction every step of the way.

These are probably the most overlooked steps of pre-production, but if you conscientiously pursue them on every project—no matter how simple—you'll save time and add polish, propelling your work to new horizons of quality.

Developing the Concept

How does a concept differ from a raw idea? Let's look at a couple of ideas and watch how they change as we develop them into concepts:

1. *The Trees of New England*; and

2. *Car Repair.*

Each of these has possibilities as a video project; but if we were to pick up a camera, or to start writing a script at this point, we'd suffer a false start. Before we can set out on our creative journey, we need a clear understanding of our destination.

Admittedly, many ideas don't deserve to survive. Who among us hasn't pulled the car off a crowded freeway to jot down a "great idea"—only to read it later and find that great idea somewhat less than overwhelming.

Take our first idea: *The Trees of New England*. This sleeper might die right on the drawing board. Why? Because, for the videographer trying to earn a buck, it lacks profitability. And for most hobbyists, it involves too much time and effort. The visual effect could no doubt be stunning, but who would purchase (or finance) a video about trees when public television carries a variety of nature shows that feature similar subjects every week?

To succeed in the marketplace, your work must effectively deliver a primary message to a primary audience. To prove worth the effort, *The Trees of New England* would have to distinguish itself from similar programming through style or content to appeal to existing markets. Another option: *The Trees of New England* could deliver its message in a way that would captivate audiences in a new market niche. *Note*: if you can see a way to make money with this tree idea, please feel free to run with it.

You may find yourself shelving many ideas that survive this kind of initial scrutiny; these ideas typically lack some element necessary to a profitable video, such as reasonable production costs or a viable market. Or through research you may discover that someone else has already produced your idea. That's okay; you can always generate more ideas. Don't get too caught up in creative decisions during these first stages of exploration. In the process of transforming a germ of an idea into a viable concept, necessity will make many decisions about a project's direction for you.

How about our second wannabe video— *Car Repair*? This one offers a multitude of development possibilities. But remember, you can't please all of the people all the time. Avoid the temptation to create a "do-all" video. As producers, we always want the largest audience we can get—up to a point. Create a repair program that appeals equally to master mechanics and interior designers, and you'll get a show without a specific destination. In other words, your project could end up running out of gas in the wrong town.

Your first move: define the audience. Let's find a target group who could use some information about car repair.

Brainstorm A-comin'

Here's where brainstorming becomes indispensable. There are as many ways to brainstorm an idea as there are people, so there are no hard and fast rules. Basically, you need to distract the left (logical) side of your brain so that the right (creative) side can come out to play.

Here's what works for me: I speak my thoughts aloud, no matter how silly they sound, while bouncing a rubber ball off the concrete walls of my basement office. This technique gets the creative hemisphere of my brain churning; my subconscious coughs up ideas from a well much deeper than the one serving my logical hemisphere. I write down the more coherent mutterings on a dry erase board as they erupt. All in all, it's probably not a pretty sight, but you're welcome to adapt this method to your own brainstorming technique.

Here's a condensed version of my brainstorming session for the car repair idea. I flip the ball. It hits the floor, the wall and then slaps back into my hand.

"Repair," I say to myself, as I continue to bounce the ball. "Maintenance ... mechanics ... men ... women ... children ... women ... smart women ... independent women ... car maintenance ... where's the need? ... when would they have the need? ... college! ... BINGO!

When young women go away to college, they no longer have Mom or Dad around to watch the oil level and check the belts. The same is surely true of young men, but I decide to target women as the larger of the two potential audiences. Should I go after both in hopes of selling more tapes? Absolutely not. Since the buying characteristics of the two groups will be different, I must tailor the style of the production to one audience or the other.

Through brainstorming, the original idea "car repair" has now become its simpler cousin, "car maintenance." Do we have a real concept now? Not yet, but we're getting there; we know our target market and our message. Still to be considered: the production's style, or the best manner in which to convey our message. This will eventually encompass shooting style, lighting style, acting, wardrobe, makeup and dozens of other factors. For now, however, we'll break style down into two parts: 1) getting the viewer's attention; and 2) keeping it.

Hook, Line and Profit

A hook is the attention-getting element that yanks viewers away from their busy day, and into our product. The need for a good hook is the same in every communication medium, whether it's an advertisement, a popular song or a training video. Human beings are frenetically busy creatures; you must seduce them into giving their attention away. After delivering this interesting hook and convincing them to look our way, we must follow through and give them a storyline that will hold their interest for the duration of the program. There are a number of ways to engage and keep the viewers' attention:

- Shock value

- Self-interest

- Visual stimulation

- Glitz and glamour

- Comedy

To decide which combination of elements will work best for our car maintenance video, we need a better understanding of our target market: 18- to 22-year-old females needing to perform simple car maintenance themselves. As with many aspects of concept development, most of our decisions are made for us as we discard what will not work—which leaves us with what will.

My gut says to skip shock value in a program that deals with cars. Self-interest is definitely an important consideration for a young lady who is both: 1) trying to assert her independence for the first time (ego self-interest); and 2) living on a budget (financial self-interest).

Visual stimulation? Our target group comes from a generation accustomed to the kaleidoscopic imagery and lightning fast cuts of beer commercials and music videos. Let's use this one.

Glitz and glamour are obvious shoo-ins for this age and gender. Comedy can be an excellent tool for communicating many subjects, as long as you execute it well. Let's keep humor in mind, too.

Simply being aware of these tools is not enough. More important is an understanding of the ways they will impact our target audience. If we can effectively use one or more of them in our production (and our marketing package), we may just have a moneymaking project on our hands.

To recap: we need an eye-catching (visually stimulating) presentation that offers college-aged females something they clearly need (self-interest) in a manner consistent with their accepted versions of self-image (glitz and glamour). If we can discover ways to enliven this delivery through the use of comedy, all the better.

Even if we are unable to meet all these criteria, we must be aware of them, so at the very least we avoid working against the psychology of our target audience.

More ball bouncing is probably called for at this point to help us predict how we'll apply these general ideas to our intended audience. But rather than put you through that again, I'll just tell you what I came up with for our sample project: *A Young Woman's Guide to Minor Car Maintenance*. The package resembles that of a concert video or a compact disc more than an instructional videotape jacket. Lots of neon colors surround a snazzily dressed college-aged woman, who leans confidently over the open hood of a small automobile. Her posture says, "I have the world by the tail, and so can you if you take a closer look at this."

The back of the jacket explains that you'll need no tools to perform most of the tasks covered in the program. These tasks are simpler than you ever thought possible, even fun once you give them a chance. Best of all, you'll feel an exhilarating new sense of independence after you master these simple skills.

Writing the Treatment

We've come a long way from the original idea. By asking the right questions, we've developed a potentially viable concept. We understand it in terms of:

- to whom the video speaks,

- how the video will speak to them and

- what the video will say.

Now we can write a treatment, which will help us pursue our project without losing sight of our concept. By clearly defining our direction in this way, we can hold true to our original vision for the project.

Depending on the complexity of a production, its treatment may be long or short. Some in-depth treatments resemble scripts; others simply document mood changes and/or visual effects, with technical annotations along the way. Regardless, the treatment should always move the reader chronologically from the beginning to the end of the program.

There's no established manuscript format for a treatment. Just try to tell a story in as readable a way as possible. The treatment for our car maintenance video might begin like this:

Project Name: A Young Woman's Guide to Minor Car Maintenance.

Statement of Purpose: The main goal of this project is to provide information about basic car maintenance to female college students under the age of twenty. These young women face the full responsibilities of car care for the first time in their lives.

In the interest of hooking and keeping the attention of the target audience, we'll present this information in a series of three music videos. Cuts will be as short as possible. A different actor/musician with a distinct personality will demonstrate each automotive maintenance task.

Most important, the tasks will not be overly technical in nature. Our audience needs to understand only the basics of car care: how to check belts, check the oil and other fluid levels, change a tire, fill the radiator, replace a burned-out fuse and so on. The frequent use of common-sense metaphors will remove any feelings of intimidation this subject may arouse in viewers.

The video jacket layout resembles that of an album cover rather than an instructional videotape. The songs contained in the program will be remakes of popular rock-and-roll songs, with lyrics pertinent to the mechanical tasks.

Summary

The opening credits emulate the digital-animated effects common to music video TV stations. These lively visual effects are choreographed to heavy guitar and powerful drums. The monolithic CTV (Car Television) logo vibrates in time with the music.

Cut to a perky female vee-jay who says, as if continuing a thought from before the latest station break, "We'll hear more of the latest tour information soon, but first let's take a look at this new release from Jeena and the Jalopies...."

Cut to close-up of female lead singer in the middle of a concert. We hear the giddy cheering of a large crowd as she introduces the next song. Her tormented expression prepares us for a tale of love's cruelty; but when she speaks, it's about how her car has done her wrong. The hand-held cameras circle like vultures on the fog-drenched stage. Her dead-earnest performance mocks the lyrics, which seem comically out of place.

Cut to a dressing room interview with Jeena. "Yeah," she says, "almost every song I write is taken from my own life. I hated that car." (She takes a drag from her cigarette.) "And I loved it. Know what I mean?" Music from Jeena's live performance fades up as the camera holds on her face.

(Music continues.) Cut to Jeena standing next to her car, a late model import. She wears the demeanor of a child instructed to shake hands with an enemy, but stubbornly refuses to do so. She casts occasional guilty glances at the camera, but refuses to look at the car, with which she is obviously quite angry. "My old car wasn't like this," she claims, shaking her head. "I could see the dip stick—easy. Check the oil and be done with it. So, you know, easy." Video dissolves to a memory sequence of Jeena opening the hood of an older automobile.

That gives you an idea of how the beginning of our treatment might read. It paints a much more complete picture than the words Car Repair. This video will probably be around 30 minutes in length; its treatment will run about ten pages, typewritten and double-spaced. If that sounds like a lot of writing, compare it to the amount of money and work required to reshoot even one minute of video.

More Treatment Tips & Tricks

Some productions, like our car maintenance video, will involve fairly hefty budgets financed by outside investors. The treatment then becomes a sales tool for communicating the project's value to potential investors.

Depending on the type of video you're producing, other uses for a treatment include:

- seeking client approval,

- giving a "big picture" of the program to the technical and creative staffs and

- making sure that you can arrive at your destination.

Perhaps the most important benefit of writing a treatment comes as a result of the writing itself. In moving from the general concept to the specific steps to develop that concept, your treatment will pass through many incarnations. Problems will crop up at this stage of the video's development; you'll solve them by revising the treatment. In overcoming each of these obstacles on paper, you will save yourself from facing them later on the shoot itself.

Production Planning Tools

Videographers have traditionally used several tools to help them navigate the circuitous pathways of production. In filmmaking, there's the storyboard, a comic book style layout of sequential drawings that tell the visual story of a movie. Some videographers use storyboards as well; but for many low-budget productions storyboards prove too expensive a luxury.

This is certainly true for our car repair video. For this production, our treatment must do the storyboard's job—by creating compelling, descriptive images with words. The treatment must clearly map out the avenues we'll travel without necessarily describing every fire hydrant and blade of grass along the way.

A general rule of thumb: gear the sophistication of your treatment to the purposes it must serve. If you need to impress the board of trustees at a major cable network and feel you are out of your league in terms of writing skills, hire a freelance writer to prepare the treatment. The earlier in the creative process you bring this person in, the more benefit you can gain from his or her experience.

Don't sell yourself short, though. If you feel reasonably sure that you can tell your video's story from the beginning to the end, in a readable way that your colleagues will understand, do it.

Planning Counts

The worst mistake: skipping these crucial planning steps altogether.

Even the simplest video can flounder if you neglect the proper planning process. The meticulous development of concept and treatment allows you to cut and polish your rough project. The goal is to move into the later phases of the work with a crisply faceted jewel that will withstand the rigors of scripting and production.

20
Budgeting Time

William Ronat

Let's say that you've planned a location shoot at a restaurant so you can get some shots for a production. You told the owner you would be there at 3 p.m. Suppose you have some other shots to do in the morning at several locations. If you didn't prepare a schedule, you have no idea how long any of them will take. Each shot will undoubtedly take longer than anticipated, you forgot to allow for travel time, the crew is hungry (don't forget time for lunch!) and when you finally get to the restaurant, you are two hours late. The owner now has to take care of the dinner crowd and you're out of luck.

You didn't get into video to become a bureaucrat. You bought your camcorder and gear to watch your visions materialize, to breathe life into ideas, to create a piece of truth where moments before there was merely air. These are laudable goals. The problem, however, is actually achieving them. And that takes planning.

Your time is valuable. Spend it like you would spend money. To make sure you get the most value from your effort, you have to do some preparatory work before your finger hits the Record button. There is a saying in the biz, "Everything takes longer than it takes." That means that no matter how well you plan, something will happen that you didn't anticipate.

You can minimize the pain by doing your homework. Many professionals spend as much as 90 percent of production time in the planning process. Alfred Hitchcock was famous for planning his films in such minute detail that he found the shooting process dull. He had already seen the movie in his head and the rest was mere mechanics. You may say, "Hey, I don't want to be bored when I'm shooting," to which I say, "Is your name Hitchcock?" All right, then.

In the Beginning

If you're serious about choreographing a video production from start to finish, you will need a script. It doesn't have to be an elaborate document. In fact, it can be an outline scribbled on a napkin (although they have a habit of disappearing during lunch). Just make sure that the script

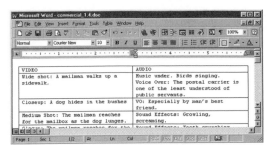

(a)

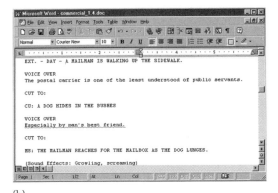

(b)

Figure 20-1 *Shot lists can be formatted in any word processing program. The top example is typical of a video production, while the bottom is more commonly used for film.*

Figure 20-2 *While you shoot, keep your shooting schedule with you (along with the script). And stick to it.*

helps you understand what needs to be shot and it will do the job.

Work with "split-format" (audio/video) scripts and "film-style" scripts. Split-format scripts are ideal for short projects, like 30-second commercials or industrial videos, while film-style scripts lend themselves to dramatic productions. You can easily use your word-processing program to set up a table and create a script that looks like Figure 20-1a. The same script done film-style would look like Figure 20-1b.

If you plan to write for the film industry, this format must be absolutely perfect or your manuscript will be tossed without a second look. There are software programs available that can make this process easier (See the *Film Script Software* sidebar).

Shot by Shot

Once you've written your script, you can begin to plan like a pro. First, break the script down into shots. In our example, we have three shots: one, a mailman walks up; two, close-up of a dog; and three, the dog attacks the mailman. Now it's time to create the next document in our bureaucracy of video, the production schedule.

Using the schedule will help you during planning in many ways. You will know approximately how long it will take to shoot shot sequences, what props and equipment you will need, how many crew members to bring and when to break for lunch (see Figure 20-2).

It can be helpful to take the split-format script table we illustrated earlier and add some more columns to it. As you can see, planning is all about detail. The script should tell you everything about each shot. Using this information, you can create a production schedule to illustrate how much time it will take to achieve the script's needs. The far-right column indicates times for each shot. Here are some rules of thumb to help you put numbers like this to your own schedule.

- The first shot of the day always takes the longest to set up. People need to get into the rhythm of the shoot, people are still groggy and equipment needs to be checked and prepared. Because of this, try to schedule your most difficult shot first. The rest of the day becomes a downhill slide.

- The first shot in a new location takes longer than the rest of the shots in the same location. If you use lighting gear or other special equipment such as wireless microphones, you probably pack them away carefully as you move from place to place. This means unpacking them at each new location. But after you are set up, each shot will take less time, because you are ready to go.

- Complex shots take longer than easy shots do. This is common sense, which does, occasionally, have a place in video production. If you set up a shot that involves moving the camera, changing the focus and having the talent juggle bowling balls all at the same time, it will take longer than a static shot of a flower. Don't ask why; it's a mystery.

- Wide shots take longer than close-ups. This is true, because there is usually more going on in a wide shot. Not always, but it's a good rule of thumb.

- It takes time to change locations. Besides tearing down and setting up equipment, you have to move it to the next shooting location. If this is across the county, you have to allow for the time that it will take to get there.

- Shots either take 30 minutes or 15 minutes to capture. For scheduling purposes, you can usually assign these times to your shots. Some shots take longer and some are done in a heartbeat. But by consistently using 30/15, your schedule will even out by the end of the day.

Stop or I'll Shoot

Once you have a script and production schedule, you're ready to shoot, right? Nope. You need to create a shooting schedule.

Shooting schedules look a lot like production schedules except for one crucial difference. All shots from one location are grouped together. This simple phase can potentially save you more time than anything else in this article. Why is grouping shots so important? Because returning to a location not only wastes time, it also sends a signal to your crew that you are not in control. And that's a real confidence buster. Let's say you are shooting at a location and trying to remember all the shots you need in your head. You finish, strike the equipment, get in the vehicle and start to drive away. Then it hits you. You didn't get the closeup. Arrrgh! Turn around, unload everything, set up the gear and get the shot. Now look at your crew's faces. Do they love you for the extra effort that you have just caused them to endure? Or are their faces black with smoldering hatred? If this scene is repeated over and over, a volunteer crew will probably not return for more. And a professional crew will not trust your judgement on other aspects of the production.

Now you have a script, a production schedule and a shooting schedule. Keep a copy of each of these documents in a single notebook when you go into the field (see Figure 20-3). You will probably work mainly from the shooting schedule. Cross off shots as you finish them and keep track of the best ones by writing down the time-code number next to the shot on the shooting schedule. This will help you find the shot when you sit down to edit. If your recording device doesn't have time code, you can note which tape (or digital media) the shot is on and the amount of time that has been used on that media. This is not as precise as time code (where each frame has a unique number) but can be helpful.

Keep a copy of your script with you in the field; just carrying the shooting schedule is not enough. On the shooting

Figure 20-3 *Electronic PDAs can also help you manage your time and take notes.*

schedule, the shot's location is the most important element, but you often need to know how the shots are going to work together in the real script. This way, you won't shoot two shots that are too similar to each other (a head-to-waist shot of the talent, for example) and try to edit them together later. Such an edit can make the talent appear to jump from place to place (which was fine on *Bewitched*, but might not be the effect you're looking for).

Put It All Together

If you have done your homework and kept good notes during shooting, your editing process should go much more smoothly (see Figure 20-4). This is harder than it sounds, because working in the field can be like being in battle, with problems and unforeseen obstacles flying like bullets. (You're trying to get audio while in the flight path of the airport; or you need blue skies and it's starting to rain.) However, let's pretend we live in a perfect world and all has gone well.

Editing is like putting together a jigsaw puzzle. If you know where all the pieces are before you start, you will save yourself a lot of trouble, which translates into time. If you create a simple show with straight cut edits, you can figure that each minute

Figure 20-4 *Better planning of your shoots will ultimately save time in post-production editing.*

of finished program will take you about an hour of editing time. If you plan to use wipes and special effects, double the estimate. If you want to experiment while editing, triple it.

Make sure you have everything you need when you go into an edit. Will you use a voice talent to narrate the show? Have it done before you start. Are you identifying on-camera interviewees with titles? Make sure that you know how to spell their names.

Taking a video from start to finish is a big undertaking. It's best to know what you're getting into before you invest your money and time. With a good plan, you will not only have more fun during the process, you will have a good chance of actually getting the darn thing done—and that's the best plan you can make.

Sidebar 1

Quick Tips

To plan effectively, you need to create the following:

- Script—Put on paper what you are trying to achieve.

- Production Schedule—Break the script down into shots and plan what props, talent and time each shot will need.

- Shooting Schedule—Similar to the production schedule, but with the shots grouped by location.

21
It's All in the Approach: Creative Approaches for Video Productions

Jim Stinson

Some informational programs use gimmicks like butter on popcorn, to hide the bland taste of the subject matter: "Hi! I'm Percy Peatmoss, and we're gonna meet some exciting lichens!" (Suuure, we are!) Though spokes-mosses like Percy went out with 16 mm projectors, promotional, training and educational programs still need what you might call a *presentation method.*

As the term implies, this is a systematic approach to laying out the content of a program. Mr. Announcer on the sound track, Julia Child behind the cooktop, the talking head in the interview—each of these is a presentation method, deliberately selected because it's well-suited to the program's subject. What are some of these presentation methods and how do you select the right one(s) for your show? Step right this way, folks; the tour starts here.

When you come right down to it, there're only a few basic presentation methods: documentary, interview, expert presenter and full script. As we look at each method in turn, remember that most informational videos use them in various combinations.

Documentary

A documentary purports to capture and display a subject as it really is, allowing viewers to draw their own conclusions from their impressions of the material. In some programs, they're assisted by narration or commentary, while in others the edited footage appears to speak for itself. (We say "purports" and "appears" because no documentary is a truly passive, neutral pipeline of information. For more on this, see *Liar, Liar!* in the October 2000 issue of **Videomaker** or at www.videomaker.com).

The documentary method works well where you want to convey a free-form impression of your subject. *Beautiful Downtown Burbank, Recreation in Bigfoot*

County, Where Your Sales Tax Goes—
these are good subjects for documentary
programs.

The most rigorous documentary form
(represented by the films of Frederick
Wiseman) uses no verbal commentary to
organize the presentation and point the
message. The entire effect comes from the
selection and juxtaposition of shots. To
the newbie, this may seem like the easiest
form of program ("Hey kids, let's showcase
Fillmore High!") but it is in fact, the hardest to do successfully. Without the guid-
ance of voiceovers and titles, the result is
often an inexpressive jumble of footage.

That's why many professional documentarians (notably Ken Burns) use multiple voices on the sound track—often a mix
of narration, dramatized voices and interview quotes. This method is easier because
it allows you to comment on the footage as
you display it. However, juggling multiple
audio sources is a sophisticated process.

For fail-safe simplicity, try mating documentary footage to voice over narration.
By scripting a single stream of commentary, you can control your presentation
more precisely.

Interview

Interviews offer ways to get variety into
your presentation, especially if you include
several people. Interviews are great for
subjects that are essentially verbal and
require some expert input.

As the sidebar, *Pictures, Words or Titles?*
explains, some topics are difficult to visualize. No matter how many photo albums
you have, they don't display family history, but only *moments from* that history.
For the actual narrative, nothing beats
Great Grandmother on the sound track.
Other good interview subjects include *Our
Corporate Five Year Plan* (interview with
the CEO) and *Coping with Depression*
(interviews with sufferers and therapists).
As these examples suggest, interview programs come in different flavors: single,
dual and multiple.

The single interview doesn't look like
a Q&A session, but like spontaneous

Figure 21-1 *Single & Dual Interviews—
Single interviews, the most popular form in
professional TV show, look spontaneous, but
dual interviews are easier to manage.*

conversation by the subject (see Figure
21-1). The interviewer is never seen or
heard, and the questions (dropped on the
cutting room floor) are phrased to elicit
statements rather than answers ("Tell us
about the Boston branch of the family").
Because they omit the overhead of questions, single interviews are the most popular form in professional programs.

However, the dual interview is easier to
manage. In this form, viewers see the interviewer and hear the questions. Replies can
be free-form in this approach. For example, "Where were you born?" "Cleveland"
is fine in a dual interview, but the answer
would be meaningless in a single interview.
Two-person interviews also offer built-
in cutaway material in the form of the
interviewer.

A more complex interview form is multi-
plevoice. Using man-on-the-street vignettes
or short sessions with the many people
connected with the topic, you weave
together a composite audio track that adds

richness and variety as well as information. If people you know have some performing ability, you might try dramatized "interviews" with historic figures or people otherwise unavailable. Be cautious, however, because voice-only acting is a highly specialized skill and amateurish results sound frankly embarrassing.

Expert Presenter

If you've watched a David Attenborough nature video ("The vegetation [*wheeze*] here at 15,000 feet [*gasp*] is, understandably [*rattle*] sparse.") then you've seen an expert presenter. This method has many things going for it. First, the expertise of the spokesperson lends authority to the whole enterprise. Secondly, he or she can often be relied on to flesh out a skeletal content outline by ad-libbing material (see Figure 21-2).

The expert is best in the field—whether that field is a studio cooking show kitchen or a construction site or the Sonoran desert. If that isn't possible, you can establish the expert on camera in interview mode and then shift his or her remarks to voiceover narration.

The simplest approach is commentary: the experts react to whatever is presented to them. At its best, this method elicits priceless observations that would never occur to a script writer. At worst, it delivers the DVD prattle of movie directors reacting off-the-cuff to screenings of their films.

One step more formal is the demonstration, anything from a construction project to a science experiment to a cooking show. A demo is more clearly sequenced (by the steps in the project or recipe) but it still offers ample opportunity for ad-lib expert commentary. A demonstration format works best when the project can be completed at a single place in real time (except for the 45 minute baking period) and when the personality of the presenter adds interest to the show.

A popular variation seen on home repair, gardening and cooking shows is the dual (and sometimes dueling) expert

Figure 21-2 *Expert Presenter—The expert presenter lends authority to your subject and can ad-lib to expand on outlined program material.*

format pioneered by Siskel and Ebert. This approach combines the virtues of the expert and interview methods, especially if one of the presenters serves as prompter/straight man to the other.

The next level up is a full-fledged lecture, either scripted or ad-lib. Since even the most dynamic expert is still just a talking head, it's good to cut away as much as possible to visuals of the subject matter. In fact, a project like this often starts with the taped lecture; then appropriate visuals are scripted and shot after the fact.

Sometimes, the effect of a lecture can be created by a skillful one-person interview. The questions select and sequence the material, and then drop away, leaving a seamless narrative.

Full Script

An expert isn't necessary when reading narration that's been fully scripted.

There are several reasons for going to the trouble of a wall-to-wall script. In some cases there are issues of legal or technical accuracy. You don't want to misrepresent details of *Employee Benefit Packages* or *Self Administration of Insulin*, and the best way to avoid doing so is by writing down (and getting approval for) every image and word.

In training and similar how-to programs, you want the clearest camera angles and the simplest language possible. In highly controlled situations like this, you'll want every sentence written and every setup storyboarded (see Figure 21-3).

A scripted program can use any mixture of presentation forms, including an on-camera spokesperson, a voiceover narrator and superimposed title buildups. You can even use interviews if the questions are closely coordinated with the script. (In real world situations, the script is often revised *after* the interviews are completed, in order to bring it into line with whatever was said.)

Full scripts and/or storyboards are almost always prepared for professional commercials, infomercials, video press releases and training programs, for one overwhelming reason: the client. Most people and

Figure 21-3 *In some situations you may want to script the narration for your talent in clear simple language.*

organizations are reluctant to spend good money unless they can see (or at least *think* they can see) what they're getting.

As we've seen, the presentation method chosen depends first of all on the nature of the topic. But real-world constraints also play a large role. What if you don't have an expert? Worse, what if you do have an expert who's a droning bore but still wants to be in the program? In situations like this, you need to know the alternative methods available to you and their suitability to your topic.

Sidebar 1

Pictures, Words or Titles?

Different types of information want different presentation media. Some things are impossible to describe but easy to show; others are the opposite. Here's a quick rundown on choosing the best medium for each type of content.

- Pictures

  If you can show it, do so. Images should always be your first choice, when appropriate, because video is inherently a visual medium. Through slow or fast motion, split screen shots and other formal devices, the medium can also display things in ways that can't be seen in real life.

- Words

  If it's an abstraction, then talk about it. "Good citizenship" can be shown by examples (voting, picking up litter) but the concept itself is impossible to visualize. That's where narration does its best work.

  Words also work well for summarizing because they deliver meaning so efficiently. "Your one-stop transmission and tire service since 1966" takes five seconds to say. You could show transmission work, tire installation and maybe a wall plaque proclaiming "Founded 1966" but these visuals would be time-consuming and lame.

- Titles

  Titles make wonderful labels and organizers. *Cliche* that it is, a bulleted agenda that builds up line by line (via PowerPoint or titling software) is still the best way to orient (and periodically re-orient) viewers to the content of the program.

  If the list is short, you can also display all the lines at once, color-highlighting whichever one is the current topic.

Combo Platters

Different viewers have different learning styles, visual, aural or textual; so try to deliver important points in at least two ways, or even three if necessary. For example, you could cover one step in a construction project like this:

- *Visual*: big CU of tab A inserted into slot B.

- *Aural*: NARRATOR (V.O.) Now insert tab A into slot B.

- *Textual*: Subtitle supered over the shot:"Insert Tab A in Slot B."

When delivering information redundantly, avoid varying its form. If the narrator says, "Now complete the assembly of the sub-widgit," viewers have to make a mental connection between this line and Tab A and Slot B. This effort can be distracting or even confusing.

22
Put It on Paper First

Gene Bjerke

Is it a dream or a nightmare? You finally have it made—full production facilities for your project. The crew is looking at you expectantly, the talent is standing around waiting for direction, and behind you is a producer looking at all these expensive people and demanding to know what you are going to do. This is no time to be considering your alternatives.

Perhaps your vision is less grand. You turn on your camcorder in a room full of tenth-reunion college chums and realize that you have no idea what you should shoot.

Whether you're a professional working against a fast-running meter or you make video for fun, everything goes a lot easier when you figure out what you're going to do ahead of time. The two best tools for this are the script and the storyboard. It's true, some people can make videos with only a few notes written on the back of an envelope; but the more detail you have, the faster and easier production will go.

There are good reasons why successful videographers use these tools. First, they help you to organize and clarify your thoughts. Then they allow you to transmit your ideas to the other people who will be involved with the production. If you're going to edit in-camera, you'll know exactly what to shoot and how much. Finally, when you're on the set and everybody is looking at you, it allows you to take charge and look good.

A good script describes everything that the viewer will see and hear in the order it will be seen and heard. A script consists of words; videos consist of pictures. To visualize what they will shoot, many people use a storyboard. A storyboard consists of a picture that shows what the camera will see along with words that describe the shot.

Types of Scripts

The script is the primary document that the videographer uses to create all the video and audio raw material and keep it organized. This last point is important, since it is sometimes not possible to shoot a video in the order in which the viewer will see it. For instance, it is easier to shoot everything that takes place in one location at the same time. You then put all the shots in their proper sequence when you edit— again, using the script to help you keep everything straight.

For our purposes, we can break videos down into two general categories: dramatic and informational. The purposes and techniques of each are different, and so are the script formats that have been developed for them. See the accompanying sample scripts for a look at how these simple rules can help you create effective documents.

The Dramatic Video

Dramatic videos are stories told by action and dialog for the audience's entertainment, such as feature films and television shows. The film format script is preferred in Hollywood for dramatic film and television productions. In this format, the writer sets the location of each scene, describes the actions and interactions that take place, and writes out the dialog. This kind of script does not indicate individual

Script Abbreviations

BG - Background
CU - Closeup
ECU - Extreme Closeup
EXT - Exterior Scene
FG - Foreground

FS - Follow Shot (Pan)
INT - Interior Scene
LS - Long Shot
MCU - Medium Closeup
SFX - Sound Effects

Film Format

EXT. OLD LOGGING ROAD IN THE WOODS

JOHN and JANET are walking down the road, discussing the possibilities for an upcoming four-generation birthday party for JANET's grandmother.

>   JOHN
>   Maybe we should hold it
>   outdoors. That way we wouldn't
>   have to rent a hall to
>   accommodate all those people.

>   JANET
>   (enthusiastically)
>   That's a great idea! We
>   could do it as a picnic in the
>   park just down the street from
>   her house.

EXT. THE PARK

As they speak, the scene DISSOLVES to the park with a banner that says "Happy Birthday Great-Grandma Schmidt." There is a pickup softball game going on in the BG and people setting up for a big picnic in the FG.

>   JOHN
>   (off-screen)
>   Yeah! We could get up a
>   family softball game, just like in
>   the old days.

>   JANET
>   And at the end bring out a
>   big birthday cake.

WIPE TO the same scene in a torrential downpour. The banner is drooping and the field is empty. We hear a loud CLAP OF THUNDER.

>   NARRATOR
>   (off-screen)
>   But that's not quite the way
>   it happened. Not only did it rain,
>   but lightning struck the bakery
>   and destroyed the fabulous
>   eight-layer cake.

Video Format

audio descriptions	video descriptions
10. LS JANET and JOHN are walking down an old logging road in the woods. QUIET MUSIC AND NATURAL SFX:	JOHN Maybe we should hold it outdoors. That way we wouldn't have to rent a hall to accommodate all those people.
11. CU Janet.	JANET (enthusiastically)That's a great idea! We could do it as a picnic in the park just down the street from her house.
DISSOLVE TO 12. LS A scene in the park with a banner that says "Happy Birthday Great-Grandma Schmidt." There is a pickup softball game going on in the BG and people setting up for a big picnic in the FG.	JOHN (off-screen) Yeah! We could get up a family softball game, just like in the old days.
13. FS Janet proudly carries a large birthday cake to the picnic table and places it in front of Grandma as the others gather around.	JANET And at the end bring out a big birthday cake.
WIPE TO 14. The same scene in a torrential downpour. The banner is drooping and the field is empty. CLAP OF THUNDER	NARRATOR (off-screen) But that's not quite the way it happened. Not only did it rain, but lightning struck the bakery and destroyed the fabulous eight-layer cake.

Figure 22-1

camera shots or moves. The basic format is as follows:

- Type scene descriptions, camera directions, stage directions, etc. from margin to margin.

- Place dialog and narration in a three-inch wide column down the center of the page.

- Type the name of the speaker in all-caps and center it just above his or her speech. Place delivery instructions in parentheses, on a separate line, and indented within the column of the speech.

- Single-space material such as: dialog, scene descriptions, camera directions and stage directions.

- Separate blocks of material with a blank line between. For example, separate:

- Lines by different characters.

- Dialog and scene descriptions or stage directions.

- Location information and scene descriptions.

- Adjacent shot descriptions.

- Transitions (such as "DISSOLVE TO").

- Type everything in upper and lower case except the following, which are all-caps:

  - Transitions.

  - Location descriptions.

  - Camera directions.

  - Characters' names (when indicating their lines and the first time they appear in scene descriptions).

The Informational Video

Documentaries and other informational videos, such as the college reunion memorial, consist of scenes that may or may not include actors. Such shows usually have little or no dialog and often have a voice-over narration. The camcorder documentarian frequently performs double duty as the narrator. The two-column video format script serves the informational video production. The left (video) column contains descriptions of the shots and the right (audio) column contains the words spoken by actors or narrator as well as descriptions of music and sound effects.

While you can use it for dramatic material, this format is especially well adapted for videos and television shows that consist of a variety of shots with narration overlaid. It's easy to see the relationship of words and pictures; the words come at the same time that you see the pictures that are immediately to their left. Create this format as follows:

- Place video descriptions in the left column, single-spaced.

- Place accompanying audio descriptions in the right column, double-spaced.

- Type video descriptions and spoken lines in upper- and lower-case.

- Type the following in all-caps:

- Location descriptions.

- Transitions.

- Camera directions (i.e., PAN, ZOOM).

- Music and sound effects.

- Type the speaker identification in all-caps and underline. Place directions for delivery in parentheses.

There is one other script format that you may want to consider. The corporate teleplay format combines elements of the two preceding formats. Most of the script is written in film format, but any off-screen narration goes into a narrow column on the right side of the page.

Storyboards

To visualize scenes, you might consider making a storyboard in which a drawing

(a) (b) (c) (d)

Figure 22-2 *Sample Storyboard.*

of the expected visual represents each shot. Written remarks amplify the drawings: dialog or narration, camera moves and so forth. The storyboard helps make it cheaper and easier to solve your visual problems on paper before you ever break out the camera.

Some storyboards are works of art in themselves, with beautiful watercolor or computer-art pictures. But this is not necessary (unless you have an ample budget or budding artist in the family). Simple sketches with stick figures or nose-on-an-egg faces are fine. Feel free to include arrows to indicate movement. A long pan may consist of two pictures, showing the beginning and end of the pan, with an arrow connecting them, showing the direction of the pan.

Since each shot requires one or more drawings, you don't usually see storyboards for long projects. They are common in the development of high-end commercials but are too time-consuming and expensive for lengthy productions. However, you might want to use a few storyboard scenes to work out something that is difficult to envision or to explain to another crew member.

The time you spend creating a script or a storyboard is recaptured when you're under the pressure of shooting. You have already solved your creative problems and can concentrate on technical details. So next time you're on the set or at an event and everybody is looking to you to tell them what will happen next, you can whip out your trusty script or storyboard and take charge.

23
Look Who's Talking: How to Create Effective, Believable Dialogue for Your Video Productions

John K. Waters

A script is a story told with pictures—but silent pictures they're not. Since 1927, when the debut of *The Jazz Singer* transformed "moving pictures" into "talkies," dialogue has played a crucial role in making successful films and videos.

But with everything else you worry about as an independent videographer—maintaining your equipment, getting the shot, getting paid—dialogue may be low on your list of concerns. Still, you don't want to underestimate its power.

Good dialogue works hard. It keeps things moving, ties individual segments together and unifies your piece. On the other hand, bad dialogue discredits your work, destroying your credibility and ultimately costing you your audience.

Whether you're shooting independent features, corporate image spots, local TV commercials or your sister's wedding, what your subjects say can make the difference between an amateur show and a powerful piece of professional videography.

Here's how to make sure what they say works.

What Is Dialogue?

Any time you put words into the mouths of your on-camera subjects, you are writing dialogue. That definition includes hosts, commentators and spokespersons, as well as actors playing parts.

The primary purpose of dialogue is to move your story forward. It accomplishes this by revealing character, communicating information and establishing relationships between characters. It can also foreshadow events, comment on the action and connect scenes.

For example: in my script *Sleeping Dogs Lie*, the hero, Ray Sobczak, is a reporter working on a story that is annoying some very important citizens. Here, a local politico delivers a veiled warning.

                    JAMIE
        What happened to you?

                  SOBCZAK
Zigged when I shoulda zagged. How's the campaign going?

                    JAMIE
Oh, I just love spending obscene amounts of my mother's money—and what your paper charges for ad space is truly obscene.

                  SOBCZAK
Something tells me your mother can afford it, Mr. Bockman.

                    JAMIE
My father, who could also afford it when he was alive, was Mr. Bockman. Call me Jamie.

                  SOBCZAK
Okay, Jamie. Think she'll win?

                    JAMIE
(ignoring him) How's the story coming?

                  SOBCZAK
Which story is that? (Jamie gazes out at the cluster of downtown buildings and the hills rising behind them.)

                    JAMIE
Salinas is growing, Ray. Over a hundred thousand at last count. But, underneath, it's still a small town.

This exchange probably won't go down in history as the most memorable in films, but it has many earmarks of good dialogue. It tells us something about the characters: Jamie is rich, has an ambiguous attitude toward his mother's campaign for mayor and has well-informed connections; Sobczak is tough, and won't let a bump on the noggin keep him from getting the story.

It foreshadows future events: people are watching. And it moves the story forward: this encounter gives Sobczak an idea, which leads him—and the story—in a new direction.

Keep It Lean

The above example also demonstrates another important quality of good dialogue: brevity. Good dialogue is a lean exchange between people, composed of short phrases. On paper, it looks like lots of white space; big blocks of type are definite warning sign that you are overwriting your dialogue.

"The good stuff is a dance of two and three-liners between characters," says scriptwriter Madeline DiMaggio. "It's a bouncing ball that keeps your audience riveted."

When it comes to writing dialogue, DiMaggio knows what she's talking about. She has written over 35 hours of episodic television for shows ranging from Kojak to The Bob Newhart Show to ABC's After School Special. A former staff writer for the daytime soap opera Santa Barbara, she is also a teacher and the author of *How to Write for Television*.

DiMaggio says the kind of close-to-the-bone dialogue you want for your videos comes only through rewriting (see Figure 23-1), "It doesn't happen on the first pass," she says. "At first your dialogue is cardboard—and that's the way it should be. It's only later, when you go back and take five lines down to two-and-a-half, and then two-and-a-half lines down to one, that you find the real gems."

DiMaggio says she plays a game with herself during her rewriting process: if she can whittle a piece of dialogue down to four lines, can she cut it to two? If she can chop it to two, how about one?

"If script writers were doctors," she says, "the best ones would be surgeons. Cut, cut, cut!"

Figure 23-1 *Rewriting and rewriting and rewriting again is key when writing dialog.*

Make It Sound Real

A tried and true technique for developing your ear for natural-sounding dialogue is to surreptitiously tape conversations and then transcribe them later.

I do this especially when I'm writing about types of people I don't know well. Ethical questions aside, this has worked well to awaken my sense of how people talk.

The first thing I noticed when I began doing this was how fragmented conversations are. The following is an example from my files.

MAN #1
Hey, what's up?

MAN #2
I dropped by the place. Thought I'd say hi, but nobody was, you know ...

MAN #1
I was over there yesterday and ...

MAN #2
... home. You know?

MAN #1
Nobody? Man, I ...

MAN #2
That's because of the, you know, holiday 'n stuff, and her car was there and everything, but ...

MAN #1
What a piece of *#@*!, man, that car ...

MAN #2
Yeah, and, you know, I left like, a note.

MAN #1
No way!

On paper, this conversation looks like an exchange between two orangutans, but they sounded perfectly normal. That's why, unless you're making a documentary, you can't just transcribe tapes of real conversations and use them raw in your scripts. And even documentaries require judicious editing.

"If you went out to a coffee shop with a tape recorder," DiMaggio says, "and went home and put what you recorded into a script, it wouldn't work. Good dialogue isn't actually real. It just gives the illusion of reality."

DiMaggio says one of the best ways to learn how dialogue sounds is to record dialogue.

"That's how I got to know Santa Barbara," she says. "There were so many characters, and they all had their own voices! I would audiotape the show and then listen whenever I was driving. When you cut off the other senses, your ear becomes much stronger."

DiMaggio also recommends audiotaping shows to develop an ear for genre dialogue.

"Comedies, mysteries, dramas—it's an incredible way to learn," she says.

Good dialogue also has a spontaneous quality, as if your characters were speaking their lines for the first time.

"When the dialogue is stilted or too formal," says corporate video writer/producer Susan O'Connor Fraser, "the audience just laughs at it. When they start doing that, you've lost them."

O'Connor Fraser is the creative director for Tam Communications in San Jose, California. She's been writing and producing videos for Fortune 500 companies for the past 15 years. Her company produced a reality-based show on paramedics in San Jose, which aired on the local ABC affiliate.

"I don't think corporate video is that much different from features," O'Connor Fraser says. "Dialogue is dialogue, and every story has its own reality. Star Wars has a reality, and so does a corporate sales presentation. Everything must play and be believable within its own reality."

According to O'Connor Fraser, one of the most common dialogue errors she sees is characters addressing each other by name too often.

"I've seen it done in every passage," she says. "It's, 'Well, John ... Well, Lisa... What do you think, John ... I'm not sure, Lisa.' It's just not real."

She says reading your script aloud is one of the easiest ways to spot dialogue errors. (See Figure 23-2)

"You're writing for the ear. So you need to find out how it sounds. You don't need actors, though they are a wonderful luxury. Just read it out loud with a friend, or by yourself while you're sitting at your computer. You'll hear many of the problems right away."

Stay in Character

When I write, I become the characters I'm writing about. This is pretty easy when I'm writing about thirty something white guys from the Midwest. But what about when the character I'm writing dialogue for is a New York cop, or a Southern doctor, or a black female Vietnam veteran with a Harvard MBA, two grown children and a neurotic obsession with alien abductions?

You simply cannot write dialogue that rings true unless you acquaint yourself with the kind of people appearing in your video. This is where real world research is essential. I'm talking about stuff you can't find in the library. But that doesn't mean that you have to spend a week on a fishing boat in Alaska or infiltrate the local Jaycees to get the right slang and jargon for your script, though those are tried and true approaches.

"If I don't have any personal experiences in my own life I can draw on," says O'Connor Fraser, "I track down the kind of person I'm writing about and take them to lunch." In her corporate work, she tends to deal with a limited number of "types," mostly from the high tech world; after 15 years she knows them well. But she still checks her "voice" with face-to-face interviews—especially when she's writing a script for an on-camera presentation by a company executive.

Figure 23-2 *Read your script aloud to make sure it sounds natural.*

"When I go out and interview a president or vice president who will be on camera," she says, "I listen very carefully, so I'm really hearing them talk. I don't want them to sound like they're reading from the inside cover of an annual report. I want them to sound very natural and comfortable, as though they were talking across the table from someone.

"Interviewing your clients is also one of the best ways to pick up the buzz words of their professions. Listen closely and make a list of unfamiliar words or phrases. Ask for clarification so you understand them in context. When you sit down to write your script, your list will prove invaluable."

Many writers just write the dialogue as best they can and then give it to someone from that character's walk of life to read. DiMaggio says she works on her dialogue, "until I'm not ashamed of it," and then turns it over to a person with whatever special knowledge her characters would have. In her TV movie script, *Belly Up*, for example, one of her characters was a man who gambled on the golf course.

"I wasn't about to take up golf to hear how guys gamble on the golf course," says DiMaggio. "So I sent the script to my brother. He gambles on the golf course all the time. In five minutes he told me things I couldn't possibly know unless I was out there. I made some changes in the script and all of a sudden it sounded absolutely real. One producer told me I wrote like a man, which, under the circumstances, I took as a compliment."

In one of my own scripts I created a character who was a professional crop duster, but I had never met a crop duster in my life. So I picked up the Yellow Pages, and a few lunches later I knew everything

I needed to know to create a believable character. (And I now know to call them agricultural aviators.)

Go for Subtext

Syd Field, author of several well-known books on scriptwriting, including the now classic *Screenplay: The Foundations of Screenwriting*, calls dialogue one of the "tools of character." That's because what people say says a great deal about them. But what they don't say often says more. The best dialogue is not only about what your characters are saying, it's also about what they're not saying. This is subtext.

"Subtext is what's happening beneath the surface," says DiMaggio. "It's the key to truly great dialogue."

Examples of subtext abound in films like the 1944 film noir classic, *Double Indemnity*. One scene in particular comes to mind, in which insurance salesman Walter Neff (Fred MacMurray) puts the make on a client's wife (Barbara Stanwyck). They fence back and forth in a conversation about cars and speeding, but driving is the last thing on their minds.

Subtext enlivens good writing everywhere—even commercials. We've watched that couple in the Taster's Choice commercials meet, woo and bed in Paris—all while talking about coffee.

Subtext probably isn't as important in most corporate video situations; still, you ignore it at your peril. Human beings talk around things. Dialogue that's too "on the nose" won't sound natural. Even the dialogue in infomercials has subtext.

Figure 23-3 Congratulations! It's a script!

Write the Right Voice Over

Voice-over narration isn't really dialogue, but many of the same principles still apply. This is especially true if the narrator is a particular character, as in the case of a host, or one of the actors, such as the Holly Hunter character in *The Piano* or Walter Neff, who narrates *Double Indemnity*.

You write voice-over narration like you write dialogue—for the ear. It should sound conversational. Even if your narrator is an omniscient voice, that voice must conform to your audience's expectations of human communication.

"When I'm doing voice overs," says O'Connor Fraser, "I still get a character in mind and write for him or her. Of course this is really important if the narrator will ever appear on-camera, but I do it even if they won't. That way, the voice is consistent throughout."

Voice-over narration can be even harder to write than dialogue. "If you think dialogue has to be lean," DiMaggio says, "voice overs have to be the best of the best. It has to be very, very thrifty. The real gems.

Otherwise it turns into an excuse for failing to write good exposition."

Practice, Practice, Practice

Writing authentic, believable dialogue is a special skill; it takes practice. But with some effort and more than a little patience, you'll get it (Figure 23-3).

"You have to realize that the script you write today won't be as good as the script you write next year," says O'Connor Fraser. "And that's okay. I'm a much better writer now than I was a year ago. I learn something with every script I write."

"We're all students, really," says DiMaggio. "No matter how long you do this, there's always something to learn. I think that's the good news. It's one of the things that keeps this work interesting."

In the end, creating good dialogue is more about listening than it is about writing. Once you begin to hear the rhythms of human conversation, the dialogue you write for your videos will improve dramatically.

So keep your ears open.

24
Storyboards and Shot Lists

Jim Stinson

Some DVDs (*Shrek* and *The Matrix*, for example) now include sample storyboards—shot-by-shot sketches drawn to visualize the action of key sequences—as bonus material. As you study these slick drawings, you'll notice that most frames are remarkably close to the actual shots they predict. Back in Hollywood's glory days, most directors (with Hitchcock a notable exception) rarely worked with storyboards; today, however, they're everywhere. Should you be using them too? That's what we're here to discover. We'll start with a look at what storyboards do.

Storyboards Visualize

Basically, pre-designed storyboards in pencil or marker predict what shots will look like. Why not just invent shots as you actually shoot? Here are three reasons.

First, storyboards let you test complicated setups cheaply on paper instead of expensively on location. Suppose your script says, "He unrolls the treasure map before him and she gasps as she sees where the gold is buried." But when you draw a high-angle insert of the unfolding map,

you realize there's no way to get "she" into the frame (see Figure 24-1a). So you try a new angle: over her shoulder (see Figure 24-1b). By moving the camcorder to center her face and refocusing as she turns into profile, you can get both her relation to the map and her reaction to it; and you haven't wasted half an hour on a setup you'd eventually discard.

Secondly, you can check your coverage of a sequence and preplan your video camera angles for variety, continuity and rhythm. Suppose you sketch three shots of the male talent digging up the treasure chest (see Figure 24-2a). Hmmm: though the sketches are from different viewpoints, they're all neutral-height medium shots and are too repetitive. OK, substitute a point-of-view (POV) closeup of the emerging chest (Figure 24-2e) and change the last shot to a low-angle closeup of his greedy expression as he reacts to the chest (Figure 24-2f). In 10 minutes of doodling, you've improved a sequence from ho-hum to dynamic.

Finally, storyboarding is essential for planning special effects. Say you want to establish a "pirate ship" by compositing stock footage of a three-master riding off-shore with our hero in the foreground

(a)

(b)

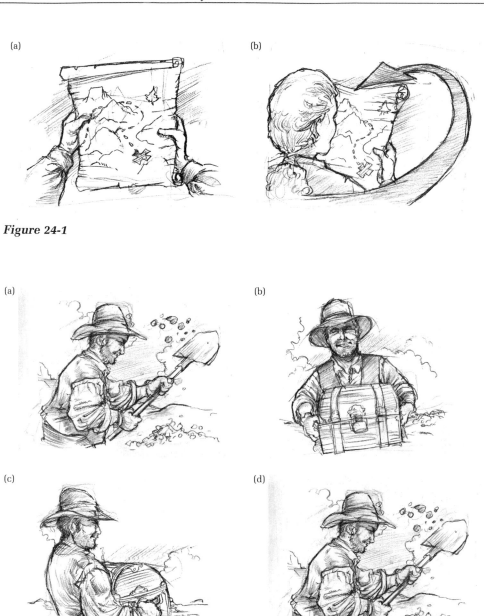

Figure 24-1

(a)

(b)

(c)

(d)

(e)

(f)

Figure 24-2

Figure 24-3

(see Figure 24-3). A sketch will guide your placement of the camera and the actor so that he'll relate properly to the scene.

Storyboard Vision

So far, you've created storyboards for your own use, but storyboards also communicate your vision to others. Verbalizing image ideas is always chancy, so it's better to show what you have in mind visually.

In the professional world, storyboards are essential for communicating with clients, first to pitch concepts and then to preview the live action. Never forget that visual imagination is like a sense of humor: many people lack it, but no one will ever admit it. The client may nod and smile as you verbalize your vision, but yelp, "You never said you'd do that!" upon seeing the footage, even if that was precisely what you promised. Prevent that scenario—put that promise in sketches instead of words.

Incidentally, you should have a professional artist draw storyboards for clients. Even though you were hired to shoot, not draw, your amateur scribbles will likely cast doubts on your professionalism. (Hey, whoever said it was fair?) If you don't have a client to impress, don't worry about the quality of your thumbnail sketches. As long as they communicate to yourself and your crew, they do the job. There are two ways to do storyboarding nowadays,

either draw them on paper or build them on a computer.

Paper and Pencil

To make a board from scratch, draw between six and 12 rectangles on a virtual sheet of paper (any word processor or paint program'll do it for you). Make the horizontal/vertical ratio 4 to 3 (4:3) for conventional video or 16:9 for wide screen. Leave enough space to write under each frame. Some people pre-print "Frame#," "action," "audio," etc., but you don't have to be that formal. Print out a large quantity of these blank boards.

Using simple lines and stick-figure subjects, sketch each setup in a frame, observing just a few conventions. Indicate subject movement with arrows in the frame. Show zooms by sketching the wide-angle position, drawing a box around the telephoto position within it and adding diagonal arrows to show whether the movement is in or out. For pans or tilts between two distinct compositions, show each one as a separate frame, with an arrow between frames to link them.

The notes written below each frame should contain some or all of the following:

- Frame number
- Sequence ("27") or sequence/shot ("27B")
- Action ("John runs past; exits frame right")
- Camera instructions: ("No pan")
- Dialogue: ("JOHN: Come back here with that map!")
- Other audio: ("SFX: bullet ricochet")
- Visual effects: ("Bluescreen for ship composite")

Computer Boards

If you're deft with a mouse (or are fortunate enough to own a pad and stylus), you can sketch boards directly on your screen.

Perhaps the easiest way to do this is with the draw tools in Corel Presentations or Microsoft PowerPoint. This approach makes frames easy to add, insert, delete or modify (see Figure 24-4).

A second method is to make individual sketches in the drawpaint software you favor, then use a graphics organizer to print them as sequential thumbnails. The ThumbsPlus software lets you add extensive notes under each image.

A third route is a publishing package like Adobe PageMaker. You can build a template page of blank frames, then either draw in each one or import an outside graphic or even location photo.

Figure 24-4 *You don't need to be an artist. Use a simple paint program to convey your ideas.*

This brings us to commercial storyboard packages. As the sidebar suggests, they can make wonderful organizers for production planning, because you can import digital photos and write extensive commentaries. However, they can be cranky and limited in drawing the shots of your particular show. Though they might seem to allow non-artists to build presentation-quality boards, the skill needed to customize their generic components is substantial.

Shot Lists

Think of a shot list as the writing on a storyboard, without the pictures (see Figure 24-5). Though simple lists of shots don't let you pre-test potential setups, they do allow you to systematically verify that you are covering every angle you need.

Often shot lists are just quick and dirty notes that help you remember everything you need in a particular sequence. You can also cull a shot list from a fully-written script if you separate video into separate columns (or paragraphs). Just build a word processor macro that will strip out everything but the scene number and the visual description.

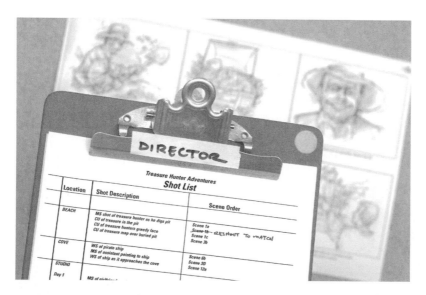

Figure 24-5 *A coordinated shot list that matches your storyboard will make your job much easier.*

On the other hand, a shot list built in a database program (such as File Maker Pro) can be the most versatile production tool in your kit. Design a database using some or all of the fields suggested in the sidebar, using each shot as a separate record. By creating report forms with different fields and sorts, you can build a working document for everyone from the director to the wardrobe person.

Sidebar 1

Storyboard Software

Commercial software is available for storyboarding but it suffers from problems that are very hard to overcome.

Most packages work by supplying a pre-drawn set of backgrounds, a grab bag of props (guns, flower pots, cars), and a repertory of characters. By selecting, placing, rotating and scaling these components, you can make very professional looking frames.

The trouble is, they can almost never illustrate your video. The script may say, "The old duchess sweeps into the palace banquet hall." But the software inventory lacks both an old woman (let alone a duchess) and a palace hall; and the drawing tools for building same are rudimentary, to put it kindly.

True, you can import custom backgrounds from programs like Bryce and characters from 3D modeling software, but expect to spend at least an hour per frame building these hybrid images. Do the math on a three-page board of 12 frames each and decide if this method is really time-effective for your project.

On the other hand, these packages can be useful in production planning if you import digital stills from location scouting and make notes in the fields provided. Shotmaster from the Badham Company (www.badhamcompany.com) is particularly versatile this way.

Bottom line: Storyboard packages have their uses, but don't expect them to draw what you can't draw for yourself.

Sidebar 2

A Shot List Database

Start your database by treating each shot as a separate record. Then add fields for every important aspect of production planning.

An Extensive List
A fairly complete set of fields might include the following (separate but related fields are grouped together):

- sequence, shot number and take

- interior/exterior and day/night

- camera setup

- audio (production, reference track, special effects)

- special equipment (like a dolly)

- shot content

- notes

- location

- talent 1, talent 2, talent 3 (etc., for as many actors as will ever appear together in a single shot)

- key prop (such as a rented vehicle), other props

- costumes

- day, date and start time

Plus any other production details you want to keep track of

A Director's List
To create a director's shot list, build a report containing these fields:

- sequence, shot number and take

- camera setup

- shot content

- notes

Then sort the list by sequence, setup and only then shot number. You'll get a sequence-by-sequence list of every shot organized by setup.

25
Budget Details: Successful Video Projects Stick to Budgets

Mark Steven Bosko

Creating and adhering to a realistic budget is important to the success of any videographer's project.

But just how do you compute that magical figure, arrive at an amount low enough to attract investors but large enough to get the job done? It's not easy. Thousands of people labor in Hollywood as budget wizards; not even they get it right always. So many variables and details can go wrong or astray; it's impossible to plan for every contingency. Most often, you just have to guess.

Still, in this chapter we'll offer a number of useful guidelines vital for budget preparation. Videographers who absorb these lessons will at least have a reasonable grasp of the basics of financial planning.

Reasons for Budgets

Video budgets both attract investors and allow you to exercise control over a production.

Since the budget is the foundation of any presentation to investors, it should be specific and accurate.

Realism is also a good idea. It's an admirable goal, applying LucasFilm-like effects to a dry-cleaning commercial, but hardly feasible when the video must come in at $499.

Most projects begin under-budgeted and under-scheduled. It's easy to understand why. A project will certainly seem more attractive to investors if you can convince them you'll finish the video for less money in less time than the competition.

But this shortsighted method of easy financing will eventually cause you suffering.

Projects under-scheduled and under-budgeted leave you with only two options once the show begins 1) the project goes over budget, or 2) the quality goes into the dumpster.

Say you tell a client $300 will do to create a training video. Then, during shooting, rain pours down; you must shut down the shoot and pay talent for a second day. You've now spent an extra $50, money intended for post-production. So will you skip the original scoring, budgeted at $50, choosing instead to give the client canned tunes? Or jettison the spiffy title effects for hand-lettered cards?

Sticking adamantly to an unrealistic budget forces you to continually compromise. This leads to a loss of quality.

There's a minimum budget for every project, a certain amount necessary to produce a video meeting reasonable standards of quality. Determine your video's destination, then calculate the smallest amount of money needed to reach it. If the available financing is less than this figure, change the project.

Keep budgeting until you have a video you can afford to make.

Step by Step

It's important to give equal emphasis to all stages of production, from writing and principal photography to music and editing.

It's easy to get excited about the shooting stage of a video project. Here is the place for lights, camera, action. Just don't make the mistake of creating an excruciatingly detailed budget for production only to carelessly slop but a few dollars to post production. You'll pay dearly.

Become familiar with the functions and costs associated with every step of the production process. Talk to the people responsible for the script, the shooting and the effects. Without such intense research, you may neglect such costs as B-roll tape, music copyright fees and catering charges.

Actual working budgets vary in size. Major Hollywood studio budgets may end up as two-inch-thick tomes, while an independent thirty-second cable spot can come in a tiny one-pager.

Regardless of size, most every budget consists of two sections: costs above-the-line and below-the-line. The former

includes cash for producer, writer, director and talent. These costs are usually fixed, set amounts. Below-the-line costs include everything else associated with production. Each line item contains many separate details contributing to the total cost. I'll examine each in an attempt to explain what makes building a budget so tricky.

Over the Line

The first above-the-line item concerns screenplay and story rights (see Figure 25-1). If your production uses an adaptation of existing work, you'll have to purchase the rights. These can be costly for a known, popular author's work, or nonexistent if the story comes from a rookie simply seeking screen credit.

Unless you come up with it yourself, you will have to pay someone some amount for either an idea or an actual screenplay. Even for thirty-second commercials, people get paid to write scripts.

Hidden above-the-line costs can include photocopying, script breakdowns and rewrites, copyright registration and legal fees associated with purchasing work.

The producer is the one who generally runs the show; and, yep, often expects payment, too. A producer is responsible for finding story, actors, crew, equipment, locations, props, wardrobe and investors. This requires an enormous amount of time, even for a small, one-day shoot. A producer's talent lies in the ability to make and keep contacts; that's what they're paid for. Obvious expenses include phone charges, travel expenses, lunches, postage, contracts and legal fees.

In Hollywood, the director is paid for overall vision. On smaller productions, the director may be you, the camera operator or even the client. With very low budgets, you can skip this item; there isn't enough discretionary cash available to afford a director.

Talent includes lead actors, supporting cast, stunt people, voice-over artists and models. In budgeting talent, keep in mind daily or hourly rates. These usually vary according to how often the person works.

Checklist Of Costs

above-the-line costs

screenplay and story rights
—purchase price of original work
destined for adaptation
—writing of original script
—script breakdowns
—script rewrites
—copyright registration
—photocopying
—legal fees
producer
—salary
—phone
—travel
—lunches
—postage
—contracts
—legal fees
director
talent
—lead actors
—supporting cast
—stunt people
—voice-over artists
—models

below-the-line costs

production staff
—camera operators
—sound recordist
—lighting technician
—makeup artist
—dialogue director
—script supervisor
—electricians
—dolly operators
—boom operators
—art director
—costume designer
—model builder
—prop maker
—set decorators
—hairdressers
—special effects technicians
—carpenters
—painters
—still photographer
—animal handlers
—security people
—first aid crew
—publicist
set operations
—camera
—lights
—tripods
—batteries
—tape
—nails, gasoline, books and more
—phone
—shipping
—catering

post-production costs

editing: equipment, for sale or rent
—music
—graphics
—titles
—special visual effects
—dubbing
—time-coding
—audio mixing
—looping
—sound effects
—tape
duplication expenses
—duplication costs
—packaging: artwork, layout, printing, photocopying, postage
advertising
—magazines
—radio
—television
—billboards
—classified
—flyers
—telemarketing
—direct sales
—conventions
—trade shows

And finally, the all-important fund for contingencies, a cool 10 percent of the total.

Figure 25-1 *Checklist of Costs.*

As an example, you might hire talent from the local actors' union for $200 a day, $150 for two days or more. Read the small print; often contracts demand that two or more days be worked consecutively. If you work your talent on Monday and Wednesday, you'll spend $400, not the planned two-day rate of $300.

For details on this intricate subject, consult Ralph Singleton's indispensable book, *Film Scheduling.*

Under the Rainbow

In an ultra-low budget affair you may spend little or no money above the line. But every production—large or small—incurs production expenses.

Depending on circumstances, production staff may or may not require significant expenditures. When the local car dealer hires you to shoot a thirty-second spot, you discover the script calls for a night shoot requiring a two-camera setup and live sound. What began simply now demands additional camera operators, lighting people, sound recorders and probably three or four grips to jockey cables and equipment.

On the other hand, your sixty-minute documentary on the mating habits of waterfowl requires only you and your camera.

Obviously, a project's length bears little relation to total costs. It's the script details that matter.

On most projects, regardless of size, the key staff members are the camera operator, sound recordist, lighting technician and makeup artist.

Support positions include dialogue director, script supervisor, electricians, dolly operators, boom operators, art director, costume designer, model builder, prop maker, set decorator, hair dresser, special effects technician, carpenter, painter, still photographer, animal handler, security, first-aid crew and publicist (see Figure 25-1).

Set operations, like staff, can demand either a large or small chunk of cash, again depending on the project. If you already own a camera, lights and sound equipment and all your locations currently exist, operation costs may be few. No need to buy or rent gear or build sets.

If your video seeks to portray a sci-fi world, get ready to dole out the dollars. The set builder needs wood, the wardrobe manager gold *lamé*, the makeup artist latex and the gaffer colored gels. The set operations segment of this budget requires great detail; include every imaginable associated cost.

It's not neurotic to include such costs as the tissues actors will need for their noses during chilly outdoor shoots. It's these little things that throw a project into disarray. Don't overlook such "obvious" items as nails, screws, bolts and glue; gasoline for automobiles and generators; rentals and permits; duplicate sets of clothing; bottles, cans, books and plants; and, of course, tape.

Again, talk to your people; learn what they require. Sometimes it's not a bad idea to ask your support staff to create their own budgets; these you can incorporate into your final estimate.

Postage and telephone fees can add up quickly. It's amazing how many long-distance calls people make in the middle of a production. And if you're on the road with a cellular, cash outflow can grow quite frightening. Same for postage and shipping expenses. If your client lives in another town and insists on dailies, you'll go broke if you haven't budgeted properly.

To cast and crew, the most important cost is catering. Believe me, you don't want to face down fifteen hungry people with nothing but a jar of peanut butter and a loaf of bread.

Post-Production Funds

The last formal segment of the budget concerns post-production audio and video editing.

Those who own their own editing equipment will find costs fairly minimal. If forced to rent, the prices can get steep. Don't underestimate the amount of editing time. This will depend on such variables as length of script, timing, client approval and number of effects.

If you've shot footage for a thirty-second spot requiring only five or six edits, an hour may be enough. If that same spot requires a rapid assault of images and sounds, you may spend two or three days in the edit bay.

You usually reserve editing time by the hour, day or week, with price breaks for longer periods. Other post production costs include music, graphics and titles creation, special visual effects, dubbing, time coding, audio mixing, looping, sound effects and extra tape.

A final cost to consider is the promotional expense associated with selling and marketing. Final product should be presented in a professional form. All videos properly labeled and packaged. You don't want to hand a client a VHS copy in a cardboard sleeve with masking tape crookedly proclaiming the title on the spine. A nice hard-shell package with a printed label is the only way to go; include these costs in your budget.

If you want your production to reach the masses, think about full-color packaging costs like artwork, layout and printing. Any worthwhile marketing effort includes mailing promotional copies to potential distributors and buyers. Estimate photocopying, postage and duplication costs.

Don't forget advertising. Magazines, radio, TV, billboards, classifieds, flyers, telemarketing, direct sales, door-to-door, conventions and trade shows whatever form you plan requires cash. Obtain quotes for ad rates during the time your ad will appear. Remember, your commercials will probably air more than a year after you've assembled the budget.

Because so much can go wrong, add a 10 percent contingency amount. This allows for unpredictable events, and lets investors know you're handling the project in a professional manner.

It's not easy to create budgets. It's harder yet to stick to them. But with a little preparation, forethought and diligence throughout the production, you could still find change in your pockets when the credits roll.

26
A Modest Proposal

William Ronat

Your phone rings. On the other end is a potential client. You like potential clients, as they represent potential profits. (Okay, so maybe you're not a professional videographer at this point. Stick with us anyway; as your skills and your reputation grow, you just might get such a call one day.)

The conversation is pleasant enough, with the potential client giving you a nebulous description of his potential video project. Then it's your turn. "What's it going to cost?" asks the potential client pleasantly.

That's the problem with some potential clients. They want to know exactly what you are going to do before you do it. And they want to know exactly what it will cost before they even know *what* they want to do.

Here's how I handle such a question. "Look," I say, "every video project is different. It's like asking how much a house is going to cost before you tell me what kind of a house you want to build. How many rooms does the house have, does it have a water view, how many acres of land? Ceramic tile? A swimming pool? You see?"

"Ah, of course, I see perfectly," says the potential client pleasantly, "But *how much is it going to cost?*"

"A million dollars," I reply.

Learn to Earn

This is the time to get some details on paper, usually in the form of a proposal. A proposal is simply a document that outlines what the video is going to accomplish, how you plan to make it happen, and an estimate of what it's all going to cost. Ahhh—we're back to the cost issue.

How can you come up with an accurate estimate of a "potential" video? By learning everything you can about the project. Who will be watching the final video—CEOs of corporations or first graders at the local elementary school? How long is the video? Will you need to shoot on Digital Betacam or is S-VHS acceptable? Are you and your crew going to have to travel to Istanbul or will everything be shot locally?

Be sure the client understands what he or she is getting. If your price is for shooting and editing, then let the client know that scriptwriting will be an additional expense. Or if you do take the job from start to finish, then outline all the steps (selecting talent, scouting locations, production scheduling, shooting, editing, and dubs). Make sure the client understands that your price includes these items only.

Before you state a price for the project, see if you can find out what the client's budget is. It may be more than you thought, which gives you the freedom to add more elements to the production. On the other end of the spectrum, the budget may be so small that it's not even possible to accomplish what the client wants. It's better to learn this sad fact early, before you invest your valuable time.

Set the Parameters

Once you state a price, the client will try to hold you to it. Client-human nature is to lock you into a price and then add complexity that will cost *you* more money. "Did I forget to mention that you could shoot on the warehouse floor only between 3 a.m. and 5 a.m.? Must've slipped my mind."

This is why you want to be specific in the cost estimating process of your proposal. If you tell him or her exactly what he or she is getting for the price you are quoting, the client won't be able to add on more complexity without that price going up.

On simple jobs, I usually break my estimate down into two parts: 1) the Treatment and 2) the Estimate and Authorization.

Earlier, we looked at how you should ask questions to learn about the client's project. With the information you learned through your questions, a natural method of creating the video will probably pop into your head.

For example, a client might be a builder of million-dollar homes. The client wants to show off the many features of the different models. Your treatment might look like this:

Classical music plays as the camera floats past the house with a breathtaking wide shot. The scene dissolves to a closer shot of the front of the house. As the camera floats forward, the front door opens and the camera (who is the viewer) is greeted by a butler. This butler (a professional actor) proceeds to give the viewer a full tour of the house.

The treatment can be as simple or as complex as you like, as long as it serves

the purpose of telling your client what the show is going to look like. If the client likes the concept and agrees on the price, you are ready to move into scripting. If there is something the client doesn't agree with, you know it before you discuss money.

Also, if the clients love your idea, they're more likely to go with you than one of your competitors. Of course, the client can always steal your idea and use another company, anyway. The unfortunate fact is you can't copyright an idea.

Author, Author

The second part of the proposal I send to clients is the *Estimate and Authorization*. On this sheet, I try to be as complete as possible, putting down my best guesses on what each part of the video will cost. There are two schools of thought on this. A buddy of mine, who also produces video, only tells his clients what the total cost of the production will be. He has found that some clients try to lower the price by eliminating parts of the video ("Look, we can save $200 if we re-use a stack of VHS tapes from home ...").

Whatever method you choose, the important item is the last line on the page. This is where it says:

Authorization: _____
Date: _____

Have the client sign and date your document and you can get started.

Does this document protect you from a client who wants to rip you off? Nope. But neither do multi-page contracts. I know of a disreputable fellow who has run up thousands of dollars worth of video production bills (though not with me, thank goodness), refused to pay, been taken to court, ordered to pay by the judge, and still refused to pay. The last I heard, he had left town—without paying.

If you don't have a good feeling in your gut about potential clients and you think they might be in the sleazy category, back off. Talk to other people in the community who have worked with these people. Are your fears legitimate? A little homework can help you avoid major headaches.

So why get a signature? Honest people (the ones you *want* to work with) stand by their promises. But even these folks sometimes have short memories. ("I never agreed to that." "But you signed this document saying you did." "I did? I'll be darned.") Leaving a paper trail helps everyone remember these little details.

What Do You Propose?

Often, a proposal is much more than just a few descriptive paragraphs with a cost figure attached.

A proposal may become a long, involved chunk of paperwork, which explains in detail how you will create a specific video project. It is sometimes written in response to a *Request for Proposal (RFP)*. Government agencies and other large corporations often send out RFPs when they need specific services, be they video production or bomb shelter construction. What they get back from an RFP is a mountain of proposals, each explaining why the proposer is the best choice to provide that service.

How can you get in on the fun of responding to an RFP? One way is to team up with a larger company which is responding to an RFP that calls for a video as a part of a larger contract.

For example, I once worked on a project where a company was creating a simulator for the Navy to train catapult officers on aircraft carriers. These officers stood on a simulated deck and looked at a large screen television showing F-14s, A-6s and other aircraft preparing to take off. The production company I worked for was the subcontractor responsible for capturing the aircraft on videotape.

As a subcontractor, the video company was only responsible for responding to a small part of the RFP. But it was important that the Navy was as comfortable with the information presented in the video portion of the proposal as the rest. If you can convince large companies in your area that you are the person to handle their video

requirements, they might call you when they need a video subcontractor.

If the RFP is for the production of a video program, you could respond as the primary contractor on the job. But be aware that these RFPs go out to dozens of companies at the same time. If you don't feel that yours is the right company to do the work outlined in the RFP, you may want to save your energy for a project you *can* handle.

Why not respond to every RFP you can find? Because creating a proposal is a lot of work. You could conceivably spend all your time writing proposals and never win any of them.

For Example

What kind of information do most agencies expect to see in a proposal? The following is the actual wording of the proposal format from an RFP from the State of Florida.

1. Table of Contents

2. Tab 1. Executive Summary—Include a synopsis of the proposal prepared in a manner that is easily understood by non-technical personnel.

3. Tab 2. Certification and References—the proposer shall provide a list of not less than three (3) nor more than five (5) different previous clients during the past 3 years as references. This part shall include the dates of the previous projects and the name, title and telephone number of a responsible employee of the previous client who is familiar with the project. The proposer must include a certification that in the previous project it was the original provider of the services.

4. Tab 3. Resumes of Individuals Proposed to Work on this Contract—the proposer shall include resumes of the individuals it proposes to assign to this project, specifying relevant educational and work experiences, and shall designate which individual will be the producer/director responsible for the coordination of work efforts of the other personnel assigned to the project. Availability of each individual shall be described, as well as the estimated number of workdays of commitment from each.

5. Tab 4. Description of Creative and Technical Approach—The proposer must provide a description of how it will produce the video programs. This description shall include the proposed production schedule of the estimated working days required to complete each part of each program, the degree of involvement by the Division, and the geographic location where the production will take place. It should also include general information about the talent (estimated number of professionals, semiprofessionals, and extras) and a general description of the proposed use of narrative, dramatics, animation and graphics.

6. Tab 5. Description of Video Equipment—The proposer must supply a list of production and post-production equipment intended for producing these programs.

7. Tab 6. Work Sample—The proposer must supply a sample in VHS format of a previous instructional or training video program with production values similar to those offered in response to the RFP. The work sample will be evaluated for both production quality and creative treatment of the subject matter.

You Get the Idea

Also requested by the RFP were a Cost Proposal Form, a proposal Acknowledgment List and a Sworn Statement on Public Entity Crimes. If you think filling out one of these puppies sounds like more work than you are now putting into entire video projects—you may be right. This is why you should feel you have a pretty good shot at getting a contract before you go after it.

The sample above, from the State of Florida, was an extremely well written RFP. A video expert was called in to give the writer advice on how a video is put together. But sometimes an RFP is written requesting strange or unworkable video solutions. It doesn't matter. You must respond to these requests as they are, even if they are bizarre.

Responding to request for proposals is a skill. You have to answer every question, dot every *i*, cross every *t*. If you don't, your proposal can be thrown out for non-compliance. It's harsh, but true.

If you can find someone who has dealt with RFPs before, it might be worth it to "partner" with him or her. It doesn't really matter if this person knows anything about video; that's your job, as long as he or she understands the language of responding to proposals.

Check with local business groups to see if they know of any retirees who used to work for a corporation. These people might have been exposed to proposal writing and they might be willing to help you learn how. They might be happy to pass on their knowledge to a new generation. If you can't find a real human to give you advice, check your public library for books on proposal writing.

Is responding to an RFP worth the trouble? Winning a contract can be extremely lucrative. But it isn't easy. If you think you can fill the requirements, I propose you give it a try.

27
Recruiting Talent

Tad Rose

Quality talent means more than just a quality performance. It may mean the difference between a one-hour shoot and a four-hour marathon.

Talent matters. Be it on or off screen, good performers can help take your project to the next level. Therefore, it is well worth the time for any producer to find ways of attracting the best talent available.

Sometimes casting is as simple as twisting your kid brother's arm, but most productions require considerable attention to the process of recruiting. Consider a request from the local school district for you to produce an orientation video. The goal is to prepare freshmen for the high school experience and to promote a safer school environment by presenting students with a variety of conflict resolution strategies. Such a project may well require talent in the form of a host for on camera interviews, a narrator to communicate important facts and statistics, teachers and counselors for expert commentary and actors to dramatize campus conflicts. Each role requires a particular skill and the right casting choices.

Determine Your Needs

A script or detailed outline is essential for determining your talent requirements. From it, you can then prepare a cast list. This list should include all significant speaking and non-speaking roles, as well as a brief description of what each role requires. For example, should the host be an adult or a teenager, male or female, clean cut or skater? If you have a clear idea what you're looking for, it will be easier to find it.

Once you've identified your needs, you're ready to start recruiting talent. It's up to you (and your budget) whether you cast professionals, amateurs or your own mother (like director Martin Scorsese), but it's important to find the best available candidate for the role. Remember that while a Hollywood cast may be beyond your budget, professional quality performances needn't be. Talent grows everywhere.

Sources of Talent

Local theater troupes, college drama departments, churches, high schools, comedy clubs and community groups are all excellent sources of talent. To tap them, contact the person in charge, explain your project, and ask if he or she can recommend anyone. Maybe he or she knows the perfect candidate. If not, perhaps he or she will allow you to post a flier announcing your audition. If you do post fliers, make sure you do it at least a couple of weeks ahead of any auditions and be sure to provide adequate information, including the type of production, roles being cast and contact number. You can also place an ad in the local paper or on an Internet bulletin board. In addition, of course, tell all your friends. Cast your net wide and you are more likely to find the talent you're after.

Auditions

There's no hard and fast rule about auditioning. Some producers have all candidates show up at the same time (cattle call), others schedule individual appointments. You could simply ask candidates to send in a videotape. I know of one producer looking for voice over talent who even had candidates call and leave their audition on his answering machine. However, if you are serious about finding the right talent, it's best to arrange face-to-face auditions and use the tapes and other demos as screeners.

Most producers provide candidates with audition materials. This can be actual dialog or narration from your script or material from another source that will allow you to evaluate their abilities. You can also allow the actors to use their own audition piece. This isn't really recommended, however, since their choice may have little relation to your project and their polished performance will not give you an idea of what it is like to work with this person on the set.

If you cannot provide candidates with audition material in advance, give them a few minutes to prepare before you put them in the hot seat. Cold readings (auditions without prior exposure to the material) rarely reveal the range and ability of your candidates.

Allow about 15 to 20 minutes per audition with five-minute breaks in between. This will give you adequate time to interview the candidates and jot down any notes between auditions. Make sure you ask about their background and experience. Show interest and be positive: This will relax your candidate and result in a better performance. It's also a good idea to tape the entire audition. This will give you the chance to review the candidates later and evaluate their strengths and weaknesses on camera.

Be sure you explain what the role entails, including the number of shooting days and any compensation your are able to offer. Don't be discouraged if your budget doesn't allow you to pay your talent; many aspiring performers will be happy to work for nothing more than a credit and a copy of the finished piece for their portfolio. Nevertheless, if you can pay a token sum, you should. It recognizes the contribution your actors are making and encourages them to take a professional approach to the project.

Evaluating Talent

For our hypothetical video, we need both an on screen host and a voice over artist to do narration. The requirements for each are different. For the host, you must consider both appearance and vocal quality, but it is strictly vocal characteristics (such as volume, diction, rate, pitch, tone and timbre) that matter in narration, since that performer will never be seen.

Casting is subjective. The goal is to match the role with the best available talent and that's not always easy. Many factors besides ability will influence your final choices. Determining the availability of your talent is a pragmatic, but important, consideration. Someone may be perfect to host the program, but if she is only available Sunday evenings after six, you will probably have to keep looking. It's also a good idea to gauge the motivation of your prospects as well, especially if they are working "for credit" (a.k.a. "volunteers"). Enthusiastic, paid performers will be more likely to show up on time and ready to perform, than those you've had to beg and cajole.

For acting roles, you may want to consider type casting. Unless you've discovered a young Brando or De Niro, it's easier for actors to play characters with traits and characteristics close to their own. If the kid who mows your lawn has a bit of an attitude, maybe he would be perfect to play the bully in your conflict dramatization. Casting close to type will often result in performances that are more natural, especially from inexperienced actors.

Getting the Best Performance

No matter whom you cast, whether best friend or a complete stranger, it is up to you to get the best performances possible. The ability to elicit good performances is the mark of a truly skilled director. It's not easy. Approaches range from the autocratic to the collaborative. However, in my experience working with both novice and veteran performers alike, I have found one thing improves performances every time: encouragement. Pointing out what was good about a given take before suggesting ways to improve it will build a feeling of confidence and security in your actors. If they know you have confidence in them, their work may lift your production to an entirely new level.

Summary

Be willing to look outside your immediate circle of friends to find the best available talent for your project. List your casting requirements, then audition to find the right person for each part. Be prepared to provide clear, concise direction to your performers. Create a positive, collaborative atmosphere on the set. And, of course, never forget to provide a free lunch.

Sidebar 1

Recruiting Talent: Best Bets

1. Community Theater
2. College Drama Departments
3. Church Groups
4. Local Schools
5. Community Organizations
6. Family and Friends

Sidebar 2

Actors Need to Know

Who – What type of person is the character? What are the traits you're looking for?

What – What will you provide? What compensation will there be, if any? Will they be required to supply wardrobe and make-up? What about lunch?

When – When will the taping take place? How long will shoots last?

Where – Where is the location of the shoot? If necessary, provide written directions and maps. Don't lose a shooting day because someone got lost.

Why – Why are you producing this video? Explain what you hope to achieve and why the actors would want to be involved.

How – How do you want the talent to dress, to speak, to move? Give direction in simple, straightforward terms.

28
The Right Place at the Right Time

James Williams

Scouting locations ahead of time is a great way to avoid last-minute surprises and big headaches on the day of your shoot.

Consider this: a scene in your short film takes place in a coffee shop. You know you could never pass off your living room as the local java joint, so you decide to shoot that scene on location. It's time to hit the road and find the right spot. There are several elements to keep in mind:

Identify Your Power Source

Power outlets are essential for lights, batteries or other equipment. For such important elements, these power sources are easily overlooked. As you scout the location, ask yourself:

- Are there enough outlets that work?

- Are outlets close enough to where you'll set up lights and camera? If not, how many extension cords will you need?

- Are the outlets grounded?

- Can the location handle the wattage of all of your equipment without tripping a breaker?

If you plan to use a generator, make sure you can place it far enough away that it won't cause audio issues or create a safety hazard.

For an event video, plugging into an outlet may not be an option, or you may need to be mobile, and you'll be using batteries. When scouting, look for out-of-the-way power outlets for recharging a spare battery.

Evaluate Lighting Conditions

Okay, so you find a coffee bar that has the exact look and feel you want. As you gaze around, you notice several large windows. Break out your tape measure, because you'll probably need to give these windows some attention.

Combining outdoor sunlight with indoor, tungsten lights can create a look that's either too blue or too orange when viewed through a video camera, particularly when human skin tones are involved.

The reason is that each light source has a unique color temperature that the camera readily picks up. It looks okay to the human eye, because our brain compensates for the color differences, but the camera simply cannot. The result is that the outdoor light looks blue and the indoor light looks orange through the viewfinder. White balancing won't always solve the problem.

The solution is to choose which lighting temperature you'd like as your primary light source, then eliminate or add filters to the other source, so all light in the room has the same color temperature.

Fluorescent lights cast a greenish hue, so most videographers turn fluorescents off altogether or swap the fluorescent bulbs with specialty bulbs that give off the desired color temperature.

As you consider your lighting situation, some questions to ask are:

- Are you using the windows as a light source?

- What are the dimensions of the windows (in case filters or light-blocking materials are needed)?

- Where are the controls to turn off overhead lights?

- If you're swapping out fluorescent bulbs, what sizes are the replacements?

Anticipate Audio Problems

Few locations are completely devoid of noise, so silence is a relative term. Scouting your location in advance allows you to hear how quiet the room really is.

Stop walking, close your eyes and listen. It turns out the room is noisier than you thought. Rumbling softly overhead is a huge AC vent. An espresso machine sputters behind the counter. A telephone rings in the next room. Traffic noise leaks in from the street.

These sounds can pose big problems for your audio track, so catching them

now allows you to make adjustments. Ask yourself:

- Can you turn off, unplug or cover up any unwanted sources of noise?

- Where is the quietest spot, and is that a good place to shoot the scene?

Bring a mic and headphones to hear how the room sounds to the camera. Check wireless mics for electrical interference or static from nearby equipment or radio towers. Can't get a clean signal? Consider a wired lavaliere or shotgun mic.

Consider the Time and Day of the Week

Most places, especially public places, look and sound different at different times of day or night. A side room may be completely quiet at 5 pm on Saturday but noisy as a roadhouse Wednesday after work. Sunlight that was soft and indirect at 9 am may be blazing into the room at 3 pm.

Some things to consider are:

- How might a change in ambient light affect your lighting plans or need for filters?

- How might changing traffic patterns, such as rush hour or sporting events, affect your audio?

Figure 28-1 Check the location's schedule to avoid unwanted surprises.

- Will other people occupy the same location while you're shooting? How disruptive will their presence be?

Consider what aspects of the location will change with the day of the week. If you're shooting on a Tuesday morning, you'll want to know ahead of time that Tuesday mornings are when the delivery guy comes. Nobody wants to pause his or her production every few minutes so delivery dollies can be rolled through the set.

Visit your locations at the same time and same weekday that you'll be doing your shoot. If that's not possible, ask someone familiar with the area what to expect at the time you plan to be there. Most people don't think in terms of poor audio or other hurdles that can hold up a production. A cleaning crew vacuuming before the place opens might not seem like a big deal to the owner, but it's enough to bring your production to a halt. Tailor your questions accordingly.

Getting the Logistics

Location scouting for video shoots and event videos is a great time to assess shot angles, camera setups and any logistical considerations. Bring a camcorder along to preview your shot list or record details of the space.

Some other observations to make are:

- Where's the best place to unload equipment and store unused gear?

- If you'll need to rearrange the room, what extra equipment or manpower will be required to do so safely?

Get Permission

Once you've found your ideal location, you'll need permission to shoot there.

Many folks are okay with letting you use their property for productions, as long as they know exactly what you're doing and how long it will take.

When asking permission, be sure to:

- Be polite!

- Be upfront and honest about crew size and time requirements.

- Explain that they will get exposure for the location and it will be noted in the credits.

Make sure the person granting you permission signs a release form, even if you've had a verbal OK. That will come in handy if anyone questions your right to be there on the day of the shoot or anytime after that.

If you're shooting in a public space, check well in advance whether a permit is required. Permit requests can take time to process and, without the right paperwork, you may find your production shut down before you even get started.

Conclusion

The day of production arrives and you're prepared. You know exactly where to turn off the overhead AC units, so they aren't picked up in the mics. You know the size and number of blankets required to block out the sunlight blazing through the windows. You have the right extension cords, the right number of lights and the right number of crewmembers to rearrange the room.

It's time to roll tape, get the shots and start planning for the next scene!

Sidebar 1

What to Bring on Your Scouting Trip

Before you walk out the door to scout locations, you'll want to bring a few key items with you. Make sure you have a notebook and pen to write down contact information, draw diagrams and record measurements. You'll also want a measuring tape to determine window sizes, room widths and the distance from outlets to where you think you'll be setting up. Bring a still camera to snap photos of the room, so you can check the details later on. Better yet, take a camcorder, so you can frame out potential shots as well. Plug in a mic and headphones, and listen to what the room sounds like on tape.

Sidebar 2

Prior to Your Shoot

Make sure you get permission to use the location, and get a signed release form to prove it. If shooting on public property, check that no special permits are required to shoot there. Finally, check in with your location contact a few days prior to the shoot, just make sure everything is still a go.

Sidebar 3

Checklist for Your Shoot

Aside from the gear you'll be using for the shoot, you'll want to have the following on the day of your production:

- Names and phone numbers of your location contacts, in case any questions arise.

- Any reference notes you took while scouting that location, especially if those notes include where to find power switches and other directions.

- Any release forms and special permits you'll need.

29
Production Planning

Jim Stinson

The worst cause of video disasters is bad planning—not just during the Pre-production phase, but right through to the end of Post-production. Professionals don't just make plans; they implement them and then they follow through on them. When you plan like a pro, you:

- *Plan the shoot* in pre-production.
- *Shoot the plan* in production.
- *Edit the planned shoot* in post-production.

This sustained planning and follow-through are essential to delivering a quality video *on* time and *on* budget.

Plan the Shoot!

The planning aspect of video creation is so often overlooked that we're breaking it down into three parts—one for each phase of production. First: *plan the shoot in*

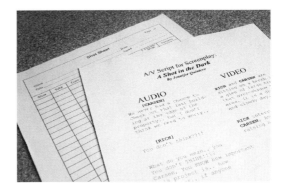

Figure 29-1 *A good script and a well-planned shot list are two of the most important planning documents needed for any serious production.*

pre-production. Of course, pre-production is nothing but planning, from first concept to final schedule. Here, though, we are focusing specifically on developing plans that you can, indeed, *shoot* and then *edit.* We'll look at scripting, casting, staffing, scouting, and budgeting. We'll also look at a new planning area: special effects.

126

In other words, pre-production planning relates to editing as well as shooting.

First, the Script

Though writing itself isn't planning, the resulting script is the basis for every single decision you'll make in prepping production. Without a complete script, you can't cast the program, design its look, determine the crew and equipment needed, list the locations or sets, budget the production, or set a schedule. Usually, an outline isn't good enough, even if it's 50 pages long. Only a true script is specific enough for planning. How about a storyboard? Storyboard sequences with complex action and/or special effects work to visualize the layout of the video, but use a written script for production planning. For nonfiction programs, a two-column "A/V" (Audio and Video) formatted script will include complete narration and essential audio in the left column and visuals in the right one. Fiction films use the classic screenplay format. For advice on how much detail to include, see the adjacent sidebar. The bottom line is this: when you get to production, you can't shoot the plan unless you've planned the shoot in detail.

Special Effects

People think that special effects are compositing and computer graphics that belong in post-production. However, the most convincing effects are fully planned in pre-production so that location, composite, and CG work can be seamlessly integrated by implementing the detailed plan. That's why you have to develop your special effects fully even before you scout locations and budget props.

For example, take a spectacular head-on car crash. To achieve the actual impact, you'll have the cars drive toward and past each other, maybe two feet apart for safety, shooting the master with a long telephoto to conceal the gap between them. In post, you plan to speed up the collision shot

Figure 29-2 *A storyboard is a useful tool for visualizing complex action and/or special effects sequences.*

and then conceal the fact that they miss each other by filling the screen with a well-timed CG fireball over the live action.

So far so good, but the secret of any effect lies in selling it with supporting shots. To make sure you get them, you need to plan high-speed shots of the individual cars, closeups of the drivers, and maybe a shot across the hood of one car after the crash, as one victim struggles out the door. You plan to put one side of the car up on blocks to tilt it and to increase the tilt by canting the camera off-level in the opposite direction. (Note to DP: choose a vague background that won't reveal the Dutch Angle shot, and throw a flickering "fire light" on the windshield, door, and struggling victim.) In post, composite a raging fire effect in the foreground to complete the gag. Every part of this must be planned, right down to the cinder blocks and the fire effect.

The moral is, you can't just say, "oh we'll do the car crash in post." Only through detailed planning both before and during the shoot can you deliver the raw materials needed to create a classy effect.

People, Places and Feedback

Even the biggest Hollywood productions are planned and developed by successive approximation: the script describes the requirements; the planners come as close as possible to meeting them; then the script is adjusted to eliminate the resources

Figure 29-3 *Scouting locations ahead of time can help you avoid a wide range of production problems.*

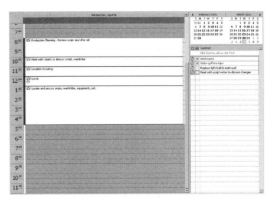

Figure 29-4 *Scheduling programs like Microsoft's Outlook can greatly help you set up a schedule for your production, and easily share with others.*

that were unobtainable and maximize those that were. This is always true with casting actors. Suppose, for instance, the script demands a slim, beautiful, enticing, evil stepmother; but the closest actress you can find is an overweight frumpy person who would look silly vamping around on screen. Happens all the time.

So you do some fast script revisions to create a frumpy, evil stepmother. By planning to fit the circumstances, you save both the actress and the show from embarrassment. Or take locations. If you can't find anyplace resembling the dungeon where the evil stepmother imprisons the heroine, you have three choices: remove the dungeon part, create it as a CG virtual set (if you have the resources), or just chain the lady up in a storeroom or something.

Again, if you plan these adjustments before production begins, you can still shoot the plan; but if you haven't invested in the planning, you're going to arrive at an unconvincing "dungeon" location and have to improvise a fix on the spot. That seldom works very well.

The All-Powerful Schedule

In reality, budgeting and scheduling are two halves of a circle. Scheduling brings the right cast members, crew, and equipment to the right location at the right time, crucial if you're paying people by the hour or day and just as important if folks are donating their time.

With good planning, you can also save big bucks (that's where scheduling and budgeting play tag with each other). For instance, if that antique fire engine rents for $200 a day, you'll want to schedule all its scenes back-to-back so you can return it as soon as possible. Oh, and how is it going to get to your location? I once rented an antique vehicle without knowing it didn't really run. At the last minute, I had to put out expensive, unbudgeted bucks for a day's use of a platform-bed tow truck.

This is also true for anything else that's time-sensitive. With meticulous planning, you'll always have the correct cast list at the proper place with the required equipment and props, all ready to shoot. Without planning, everyone ends up standing around, and that's not good. And if it rains or something else goes wrong? A planning pro will have a contingency plan: a way to shoot something else until you can resume the original schedule.

Money, Money, Money

Professional production accountants must keep tiny altars to the Spirit of Murphy, on which they burn symbolic dollar bills, because on a shoot, anything that can possibly go wrong will go wrong. Corollary #1: everything that goes wrong costs money. *Everything.* It goes without saying that good production planners budget the show line-item by line-item, right down to cold cream for the makeup department. Then they run an eagle eye over every aspect of production. Does one character throw a vase at another? How many takes might that require, and how many replacement vases? Does one sequence call for actual snow? What will the weather be like and how many days might be lost while waiting for the fluffy stuff to start falling?

Obviously, every production is different. If you're taping the CEO's speech in her office, you're probably very safe. If you're covering whale migrations from the subjects' POV, good luck. Since you don't have unlimited funds, you can't just say, "well, whatever it takes." You have to cast a cold planner's eye over every script page to spot every place that could run over budget. Then you add a contingency fee for protection. Then you double it, and pray. That's it for creating a production plan. Now, let's see how that plan structures the actual shoot so that you can end up editing the show you started out to make.

Shoot the Plan

Following the plans you made in pre-production sounds like an obvious idea—but it's tougher to do than it looks.

Plan the shoot, shoot the plan, edit the planned shoot. That's the mantra we introduced earlier. Talk about obvious! Not so fast. If that deceptively simple rule were routinely followed, Hollywood epics would never overrun their schedules and amateur productions would never look embarrassing (assuming they didn't crash and burn before completion). So let's review reasons for staying on-plan, gremlins that attack production plans and ways to protect yourself against disasters, both serial and parallel. The underlying concept is that crucial decisions are made in pre-production planning that will affect everything that follows, all the way through to the end of post-production. A good planner keeps that long timeline

in mind, the way a good chess player thinks many moves ahead.

Stick to the Plan

Sticking to a plan no matter what, seems sort of, well, retentive; but there are several reasons for resisting changes or at least studying them very carefully before making them. First, remember the law of unintended consequences. Even small productions are complicated organisms with many interdependent parts. If you decide to shoot, say, scene 22 instead of scheduled scene 14, the cast, location and time of day might be fine—but what about the actor's distinctive Grateful Dead shirt, which got all muddy in scene 13 but has to be clean again for scene 22? Thinking fast, you run it through a Laundromat during lunch break. Uh-huh, but when you go to scene 14 later that shirt has to be dirty again—with *exactly* the same stain pattern as before it was washed.

So things start to domino. Cleverly, you have the actor play scene 14 without the shirt, adding a line like, "Boy, I hope I can get that shirt clean; it's an heirloom." Right away, you've handed the editor two problems. Since the action is continuous

Figure 29-5 *What might seem like a minor change in wardrobe can quickly turn into a large out-of-control, chain reaction avalanch that could bury your production. You did such a great job planning, now do a great job of following it.*

across scenes 13 and 14, the character has no off-screen time in which to take off the shirt. Major jump cut. Also, the added line tells viewers that the shirt's valuable, which is totally irrelevant to the story and distracting from the point of the scene.

You're already thinking of fifty things at once, under time and money pressure to move, move, move! If you must make alterations, take the time you need to think them through. The second moral is that post-production is very demanding. Once you wrap production, it's expensive and often impossible to re-open the shoot for vital pieces that are missing or mismatched to other pieces.

The Enemies of Planning

The first big foe of systematic shooting is good ol' Murphy's Law in all its many forms.

Things go wrong; stuff happens; you have to roll with the punches. Outdoors, time and weather are huge factors. Obviously, you can't shoot if it's pouring rain, and even if it hasn't started yet, the light in that sullen overcast before the storm doesn't match yesterday's sunshine. As for time, an equipment malfunction held up the shoot until yesterday's pearly dawn turned into high noon.

Whether outdoors or in, personnel are always a problem, especially when they're not getting paid to show up on time and keep working all day. You might limp along without a certain crew member, but if the performer isn't there, the show doesn't go on. Inanimate objects are just as bad. People bring the wrong wardrobe; props are missing, equipment malfunctions. When you arrive at the gym where you got permission to shoot the "hurricane disaster relief center" you find it's been decorated for the Senior Prom. Above and beyond Murphy, there's another threat to shooting as planned: your own creativity. You show up at the vacant lot to find that there's a carnival set up there. Wow, what visuals! What production values! Thinking fast, you replace half your planned setups to exploit the unexpected dividend. Or maybe it's just a brainstorm on the set: hey! Why not do it this way instead? Either way, you risk omitting stuff the editor will need and adding stuff that doesn't belong in your program.

Cover Your Caboose

No shoot is ever completed exactly as planned, but you can minimize the risks by following a few vital procedures. First, always have plan B ready. If weather might be a problem, identify indoor scenes with the same cast and have the locations, costumes and props standing by. If performers are flaky about showing up, know where to

Figure 29-6 and Figure 29-7 The script says the scene takes place on a sunny day and it's pouring out. Instead of re-working the script, you should have a "plan B" (and maybe a "plan C"), for when the inevitable Murphy's Law occurs.

find them and how to shoot around them in the meantime. The trick is to identify the vulnerable parts of your plan in advance and have alternatives ready to go. Second, learn how to adjust plan A. Understand that a simple thing like a dirty shirt can ripple all the way to post-production. Take the time and care to work out all the implications of proposed changes.

Next, know when to quit. Nothing is more frustrating than doing all the work of getting a day's shoot together and launched, then sending everyone home again. Your instinct is to say, okay, let's call Fred and Wilma and see if they can go over to the church and shoot their stuff today, and try to rent that '57 Chevy, oh, and phone the church sexton, and…. Uh-uh. This kind of desperate improvisation may keep your crew busy, but the results will be hasty and undercooked. You have to develop the good judgement to know when you're licked for now so that you can live to fight another day.

Finally, review your footage, preferably before you wrap at any one location, but at least at the end of every shooting day. In even the most professional production, you're going to find stuff that's inadequate, wrong or just plain missing. Before matters go any further, make the notes you need to get pickup shots, to retake bad stuff, to re-think and re-stage sequences that plain don't work. Then plan the reshoot as

meticulously as you planned the original. When post-production starts, you'll bless yourself. Speaking of which, time for the exciting conclusion: *Edit the Shoot You Planned.*

Edit the Plan!

If you planned the shoot well, editing the plan should be a snap. Planning for post-production will refocus your vision of the program you want and then help you create it with the material you've got.

Post-production is supposed to fulfill the promise of pre-production (the script) and production (the shoot). Editing, they tell you, pulls everything together and delivers the program envisioned by the producer, director and sponsor.

Figure 29-9

Figure 29-8 *The people who make six-digits plus making movies view their "dailies" at the end of each day and so should you. Just make sure you don't accidentally leave the record head in the middle of a scene and record over your work.*

Figure 29-10 *Make sure producers acquired all the planned video and audio by checking the footage against the shot list and marking where you need pickup shots or changes.*

As usual, reality falls short of theory, because editors almost never get exactly the raw material they expected, and they don't always shape it as well as they might. Earlier, we talked about planning the shoot and then shooting the plan. Let's wrap it up here by seeing how to carry planning forward into post-production. In a nutshell, you work as hard as you can to complete the original vision, and, where that's impossible, to make the best program you can with what you've got. To do this, you systematically evaluate and deal with your raw material and then systematically mold it throughout post-production. In both cases, "systematically" implies that you're doing some planning of your own.

In the best production setups, the editor is in on the shoot, evaluating each day's footage and providing feedback to the director to ensure that he can edit the show to the original plan. Too often, however, the editor joins the process after shooting wraps and is presented with a done deal: here's the stuff, now build a program. This is the real-world situation we'll talk about here.

Planning for Post

First off, a good editor is not an *auteur (a director who is believed to be the major creative force)*: Your job is not to express your own vision, but to carry out the vision of the writer, director, producer or whoever

it is that presides over the production. With that in mind, you should take your very first step even before you start screening footage: you should discover (or recollect) what the original plan was—what the program was supposed to be. Typically, that means reviewing the concept with the producers or at least closely re-reading the script. Only when you have the original concept freshly in mind can you start dealing with the footage.

The obvious next step is to review all the raw material, constantly comparing it to the program concept. First and foremost, did they shoot all the material needed? (You'd be surprised how often they didn't.) Does the footage they did shoot do its job: Are the establishing shots and closeups and inserts taken from the right setups of the right stuff? Is the technical quality uniformly up to par? And don't forget the audio. Is the production sound of good quality (or even usable)? Did they lay down background tracks, presence tracks and wild sound effects? Have they planned the music to use and how to use it, or are they leaving that to you?

After a thorough review of the raw material (and a yellow pad bristling with notes), you're ready to plan your post-production strategy. First of all, what absolutely *has* to be shot (if overlooked), or re-shot (if loused up)? For example, your documentary on glass blowing covers the whole process of making a vase, from molten glass

Figure 29-11 and Figure 29-12 *A plentiful supply of cut-aways will save an editor's ... reputation. If you can get to the production crew before they shoot, request cut-aways.*

to finished.... Whoops! The beauty shot of the completed work is badly lit and out of focus. Try as you might, you can't think of a way to drop the poor shot and edit around it because it's the whole point of the program. So it has to be re-shot.

And as long as they have to send a crew back out, what *other* shots can you improve? What missing angles could be picked up? (Which is why they're called "pickup shots.") Sooner or later, you'll run up against a wall: you can't get more coverage of the master glass blower because she promptly retired and left for Maui. Now your strategy shifts to developing plan B. Studying the footage you discover two things:

- There are several shots (some with multiple takes) in which her body blocks the furnace opening, so you can't quite see what she's doing.

- You have some inserts of her assistant's bare hands and arms that look similar to hers.

Gotcha! Plan B is to support shots of the blocked furnace door with narration explaining what she's doing (even though she was doing something else) and shoot the missing inserts with the assistant's hands and arms subbing for the Master's. In summary, then, you evaluate your raw materials, reshoot where it's feasible, and plan workarounds where it's not. With plans A and B implemented, you do your best to create the finished program as originally envisioned.

Planning the Edit

With your post-production strategy worked out, you're ready to turn the raw footage into a work of genius. Here too, you need a systematic plan, though admittedly, the plan is much the same for most editing jobs.

The problem with digital post is that it encourages you to do everything at once: find the shots, assemble the sequence, trim to length, build the tracks, add CGs and graphics, repeat with the next sequence and so-on. Completing one sequence at a time, you're more likely to end up with a bunch of individually fine pieces that refuse to fit smoothly together. Instead, it's generally (though not always), better to work vertically instead of horizontally: go through the entire show, doing one job— building just one layer—at a time. Here's how it works:

First, break out and catalog all your footage at once. Why? I can't tell you how many times I've plugged a hole in one sequence by remembering a shot I could steal from a different one. You need a mental inventory of all your footage before you start. Then assemble your show, sequence-by-sequence, to be sure, but without worrying about fine-tuning. Once you've previewed the result, you'll have a good feel for the way the program's coming together. Now do your tuning, trimming shot lengths, adjusting cut points, pulling whole shots that turn out to be superfluous. By working the whole program at once, you keep a feel for its rhythm and pace.

So far, you've had just the production track, if any. Now it's time to pull things together with audio, laying presence and background tracks, adding sound effects, timing narration, selecting and adding music.

Finally, you're ready for CGs and graphics: transitions, titles and the like. Again, seeing the show as a whole will help you keep them consistent. And don't forget the DVD (which will almost certainly be your release format). As you polish the show, start looking for the material to repeat as backgrounds for main and sub menus.

So do your strategic post-production planning by evaluating your materials and deciding what to do with them; then do your tactical planning by working through the editing process one careful layer at a time.

Sidebar 1

How Detailed a Script?

Whether scripting in the A/V or screenplay formats, you do not—in fact, *should* not—specify camera angles and individual shots. For instance, if the story calls for a character to window-shop along a street, it's enough to write:

> Marcie walks down Main street, looking in shop windows, pausing at some, then moving on. Halfway along, she spots something in a window. It is the statue of a black falcon. Surprised, she gets her courage up and enters the store.

Notice how the paragraphing suggests a rough breakdown of the scene content, but without trying to do the director's job. Any director worthy of the title will know how to distribute that action among appropriate setups. On the other hand, the production manager can learn enough from the description to schedule the "Marcie" actor and plan for a small town street, an antiques or pawnshop and a Maltese Falcon prop. In short, the script is detailed enough for planning, without being too restrictive.

Sidebar 2

Your Key Collaborators

You know you've reached the big leagues when you can have three key people beside you throughout the shoot.

- *Continuity.* If the script is the basis for the shooting plan, the continuity person is the guardian of that script. Did you get the closeup? Do you have the insert of the pistol in the drawer? Did you overlap the wide shot and the medium shot enough to provide good edit points? A good continuity person will catch every problem and let you know. No matter how creative you're being or what else you're thinking about, *listen to continuity*!

- *Production Manager.* A good production manager knows who is available, which locations are open and when the rented '57 Chevy is coming. If you have to change the plan in real time, the production manager can figure out a workable alternative. Never make changes in the plan without consulting the person who is directly responsible for it.

- *Editor.* Continuity can tell you if you have full coverage and matched action; but only the editor can cut things together in his or her head and predict whether the result will be effective. When allowed the luxury, I like to have the editor on the set, making sure the shooting plan is being followed—and that it was a good plan to begin with.

Sidebar 3

Evil Temptations

As you work, you'll be vulnerable to three terrible temptations. If you give in to them, you risk distorting, degrading or even ruining the original program plan.

- First, never blow off problems. "I'll stick in a dissolve." "I'll run it in slo-mo." "I'll cover it with voice-over" or just plain, "Ah'll think about that t'morra." When you encounter a problem, deal with it, solve it, do it now! If you don't, these little difficulties tend to accumulate until they overwhelm you.

- Second, don't talk yourself into inadequate fixes. "That's good enough." "Oh, nobody will really notice." "Those shots cut together well enough." No, no and no. You're always under deadline pressure and it would really, *really* help if you could get away with things; but when you screen the finished product, they'll jump up and wave at you, every one of them.

- Finally, don't make every sequence perfect in and of itself. Always recall what it's supposed to do and how it's supposed to fit in the program as a whole. Sure, you got such amazing footage out of that car chase that you just have to use it all; but it makes the sequence way too long and too important in the story as a whole. So don't get hung up cutting each gem, without regard to the whole necklace.

PART III
Production Techniques

Tips for capturing the highest quality video and sound.

30
Framing Good Shots

Brian Pogue

The images you record are the building blocks and foundation of your video productions. As your foundation, some thought and planning should go into how your shots are composed. A well-composed shot grabs and holds your viewer's attention. It also influences the mood of the scene or the comfort level of the audience.

When done right, the composition will not draw attention to itself. Instead, it will instill a sense of normalcy and stability. On the other hand, a poorly composed shot will have the opposite effect. It will distract the audience, or worse, make a scene entirely unwatchable.

In this article we'll give you some basic composition guidelines that experts use as their foundation, as well as some common pitfalls you should try to avoid.

The Rule of Thirds

A basic rule of composition is the rule of thirds. This guideline gives you ideas on where to place your subject within the frame. Though your tendency may be to position your subject dead center on the screen, the rule of thirds will give you a more compelling picture.

First, imagine that two vertical and two horizontal lines divide your viewfinder into thirds. (Think of a slightly elongated tic-tac-toe board.) The rule of thirds suggests that the main subject in your shot should fall on one of the points where these imaginary lines intersect. The resulting image will be much stronger than if you simply place your subject in the crosshairs (see Figure 30-1).

When videotaping a person, that person's eyes are your main focal point. Whether using a wide shot or a close up,

Figure 30-1 *Eye Liner—Keep the eyes on the upper-third line, even if you lose the top of the head or hair.*

(a)

(b)

Figure 30-2 *Look Room—The left image doesn't leave any look room. The framing in the right image is much better.*

compose the shot so that the person's eyes fall on one of the uppermost imaginary intersections. The intersection you choose depends on which direction the person is looking. Frame someone looking screen left on the right third of the screen. This places the subject slightly off center and builds in another element of composition called "look room."

Look Room, Lead Room and Head Room

Look room is the space that you leave in front of someone's face on the screen. This space gives the person room to breathe, as well as gives the impression that the person is looking at or talking to someone just off screen. If you don't leave enough look room, your subject will appear boxed-in and confined (see Figure 30-2).

Be aware that the amount of look room necessary is dependent upon the angle of the subject to the camera. A person looking directly toward the camera will require less look room than someone shot in full profile.

Moving objects such as cars require a similar buffer called "lead room." Allow extra space in front of a moving car so that the viewer can see that it has someplace to go. Without this visual padding, the car's progress will seem impeded.

Head room is another element you should consider when framing your subject. Headroom is the amount of space between

the top of someone's head and the top of the frame. If you leave too much space, the person will appear as if sinking in quicksand. If you don't leave enough room, the person will seem in danger of bumping his head. By positioning the subject's eyes on the top third imaginary line, you will be building in the proper amount of headroom.

When considering head room, be sure the shot is loose enough so that you see part of the subject's neck or the top of the shoulders. If not, you'll end up with what looks like a severed head on a platter. However, don't be as concerned with cutting off the top of someone's head. Viewers do not perceive this as abnormal as long as you frame the actor's eyes where they should be.

The Background

Many composition pitfalls lie in the subject's environment. Trees and phone poles, vases or pictures on walls may all cause problems.

Be aware of lampposts, trees or other such objects that are directly behind your subject. A flagpole protruding from the top of an actor's head looks ridiculous, as does a vase that may seem balanced on someone's shoulder. Likewise, a power line running through the frame may appear to be going in one of your subject's ears, and out the other. Steer clear of any such visual distractions (Figure 30-3).

Even if these objects are not directly behind your subject, they can still cause

Figure 30-3 *Watch the Background—Poles protruding from your subject's head can be distracting. The receding lines in the shot on the right add depth.*

Figure 30-4 *Natural Frames—Look for objects (natural or artificial) in the environment that act as natural frames.*

problems. A lamppost running vertically through the middle of the frame will not only disrupt the balance achieved by the rule of thirds, it can also isolate or box in the subject. It may also take away the look room that you've built into the shot. Be aware of these background objects, and work to avoid them whenever possible.

Framing Using Objects

While objects in the background can cause problems, objects placed in the foreground can lend a hand. This technique can add depth and character to your shot.

Try using something in the environment to obstruct part of your shot (see Figure 30-4). Place a piece of furniture in your foreground and shoot past it by framing it to the extreme right or left. You can shoot through open doors, where the doorjamb frames the edges of the screen.

Be careful, however, not to overdo it. Using the environment to frame your shots should not be so blatant as to distract from what is happening in the scene.

The Ultimate Goal

Good composition is a means to an end. When it's done well, the audience should not notice it. Instead it should help create a mood, or at the very least, a sense of normalcy and stability. The next time you watch a movie, pay attention to how the cinematographer frames the shots. You'll notice that he or she uses the rule of thirds as a foundation, and builds from there.

31
Shooting Steady

Dr. Robert G. Nulph

Shooting steady video is perhaps one of the most fundamental skills of good video production. If your camera isn't steady, your shots will be difficult to watch (unless you provide a healthy dose of seasick pills). In this chapter we will take a look at various ways you can shoot good solid video every time, no matter the subject or the situation. We'll start out with the fundamentals of shooting handheld video and move towards more sophisticated electronically aided methods for keeping your video smooth and steady.

Shooting Fundamentals

Shooting handheld video is perhaps the most difficult way to capture images on tape. No matter how steady you think you are, even your breathing can make the camera move and shake. If you find yourself in a situation where you must shoot handheld, there are a few things to keep in mind.

One of the most important things to remember about camcorders and their lenses is that zooming emphasizes movement. The closer you zoom, the more your movement is magnified. Because of this,

when you are shooting handheld video, you should get as physically close to your subject as you possibly can and zoom out as far (wide) as the camcorder's lens will allow. This will give you the steadiest shot possible.

The second step towards good handheld shots is maintaining good posture. Keep your back straight; legs shoulder width apart; knees slightly bent; and your elbows close to your body. If you are handholding a small camcorder with an LCD screen, hold the camera with both hands in front of your body, elbows tucked into your sides. If shooting from the shoulder, tuck your elbow into your side and use your right hand and arm for support, while your left hand controls the focus and iris.

If you have to move while actively shooting, do so slowly and as smoothly as possible, keeping your subject composed well in the shot and maintaining good solid posture throughout the move.

The World around You

If you find yourself in a situation where you don't have a tripod, any solid surface

Figure 31-1 *Rock Stable—If you find yourself in a situation where you don't have a tripod, any solid surface can act as a camera platform. Set your camera on a rock, fence post or parked car, or lean up against a tree or the edge of a building.*

Figure 31-2 *Required Equipment—Every videographer should own a good tripod. A tripod lets you shoot solid, steady video with little effort.*

can act as a camera platform. Set your camera on a rock, fence post or parked car, or lean up against a tree or the edge of a building (see Figure 31-1). Use a table or chair to steady your shot. If shooting on the beach, lay some plastic down and steady the camera on the sand, or set the camera up on the steps of the lifeguard tower.

When using a solid platform to shoot from, you will most likely have to tilt the camera to get the best shot. Once again, objects around you might be useful: credit cards, cardboard, newspapers, pencils, even gum wrappers can be used to stabilize your shot. Once you compose your shot, press the record button and take your hands away.

Tripods

Every videographer should own a good tripod (see Figure 31-2). A tripod lets you shoot solid, steady video with little effort. There are, however, some things you need to keep in mind when using a tripod. Always set your tripod and camera up so that one of the three legs is pointing towards your subject. This will create a space for you to stand in between the other two legs. If you know you are going to pan in one particular direction a lot, point the front leg of the tripod halfway between the farthest left and farthest right,

your subject will move so you won't have to walk around or step over one of the back legs.

When adjusting the height of your tripod, use your subject as your guide, instead of setting it at a level that makes you feel comfortable. Set your tripod up so that the camera, when completely horizontal, is pointing at the neck of your subject. Unfortunately, this might mean that you will find yourself in some uncomfortable shooting positions, but that's a small price to pay for better-looking video.

If you do not have to move the shot and the subject will not be moving, lock down the tripod, press the record button and let go. If you do need to move, position yourself with the camcorder so that you are as solid and comfortable as possible and slowly move in the direction you have planned. Always plan and rehearse camera movements before making them.

Steadicam Flyer

A Steadicam flyer is like a hiking stick with a camera mount at the top. Steadicam flyers are primarily still-camera tools, but can be quite handy when you must be mobile and you still need to shoot steady video. You will often see camera operators on the sidelines at football games or other sporting events using monopods. The Steadicam flyer is lighter and more

Figure 31-3 Fly Right—Handheld counter-balanced supports allow you to move freely while shooting and produce gliding, shake-free video.

manageable than a tripod. While the Steadicam flyer prevents vertical movement of the camcorder, it does nothing to stop the horizontal or tilting movement.

Flying Supports

If you have a little extra cash in your pocket, you might want to check out one of the many types of flying camera supports on the market (see Figure 31-3). These handheld counterbalanced supports allow you to move freely while shooting and produce gliding, shake-free video. The most famous flying camera support is the Steadicam and the brand name has become a shorthand for the entire class of products. Beyond simple handheld devices, you can get complex vests and harnesses that will help you hold the camera during long shoots. The professional gliding

camera stabilizers are so smooth you can barely tell the camera is not sitting on a tripod. One note of caution: if you are considering buying one, try it out first to see if it will work with your camcorder.

You can create a flying camera support of sorts by mounting your camcorder onto your tripod or monopod and lifting it off the ground, using the weight of the legs to act as a counterbalance for the camcorder to keep it upright. This will not produce anything close to the results you'd get from a precisely engineered and finely balanced flying camcorder support, but you may be pleasantly surprised at the look of the shots.

Image Stabilization

Image stabilization is the video engineer's gift to amateur videographers. Your camcorder's built-in image stabilizer seeks to smooth out handheld video, minimizing camera shake. Image stabilizers are found in most camcorders today. There are two types: electronic and optical. Optical is generally better, and is typically found on higher-end camcorders. Although they can be quite handy if you find yourself in a situation where you must shoot handheld, they do have a couple of limitations. First, electronic image stabilization can reduce the overall number of pixels on the CCD that are used to capture an image. This can result in a general softening of the picture (see Figure 31-4). Second, when the stabilizer is used during a pan, the smooth pan might jump slightly from one point to the next as the stabilizer tries to correct your intentional movement. Still, image stabilization, both electronic and optical, can be a shotsaver when shooting handheld.

Keep It Steady

There are times to move the camera and times to hold it still, but, unless you are trying to create an earthquake effect, there are seldom times when shaky video is good video.

Figure 31-4 *Oversized CCD—Electronic image stabilization can reduce the overall number of pixels on the CCD that is used to capture an image. This can result in a general softening of the picture.*

Sidebar 1

Time Is of the Essence!

You should never handhold shots that demand rock solid video. Long interviews, cutaways of objects with vertical or horizontal surfaces and steady landscapes should never be handheld. Moving subjects, shots with camera movement already built into them, such as pans and tilts, and shots where the camera physically moves from one place to another can easily be handheld. Always plan your movement and move steadily and in one direction.

32
Make Your Move

Michael Hammond

Unlike our counterparts in still photography, those of us shooting video have a wonderful advantage—motion. With some imagination, a steady hand and a good tripod, you can take your viewers on a great visual ride. Let's review a few creative moves that you can all use to add interest in your videos. Keep these in mind as you plan your next project and work them in where they seem to fit.

Movin' on Up: The Pedestal

The pedestal move is a great way to add some vertical action to a scene. It allows you to create some anticipation with a viewer, to add a greater sense of height and importance to a subject and to link more than one subject in a single shot.

A pedestal move involves moving the entire camera vertically. The move is named for the adjustable center post found on many tripods. Unlocking this center post allows you to raise the camera while the tripod legs remain in a fixed position. Not all tripods have a pedestal that allows you to make a nice, smooth move. In some cases a tripod isn't practical,

so you may make this move as a handheld shot (see Figure 32-1).

The trick is to keep the vertical movement as steady as possible and to set your viewfinder before you start shooting. If you're working with a camcorder that has a flip-out LCD screen, by all means use it. Try to position the screen so that you can keep the framing in sight throughout the entire shot. If, for example, you're shooting a person's foot and moving up the body to end on the face, here's how to approach it. Frame up a nicely composed shot to start and check for clear focus. Since you're starting at almost ground level in this example, begin from a bended knee position with the camera directly in front of you, elbows resting just above your knees. Slowly lift the camera with your arms and then begin to stand as you rise up through the shot. Keep your elbows tucked in as close to your body as possible, and practical, to help keep things steady until you reach your end position.

This move could be great at a wedding to reveal a bride's dress. An example of linking subjects with this move might be starting on a full-screen shot of a house For Sale sign and then doing a pedestal up to reveal the home behind it.

Figure 32-1 *Pedestal—A pedestal move involves moving the entire camera vertically.*

Keep on Truckin': The Truck Move

In a trucking move, you, the tripod and the camera pick up and move to the left or right. This move is great for following, or creating a stronger sense of action. Let's say you're shooting someone jogging. If you just pan the camera to follow the runner, you'd need to be on a pretty wide shot and there would be a pretty significant change in the backgrounds and perspective as you follow the subject left or right. It also isn't as dramatic. Set up a trucking shot and you'll see the difference. Choose a distance from the runner, let's say you want to keep him full-body throughout the shot, and set up alongside of him with good focus. Unless you've rented or purchased a Steadicam or some other kind of stabilizing gear, if you actually jog beside the subject yourself the video will likely be unusable. You need some wheels! Without going to great expense, you can use an automobile, a wheelchair or a child's wagon to provide your motion (see Figure 32-2). Whatever you choose, be sure you have a partner to get you moving and keep you safe and stable while you're shooting. If possible, start moving the camera first, then cue your subject to start running. Settle on a comfortable speed and nice framing. Lead room is important in trucking shots. Give the subject some space between his nose and the edge of your frame so it looks like you're leading him and not trying to play catch-up. If you don't like the profile you get from trucking right alongside the subject, pick up some speed and get ahead a bit. This allows you to see more of the runner's face and changes up the background for some interest.

Taking Flight: The Flying Camera

The flying camera move gives you an opportunity to take your viewer on a ride. Think of this as taking on the point of view of an insect moving in and around subjects. I started using this type of move when my oldest child was a toddler. Fly

Figure 32-2 *Truckin'—In a trucking move, you, the tripod and the camera pick up and move to the left or right. Without going to great expense, you can use an automobile, a wheelchair or a child's wagon to provide your motion.*

around at kid level to make the viewer more an active part of the child's world. Of course, it works for shooting adults, too.

Let's say you want to capture some treasured moments of a child eating in a highchair. You might hold your camera at your waist with arms tucked into your stomach for stability. Begin the shot from behind the child, showing someone feeding the little one, then arc around the chair to the front. For more action, you could begin with the camera held high, coming down and around the chair. The opportunities with this one are endless. Picture a table with a great spread of food. The camera starts high, taking in most of the table from above, then sweeps down and runs the length of the table, flying past all of the treats. For a smooth move and good focus throughout the move, it works best with the lens zoomed out wide.

Guud Eeevening: The Hitchcock Zoom

This move is one of the most dramatic, and it requires a bit of practice. Alfred

Hitchcock made use of this camera move, and the film *Jaws* used a similar version of it. When done well, this move gives the appearance that the main subject is stationary as the background crashes in or flies away. Set the shot up by framing the subject with the lens zoomed out wide (see Figure 32-3). Begin to dolly away from the subject as you simultaneously zoom in to keep the subject the same size in the frame. The optics of the lens provide a unique look. Timing is important here in matching the dolly speed with the zoom, but when it all works it leaves a very dramatic impression with a viewer. Try the reverse, as well, by dollying in while zooming out. Great moves with powerful results.

Walkin' the Walk: The Walking Shot

This is a favorite of mine because it's easy to execute and adds zip to a normally dry shot. Rather than a static shot of your subjects walking, move with them. For a shot of two people passing by from behind, hold your camera about waist level with a wide lens and begin to walk ahead of your

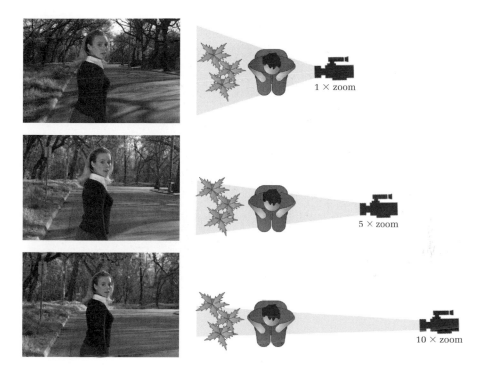

Figure 32-3 *Hitchcock Style—Dolly away from the subject as you simultaneously zoom in to keep the subject the same size in the frame. This move gives the appearance that the main subject is stationary as the background crashes in or flies away.*

Figure 32-4 *Walking On By—Begin walking backwards, cueing your subjects to walk toward you, passing you on either side as they exit your shot.*

subjects. Cue your subjects to start walking and overtake you, entering the frame from behind, one on either side, and continue walking away (see Figure 32-4). The reverse of this would be for you to begin walking backwards, cueing your subjects to walk toward you, passing you on either side as they exit your shot. You can give this last one an even more interesting perspective by zooming out as you walk backward.

Sidebar 1

Easy as 1-2-3

Unlike still photographers, videographers can move their cameras to create action or cover several focal points in a single shot. This means your composition—what you choose to include in a shot and where you choose to put it—will change as you move. It may help to think of every move that you make in three distinct parts.

1. Beginning Composition. This is where the shot begins. Choose carefully what to include in your scene and how to arrange it all for good balance. Identify this composition before rolling tape.

2. End Composition. This is where the camera comes to rest. Again, identify this composition before you start recording and try to achieve a good overall balance in the shot.

3. The Bridge. This is the camera move that connects the beginning shot with the end position. Practice the moves you intend to do as much as possible. Work to make the move smooth, maintaining good composition and focus. You may shoot a move several times adjusting the speed of the bridge for editing options.

Sidebar 2

Shoot Like an Editor

This old adage is good to remember while shooting. It'll be of great help during editing if you think through all of the possible uses of what you record as you plan your shots. This means if you're doing a camera move, record it several times at several speeds. If you've recorded some fast moves and a few slower versions, you've covered your needs for whatever pace you use in the final production. It's always a good idea to record a version of the shot without a camera move, just in case. You may find when editing that you don't have time for a camera move after all, and trying to freeze a shot—extracting a still frame from a moving shot—may not provide the quality you're looking for.

33
Use Reflectors Like a Pro

Jim Stinson

Reflectors are so versatile, useful and simple that professional videographers deploy them even in high-rent productions. Advanced amateurs may know how to use reflectors for outdoor fill light, but that's only their most obvious application. So let's conduct a quick flyover of professional reflector techniques, both outdoors and in.

First, let's take a quick taxonomy of reflector species. Reflectors are either rigid or flexible. Rigid reflectors may be faced (in order, from brightest to softest) with shiny aluminum, matte aluminum, wrinkled aluminum or white paper. Paper-faced reflectors are usually foamcore: rigid Styrofoam sandwiched between paper surfaces and available at any art or craft store. (Tip: pay the modest premium for one-inch-thick boards. They far outlast thinner ones.)

Flexible reflectors are usually cloth spread across thin metal hoops that can be folded for storage. Fabrics may be metallic for greater reflectivity or plain for a soft, diffuse effect. They come in white or sometimes gold, for reasons detailed in the sidebar.

Which to choose? Flexible reflectors are light and easily stored, but they're unstable in any breeze, making their light waver visibly on-screen. Hard reflectors are cheap to buy (or easy to make for almost nothing) but they're bulky and rigid, making them difficult to transport and store away.

Since these critters are most often used in wide open spaces, let's see how to employ reflectors outdoors as key, fill, rim or background lights. (NOTE: For simplicity, we'll describe everything via a clock face metaphor, with the subject at the center and the camcorder at six o'clock.)

Reflector Key Light

With the sun shining, why make your primary light a reflector? Often the sun's in the wrong position or the subject's standing in adjacent shade. In fact, the sun can become a gorgeous rim light, outlining the subject's head and shoulders and separating them from the background.

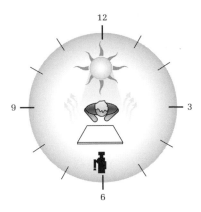

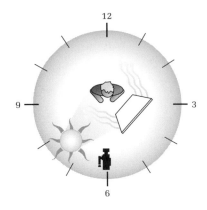

Figure 33-1 *Below the Shot—Start by placing your subject with the sun behind her (between ten and two o'clock). Then use a white reflector placed between four and eight o'clock, close to the subject and just below eye level, to fill in nose and chin shadows.*

Figure 33-2 *Key Reflector—More often, we'll use the sun as the key and the reflector for the fill, with each light source placed between three and nine o'clock, though I personally limit the arc to four to eight on our clock face.*

Start by placing your subject with the sun behind her (between ten and two o'clock). Then use a white reflector placed between four and eight o'clock, close to the subject and just below eye level, to fill in nose and chin shadows (see Figure 33-1). If you want to get fancy, use a reflector on either side, with the key unit closer, so the subject is lighter on that side.

A reflector key light also works well when the subject is in the shade. Bounce the light in, moving the reflector in or out until it is two to three times as bright as the ambient shade light creating the fill.

Reflector Fill Light

More often, we'll use the sun as the key and the reflector for the fill, with each light source placed between three and nine o'clock, though I personally limit the arc to four to eight on our clock face (see Figure 33-2). As always, place the reflector just slightly below the subject's eye level to fill nose and chin shadows. Too high a position delivers a Hitler moustache effect and too low creates a vampire. If the sun is at seven to eight o'clock, you can often get a nice effect with the reflector all the way around to three o'clock, filling the subject's profile.

Every type of reflector can and should be used for fill. For closeups, a diffuse white card looks most natural, but its intensity is too low for the throws required in longer shots. If you're short-handed, have subjects aim a white card, held below the frame line, up at themselves for their closeups. It often works great.

When higher intensity is needed, bring in the aluminum or metallic fabric models. They have enough punch to keep the reflector out of camera range and still work effectively. Always try to use the softest version that will deliver enough fill, starting with a metallic fabric model.

Using aluminum reflectors for key or fill light requires care, because they throw a hard, narrow beam and they can make subjects squint unattractively. Make sure you place them far enough away to reduce their intensity.

Reflector Rim Light

Those hard aluminum surfaces are perfect for rim-lighting the subject, especially when the sun is between four and eight o'clock. Place the reflector very high and opposite the sun or as nearly opposite as possible while staying out of frame.

Rim lighting works best when a second reflector is delivering fill light, as described in the previous section. If the sun is close enough to six o'clock and low enough in the sky, fill light may be unnecessary, but the golden glow of rim light might look wonderful.

When the subject is in shade, rim lighting doesn't work, unless the protected spot is just outside a sunny area. A hard aluminum unit in the sun can often bounce light off a second hard unit in the shade and back onto the subject's hair and shoulders. That's what bright aluminum reflectors are for: very long throws of relatively narrow light beams. In bright sunlight, I've seen hard aluminum units set as far as 100 feet away, from which position they can spread a broad, diffuse light on subjects without hurting their eyes (see Figure 33-3).

Reflector Background Light

Suppose you have a subject in the sun with, say, a shaded building wall as background. That makes for great facial exposure, but often a boring background. To spark it up,

fill in the backing with one or more hard aluminum reflectors (softer models are too low-intensity to work) (see Figure 33-4a).

Here, the keys to success are angle and distance. If the wall is parallel to 12 o'clock, behind the subject, try to get the reflector as close as 11 o'clock (sun angle permitting) to rake the background with an oblique wash of light (see Figure 33-4b).

If you have the resources, aim multiple reflectors at different areas of the background (I've used three or four). With care, you can produce a variegated and interesting wash of light that looks quite natural.

Or you can go a step further and use an improvised cookie. A cookie, short for "cukaloris" (a word lost in the mists of theatrical history), is a stencil pattern

Figure 33-3 *Versatile Sun—The sun produces plenty of light for a reflector to be used as a fill or light.*

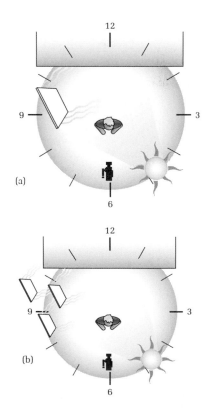

Figure 33-4 *Background—Suppose you have a subject in the sun with, say, a building wall as background. That makes for great facial exposure, but often a boring background. To spark it up, fill in the backing with one or more hard aluminum reflectors (softer models are too low-intensity to work).*

of leaves, bars or whatever you like that is placed between a spotlight and a surface. Cookies create interesting light and shadow patterns.

Hard aluminum reflectors throw a concentrated light beam that you can place cookies in front of to create surface patterns. To control the effect, move the cookie closer to the reflector for softer edges or farther away for harder ones. Because of the large surface areas of reflectors, the cookies must be much larger than those used indoors with spotlights. Outdoors, I sometimes improvise and use a dead branch with leaves still on it. Even if the leaves move in the wind, the effect on the background is quite natural.

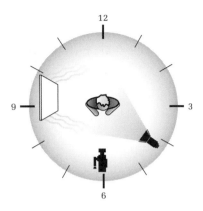

Figure 33-5 *Indoors—If you're working with just one spotlight, use it as a key light and place a large, white card out of frame on the opposite side. The result is a very soft natural looking fill light.*

Reflectors Indoors

Reflectors are not as versatile indoors because the light sources they depend on aren't as powerful as sunlight. Even so, you can easily use them to make one light do the work of two.

If you're working with just one spotlight, use it as a key light and place a large, white card out of frame on the opposite side (see Figure 33-5). The result is a very soft, natural looking fill light. You can even soften the naturally hard spot beam a bit with spun glass diffusion (e.g., a furnace filter) and still put out enough light for the reflector.

Even if you have more spotlights, you may want a softer look to your lighting

design. To achieve it, turn the lights away from the subject and bounce them back in with reflectors. In this application, metallic cloth or crinkled aluminum types work better than ultra-soft white cards. Carrying this to its logical conclusion, I've seen studios with 8×8 foot white walls on roll-around stands that make jumbo-sized reflectors delivering window light quality soft illumination.

So there's a quick rundown on reflectors. Once you see how versatile they are, you'll realize that reflectors aren't lights for poverty-stricken productions: they're versatile tools that pros use all the time.

Sidebar 1

Going for Gold

Foamcore, cloth and even some hard reflectors can be colored gold instead of white. Hoop-and-fabric units are sometimes two-sided, with one side gold and one side silver.

Gold reflectors are very useful for warming up the light they throw. Here are just a few ways to use them:

- To simulate the magic hour look of sunset.

- To counteract the naturally bluish cast of open shade.

- To warm up one light source (also useful in creating day-for-night effects).

- To add glamour to closeups, either as fill light or as a warm rim light on hair and shoulders.

The most economical way to acquire a warm reflector is by buying a piece of tinted foamcore. Instead of true gold, try a lighter yellow color to start, then experiment until you find what suits your needs.

Sidebar 2

Zoom In

A telephoto lens is excellent for closeups. Not only does it flatter human faces, but it includes less background, letting you sneak reflectors as close as even the eleven o'clock position.

34
Applying 3-Point Lighting

Dr. Robert G. Nulph

We are often told, "you have to know the rules before you can break them!" In the case of lighting, the rule for good lighting involves the use of three-point lighting. In this column, we will provide pictures and diagrams that will give you the rules you need to produce good lighting in simple situations. Once you master three-point lighting, you will be ready to move on to creating realistic quality lighting for your video productions.

Key, Fill and Back

The key light is the main source of light in a scene. You place the key light in front or to the side of the subject depending on the situation. The more dramatic the light needs, the further to the side you should place the light. Usually you place the key light at a 45-degree angle above the subject and 45 degrees to the side (see Figure 34-1). If the light is correctly placed, it will create a shadow that pleasantly slants down the side of the subject's neck as well as the side of the

nose giving a three dimensional look (see Figure 34-2c).

The role of the fill light is to fill in the shadows created by the key light. The fill light also gives the image a sense of time, place, mood and drama. The fill tells the viewer the brightness of the location where you are shooting. To prevent secondary shadows, it is best to place the fill light in front of the subject and closer to the camera lens than the key (refer to Figure 34-2b). This light should always be some degree less bright than the key and, as described below, is best if it is a soft light.

The backlight is essential to three-point lighting in that it separates the subject from the background. To set up a good backlight, place the light behind the subject and opposite the main light source (key light). The backlight should be set 45 degrees above the subject so that its light falls on the back of the subject's head and the top of the shoulders (see Figure 34-2a). Use more backlight for brunettes and less for blondes.

When you put all three lights together, it should create a very pleasant and natural

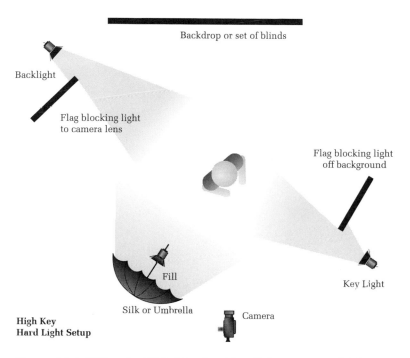

Backdrop or set of blinds

Backlight

Flag blocking light
to camera lens

Flag blocking light
off background

Fill

Key Light

Silk or Umbrella

Camera

**High Key
Hard Light Setup**

Figure 34-1 Without a fill light, a hard key light can cast a high contrast and harsh shadows. Keeping the light low and directly in front of your talent will minimize the effect.

looking three-dimensional image (see Figure 34-2d).

High Key versus Low Key

If the fill light approaches the intensity of the key light, the contrast is reduced and is often called High Key Lighting (see Figure 34-2g). You would use this type of lighting if you did not need to create a dramatic mood or just wanted a low contrast scene.

If the fill is a great deal less intense than the key light, the lighting is called Low Key Lighting (see Figure 34-2f). You would use this type of lighting for dramatic scenes, scenes shot to look like nighttime or dramatic interviews. To set up this type of lighting, place the key light farther to the side of the subject and reduce the intensity or eliminate the fill light (see Figure 34-3).

Hard versus Soft Light

The quality of light can be either hard or soft. Hard lighting comes from small lighting instruments that create hard-edged shadows. You can create soft light by making your lights bigger by diffusing their light with large silks, umbrellas or softboxes. You would use hard light to create intense dramatic lighting with sharp-edged shadows. However, if you want your subject to look soft and smooth, use a soft light setup. Note the softer look in Figure 34-2g versus the harder look in Figure 34-2i.

You can also use soft lighting for both high and low key lighting. You will find a lot of high key soft lighting used in interviews and news shows (see Figure 34-2h and Figure 34-4). You place the lights in basically the same places as the hard light high key setup (Figure 34-1). However, it

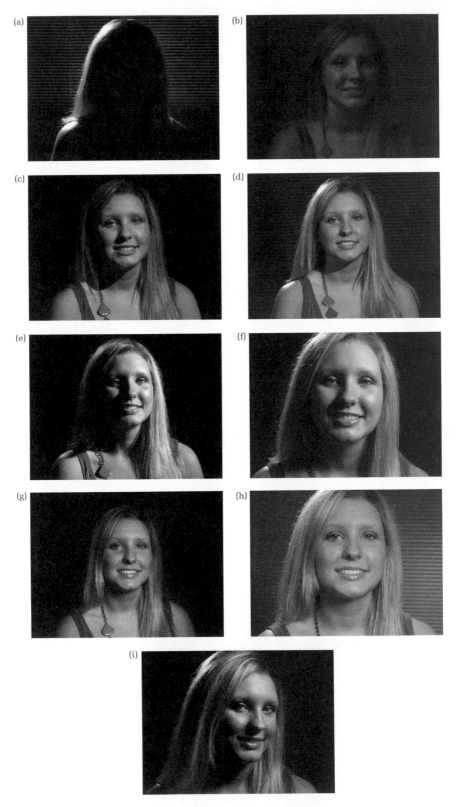

Figure 34-2 *Lighting helps create the mood of the scene.*

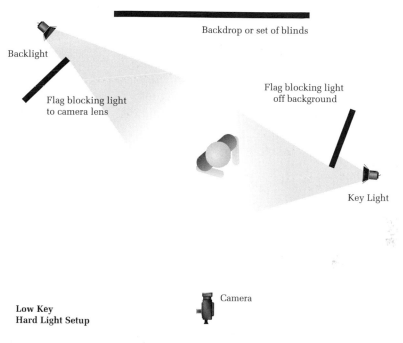

Backdrop or set of blinds

Backlight

Flag blocking light
off background

Flag blocking light
to camera lens

Key Light

Camera

**Low Key
Hard Light Setup**

Figure 34-3 *Without a fill light, a hard key light can cast a high contrast and harsh shadows. Keeping the light low and directly in front of your talent will minimize the effect.*

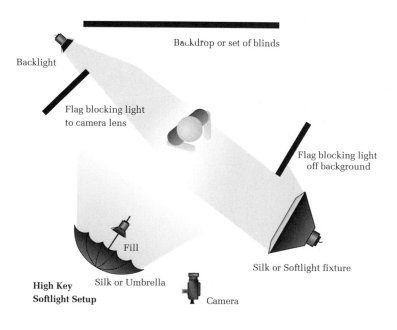

Backdrop or set of blinds

Backlight

Flag blocking light
to camera lens

Flag blocking light
off background

Fill

Silk or Softlight fixture

**High Key
Softlight Setup**

Silk or Umbrella

Camera

Figure 34-4 *High key soft lights will cast soft, even light on your subject. Soft boxes or umbrellas are a perfect tool for this effect.*

can also be used to create soft and dramatic shots using a low key setup by eliminating the fill light and moving the soft light more to the side of the subject.

Mastering It All

Whatever your lighting situation, always ask yourself, "what is the quality and position of the main light source?" Place your key light so that it best approximates the look of that major light source. The fill determines the level of the ambient light in the scene and the backlight, which is as intense as the key light, completes the setup. You are now ready to break the rules.

35

A Dose of Reality:
Lighting Effects

Robert Nulph

The firelight flickered against the cabin wall, warming the cool blue light of the full moon filtering through the tattered curtains. Suddenly the ominous blue then red flash of police lights filled the small room and Carson knew his game was up.

Suddenly the director yells, "Cut!" and the camera pulls back to reveal two Hollywood flats painted to look like cabin walls and a squadron of techies moving a myriad of lights and other equipment to new locations. Nowhere in sight in the cavernous sound stage is there a squad car, a full moon or a flickering fire.

For years Hollywood and independent filmmakers as well as corporate video producers have used lighting techniques to make us believe things exist that aren't really there. You can too! It is all a matter of collecting the right lighting instruments and accessories and adding a large dose of imagination. Mix them all together to give your scene a large dose of reality. Throughout this chapter, we'll look at a variety of ways to bring reality to your scenes. It is all in the power of lighting.

Mr. Sun and Mr. Moon

It's a good idea to always plan the outdoor and daylight shots first for your productions, because you have more control of indoor lighting than you do over the weather. All you need to make sunshine or moonbeams is a small, powerful light source and some colored gel. You can create sunshine, even at night, by placing a powerful light (1,000 watts or so) outside your window. (It is not advisable to do this if it is raining.) Make sure you place it at an angle similar to that of the sun at the time your scene takes place and is out of the camera shot. It works best if you use a small, intense light to create the light of the sun or moon because you want to imitate their qualities. If you think about it, the sun and moon are very small intense lights that throw very hard shadows. A big soft light will not do the trick.

To recreate the sun, you have to determine what time of day your scene is taking place. If your scene is in the early morning, you may want to place a single blue gel in front of the light. For midday, use

Figure 35-1 *Shine a light through a set of mini blinds to imply the existence of a window.*

no gel and for evening, use a yellow/gold, orange or red/orange gel, going towards the red as the day progresses. A light shining into a hard gold reflector and reflected through the window makes a fabulous evening light.

To recreate the moon, place two Color Temperature Blue (CTB) gels together in front of your light. Dim the lighting in the room to pick up the color of the moonlight and create the feeling of nighttime.

If you are creating the sun or the moon on a sound stage or other big room, you can also create windows through which they can shine. Place a window frame just out of camera shot so that its shadow falls across the floor and the background wall. Set up window blinds (Figure 35-1) and let the light filter through the slats. You instantly have a wall with a window.

Cars and Cops

With a little mechanical skill and a good sense of pacing, you can easily imitate car headlights, city streetlights, the flashing lights of a squad car or a searchlight being used to find the bad guy. You'll also need a couple of small, focusable lights that you can gel.

One of the easiest yet most effective lighting effects you can use is the imitation of a car's headlights. Using a four-foot long 2 × 4, mount two narrow beam lights about two feet apart. Slowly sweep the beams of light at an angle across the darkened back wall of your set. Instant car lights. If you are shooting a scene in a car at night, you can use the same technique both for cars passing you from the other direction as well as those coming up from behind.

In the same driving scene, you can imitate the passing of city streetlights, by rhythmically passing the beam of a powerful flashlight over the hood of the car, avoiding the camera lens. A flashlight works well because its lamp has a yellow color temperature and should look different from the lights you are using for headlights.

If your characters get in trouble with the law, you can fill the car or house with flashing blue and red lights by rhythmically passing a double or triple blue gelled light then heavily gelled red light past the background or interior of the car. The Lowel Omni light has a comfortable soft rubber grip that allows you to move it around without being burnt. Focus your light's beam to the tightest setting possible and pass first the red then the blue past the set. You can flash the set, tilt the beam to the floor and pass it again. With two people, it is a bit easier, but one person can handle it. Take the gels off one of the lights, put on a yellow gel, widen the focus on the beam and you have just created a searchlight.

If your scene occurs on a city street or in a seedy motel room, you can add the pulse of a red neon light. Reflect a diffused red-gelled light onto the background or into the interior of your car. By turning the light off and on or moving a flag to cover the light occasionally, you can imitate the stuttering of an old neon sign. Add a few sound effects and your characters are in for a long and dramatic night.

Living Rooms

Fireplaces, televisions and lamps that you see used in video and movie scenes more often than not don't really work the way we think they do. You can create it all through the magic of lighting.

If your character is supposed to be watching television yet you don't see the front of the set, you can create a very believable TV light. Get an old TV set, remove the picture tube and tack a double CTB gel to the front. Inside, place a lighting instrument that has a good quality switch on its cord. Quickly turn the light off and on; pausing at times for longer lengths of both light and dark. A television is never always bright so the flickering makes it look more realistic.

Of course, you could always plug in an actual TV set, but hey, that would be too easy.

If your character is sitting before a warm fire, you can create the effect by setting up a small, diffused light, angled up from floor level. In front of the light, hang inch wide strips of red, yellow and orange gels on a broomstick. Gently shake the gels in front of the light to create the feeling of firelight movement, as in Figure 35-2. Another method uses a round wheel (like an old bicycle wheel) covered with various orange, red and yellow gels cut with holes and layered to provide a variety of combinations and the occasional flash of real light. Turn the wheel slowly in front of the light to create the movement of the flame. Again, add sound effects and bake to perfection.

For lamps that you will see on the screen, the first thing you need to do is remove the regular bulb. A sixty-watt bulb will cause the lamp to glow on camera and look much brighter than it should. Place a 15-watt bulb in the lamp to provide a soft internal glow and supplement the light with a diffused

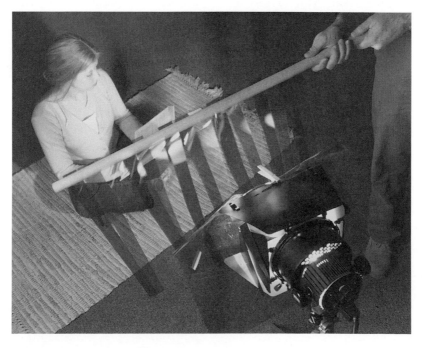

Figure 35-2 *Red and yellow gel strips waving in front of an orange-gelled light create the illusion of firelight.*

600-watt or more lighting instrument. Be sure to flag the light so that its beam does not fall on the lampshade of the light you are trying to use. If you place the lighting instrument just off-line from the real light, you can light your character in a warm glow that will look like it is coming from the lamp beside him.

Water, Water, Everywhere

Sometimes, the script calls for water ripples reflecting in your character's eyes or on her face. Often, it just isn't very convenient to set up lighting to get this effect using a real water source like a creek or lake. Don't worry, it is really a quite simple effect to recreate. All you need is a deep pan like a roaster or a painter's roller pan. Carefully break up a mirror into two to three inch pieces and place them in the bottom of the pan, face up. Cover the mirrors with about three inches of water. Shine a small, intense light into the water so that the light reflected from it falls onto the face of your character. (See Figure 35-3.) Gently lift one end of the pan up and down to create a soft ripple effect. You should see water ripples in your character's eyes. If your scene occurs at night, add a CTB gel to your light. Add a few seagulls, some

Figure 35-3 Light reflected off of water and broken pieces of mirror create a shimmering pool side effect.

water sounds and you're ready for a day or night in paradise.

Reality

Always be aware of the world around you. Look at the light that makes up our world, its reflections, its colors and the shadows it casts. If it occurs in the real world, you should be able to re-create it for the camera. A bit of knowledge, a dose of imagination and a touch of lighting magic can create any reality you wish.

36
Outdoor Lighting: What You Need to Know to Shoot Great Footage Outdoors

Michael Loehr

How do you light the outdoor scenes in your videos? Do you plan and stage each shot carefully to make the most of the sun's glow? Or do you just switch to outdoor white balance, call out "Action!" and roll tape?

Even if you choose the latter, chances are your videos still look pretty good. Today's camcorders work well enough in daylight to make very acceptable pictures, even with no attention to lighting.

Maybe that's why videographers don't worry too much about outdoor lighting. Perhaps they think making the best use of sunlight requires expensive instruments and tools they can't afford. Perhaps they just never learned the tricks of managing sunlight in a video project.

That's where this guide can help. In this chapter are some of the popular outdoor lighting techniques. They can help subjects look more natural on video, and improve the overall look of your projects.

You'll learn what tools and gadgets you need to make the most of sunlight. You can build many of them with inexpensive stuff from art supply and hardware stores. We'll even teach you how to create the illusion of a dark night in the middle of the afternoon.

So start taking advantage of what may be your greatest asset as a videographer: the sun.

Principles of Light

The fundamental principles of good lighting apply whether you shoot video indoors or out. However, sunlight presents unique challenges to videographers. On almost any given day, there is more than enough light outside to shoot a scene. At first, an abundance of light seems like an asset. However, the hundreds and thousands of lumens cast by the sun can actually cause problems for your camcorder. Not technical problems, but aesthetic ones.

At its brightest, the sun can shed more than 10 times the light of one typical indoor instrument. When it shines brightly, it also casts very dark shadows.

In video lingo, the difference between these light and dark areas is commonly called the contrast ratio, or *contrast range.*

Our eyes can compensate for the high contrast range of a bright day. Our camcorders, however, don't react as well. They require a much lower contrast range, especially to capture detail accurately. (Of course, our eyes also see better when we lower the contrast range, which is why we often wear sunglasses on sunny days.)

On bright days, the contrast range is usually too high for your camcorder to make good pictures. If you shoot without any lighting equipment or assistance, the sunlight won't flatter your subjects. Dark shadows may leave unpleasant or unnatural accents on facial features. Your images may also look washed out.

A high contrast ratio also affects your camera's automatic iris feature. You may have noticed that when the auto iris is on, its position changes constantly while you shoot.

As you move into a shadowed area, the iris opens to allow more light into the lens. As you move back to the bright areas, it closes again to avoid overexposure. That means you might get even, natural lighting from one angle, and harsh, overexposed lighting from another. The constant movement of the iris makes maintaining continuity between different camera angles difficult. It's also very distracting mid-shot.

The goal of outdoor lighting design is to lower the contrast range without damaging the natural look of the subjects and the outdoor setting. You want a lighting setup that looks the same to your camcorder, no matter where you put it. To do this, you need to brighten the dark, shadowed areas, and perhaps even lower the overall

light level, depending on how brightly the sun shines.

Tools and Tricks

If you're shooting indoors and need more light, the standard practice is to plug in a light and point toward the dark areas. Outside, you do practically the same thing, only with different tools.

You only have one light source—the sun. It doesn't need extension cords or power outlets. Even better, it will usually give you more than enough light to work with.

All you must do is redirect some of that excess light toward the shadowed areas of your set and your subjects. The best, most affordable tools for redirecting light are reflectors and diffusers; they will point light in different directions, and alter the way it falls on a subject. Light will bounce off a reflector, and pass through a diffuser.

Learning to use reflectors is easy. Their behavior is somewhat constant, given the fact that light bounces in predictable angles.

Reflectors vary, however, in three ways: 1) how much light they reflect, 2) how large an area their reflection covers and 3) the color of light they reflect.

Foil or mirrored surfaces reflect the most light over a small area. Pure white surfaces usually cover larger areas, but with less light. Some reflectors have a gold foil surface; these bounce light with a warm, rich quality that really flatters skin tones.

Diffusers filter direct beams of sunlight, spreading them evenly over a large area. Like reflectors, they're easy to use and fairly predictable.

A material's porosity and transparency determine its diffusion characteristics. Dense or very cloudy materials allow less light to fall onto the subject. Highly porous materials allow more.

Diffusing sunlight is probably the most effective technique for taming unpleasant shadows and reducing contrast. It does an excellent job of brightening dark areas, while retaining much of the outline and contour.

Figure 36-1 *An overhead canopy of diffusion material (a, before) can help to control excessive contrast from the sun (b, after).*

Figure 36-2 *When shooting in direct sunlight (a) a simple reflector can bounce light back into dark areas to improve contrast (b).*

To use a diffuser, simply suspend or position the material between your subject and the sun. Where you place the material and how you angle it depends on the look you want. To create shadows on the face, place the diffuser close to the subject and off to one side. To spread light evenly and minimize shadows, place the diffuser above and away from the subject, angled down slightly as in Figure 36-1.

Experiment with the diffuser to determine the most effective position for your particular scene. No matter where you put it, your camcorder will make better pictures with diffused light.

There are, however, a few drawbacks to using diffusion. It simulates the light you might see on a slightly overcast day, especially when you suspend the diffuser overhead. This lighting tends to be flat— some subjects may look bland under diffused light.

One solution: bounce more sunlight toward the subject. This highlights the subject and slightly increases the contrast range.

Or you can abandon diffusion altogether and bounce light around the scene with reflectors instead. By using reflectors, you can maintain the look of a summer day and still reduce contrast.

(a)

(b)

(c)

Figure 36-3 *If you must shoot during the day, try to get your subject out of the sun (a) and into the shade of a tree (b) or a building (c).*

Position the reflector to bounce excess sunlight toward shadowed areas, as in Figure 36-2. This lets your camcorder use more incoming sunlight without washing out your subjects.

If you're shooting at midday, unpleasant shadows may appear on your subject's face. The simplest solution is to move your subject out of the direct sun, if possible (see Figure 36-3).

Another solution is to use a reflector. Try putting the reflector below the subject's face; this should help eliminate the shadow. Be careful to avoid the "monster look," however. Strong light from below the face is a classic horror film technique, hence the name. Unless you want your subject to look frightening, make sure the reflected light flatters the face. Reposition the reflector as necessary to eliminate the monster look.

One last tip: videographers on the go may prefer reflectors to diffusers. Diffusers can sometimes be cumbersome to set up. Reflectors offer better portability, and still solve many outdoor lighting problems.

Simple Solutions

Other very effective and inexpensive outdoor lighting techniques involve simply staging a scene in the proper place with respect to the sun.

You've heard the saying that the sun should always be behind the camera when you shoot. True enough, but it doesn't tell you whether the sun should be to the left, the right or directly behind the camera. Many videographers default to the center position, where the sun sits directly behind the camera. This is a bad idea for two reasons:

1. It puts the sun in the subject's face, which almost guarantees squinting eyes in the shot (see Figure 36-4) and

2. the shadow that you and your camcorder cast is likely to wind up in the shot.

You can avoid these rookie moves by adopting an outdoor version of the classic three-point lighting setup, which is used to add more light to indoor shooting situations.

Figure 36-4 *Direct sunlight hitting your subject from the front causes squinting eyes.*

In the three-point setup, one light serves as the main or "key" light. It provides most of the light for a scene. It's positioned to light one side of the subject, angled approximately 45 degrees horizontally from the subject.

A second, less intense light shines on the opposite side of the subject. Called a "fill" light, it balances the shadows that define contour and shape. It's often somewhere between one half and two thirds as bright as the key light.

Sometimes a third light adds backlight. A *backlight* separates the subject from what's behind it, and provides shoulder and hair highlights on people.

Here's how you can adapt this three-point setup to outdoor lighting situations. Instead of standing with the sun directly behind you, change your position so that the sun shines from behind you over either your left or right shoulder. In this position the sun becomes a key light, shining light on one side of the subject's face.

This takes the light out of your subject's eyes and lowers the chance of your shadow appearing in the shot. When the sun shines at an angle similar to a key light, the shadows will fall away from you and the subject, and hopefully out of the shot.

You can also add a very inexpensive fill light by just using another reflector. Once you've established the sun as the key light, either clip a reflector to a spare light stand, or have an assistant hold a reflector near the subject on the side opposite the sun. Rotate the reflector back and forth to bounce light onto the "dark" side of the subject. Move away to lessen the intensity, closer to raise it.

If you have another spare reflector, particularly one with a foil surface, you can simulate a backlight. Stand just off camera behind your subject, on the side with the key light. Point the foil side toward the sun and rotate it until the reflection lights up the back of your subject. Presto! Instant backlight.

Occasionally you will encounter outdoor settings where the background is as brightly lit as the subject. This is another aesthetically unpleasant situation.

When the subject and background are both very bright, they conflict with each other, creating an image viewers will find difficult to watch for very long. To solve this problem, you must highlight the foreground subject. Instead of trying to reflect more light onto the foreground, try shadowing all or part of the background.

The technique is subtractive lighting, or "flagging." It involves using a card called a "flag" to block sunlight from hitting certain areas. You can buy ready-made flags from video stores, or build your own from black foam boards. In a pinch, a reflector will work as a flag, but black foam board is better. The reflector's white surface sometimes bounces light where you don't want it.

To shadow the background, position the flag behind the subject, just off camera on the key light side. Angle it so that it casts a shadow on the background. You may need to move the subjects away from the background to avoid casting a shadow on them as well.

Position Problems

Because the earth rotates in space, the sun's position, intensity and color balance change through the course of a day. This can create problems for uninitiated videographers. Understand these changes, however, and they can become tremendous assets.

If you shoot a series of scenes during an entire day, you'll notice the lighting changes from scene to scene. Shadows gradually change position, density and direction, and the contrast range changes. Color temperature also changes throughout the day.

For example: a scene shot very early in the morning will have long horizontal shadows, a slightly orange glow and a lower contrast range. A scene shot in the same location at midday will have dark vertical shadows and a much higher contrast range.

You will experience difficulty when you try to edit these scenes together. Differences in shadow placement and color balance will reveal that you shot the scenes at different times (see Figure 36-5).

A diffuser is an excellent way to prevent such problems. Diffusing sunlight hides the movement of the sun across the sky, and disguises the time of day. Sometimes the earth's atmosphere provides its own diffusion in the form of cloud cover. If the forecast says the clouds will hang around all day, you may not need to set up a diffuser at all.

Many projects call for dramatic use of light and shadow to convey specific moods or emotions. If yours is such a project, avoid using diffusion; it lessens the impact of shadows. Also avoid shooting in the middle of the day, when shadows make subjects look less than their best. Instead, shoot your footage either late in the day or early in the morning, when the shadows are most flattering.

When the sun is near the horizon, its color temperature is different from when it's high in the sky. At noon it casts a white light high in color temperature, usually around 5,600 K (Kelvin). Your camcorder's outdoor filter works best with this type of sunlight.

At dawn and dusk, however, the sun is lower in the sky, and its glow is a warm, golden-orange color. Videographers often call this period the "golden hour," since it

(a)

(b)

Figure 36-5 *Shooting in the evening or early morning results in a soft light (a). Midday sun is brighter and harsher (b).*

usually lasts right around an hour. Its color registers much lower than the 5,600 K light of midday—usually around 3,100 K.

Consequently, your camera may react differently when switched to the outdoor setting. If you white balanced early in the day under regular 5,600 K light, the video will turn more and more orange as the evening progresses. If you don't want this look, simply white balance your camera at the beginning of every shot.

While this change in color temperature may prove inappropriate, it can also be perfect for certain types of shots. The golden hour's long shadows and warm lighting make it an ideal time to shoot dramatic or romantic scenes.

Be aware that the moment only lasts a short time. You can extend the golden hour a little by reflecting sunlight off a gold-surfaced reflector. However, once the sun either disappears in the evening, or reaches a 45 degree angle above the horizon in the morning, the golden look will be difficult to maintain. If you know exactly when the golden hour will happen, you can plan to take advantage of it on your next project.

On very rare occasions you may need to add artificial light to make an outdoor scene suitable for shooting. This is most common when shooting under either very dark clouds or heavy shadows. In these cases it may be appropriate to use your indoor lighting instruments instead of reflectors to light a scene.

Remember, the color temperature of sunlight is much higher than that of indoor studio lights. To use indoor lights outdoors, you must put a blue gel in front of them. Also be aware that indoor lights shine a very small amount of light when compared to the sun. You may need two or even three instruments to light a subject adequately outside.

Night Lights

Shooting outdoors at night can be trouble for professional and amateur videographers alike. Even with low-light camcorders, it's still very difficult to get good pictures without adding artificial light.

To solve this problem, use a technique called day-for-night shooting. It involves shooting a carefully staged and controlled scene during the day, making it look as if it were shot at night.

Day-for-night shooting isn't easy, and it isn't always effective. To make it work, you must create an illusion of nighttime that will fool your audience. To do this, pay close attention to how your eyes see at night.

Pay close attention to colors. At night our eyes don't see colors as well because of the lower light level. The same is true for our camcorders. Dress your subjects in muted colors to keep the color intensity down.

If your camcorder has a monochrome mode, consider using it instead of the color mode; this will help reduce the amount of color in the scene. Some editing VCRs have chroma controls or monochrome switches, which can also mute color intensity.

Consider buying a blue filter for your camcorder. This helps create the illusion of moonlight by turning sunlight blue. Most video stores carry a selection of filters to fit your camcorder. Be sure to get one that fits your model's lens.

When combined with the other techniques, the blue filter greatly enhances the nighttime look.

If there are any ordinary lights in your scene—car headlights, porch lights, window lights—switch them on. Indeed, before you shoot you should turn on any and all lights normally on at night.

You also must know how to disable your camcorder's auto iris and auto white balance circuits—if it has them. When activated, an auto iris circuit lets the optimal amount of light into the lens to make pictures.

With day-for-night shots, you want to limit the light entering the lens. You can only do this when you turn off the auto iris.

The same applies to auto white balance. If active, the feature will try to get an accurate white balance, even with the blue filter on the lens. The goal is to fool the camera and ultimately the audience, so switch off the auto white balance.

With the circuits off, white balance the camera without the blue filter. Place the filter on the lens, and manually close the iris until a small amount of light enters the lens. Let enough light through to distinguish your subjects, but not any more than that.

The result is the nighttime look: a grainy bluish image with muted colors and contrast. If your editing VCRs allow it, try lowering the black level and raising the luminance during post-production.

This increases the contrast enough to match what our eyes typically see at nighttime.

Wrap It Up

Enhancing your outdoor shoots with reflectors and diffusers is more art than science. The techniques reflect personal preference as much as rigid rules.

So use reflectors and diffusers to express your own visual ideas more effectively.

The best way to learn is to experiment with them.

Stage a simple scene outside, and then create four or five different moods by just changing the lighting design. This'll teach you how sunlight works, how to make the most of your tools and how your camcorder reacts to sunlight.

Experiment, too, with different materials and techniques. You may discover a style that becomes the signature element in your videos.

37
Audio for Video:
Getting It Right from the Start

Hal Robertson

So, you've bought a shiny new digital video camera and you're blown away by the image quality. But what about the audio? Audio is possibly the most overlooked element in video production. That's too bad because audio quality can make or break any video project, regardless of budget.

You may be able to fix some things in post-production, but why go to all the trouble when you can get it right the first time? This article explores 10 tips for gathering the best possible audio on your next shoot. Some are commonsense tips, but many are hard-earned lessons from the field.

1—Plan Ahead

When shooting on location, a smart videographer scouts the site before the shoot, looking for ideal lighting and backgrounds to produce the best image possible. For your next shoot, scout with your ears too. Listen for traffic noises, machinery, animals and aircraft—anything that might ruin the audio during the shoot.

Depending on your topic, some background noise may be acceptable or even desirable. Just make sure you can hear your subject over the ruckus.

2—Use an External Microphone

Unless you have a high-end professional camera, your built-in microphone is absolutely worthless for anything more than your 3-year-old's birthday party. First, the microphone is built into the camera's body, and is very sensitive to noise from zoom, focus and tape drive motors. The second problem is a matter of distance. Even though you can zoom in on a subject from across the room, the microphone is stuck 20 feet away. Trust me, you need an external microphone.

3—Choose the Right Microphone for the Job

OK, I've convinced you to use an external mic, but what kind? There are four basic types: handheld, lapel, shotgun and boundary (see Figure 37-1).

Handheld mics, typically used by news reporters, add a newsy feel to your video. Directional handheld mics minimize background noise while non-directional mics collect the audio flavor of the scene.

News anchors and sit-down interview participants often use lapel, or lavaliere microphones. They are useful anytime you want to get close to the source, but minimize visual impact.

Shotgun microphones, highly directional and often used on TV shows and movie sets, usually suspend from a boom or "fishpole." Shotgun mics typically hover just out of the video frame and point directly at the subject.

If you shoot legal or corporate video, the boundary microphone could be your new best friend. Boundary mics turn an entire table, wall or floor into a pickup surface. Unfortunately, their incredible sensitivity is a double-edged sword. They clearly pick up voices from every direction but also amplify shuffling papers and air conditioner noise equally.

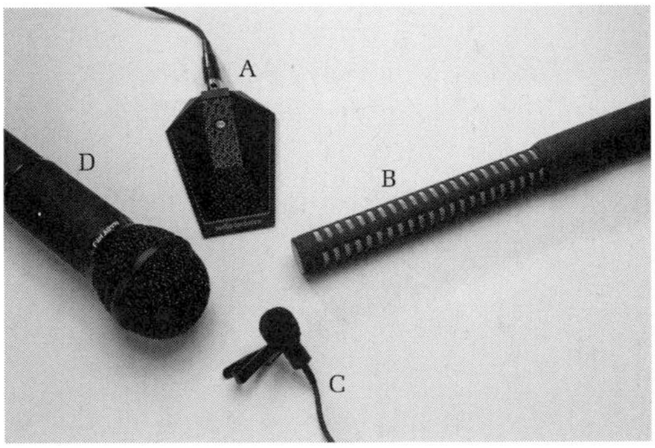

4—Use a Windscreen

You're familiar with the effect of wind blowing into a microphone. The resulting rumble masks all but the loudest sounds, making the audio useless. Subjects speaking close to a microphone also produce small blasts of wind from their mouths. One of three basic windscreens will minimize or eliminate these problems altogether.

Foam windscreens are the most common since they are inexpensive, and work great for both handheld and lapel microphones (see Figure 37-2). Although shotgun mics also use foam windscreens, the pros usually use a special type called a zeppelin. This special-purpose windscreen gets its name from its shape. It looks like a long, skinny blimp. Porous cloth or fur typically covers the mic and blocks the wind, while letting sound through unharmed. A shotgun microphone mounts inside the zeppelin where the entire mic is protected from audio-wrecking wind noises.

When you record the narration for your next video, consider using a hoop-style windscreen to improve the sound quality. Hoop screens are usually about six inches

Figure 37-1 A. Boundary Mic—Also PZM, lies flat on a table or surface and is typically used for miking people sitting around a table.
B. Shotgun Mic—Usually has a highly focused pickup pattern and is best at gathering sound at a distance or in a noisy environment.
C. Lapel Mic—Is very small and can be hidden on or around the subject to completely conceal its presence.
D. Handheld Mic—Comfortable to hold in the hand, it is commonly used by television newscasters, singers, public speakers and talk-show hosts. It's ideal when you want the talent to directly address the camera.

Figure 37-2 Screen Test—A simple foam windscreen can do wonders to minimize outdoor gusts and plosives in the voice.

in diameter and covered with one or two layers of fine mesh cloth. Recording studios worldwide use this type of windscreen on critical vocals, and you can too.

5—Position Microphones Properly

Some simple attention to microphone placement can make a dramatic improvement in sound quality. Take the shotgun mic, for example. Its extreme directional characteristics and high sensitivity make it great for picking up audio from a distance. But point a shotgun up at your subject from the ground (instead of overhead), and you might pick up birds singing in the trees or the 3:30 flight to Albuquerque.

Misuse of lapel microphones is just as easy. Ideally, they are worn on the outside of clothing, attached to a lapel, tie or shirt. However, hiding lapel mics under clothes minimizes wind noise and visual distractions (see Figure 37-3). This location guarantees a muffled sound and the sound of cloth rubbing on the microphone. If wind is the problem, try positioning your subjects with their backs to the wind. If cosmetics are the issue, try a smaller microphone, a less distracting location or a shotgun mic.

6—Learn to Deal with AGC

Automatic gain control, or AGC, is built into many cameras on the market. This seemingly magic circuit constantly monitors your incoming audio, then keeps the loud sounds from getting too loud and the soft sounds from getting too soft. Sounds like a great idea, doesn't it? It's not a bad idea, but problems crop up later during editing when you try to match clips from different takes. One take will be loud and strong, but another will be softer with more background noise. Now what are you going to do?

There are a couple of solutions. First, have your talent re-take the material, starting before the break point. This will get the AGC working in a similar range to the previous take, making your edit point more consistent. The second method is to turn the AGC off. This only works on certain camcorders, but if yours has this feature, use it. You can adjust the audio level manually for consistent sound, take after take.

7—Monitor with Headphones

If your camera has a headphone jack, buy a pair of good headphones and keep them in your camera case (see Figure 37-4). The next time you shoot, you will hear exactly what the microphone hears, making mic positioning easier. You will also catch bad connections, dead batteries and background noise before you commit it to tape. This is an absolute must and will save you much frustration and embarrassment.

Figure 37-3 *In or Out?—It may be tempting to conceal a lapel mic in the clothing; however, it will cause the audio to be muffled and the sound of rubbing cloth to be picked up.*

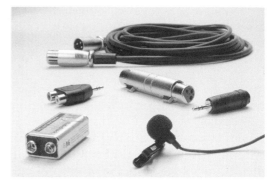

Figure 37-5 Hooking Up—With a variety of cables, adapters and spare batteries you'll be prepared for every audio occasion.

Figure 37-4 Listen In—Always use headphones when using an external mic.

8—Get Connected

Audio cables and adapters are a necessity for the videographer—just make sure you have the right ones before you shoot (see Figure 37-5). Wireless mics often need jumper wires to connect the receiver to the camera. Professional microphones use three-pin XLR connectors that won't plug into most consumer and prosumer cameras. For these mics string together several adapters or buy an interface box. If you're connecting to a sound system or other audio equipment, bring every adapter you own to the shoot. You'll need them.

9—Get In Close

Regardless of your microphone choice, the closer you get it to the subject, the cleaner your audio will sound. Position the handheld or lapel mic a little closer than you previously had. Boom in as close as possible with the shotgun. This technique also reduces background noise and further improves your audio.

10—Bring Spares

Spare cables, spare adapters, spare microphones and spare batteries. This tip will save your skin in an emergency and give you some creative freedom. Perhaps you get to the shoot and discover your single lapel microphone won't work because there are two subjects speaking. Your spare shotgun or handheld microphone will work even better and you'll look like a very smart cookie.

Take these ideas to heart and your next video production can sound match the sound of a professional studio. In a future chapter, we will explore how to create professional sounding audio in the edit suite.

Sidebar 1

An Audio Horror Story

Last year I shot a video for my church in a city park. I scouted the site and found a great location for audio and video. What I failed to notice was the railroad behind a wall of trees on the east side of the park.

The day of the shoot threatened rain, so we had to work quickly. Unfortunately, we had to stop shooting twice for a passing train—destroying 20 precious minutes of clear sky. We got the video done, but we also got wet packing the equipment back to the car. Lesson learned.

Sidebar 2

Watch with Your Ears (or Listen with Your Eyes)

Still not sure what type of microphone is best for your next shoot? Broadcast TV shows offer a valuable and free resource of audio examples to help you decide what microphone to use.

News broadcasts provide the perfect opportunity to listen to the differences between lapel mics (anchors) and handheld mics (field reporters). Close your eyes and carefully listen to the variety of audio sources.

Most sitcoms and dramas offer a chance to examine the sound of a shotgun microphone in action. If you listen closely, you'll begin to notice when the mic isn't pointed exactly at the subject.

38
Outdoor Audio

Hal Robertson

Ah, the great outdoors. It's a video shooter's dream come true. Loads of free lighting, gorgeous backgrounds and breathtaking scenery—what more could you want? At least visually, shooting outdoors is a wonderful idea. For audio, however, an outdoor shoot presents a new set of challenges. Learning to deal with these challenges is a combination of the right tools and knowledge of all the variables. Grab your walking stick and camcorder and join us on a hike through the backwoods of outdoor audio.

It's Not Nice to Fool Mother Nature

If you plan to shoot outdoors, rest assured you'll have to deal with less than ideal weather conditions from time to time. Of particular concern are the detrimental effects of rain and snow on your precious (i.e., expensive) audio and video equipment. Wet weather and electronic gear mix like oil and water, so you'll do well to prepare for the worst.

First, and most important, is to keep the water out of your camera. Surely you've seen the advertisements in the back of ***Videomaker*** for rain slickers made specifically

for cameras. These are excellent accessories for those who shoot outdoors on a regular basis. The occasional outdoor videographer, however, can make due with a simple plastic trash bag. Cut a hole for your lens in one corner of the bag and a hole for the viewfinder in the other corner. You'll still have easy access to the controls from underneath, although it will be difficult to use a flip-out LCD and certain viewfinders. It's not as waterproof as the rain capes with watertight lens holes, but a trash bag might be sufficient in a light mist.

Zipper sandwich bags come in handy with your audio equipment (see Figure 38-1). A wireless microphone transmitter pack doesn't like the wetness any more than your camera, so keep it dry too. You'll need a knife and some gaffer's tape to complete the task, but the finished project will keep your transmitter dry and away from the repair bench. Wired microphones fare better in the elements, but it's still a good idea to keep the connectors dry with a simple wrap of electrical tape. The same applies for battery doors.

Exposed microphones—whether hand-held, shotgun or lapel—are more of a sticking point. It's never a good idea to

Figure 38-1 *Bag It—Zip up the delicate electronics in a sandwich baggie in extreme environs.*

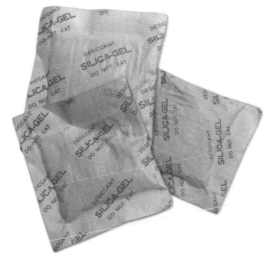

Figure 38-2 *Do Not Eat—Silica gel packs in your camera bag can absorb moisture.*

get a microphone wet, regardless of type or application. For a quick outdoor shoot, a simple foam windscreen will keep the microphone dry enough, but extended shoots require measures that are more drastic. While you can cover your microphone with the same bag as your camera, the audio will suffer. Not only will you hear the drops of rain falling on the plastic, the covering will dramatically change the quality of the sound. Honestly, there isn't a simple fix for this problem. There are professional windscreens that make notable improvements, but the price may be out of reach for many casual shooters. If you're using a lapel microphone, it's possible to secure the element under your talent's clothing or even under the brim of a hat. These are extreme measures and will negatively affect the sound quality, but it's a reasonable tradeoff if the alternative is to abort the shoot.

Although not specifically audio related, it's a good idea to avoid rapid shifts in temperature and humidity—your audio and video gear won't like these changes and may rebel. Condensation (when moving from cold to warm environs) will produce everything from random glitches to a complete shutdown to fried circuitry. You can minimize these effects with two simple techniques. First, place several packs of silica gel in your camera case to absorb excess humidity (see Figure 38-2). Second, when moving from a cool environment to a warm one, give the equipment several

minutes to acclimate. You'll eliminate the embarrassment of an equipment failure and save wear-and-tear on your gear too.

The Windscreen Is Your Friend

Whether you shoot in wetness or not, every outdoor shooter has to deal with wind noise. Uncontrolled wind noise can render your audio useless and there is no way to repair the damage in post-production. Regardless of the audio you capture outside, your microphone needs a windscreen.

The most common type of windscreen is made from open-cell urethane foam (see Figure 38-3). Although available as an accessory for virtually every type of microphone, some microphones come with the windscreen permanently installed. The windscreen's task is simple—keep the wind out of the microphone. Foam windscreens vary in their ability to accomplish this mission, but they're inexpensive, readily available and work well in many situations.

In more extreme conditions, you'll need a professional windscreen—often called a windsock or zeppelin. These windscreens differ in size and construction, but most often use a special cloth stretched over an open frame. The microphone is enclosed

Figure 38-3 *Foam Fun—Cheap foam covers can help eliminate wind noise.*

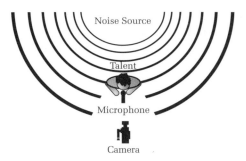

Figure 38-4 *Block It—If you're shooting a subject using a handheld or lapel microphone, position him with his back to the noise. His body will block a great deal of noise and can make an impractical setup feasible.*

inside the frame and the cloth blocks the wind from entering. The completed assembly looks something like a blimp, hence the zeppelin reference. The windsock is effective at eliminating wind noise, but costs a good deal more than the common foam windscreen. In addition, the length and diameter of your microphone factor into the design of the enclosure. For shooters in brutal wind conditions, the addition of a fuzzy fur cover to the windsock can eliminate the detrimental effects of wind noise up to 60 miles per hour.

Dealing with Background Noise

Whether outdoors means mountain streams or traffic jams, you have to deal with unwanted noises in your audio. These may manifest themselves as simple, random interruptions or as a constant roar that all but obscures the sound you *want* to record. In any case, there are weapons at your disposal to minimize these effects.

The simplest technique is to use natural barriers to block the noise. If you're shooting a subject wearing a lapel microphone, position him with his back to the noise. His body will block a great deal of noise and can make an impractical setup feasible (see Figure 38-4). You can exploit other barriers such as buildings, rocks and trees to similar effect. When using directional handheld or shotgun microphones, utilize the built-in null points to your advantage (see Figure 38-5). You can leverage this

Figure 38-5 *Aim for the Mouth—It is important to point directional microphones correctly.*

knowledge of pickup patterns by placing the microphone where it will pick up the maximum amount of sound you want and a minimum of the sound you don't.

On the other hand, you *are* shooting outdoors and your viewers associate certain sounds with being outside. If the area you're featuring contains colorful audio, capture several minutes of sound on tape after the shoot. Back in post-production, you'll have a way to cover abrupt edits and scenic shots that don't have acceptable audio. Properly blended, these patches will sound perfectly natural, plus you'll have another soundscape for your audio effects library. It is better to have the option to add ambient noise back into the mix in post than to try and remove it.

Shooting in the great outdoors can be challenging, but some preparation and practice will have you ready to tackle those projects, and you'll have some impressive audio to show for your efforts.

Sidebar 1

DIY Windsock

Professional microphone zeppelins or windsocks can cost several hundred dollars and aren't worth the cost for casual use. A few dollars and a trip to the fabric store will supply most of what you need to build a simple windsock. First, pick up a small roll of fiber batting—the type used to fill quilts and blankets. Next, buy some costume fur with a nap of one inch or longer. Installation is simple. First, wrap some batting around your microphone, securing it with rubber bands. Then, do the same with the fur if you're shooting in strong winds. This setup will likely thin out the sound, but wind noise won't be as much of an issue.

Sidebar 2

Listen Closely

Most shooters know to monitor their audio with a pair of headphones, but monitoring outdoors adds some complexity. Many camcorders offer skimpy headphone amplifiers, so you have to make the most of every milliwatt. Start with a pair of sealed-cup (circumaural) headphones. These will block outside sounds and allow you to concentrate on what's coming through the microphone. Several manufacturers offer excellent sealed-cup models, but try them with your camcorder before buying if possible. As you sample several brands, you'll discover that some headphones play much louder than others. Find the best tradeoff of sound quality versus volume and you'll have an audio reference that will serve you well in every circumstance.

39

Stealth Directing: Getting the Most Out of Real People

Michael J. Kelley

It must have been Take 30, but we weren't quite sure because we were no longer using a slate, nor did we stop tape in between takes, for fear of losing the little momentum we had gained. The talent was a beautiful young woman who had volunteered for the part. She was well cast by the bank's producer. Her considerable knowledge of the subject matter meant that she had her lines down, but her lack of experience in front of the camera made this training video laborious to capture. Even worse: The experience was completely humiliating for her, the performance was indeed embarrassing and she would very likely never again volunteer for a shoot. It can be difficult to coax an agreeable performance out of an amateur, but it can be done.

Be Realistic

Professionals know that to deliver a compelling performance, the talent must be comfortable not only with the script, but also with being the center of attention, where lights, microphones, camera and production crew all hang on every move. This alone is a tall order for most people: Remembering lines is one thing, but putting it all together with eye lines (where the talent should direct their gaze), blocking (where they should stand and move) and interacting with other players and props in a well-timed and natural way reminds us all why the really good actors deserve the big bucks. Even under the best of circumstances, it's not easy to deliver a believable performance.

Using real people is a calculated risk. The successful director manages an exercise in stealth, regardless of the size and scope of the production environment. Most of the management techniques that typically apply to pros can be tossed out from the beginning. From pre-production coaching to the first rehearsal, all the way to the last shot, the director of amateur talent is most successful when being downright sneaky.

Figure 39-1 *Ready Off the Set—Ready the talent off of the set, preferably in an environment which is both familiar and relaxing.*

Tread Lightly

Standard techniques, such as on-camera rehearsals or calling for "places, lights, camera, action," just don't work. The pressure while waiting on the set is generally too much for amateur talent to bear, so much so that, while the shot is prepared technically, the stealthy director can best use the time to ready the talent off of the set, preferably in an environment which is both familiar and relaxing (see Figure 39-1).

Aside from any artistic or technical prowess, the director is equal parts coach, babysitter, mentor, friend, psychologist, boss and dentist (as some "teeth" can be extracted more painlessly than others). The director is also much like a valve, constantly bleeding off pressure while developing an acceptable flow. Finally and always, the director is also a good writer (able to adapt scripts in a heartbeat), editor (able to adapt to new sequences as they occur), and actor. You, as the director, must invisibly manage your own pressures sufficiently to give every attention to the fragile talent. Normalizing the talent's pressures is your primary task, for, without an acceptable performance, all of the rest is but a drill.

It's crucial that you be so well organized that your manner is relaxed and friendly, stress-free and even playful. Much of this has to do with doing your homework and providing ample time for the scene to be captured. Advanced preparation really pays off here, and a flexible production timetable which is able to cope with surprises, delays and unanticipated bits of serendipity is a must.

For most people, being in front of a camera is an exciting experience, complete with ego attachments, unfounded expectations, vain fantasies and delusions of grandeur. Given a little extra time, a clever director can use all of that energy to great advantage.

Call Talent Last

It's best if the set is fully prepared before the talent ever arrives (see Figure 39-2). Stagger your call times, call the talent in as late as possible, and, by all means, do not over-rehearse your talent. Repeat your technical run-throughs separately until they are consistently on the mark. This is where the sneaky part starts: With the talent arriving fresh and full of anticipation,

Figure 39-2 *Last Call—It's best if the set is fully prepared before the talent ever arrives.*

the director should focus all attention on the talent, perhaps assigning a production assistant specifically for the talent if possible. The whole crew should be welcoming and relaxed. This first impression cannot be overestimated. Setting an inclusive stage makes every difference, so always provide the time for the talent to be fully introduced to the crew and the environment.

Prep Off the Set

Next, get the talent off the set. Applying makeup, tending to hair and wardrobe or even wiring a concealed mike may make the talent feel important, but it also ups the pressure. These tasks are all best accomplished off-set. It's also a great time for the director to distract the talent by casually discussing the shot and how the talent will deliver his part (see Figure 39-3).

Show Time!

With the crew in position, the tape cued and everyone at the ready, escort the talent to the fully lighted set. As the director

leads the talent through his blocking, perhaps even giving an example of how lines are to be delivered, the crew is on full alert, keenly watching for the roll cue which may be as subtle as a silent nod or a flick of the hand. With the talent slowly and carefully massaged into place, the director should casually call for a rehearsal; that's often the cue to roll tape too. No tally lights, no calls for "Action!", no extra pressure.

If all goes well, you may have your shot finished before the talent even knows you've started. Recording "rehearsals" sometimes yields the freshest, least self-conscious delivery. Of course, many performances improve with a little work and encouragement from you, but even when conducting interviews, you'll find that the best performances come from talent that is fully prepared in advance of ever reaching the set and is then gently coaxed through short segments with as little hoopla as possible.

After all, real people are often very talented, attractive and capable, if only the director and producer take the time to conceal the pressures of the process and prepare for what may be the performance of a lifetime.

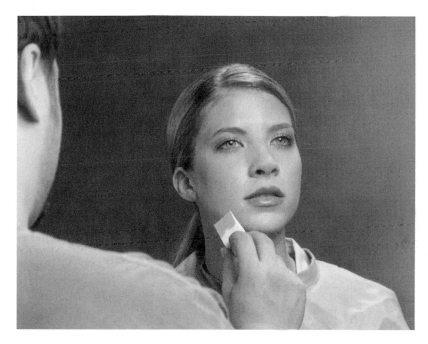

Figure 39-3 *Off-Set Application—Applying makeup, tending to hair and wardrobe or even wiring a concealed mike may make the talent feel important, but it also ups the pressure. These tasks are all best accomplished off-set.*

Sidebar 1

Craft-Services Prep Pays Off

A thoughtfully catered table can offer needed liquid refreshment and nourishment. Find out your talent's preferences ahead of time and provide meals which are appropriate for the time and length of the production day. The talent may be a strict vegan or allergic to the almond torte you specially prepared. You want to fuel the performance, while calming the performer, so have choices. Snacks of fresh fruit are always crowd pleasers. Carefully regulate the use of sugar and caffeine, and save the champagne for when the shot's in the can. Whatever you do, give the talent plenty of water, but don't let her use ice, as it may constrict the vocal chords.

Sidebar 2

It's in the Eyes

Interview subjects are usually experts in their fields, but most experts aren't performers, so it's up to you to give the talent every encouragement. Choose your questions carefully. Don't put your expert on the spot and, if an answer is difficult, move along and come back to a rephrased version of the question later on. Your body language is very important: Attentive, upright posture and focused eye-contact, coupled with an open, pleasant smile and nods of encouragement, will all help your talent to feel relaxed and conversational. Have him tell his stories to you in his own words, and have the stealth camera crew there, almost invisibly capturing every nuance.

40
What Were You Thinking?! Pet Peeves of the Video Pros

Jennifer O'Rourke

Have you ever wanted to wrestle a camcorder away from Uncle Buck while at a family function or public event and scream into the lens, "What are you THINKING!!??"

We have to admit, as experienced shooters and editors, that we've had to squelch the impulse to take control of someone's camcorder from time to time. We also know that many shooters, editors, directors and producers have had similar tongue-biting moments when dealing with people within the profession. So we polled our various video associates for their pet peeves and I added a few of my own. Do you see yourself or someone you know in this list?

Subliminal Message

A flash frame in a finished project is the number one "fingernails on a chalkboard" peeve of mine. When they are meant for effect, flash frames are a great editing technique. But when it's just sloppy editing it presents a poor production. After working hours, days, maybe even months on a project, step back and watch it, really watch every frame that passes by. Watch for continuity. Watch for match editing, and above all, watch for those dangling flash frames. You don't want to discover the mistake as it goes live on the air, debuts at the major stockholders meeting or shows at your grandma's lifetime achievement party.

Figure 40-1 *A flash frame, in this case a single frame of black that inadvertently snuck in when two clips were not joined properly, will be subconsciously noticeable to the viewer. Be sure to catch and remove these.*

Steady as She Goes

Have you watched someone's footage (not yours, of course!) that looks as if they're trying to create the next *Blair Witch Project*? But they're only shooting little Janey's ballet recital.

In the Olden Days, camcorders were big and bulky ... and heavy. The shoulder-mounted weight of the camcorder gave you ballast that helped make shooting steady. But nowadays, with mini this and mini that, everything is small, and small is not good when it comes to shooting video handheld. Use a tripod. If you don't have one, or it's not available, hold your arms close to your sides, tuck the camera in and bend your knees. Or lean against a tree, balance the camcorder on something or even cup the camera under your arm. You have to become a human tripod, and by all means, if you're shooting something at an extreme distance without a tripod, don't zoom in! Trust me on this one, it will not enhance your video. Either get closer, steady the camera some way, or accept that you're going to be stuck with an extreme wide shot. An out-of-control picture that looks like it's in the middle of a hurricane can make your viewer sick, and his eye tends to concentrate on the frame edge rather than the subject matter.

Watch Out for That Tree!

How many times have you seen this? A medium shot of a person talking into the camera with a tree, telephone pole or lamppost growing from the back of his head? Or maybe it's high-tension wires seeming to grow through her ears? Too many people work hard at framing their key subjects in the picture, and forget to look at the rest of the scene. Pay attention to foreground and background, they are just as important to a well-composed picture as the main subject is.

We're always talking about the "Rule of Thirds" which good Videomaker readers all know: by moving your subject from dead-on center, you will create a more

Figure 40-2 *When composing your shots, always remember to pay attention to what's happening in the background, so you don't end up with a telephone pole growing out of someone's head.*

interesting scene to enjoy. But you also need to look at background and foreground to escape the tree-through-the-head shots and to add depth and interest to a picture.

Get Set, Lock Down, SHUT UP!

If a picture is worth a thousand words, then a talking videographer is worth the price of a bad joke. Listen to the pictures you're recording: can you hear the sound of birds chirping, children laughing, kites whooshing and brooks babbling? If all you hear is yourself narrating, you just ruined one of the most important parts of your video story: NAT SOT (NATural Sound On Tape).

I once shot a news story on how the California drought years were ruining the natural habitat of rare fish in the mighty Kings River. While shooting my B-roll, the reporter on the story kept up a continuous dialog with the Parks Service representative we interviewed earlier. Later, the reporter asked for sound full of the once roaring but now babbling river, and all I had was her chattering. Instead of a babbling river, I used her babbling conversation as my NAT SOT full volume, and she learned her lesson. You can enhance any story, documentary, or vacation video with the sound all around us, or ruin it with babbling ... well, people.

Following interviews, news shooters and documentarians will often record a minute of "room noise" or outside noise to use as "sound full" (recorded full volume) without narration, or sound under to enhance the ambience of the scene. Stop and listen, really listen, to the silence, and you'll hear it's full of noise, from computers and air-conditioning inside, to the distant barking beagle or lawn mower buzzing outside. When shooting, always remember to hear, not just see, the picture, and use it appropriately. Be aware that the air-conditioning or barking dog might ruin your video, but used right, it could also enhance the story.

Figure 40-3 *In video, as in most visual arts, less is more, and too much information can lead to a busy, confusing look.*

Edit Thyself

Oh, this is my biggie against myself. It's hard to edit down your favorite scenes. Think about it this way: Remember those times when you've looked through someone's collection of still photographs? You quickly flip through some, pause over others, and pass by the blurry close-up of the photographer's foot. You naturally pass some shots with nary a glance, and spend a great deal of time with others. You are editing. In addition, let's face it, some still shots are accidental, and if the photographer needs to explain, "oh, that was a mistake ..." then he should have "edited" them out before he handed them to you. The same goes for editing video. Less is more. As hard as it is, remember to always leave them wanting more, not waiting for the end(less) credit roll so they can bolt for the bar.

Lost in Translation

This one drives me so batty it's made me scream at the TV like a crazed idiot. Producers of some local commercials, bless their sometimes low-budget hearts, try too hard to throw in every trick in their effect banks and overlay video over video over video so badly that you have no idea what the product is that they're selling.

Remember this, if you're laying one stream of video over another, don't compound the frenzy by using shots of moving video moving all over the place, and don't use busy complicated video clips.

Remember the KISS rule: Keep It Simple, Spielberg.

Burned Out

We're easily sated with the overused cheesy effects in 1980s sitcoms, but is anyone else starting to feel the same way every time you see the "Ken Burns" effect? You'll either see every tracking and zooming on every still, or they track waaaay too quickly, especially when panning, thus losing the subtlety and beauty of the effect.

I love the effect, if done correctly. If you do zoom in on picture "A," then you should begin your next shot tight on picture "B" and zoom out. This is a lot less jarring to the viewer, and has a more fluid flow. If you're tracking and zooming to a particular spot in the picture, don't track too quickly. The original reason for this effect is that going from a moving picture to a still shot has an abruptness that bothers the eye. But editors have now so overused the pan-and-zoom that audiences want to yell, "Enough, already ... you're NO Ken Burns!" A simple dissolve sometimes is all the effect you need, and subtlety is the key to good pan-and-zoom.

Walk Don't Run. Hey, Don't Walk Either!

Some people just can't seem to settle down and ... well ... shoot. Anyone can record events as they happen in front of a camera. Just turn on the camera, press "record" and wave it around. But if you're chronicling the events of the world around you, you should NOT be a part of the action. Walking down the street, waving the camera back and forth, gathers nothing good, and loses the essence of the event. Settle down and record from a distance. Short, far, it doesn't matter. Sure, an occasional POV (Point of View) shot is fun, and putting the camera into the action makes for more interesting video, but not every shot.

Even worse is what I call the Waving Camera Syndrome. This looks like an indecisive "which way did he go, Joe, which way did he go," shot. I've seen news photographers do this, too. The shooter follows the action, then sees something else in his peripheral vision and swishes over to that, only to decide that the first shot was better after all, then swishes back. Unless he's shooting a one-camera baseball game where the action happens all at once all over the field, he just ruined both shots. Professional videographers know when it's proper to swish quickly from shot to shot. They always begin each shot from a steady still position, then swish to follow the action, ending the shot at a still position. It gives the eye the chance to settle down before the next clip. Learn to make a decision, follow through with the shot, then quickly frame up, compose and focus for the next shot.

Figure 40-4 *Video "footage"—shots of your feet when you thought the camcorder was off—are a common mistake of the beginning videographer.*

It's not that hard and it makes for a much more visually pleasing video.

And Finally

Keep the zooming to a minimum. Just because your camcorder has a zoom control, doesn't mean you should always use it. The stationary shot with the subject matter supplying the action is most often all the movement you need. When you do zoom or pan the camera, start and end your shot with a still shot.

Of course, our **Videomaker** readers are savvy shooters and all know these simple rules, so you can pass these tips to your next door neighbor, Uncle Buck or the parents at school afflicted with the waving camera syndrome. Meanwhile, keep your eyes and ears open and clean up these production peeves for us, OK? That way we can start picking on something else.

41

Makeup and Wardrobe for Video

Carolyn Miller

Though many people equate makeup and wardrobe with high-budget Hollywood productions, even the most modest video can greatly benefit by simple, inexpensive attention in this area. Wardrobe and makeup (this includes hair, as well) are closely tied to the whole look and style of a piece. They help tell the story and offer important visual clues about the characters—whether they are actors, spokespersons or interview subjects. They can subtly but significantly enhance your presentation—or, if you haven't done your homework—seriously undermine it.

Even if you intend to shoot your subjects in all their raw, unblemished uniqueness, disregarding these "vanity" concerns can turn your searingly honest piece into an unintentional comedy. Do you really want your audience distracted by a bald head that gleams like a light beacon, by patterns on shirts that take on an animated life of their own, or by clanky jewelry, jarring color schemes, or faces that look like floating heads? If not, then you're going to have to devote some time to makeup and wardrobe.

Planning Ahead

Like every other aspect of making video, it's a good idea to think about wardrobe and makeup well in advance of production. As you envision your completed video, ask yourself what overall look you're striving for (for example, glamorous, upscale and sophisticated; or hip, young and wacky). Clothing style, colors, makeup and hair should all support this look. Susan Stroh, a Los Angeles–based pro who over the years has worn many hats on industrials and documentaries (producer, director, script supervisor, writer), calls this "image positioning," a term that is borrowed from the world of corporate marketing.

Even if you're using real people in your video, as opposed to actors, you'll want to make sure they are dressed in a way that fits their role in the piece. You probably don't want your CEO to be wearing jeans, or your auto mechanic in a suit and tie. But then again, your concept may call for exactly that. Just make sure you convey your vision to your subjects.

Joan Owens, a veteran Hollywood documentary producer, director and writer (TV's *Hunt for Amazing Treasures* and *Zoo Life with Jack Hanna*) feels the goal of documentaries is to capture people as they usually are, in clothing that reflects the flavor of their specific world. "Sometimes people want to make a good impression for the camera," she notes, "and dress more elegantly than they normally would."

Joan encourages her subjects to wear appropriate clothing, and also makes sure they have wardrobe changes for all the scenes they'll be in. For instance, while making a documentary about the recovery of a Civil War submarine, one of her subjects needed an outfit for an on-camera interview and a very different type of outfit for a scene on a fishing boat to re-create an event from the past—and both scenes were to be shot on the same day. Sometimes, though, you'll want one of your performers to wear the same outfit throughout the shoot. Joan points out that Jack Hanna, as host of his wildlife series, always wore a safari jacket. It not only clearly reflected the theme of the series, but also made it easier to mix and match scenes in the editing room.

Special Considerations

One important wardrobe consideration is whether or not you'll be shooting chroma-key scenes, to electronically "transport" your talent to a different set. If your chroma-key background is blue or green (sometimes called "shooting bluescreen" or "shooting greenscreen") you want to make sure your talent is not wearing the same color garment. Otherwise, there will be a gaping hole in the talent's clothing, filled in electronically by the chroma-key set.

You should also scout your locations in terms of your overall wardrobe approach. You'll want your talent to be dressed in colors that will harmonize with the set and not clash with it. And outfits should be thematically appropriate to the environment, too. For instance, if one of your locations is a rough-hewn hunting lodge, your talent

will look better in a casual suede jacket than in a tailored business suit.

During the planning stage, also give some thought to the physical appearance of your on-screen personalities. If you're aware of facial features that may present special problems—acne scars, closely set eyes, a very round face—you'll want to make sure you've got items in your kit that can handle this. It doesn't mean, though, that you should attempt to turn them into something they're not.

Greg Braun, a Chicago-based Director of Photography who owns his own business, G.B. Productions, specializes in high-end work for major corporations and has strong views on this subject. "I'm not trying to re-create the person in any way," he states emphatically. "But I do want to enhance their appearance—to make them look their best."

If you realize you're going to be faced with makeup challenges that are beyond your abilities, it may be necessary to call in a professional. This may be especially true if you're doing a fictional piece. Both makeup and wardrobe can be extremely demanding in fictional dramas, particularly stories set in a different era. In projects like this, specialists can be a big asset. This doesn't have to be as expensive as it sounds, as long as you're resourceful.

Producer-director David Phyfer, based in Geneva, IL., has a number of ideas about how to get assistance without spending a fortune. His company, Stage Fright Productions, makes educational and children's videos on less than lavish budgets. David suggests that community businesses might help out. A local store might offer clothing, costumes or shoes in return for a scene set in their shop; a beauty salon might provide hair or makeup services on the same basis. You might also be able to get wardrobe items in return for guaranteeing product placement in the video, or an on-screen credit.

Wardrobe Do's and Don'ts

Once you've decided on your wardrobe approach, you'll want to go over it with your talent, since in most cases they'll be using their own clothing. Here are a few examples of what your talent should not wear:

- fabrics that wrinkle easily, like linen

- baggy clothes (they make people look heavier than they really are)

- shiny or noisy jewelry; dangling earrings

- silk (it rustles, causing sound problems, and shows sweat stains quickly)

- hats, unless necessary for the identity of the character (they cast shadows)

- fabrics with tight patterns, like checks, stripes, herringbone and houndstooth (they create an unstable, vibrating, jumpy effect called a moiré pattern)

- clothes and shoes that display brand names or commercial logos

- outfits in the latest style (fads will quickly date your video)

- deeply saturated colors, especially red (video doesn't handle them well and they tend to bleed when duplicated)

- bright white or extremely dark colors

This last point deserves special attention. While it's true that video cameras are able to deal with sharp contrasts in tone better than formerly, it's still challenging to light someone wearing bright white or very dark clothes. White, for instance, picks up all the light, and to compensate, faces tend to be underexposed.

Joan Owens recounts an incident illustrating the problem with white. She was writing a documentary set in an exotic foreign locale, and the cameraman shot a great scene of the American ambassador riding a motorcycle through the city streets wearing a white tee-shirt—"a wonderful Marlon Brando image." But when the footage came back, everything was too dark, virtually unusable, to compensate for the white shirt.

Extremely dark colors are equally difficult, and sometimes create bizarre effects. Los Angeles producer-director Bob Silburg,

who's done hundreds of PSAs (Public Service Announcements) and short videos, ran into this problem with a PSA featuring Jack Lemmon. The subject matter was quite serious, so he'd asked his star to wear a dignified navy blue blazer. Unfortunately, the office they were shooting in had dark walls, and as a result, Jack Lemmon "… looked like a floating head without a body." Luckily, Bob was able to solve the problem by tweaking the backlighting.

For wardrobe colors, David Phyfer recommends pastels and pale shades—light blue shirts and gray jackets, for instance. "Avoid sharp contrasts between dark and light," he advises, "and pull your colors together as much as possible."

When it comes to fabrics, natural materials like wool and cotton shoot much better than synthetics. Susan Stroh, for one, pays close attention to fabrics and textures, believing they help convey the message of the video—tweed and corduroy for an earthy look, for example, and damask for a luxurious look. She feels simple clothes work best for women, and are the least distracting. She prepares a detailed wardrobe checklist for her talent, and instructs them to bring duplicates, or near duplicates, of shirts and blouses, in case of spills or stains.

For most productions, it's a good idea to have talent bring three completely different outfits, including shoes and accessories, to provide ample choices. Men should bring a selection of ties, and women might be asked to bring some scarves.

On the Set

Most women in your cast will probably apply their own makeup and do their own hair. They should be encouraged to strive for a natural look, which works best for a video camera, unlike heavily exaggerated makeup, which works better for the stage. A good foundation is important, because it covers blemishes and evens out color. But if a woman is inexperienced in applying it, watch out for makeup lines around the eyes and jawline, where the foundation leaves off and the skin begins. You might also need to add some blush to emphasize her cheek bones or chin, or eyeliner to make her eyes look larger.

Though men need makeup, too, some are uncomfortable with the idea and even professional actors rarely apply their own. Greg Braun, who shoots many top executives, is careful to make sure none of their subordinates are nearby while he's doing their makeup—the last thing they want is an audience. And he jokes a little to put them at ease. "This is what made Charles Bronson so handsome," he might say as he dabs on the foundation. He works fast, completing the job in two to three minutes. Bald heads—"chrome domes"—are a common challenge. He uses a fat makeup brush and loose powder to remove the shine. Greg carries three different shades of powder and three shades of foundation to cover the range in skin tones.

Once your talent is made up, dressed and ready to go, don't forget to check them out in a color monitor before you shoot. You're sure to catch things you hadn't noticed with your naked eye—smudged mascara, a crooked collar, or a moiré effect on a tie. But after you've made the necessary adjustments, don't think your makeup and wardrobe duties are over. As you shoot, be alert for wrinkled shirts, bunched up jackets and faded lipstick. Fly-away hair and glint from buttons and eyeglasses are extremely common problems. And then,

always, there is facial shine—oil and sweat brought on by the heat and tension. But before you add more makeup, blot off the moisture and oil with a tissue. Otherwise, you might get caking and streaks.

For fly-away hair, experts recommend spraying your hands with hair spray and lightly patting the hair, rather than spraying the hair directly, which can result in an unnatural "crispy" look. Shiny buttons and jewelry can be dealt with easily with dulling spray, although be cautious with costume jewelry, which could be damaged. Eyeglasses are a tougher problem. Dulling spray could ruin them, and there aren't any other good substitutes. You might have to take care of the glint on glasses by lighting adjustments or re-positioning the talent.

Finally, pay close attention to continuity, making sure wardrobe and makeup are consistent from scene to scene. Carelessness here can give your video a sloppy look. If possible, have an assistant keep notes as you shoot. Is there always a hanky in that pocket? How is the scarf draped? Is there a lock of hair tucked behind the right ear?

Clearly, there's a great deal to consider in terms of makeup and wardrobe, and some of it is quite minute. But each detail contributes to the overall quality of your production. Yes, your mother may have tried to convince you that beauty is only skin deep. But when you're making videos, the visual appearance of your performers is hardly a superficial matter.

42
Let's Make a Documentary

Randal K. West

To Dream a Possible Dream
Few other communication forms have the power to reveal a unique perspective, capture imagination and even motivate change. In this article, you'll discover how you can move your story from dream to distribution.

Walk onto the working set of any television production studio and almost every person on the crew has a documentary they are just posting, getting ready to shoot or trying to fund. Why? Because everyone from the Director of Photography to the Key Grip has a story, they feel compelled to share with a larger audience.

True, the percentage of would-be documentary filmmakers is potentially greater within the film/television community than among antique car salesmen, but there are many people from all walks of life who want to share their story or a significant piece of history through documentary filmmaking. In today's world dominated by high tech gizmos and reality TV, documentaries have never been more popular and the equipment to shoot and edit them more accessible and inexpensive.

Is Your Story Compelling?

The founder of our agency and I were approached one day by a reasonably well-known and respected individual in our community. He wanted to pitch a documentary idea to us for possible production by our company. The man went on to explain that although he still seemed to exist as a "regular" guy in our community, since his divorce he had lost everything and was living between his car and an abandoned building. We asked many questions, but despite his having managed to hide his status from the rest of the community, there just wasn't a strong enough plot line to hang a documentary on. We felt horrible for the guy but there was no universal truth, no significant lesson to be learned that we felt warranted filming a documentary.

Two months later a woman named Patti Miller came to my office and described how 40 years ago as a Drake University junior, she had traveled to Mississippi to participate in the Freedom Summer, in order to help African Americans sign up to vote. Patti, "a lily-white Iowa girl" was fundamentally affected by her experience, an experience shared by others who had participated. She pointed out that the fortieth anniversary of Freedom Summer was approaching and many of the volunteers were now in their fifties and sixties. Patti's story was a part of history that could easily start to slip away and the 40-year anniversary presented a seminal opportunity to share the story. The story moved me, and my crew and I headed to the South to start filming. Patti's story had universal appeal and importance. We decided that we would tell this story of national racism, politically controlled hatred and the individuals who fought oppression through the very personal eyes of one Iowa undergraduate female, alone and out of her home state, for the first time in her life.

Tell Me a Story

What's your story? Is it universally applicable? Is it simply a slice of life anecdote, but very funny or very profound? Would someone who doesn't know you care or benefit from becoming aware of your story? Is it a scholarly piece addressing an issue or topic discovered through research and others should be made aware of? Could others benefit by seeing the world through your eyes, watching you follow a particular person or group of people around as they do what they do? If you can find a way to turn your personal experience into a universally shared or recognized experience, you have the foundation for building a documentary. At this point, identify your eventual audience and keep them in mind as your documentary morphs toward its final form.

Putting It Together, Bit by Bit

So, you've got your story, now what? Old fashioned as it may seem, try to get all

Figure 42-2 *You may not have used index cards since grade school but they are a great tool to help you and your creative team pre-visualize the project.*

the elements of your story written down in simple outline form using 3 × 5 index cards. Keep it loose, put each element on one 3 × 5 card so you can shuffle and re-shuffle them. Lay your story out and look at it. Examine all your possible elements. (Of course, you can do this with a computer too, but the index cards work well for sorting out thoughts and ideas.)

If you have old 8-mm film from your youth, log it and list it as an element. Do you have old photos or access to old newspaper articles? Who are the people you want to interview and what subject matter will they cover? Record every element and every topic on a card and separate the cards with only one topic or element per card. Lay them out in an order that makes sense to you and use this to create your first outline. *Keep these cards!* You will use them over and over again.

Figure 42-3 How will the finished piece look (or how do you hope it will look)? Storyboards or large sketches will further help you communicate with your crew to assure everything proceeds as smooth as possible once the camera starts rolling.

Figure 42-4 A detailed budget is an extremely important part of your pre-production planning. You don't want to be halfway through your project to realize the funding is depleted. Factor in every possible expenditure and then add a 10% contingency.

Dramatic Structure

Every story needs three things, a beginning, middle and end. You must define where these points exist in your story. Does your story have a great hook that will involve the audience from the outset and hold them? Is it most effective when told chronologically or should it jump around in time? Will your story be narrated, will you write the narration or will the subjects you interview tell the entire story in their own words? Will it be a combination? You must discover what is most dramatic and engaging about your story and tell it in a way that highlights those points.

Tone and Treatment

How do you want your story heard? Do you want to create a formal documentary with voice-over narration and drops to interviews and B-roll, or do you want to do a cinema vérité piece where the camera seems to just exist as it captures everything around it? Many documentaries these days have the raw reality look of the *Cops* TV show with hand-held cameras loosely carried on shoulders. Other documentaries use guerilla tactics; they surprise people by simply shoving a microphone in their face. Michael Moore is famous for this.

An Emotional Center

Regardless of your choice of treatment or subject matter, almost every documentary needs an emotional center. The audience needs someone or a group of "someones" to care about. A message or idea is not enough. The characters in your documentary will carry your plotline as strongly as your storyline. Very few documentaries based solely on intellectualism succeed. Give your documentary some heart and some emotion. Give us someone to root for.

Formulating a Plan

As soon as you have determined the structure and treatment of your documentary, you are ready to take your outline and create a projected timeline and budget. In order to create a budget you must decide the format in which you want to shoot your project. Will you shoot film or video? What type? How often will you need sound? Will you be lighting with instruments or will you be shooting in available light? How many days and in how many locations will you need to shoot? How big of a crew and how much equipment will you need? How long and with what means will you edit?

After you answer these questions, you will be in the best position to get close to a bid for creating your project.

Go Find Some Funding

Collect your outline, timeline, bid and distribution plan (distribution will be fully covered in Part III of this series but it must be fully fleshed out in your pre-production planning if you wish to raise funds from someone other than your parents or credit cards). Create a printed proposal using these elements to pass for your fund-raising efforts to support your project. Documentary film budgets can run the gamut from low-budget to multi-million dollar ventures, but many make it on a very limited amount of hard capital. Documentary filmmakers as a group are notoriously successful at getting "sweat equity" from people who volunteer their equipment and their expertise for a stock in the project. There will always be some hard costs though, and if you are not in a position to cover them yourself you should see an attorney and get help setting up a simple system that will enable you to accept funds on behalf of your not for profit project. Some filmmakers seek financial support by asking existing non-profit organizations to sponsor their project, then take in the funds, and allocate them back to the filmmaker.

FULFILLMENT OF THE DREAM

Considered an art form by many, documentary video production has its own special challenges and rewards. Now let's explore how to plan your approach, find your subject and begin the process of bringing your vision to fruition.

Once you've chosen your topic for your documentary, you still have many choices facing you. How do you want to approach your subject? Will your documentary

Figure 42-6

seem to have a passive feel? Will the story be told by the people who are interviewed as the story comes out in their own way, or will an aggressive interviewer (Michael Moore) drive the interviews, or will you mix interviews with written narration to be delivered in voice-over? Will your documentary be a balance view of an issue where both sides are equally and fairly explored? What criterion should help you make these decisions?

Point of View

Whose story is it really? You can choose to not have a "voice" in your documentary and make it "news" style and as impartial as possible or you can choose the individual or group that is most affected by your story and let it be their story. This doesn't mean you can't explore both sides of an issue, it just means that you are going to put a real face on one side of the issue and allow personalization of the story. A compelling documentary should not only be factually correct but it should be engaging and emotionally compelling. You can also personalize both sides of a story. We have said for years in the advertising business, "Don't just sell the steak, sell the sizzle." Find the sizzle in your story because that is what is going to eventually get you distribution and remember that even a personal story should have some universal appeal.

Sound Issues

Never take sound for granted. Nothing ruins a video that is shot on a budget quicker than bad sound. I always fight to

Figure 42-7 *Sound matters. Pay attention to your setup and shoot on location for great emotional reactions.*

get a sound person who is solely responsible for sound because it is that important to me. If we truly can't have the extra body I will listen for sound as I direct as I don't feel a camera operator can split his attention well enough to both shoot and listen effectively at the same time. That said, there have been times when I have both shot and monitored sound, you just increase your percentage chance of having a problem. Use a lapel mic on the person you are interviewing and if possible put a pole mic on the other channel right out of your shot. Blending these two microphones together in post will give you a rounder and fuller sound. If you only have access to one mic make sure the sound is as pristine as possible. Listen to the room before you shoot and turn off air changers if you can. Also take the time to record room tone (everyone sitting in the room making no noise for 30 seconds), or outside ambient sound, as this will help your editor remove background noise in post.

Shooting

If you don't know the camera well, you can probably survive mostly on factory settings. You do want to be aware of the iris setting and watch out for backlight that becomes overwhelming. Be sure to white balance every time you change locations. When in doubt keep your shots

simple and clean. As you gain confidence you can shoot "walk and talks" but when you're starting just find a safe, pretty environment and shoot.

Conducting Interviews

I rarely have a subject speak directly to the camera. Unless they are doing a direct appeal to the people watching the video, they should not speak directly to the lens. Sit directly next to the lens either to the left or right with your eyes at the same height as the lens and have them speak directly to you. Don't feel like you have to just jump right into the subject of the interview. If you don't know them, spend some time getting to know them. Ask about what they like to do. Find out who they are and then lead them into the subject you want. The cheapest component of your project is the videotape so let it roll. This is a technique to make them feel more at home in front of the camera but sometimes you also discover gems you didn't think you'd find. Also, *listen!* Don't be so wrapped up in the questions that you have planned to ask that you don't listen to what is actually being said. Ask unscripted follow up questions and closely explore their reactions. Let them control some of the content of your interview. Be very open to finding a surprise and letting it blossom into something wonderful.

B-Roll

Keep track of everything your interviewer says and keep in mind possible B-roll shots that could highlight what is being said. A-roll is when the camera is on the subject and the words are coming out of her mouth. B-roll is footage without sound that is shot to break up the talking head portions of an interview and is inserted in place of the talking head during the post-production process.

Documentaries many times rely on old pictures or licensed stock footage but

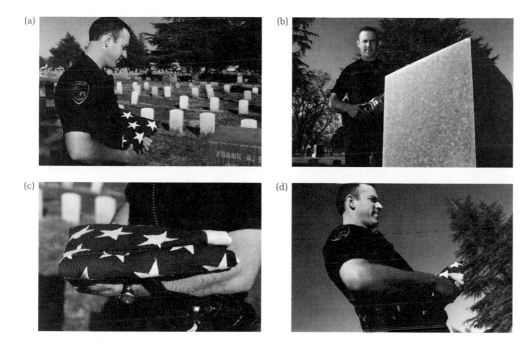

Figure 42-8 *Shoot plenty of cutaways and angles. Your B-roll shots will be invaluable for insertion over your interview audio.*

those elements can be expensive even for smaller projects and the licensing can limit how and where you can show the finished piece. Reenactments are a way to create footage that can help fill the needs of the project. If you are doing a piece about the sixties, you can find old civic buildings that still look as if they are in the sixties. Go to someone's attic or to a thrift store, locate appropriate wardrobe and create your own footage. You can pull this footage into sepia tones or make it black and white in post. You can blend this created footage with the old photos you can find and it will give the piece a sense of movement.

Figure 42-9 *Go back to the locations where pivotal events happened within your story to give your audience some additional perspective.*

Discovery In the Moment

If your documentary is taking a person back to an event or a moment that changed his/her life, if you can afford it, don't just talk about it but go there. Shoot the first time they see this place after so many years and let them just describe what and how they feel. If there is a significant person who helped them at one time, don't just talk about it, shoot them meeting, and get the energy of that exact moment.

Finding Your Vision

Every documentary should begin as a blank sheet of paper or a canvas to paint upon. What colors you use and what format

Figure 42-10

should come from a combination of you as an artist and the content of your story. Content should always dictate form but you are in this equation as well and it will be your passion that drives this project. Five filmmakers could attempt the same topic for a documentary and each would mostly likely create a piece that only resembles the others by subject matter and that is as it should be. Find what excites you then find your own means to express it.

What's left? Distribution. *How* do you get that video seen? First determine *Who* is your audience and *Where* they will most likely go to view your Masterpiece.

SHARE THE DREAM

You found the "story" that needed to be told, you scraped together enough funding to shoot and post it and now you have an end product that you and your small circle of best friends think is great ... but now what?

Festivals are one of the first places you should look to get your project noticed. Start by building lists of potential places to show your film and group these into at least two categories: 1) Festivals that are well known and often lead to distribution. 2) Festivals that are grouped by production type or topic, i.e., an all female film festival if your work was all done by females, or a film festival that celebrates stories from the south for documentary about Freedom Summer in Mississippi. Most festivals will involve some cost to enter and you need to count this as a loss even if your film doesn't make the selection cut.

Your Own Backyard

Look locally. There are at least 15 film festivals each year in Iowa that feature projects created within the state. Contact your state (or even county) Film Commission and get a list of all the local film festivals. If you can, speak with someone in the film office and tell him or her about your film. Their job is to promote films produced in state, so allow them to offer their suggestions for local distribution and attention.

Public Television

Accessibility to public television will vary greatly from state to state and even regionally. Iowa, for example, has a very developed Public Television programming department that is very accommodating in terms of providing information and support for our documentaries. They even offered seed monies for one of our projects, but we decided to self-fund and maintain complete rights until the project was completed. They did, however, refer us to ITVS (Independent Television Service), which is a service that assists filmmakers and showcases independent producers.

Unfortunately, much of what you have heard about the state of Public Television is probably true. They still seek first-quality programming and though open to documentaries, they are no longer the land of "milk and money." Public Television has become quite dependent upon grant and gift monies to support project funding.

Cable Distribution and Television Syndication

What cable outlet or Broadcast channel is the best possible match for your project? As more and more channels become available, the appeal of each channel becomes more selective and niche oriented. Many cable channels run a high level of documentary programming and much of it is tied to a

(a)

(b)

(c)

Figure 42-11 *A satellite uplink sends video to a satellite, a microwave dish sends video to a TV transmitter and movie theaters send video straight to the viewer.*

very specific topic, (E Entertainment, Style, The History Channel, Bravo). Some Cable Channels are connected to entire cable networks. The Discovery Channel is a flagship cable station connected to 14 other cable stations including Animal Planet, The Learning Channel, The Travel Channel, and FitTV. If you contact the Discovery Channel distribution office they can send you the required forms for submission and will help move your material to the proper cable outlet.

The Internet

The Internet is exploding with showcase opportunities. Many Websites allow for very extensive streaming video. Does your project relate to or help clarify some aspect of someone else's Website? Could a portion of your documentary play on their Website via streaming video and then be offered for purchase? Do you have your own Website where you can sell your end product? If not, and your documentary is one that people might purchase if they knew it existed, you probably should be selling it through a Website. Make sure the site is clean and simple and has a shopping cart that allows others to purchase your documentary in a variety of either downloadable formats or DVD.

Vidcasting

Vidcasting (also known as video podcasting, vodcasting and other names) is different than streaming. It is a method of transmitting up to broadcast quality video via an RSS feed [Really Simple Syndication] to a computer. This method of video sharing provides a low-cost, broad and immediate marketplace for video distribution by enabling users to receive continuous, high quality updates directly to their personal computer. Independent producers and filmmakers can benefit greatly from this technology as it enables them to cut out the middleman and make their videos instantly accessible to a wide audience at TV broadcast quality.

Independent filmmaking, especially documentary filmmaking, is by nature a challenging area of video production and finding a viable distributor presents a special challenge all of its own. If you are new to the documentary arena, this is an opportunity for others to see examples of your work and for your exposure to networking and marketing opportunities.

If you are ready to start selling or marketing your work you can create a sample or a trailer of your documentary and encourage those who see your sample to go to your Website to purchase the entire piece.

Educational Video

An Internet search for educational videos will bring up a substantial list of

Figure 42-12 *A well-designed Website may be the best tool available to get your project in front of thousands of eyes across the globe.*

catalogues and services that specialize in videos and documentaries appropriate for classroom and educational purposes. If your documentary qualifies as a possible option in one of these catalogues, it would certainly be worth further investigation. Be prepared to create a study-guide for your documentary if they request one.

Finding Funds for Distribution

Fund-raising to help find distribution outlets and marketing opportunities for your project is different than looking for "seed" money. You already have a relatively finished end product and now you simply need help finding ways to get people to see it. In our small town, there are many known businesses that routinely give to special projects. The cost of underwriting the marketing for your documentary will probably not be much more expensive than underwriting a good-sized event for your town or for an organization.

Take your outline, your budget and a one-page synopsis of your project which includes not only your subject matter but why your "subject matters," along with possible areas for distribution to the meeting. If you can create a short 3–4 minute DVD that can function as a sample reel of your documentary, it can be a very motivating portion of your pitch. Take a portable DVD player to the meeting just in case. Have a detailed marketing plan for your project that shows all the festivals you plan to enter, all the ways you want to present your documentary and the costs for this exposure.

Figure 42-13 *Organizations such as the Foundation Center can assist video producers with fund-raising right from the Internet. (www.foundationcenter.org.)*

You don't need a formal business plan at this point, unless you are truly attempting to raise a substantial amount of money. If that is the case you will need to create a formal business plan that includes projections for how the money will be returned to those who invest. Many documentary filmmakers have been very successful at raising dollars in support of their

endeavor while promising no more than a credit listed at the start and finish of the documentary. PBS won't allow much more than a simple acknowledgement of support. You do, however, need to know how you plan to accept the funds if an individual or a company offers them to you. If PBS partners with us on one of our projects, anyone wishing to donate to the project designates the funds as a gift or grant to Iowa PBS. PBS then re-allocates the funds back to the project. Sometimes the organization which functions as the "pass-through" will charge a "processing" percentage to cover its time and effort.

Last Thoughts

We have now traveled the full course of documentary filmmaking. We have discussed finding a subject, defining your style, the technical requirements for bringing that vision to video and how to market that video to a group of people. Like any artist or craftsman, you are now equipped with the necessary tools of your trade. I look forward to one day hearing a breathless documentary filmmaker at the Academy Awards stating how an article in *Videomaker* Magazine helped get you started. Hey, I can dream too you know!

Sidebar 1

Budgeting

Once you have made the initial choices about your documentary you will need to create a budget that reflects accurate estimates of the costs involved. First estimate how many days of shooting it will take to film your documentary. Divide the total into days when you will record sound and days when you will just shoot images. In the industry, they call this type of film/video budgeting as defining your "Day of Days." Create a proposed set of crew costs for both types of days. Even if your crew is volunteer, you will still need to consider food, travel and ancillary costs. Next create a list of equipment for each type of day and project any "real" or "hard" costs. Determine if you will have to rent support equipment (sound, lights, etc.,) and get estimates for this equipment that you can put in your budget. Will you have to get permits or insurance to shoot in any of your locations? Include these and any projected expendables, such as videotape, in your projected budget.

If you plan to use much of your own equipment (camera editing system) and these will not constitute "hard" costs in your budget, create an "in-kind" contribution section of the budget that demonstrates the savings created by your "sweat-equity" (volunteered hours) and owned equipment. This is helpful when soliciting contributions to cover the remaining "hard costs" because potential investors can see exactly where you allocate their contributions. Create a post-production budget and be sure to include both editing time and costs for licensing stock footage, existing film footage, photos or music.

Video/Film budget templates exist on the Internet that can help you create your budget, just be sure to eliminate any line items that don't apply to your project.

Sidebar 2

Why Doc?

Documentary filmmaking is the art of telling real stories in imaginative, entertaining and insightful ways. A documentary can retell an old story with a new twist, or present a never before heard of issue, person, place or event that has universal appeal. It can be fair and impartial, presenting both sides of a split issue, or pure propaganda. A documentary provides its audience with an intimate look into the lives and worlds of the people and places captured therein. There are documentaries that explore major historical events and ancient civilizations, documentaries that take us from the bottom of the ocean to the top of Mt. Everest, works that can show us the lives of a local quilting group, or teach us to ride the most powerful and impressive ocean waves. Documentary filmmaking is about finding a subject that you are passionate about and using the medium of video/film to share that passion with a larger audience. The key to finding a good subject for your documentary is starting with a personal experience or opinion that you know is shared or opposed by others, and finding a way to educate your audience about that subject in an entertaining and thought provoking way.

Sidebar 3

Release Me

Devising an effective paper trail for your project is not the most fun you'll ever have as a documentary filmmaker, but it is an essential step for avoiding potentially costly legal suits. It doesn't matter if everyone appearing in your documentary is a friend or family member, you should still have them sign a simple release allowing you to use their Name and Likeness at no charge to you. I have witnessed too many cases where someone who was fine with being shot initially, but insisted later upon edits or complete removal from the finished product. The way to protect yourself is to get a release before you shoot them.

"I hereby consent and authorize the use of my name and likeness, which may appear in any film, videotape or still photograph released by (you and your address), in connection with the distribution of an as yet untitled documentary (The Documentary).

I hereby authorize (you) and/or his/her assignees to use, reproduce, sell, exhibit, broadcast and distribute any promotional materials containing my name and likeness for the purpose of The Documentary.

I hereby waive any right to inspect or approve the finished videotape, soundtrack or advertising copy or printed matter that may be used in connection therewith or to the eventual use that it might be applied."

You will need each individual to state whether he or she is over or under 18 or 21 years of age, depending upon the legal age of adulthood in your state. If he or she is under that age, you will need to have a parent or legal guardian undersign the release. He or she should provide you with name, address, date of birth and signature and you should have a witness present at the signing. Some producers also state directly in the release that there is "now nor will their ever be any recompense for this recording" if that is in fact the case. I realize that this sounds a little like overkill but these kinds of releases aren't often read before the shoot, but they may save your project down the road.

Sidebar 4

The Purpose of a Documentary Is:

Depicts the real lives and opinions of the filmmaker and/or his subjects
Offers a fresh perspective on an old problem, or presents an entirely new issue
Communicates a shared experience in an intimate way
Universal accessibility
Motivates people to think and take action
Entertains
Niche filmmaking, speaks to a specific audience determined by a shared interest
Teaches audiences
Arranges perspective to support or refute one or both sides of a split issue
Real
Yet dramatic
Follows local and global politics, events or characters
Insightful and imaginative
Looking at life
Medium of video/film

43
How to Use Available Light

Garret C. Maynard

If you show up on a shoot or have a spontaneous need to roll tape with no light kit: relax. Today's cameras and their ever-improving contrast ratios and light sensitive electronics are very forgiving. However, if you're not so lucky to have the ideal situation in which to make use of the sensitive electronics, here are some tips to help you get that shot and look like a pro.

Available Light Indoors

Indoor lighting scenarios are innumerable, but, for the most part, you will be dealing with sunlight and incandescent mixed sources in the day.

The first tip is a no-brainer: don't place your subject in front of a bright window. Move the subject to a place where the light source (window) falls on the front. If that is impossible, frame the shot tighter so most of the window is not visible. In most cases, the auto iris of the camera will adjust as you remove the light source so exposure will not give you an undesirable backlight or silhouette effect. Turn on as many lights as possible to offset the stronger sunlight behind the subject. Use the manual aperture setting to counteract the camera's desire to overcompensate. In situations where you have a choice to use sunlight or incandescent, use the former. Sunlight is more colorful than the house lights. Remember to white balance for the dominant light source and, if the light varies a lot in the shot, write down the f-stop for the lightest and darkest spots in the shot and then, using the manual setting, place your final f-stop in between the two readings. When all else fails, use the backlight button, but be proactive. Make the light work for you. Don't let the light make you work.

At night with incandescent light sources, you'll have more freedom to move both the subject and the light. Again, it's a good idea to keep the light source out of the frame, but this time you don't have to compromise framing, just move the light. Another reason to remove the light from the frame is because table and floor lamps (practicles) sometimes leave a halo around the subject when placed in the frame. The light falling on the subject should be the brightest spot in the frame, with as few deep shadows as possible. Try to mold the light across from one side of the subject to the other so the difference between lighter and darker helps create the illusion of three dimensions.

Figure 43-1 Don't place your subject in front of a bright window. Frame the shot tighter so most of the window is not visible.

Available Light Outdoors: Nighttime

We've all come across the difficulties of lighting outdoors at night. If all you have is the porch light, try to bounce the light or at least remove the light source from the frame. Don't place the subject directly below the light, this will cause harsh shadows under the eyes, nose and chin. Headlights from a car can work but they are hard and will act like spots: try bouncing them also to diffuse the light. I've seen flashlights bounced off clothing work, but this is really tricky. Moonlight is unlikely to work well, no matter how bright it looks to your eyes. In any event, move your auto focus and aperture to manual. At such low light levels, the auto sensors do not work well.

Available Light Outdoors: Daytime

A sunny day is okay, but overcast is a better situation. An overcast sky throws diffused light, creates very little shadow and you can shoot all day. If there is full sun, your subject may cast deep shadows, since sunlight is very hard. The stronger and higher the sun, the deeper and more contrasty the shadows, so there's not much opportunity to create 3D molding. Try to avoid shooting from 11:00 am to 2:00pm. During this time, the sun is high and creates overhead lighting, which is very flat. In this situation put your subject under a tree in the shade, but don't show too much of the sky as background, since the dappled light under a tree will contrast strongly with the full sunlight in the background. Keep the camera angle higher so you can avoid too much bright sky or a hot background. Sunlight provides plenty of light for a reflector, however. Position your subject in the shade and then use a reflector to bounce sunlight onto your subject. This is really an ideal situation.

If you have to deal with varying light intensities, because the subject is moving, for example, set the aperture to manual, take a reading of the brightest and darkest areas and then set your f-stop or aperture in between the two. If full sunlight with a beach or snowscape setting is unavoidable, at least position your subject with the sun to the side so she doesn't have to squint directly into the sun. If available, you can bounce light from the sun with a white sheet, poster board or foam core. You don't need a big piece, just enough to illuminate the face. The upshot is to avoid sharp shadows and great contrast. Some shadow is good on people, because it results in a stronger three-dimensional look. In shooting inanimate objects, less shadow is desirable because you want to see all the detail that shadows may hide.

If the light is too hot, your camera may overexpose the shot or overcompensate in the auto mode. What you really need is a neutral density filter, even a cheap one. These gray filters don't change the quality of the light, just the intensity. They screw on to the front of your lens and come in two-stop

Figure 43-2 *To avoid having the subject washed out amongst the bright light (left), use a piece of white foam core to bounce sunlight back to the talent (right).*

Figure 43-3 *Candles can provide soft illumination in places where on-camera lights are frowned upon.*

increments. Also, if you want to shoot sky and create fuller and deeper looking images, try a polarizer, it acts like an ND filter but changes the quality of the light much like polarizing sunglasses.

Candle Power

Most of the time, you will have at least some control over your lighting. It's all in how you apply your creativity to solve the problem that will allow you to get the best exposure. These tips will help but you can come up with your own problem-solving ideas if you are thoughtfully patient.

One time, I shot a wedding in which I had only candlelight, and very little of that, during a portion of the reception. The host would not let me use my camera light. I told him I could not get a good exposure with such limited light. He shrugged his shoulders. I knew the client would be asking later why the interviews were so dark. I thought of how I could exploit the situation to solve this problem. If I could not bring light to the subjects, then I would bring the subjects to the light. I gathered as many candles as possible, put them on a single table, and then brought subjects to the table to conduct interviews. The final results were actually better, more natural and lovelier than if I had whipped out my artificial light kit.

Sidebar

Cheating with Dimmers

In an indoor situation where you have bright light from a table lamp or floor lamp, try using dimmers. Dimmers are very easy to make and you can safely wire one into an extension cord without too much trouble. If you are in a situation where the lights are bright just whip out your handy dandy home made dimmers and make that light as bright or dim as you want without the need to rearrange the furniture. The color temperature of the light will change, but as long as you white balance first, you should be OK.

44
Practical Special Effects: A Baker's Ten to Improve Your Video Visions

Bernard Wilkie

Most videographers fall into one of two groups. First, the snapshotters—people who record scenes until their tapes are full, then view the disconnected events using the search button. Second, videographers and pros, who edit their tapes and employ all the techniques and processes necessary to obtain professional results.

It's not that people in the first group are unimaginative. They may not want to assemble their pictures or lay down soundtracks, but often they do wish to add variety to their videography. Thus this chapter can serve snapshotters as well as the more advanced. This list of special effects may also remind the experts that simple solutions can be the best.

Deep Water

Children mucking about in the pool occupy many tapes. However, all the action commonly occurs above water.

More exciting footage is possible with an underwater periscope, enabling videography beneath the surface. Camcorders become underwater cameras without the need for expensive blimps or aqualung equipment.

The *periscope* is simply a rectangular box with a sheet of glass cemented into the bottom of one side. It contains two mirrors, one at the bottom, one at the top. Surface-coated mirrors provide better pictures, but even ordinary mirrors will produce good results.

Set up the periscope poolside and record events above or below water while holding the camera and peering through the viewfinder in the usual manner. Weight the device to overcome its natural buoyancy. Clamp it to something solid, like the pool steps. Those going to sea can mount the periscope on a boat or sink it into the water for shots of marine life.

Another trick to improve waterside close-ups involves the simple trick of placing a shallow tray filled with water and broken pieces of mirror below the picture. Ensure that the sun's reflections fall on or around your subjects. Then tickle the surface of the water with your fingers. Voila! The ripple effect says your subjects are waterside though they may really be nowhere near water at all.

Sound Skills

Sound is perhaps the greatest special effect of all.

The videographer seeking to create the atmosphere of a shopping mall need only shoot characters looking into a store window. Sound effects added later will provide the essential ingredients—children calling, skateboards whirring, the voices of people walking by, a distant police siren.

For the best location atmosphere, shoot scenes where you can capture the best and most interesting off-camera sounds. When on vacation, don't always aim for peace and quiet. If you want footage of your family on a foreign railway station platform, wait for the moment the train pulls out.

When creating a drama, always think sound. Sound can often say more than pictures. Imagine a scene with two people watching TV. Suddenly they react to the sound of squealing tires on the road outside. The sound of the crash that follows has them leaping towards the window. The skillful use of sound effects has fooled viewers into believing something horrific really did occur.

Bet you didn't know you can create a simulated echo using a length of garden hose and a funnel. Just stick the funnel in one end of the hose. Place both ends close to the microphone of a cassette recorder. Then speak. The effect is certainly weird.

Different lengths of hose produce different delay times. This contraption is useful for adding echo or creating monstrous outer space voices.

An even better echo results from linking funnel, hose and microphone to one input channel of a stereo recorder while using the other channel and a second mic straight.

Mirror Dimension

Video pictures are two-dimensional, with height and width but no depth. This fact is used repeatedly to fool viewers.

The scene outside a window may be only a painted backcloth, but who can tell? A photograph of an object can look the same as the real object. Use photos when you can't acquire the real thing—a priceless museum exhibit, for example. Photographs, or even photocopies, can simulate multiple items such as meter dials or control panels.

The fifty-fifty semi-coated mirror, or beam-splitter, is a most useful piece of videography equipment. Used to superimpose one picture over another, it works because half the light passes through the glass while the other half reflects back from the surface.

Often employed to produce ghostly apparitions, it also has other, less spectral, uses. For instance, superimposing captions over pictures. With the mirror placed at a forty-five degree angle to the lens, illuminate the words as they appear. This technique can create opening titles, or overlay words or arrows on a demonstration video.

Superimpose graphics with a box housing the mirror and shielding it from stray light. Stand the rig in front of the camera. Light the caption from front or back. If lit from the front, place the lamps to either side. To remain in focus, the superimposed material must lie approximately the same distance from the camera as the main subject.

Used with a spotlight, plain mirrors stuck to a revolving drum provide a strobe effect. Two stuck back to back simulate the flashing lights of emergency vehicles.

Gun Fun

It's not unusual to see a TV actor, chest riddled with bullets, stagger and fall to the ground. If he seems to move awkwardly it is probably due less to his supposed wounds than to the fact he's trying not to trip over the operating wires running up his trouser leg.

This effect, using small explosive squibs secreted under clothing, is too complex and dangerous to discuss here. But there do exist safe alternatives, which, if used imaginatively, can appear as convincing as those in the movies.

You can use a bicycle pump for bullets in the chest. Record as a separate closeup, for it works only with a short tube close to the pump.

Suck some fake blood into the tube and seal the end with a small piece of tightly stretched party balloon. Hold the balloon in position with several turns of a rubber band. Placed under thin cloth, the pump will rupture the diaphragm, flipping the cloth realistically and producing a spatter of gore.

For continuity, shoot the garment on a stuffed sack. Then remove and place on the actor. A limp balloon containing blood and worn under a garment will produce a spreading stain when punctured by a spike attached to a ring worn by an actor. The flow will increase by keeping the hand in place and pressing hard.

A rat-trap set up behind scenery can punch out a piece of wall or knock a hole in a door. The hole must be pre-made, filled with appropriate material to disguise its true nature. Insert a captive peg from behind. When struck by the trap the peg ejects the filling, leaving a hole.

Rat-traps can also simulate a bullet hitting a mirror. Protect the front with a sheet of rigid plastic and cover the back with self-adhesive vinyl. This is essential to produce a really good shattering effect; without it the glass just breaks.

A bicycle pump with some talcum powder in the barrel will produce a convincing spurt of dust from rocks or concrete. Use energetically and apply a good ricochet effect on the soundtrack.

No bullet effect will impress without realistic sound. Conversely, a poor effect can often pass with a professional soundtrack liberally sprinkled with gunshots.

Smoke and Flames

This can be a touchy area; as always, **Videomaker** does not recommend you endeavor to create sequences involving fire, smoke or explosions without assistance from experts.

Movie and TV producers often rent an empty house or store when they need to create an outdoor fire sequence. To record in a studio is too impractical and too expensive.

However, property is property, so these big fire scenes are rigidly controlled to ensure they don't get out of hand.

In many cases fire can be simulated without actual flames. At night, backlit smoke rising from behind a building suggests it's on fire. Rooms powerfully lit, with smoke pouring from the windows, imply a house afire. Stretch a clear plastic sheet behind the window and pump smoke up underneath it. This ensures maximum effect at the window while preventing too much smoke from filling the room.

But the fact there's no flame doesn't guarantee total safety. Always ensure crew and artists have a clear exit to the outside. No one should have to stumble around in thick smoke and darkness.

Smoke, of course, is essential for all fire sequences. Much depends on the sort of smoke used. In moviemaking there are two types: pyrotechnic, and machine-made. Of the two, only the smoke machine is controllable. Pyrotechnics, once lit, will burn to a finish.

You can rent smoke machines; those who don't know where to look should contact a local theater or TV studio.

Smoke from reputable machines should cause no breathing problems, even when discharged indoors. Pyrotechnic smoke is appropriate only for exterior work or in places where it won't be inhaled.

Movie studios produce controlled flames by igniting propane. The gear usually consists of a fireproof and crushproof hose with a shut-off valve and pressure reducer. At the business end is a length of copper tube terminating in a sort of flattened funnel.

You can smatter small areas of flame around a set by using absorbent material treated with a dash of kerosene, burned on metal sheets or fireproof board. With the appropriate amount of smoke this will simulate the aftermath of an explosion.

House Mess

Many videographers must shoot in their own homes, which can cause problems when trying to capture scenes of dirt and degradation. Fortunately, it's usually possible to obtain materials easily cleaned up at the end of the day.

Freely spread sawdust, dry peat, coconut fiber, Fullers Earth, rubber dust and torn-up paper; all will disappear beneath broom or vacuum at the end of the shoot.

It's not easy creating convincing scenes of mess and filth. The camera has a habit of prettifying even the nastiest setups. It's therefore often necessary to exaggerate the dirty scenes.

For oil, food or paint spills, pour liquid latex onto a sheet of glass or metal. When set, spray paint the mess with any color. Peel off to provide a movable puddle; place where required.

Dead and dried vegetation often complement this sort of scene. Torn plastic sheeting sprayed nasty colors and wrapped around pipes, faucets and radiators also looks good.

To make metal appear rusty, wipe with a smidgen of petroleum jelly. Then blow cocoa atop the grease.

Cobwebs are great for dirty scenes, produced by spinning liquid latex in a special device called a cobweb gun. These guns are for rent, the fluid available from TV and theatrical supply houses. Spin webs over a collection of objects bunched close together for the best effect. Cobwebs won't straddle open spaces; string thin cotton across voids. Blow talcum powder onto cobwebs to make them visible. Don't apply to absorbent surfaces.

Caption Making

Electronic devices to produce lettering for videos are now available, either as separate equipment or as integral camera circuitry. Stick-on or rubdown letters come cheap and offer a variety of typefaces. Even magazines and newspapers will produce usable opening titles.

No one wants to engage in the laborious chore of cutting round letters with a stencil knife. But if you cut the letters or words as rectangles from white paper you can stick them to a white backing, the joins between painted over with white artist's paint or typing correction fluid. Photocopied, the joins disappear.

You can apply rubdown lettering or reusable vinyl stick-ons to a sheet of glass and place over various fancy papers or illustrations. You can also place the glass in front of three-dimensional objects like flowers or coins. Tabletop captions are simple to produce and offer more variety than stereotypical electronic images.

A tracing paper screen and a slide projector are also useful for graphic backgrounds. You need not project slides onto a flat screen; you can project them onto textured surfaces like rumpled cloth, rough plaster or piles of snow.

Interesting animations can result by fixing the lighting, the camera and the lettering to a common mount in which loose objects such as marbles, sea shells, sand, sugar or liquids are free to move around. When you tilt the rig, the camera perceives no movement of the backing; meanwhile, the loose objects react strangely, defying gravity and moving in a random and seemingly unpremeditated fashion.

President Matte

Miniatures are models placed in front of a set to extend the scenery or provide an effect unobtainable by other means. Mattes perform a similar task, but are simply flat paintings on glass.

This is an oversimplification, because there also exist creatures like "hanging miniatures" and "traveling mattes." But these characters would take us into deep technical water, and we're interested here only in the simple stuff.

Say the action occurs in the oval office of the White House. They won't let you tape there, and a recreation would eat up your entire budget. So go for the special effect.

You may have to hire a table and some chairs—pretty safe stuff, because who, after all, recalls exact details of the White House?

Sensibly, you'll video your fake president against an easily obtainable neutral wall. But at some point you'll have to show the room, or at least a convincing recreation.

One option is a *matte*. If you can procure a talented artist, take a large pane of glass, mount it on legs and position it between Mr. P and the camera. With constant reference through the camera viewfinder the artist can paint the oval office, leaving a hole in the middle to perceive Mr. P, his desk and the back wall.

Suppose you don't have such an artist. So get a photo of the scene, blow it up, cut out an area where Mr. P will sit and, if your photo is black-and-white, add some color washes. There. The White House.

Miniature Quixote

Let's try a second example: the story of Don Quixote, the man who tried to kill windmills.

Unable to take your unit to Spain, you'll use plaster-of-paris, sawdust, sand, cardboard and other materials to construct a *baseboard model* of a sandy plain. On the horizon position a model windmill with motor-driven sails. Finally, mount the model on a rig supported from one side only. Put in a sloping floor in the studio and cover it with sawdust and sand. At the back paint a ground row to provide the horizon.

Finish up with three components: the sky backing, the main scene on the floor and, sticking in from one side with its supporting leg out of vision, a model of a sandy plain and the windmill. Make sure everything lines up and adjust the lighting to insure a complete blend.

When using a miniature, join the model to the set along natural boundaries—hedges, woods, roads—where the foreground, which we see as the background, will blend unnoticed.

Don Quixote will stand on the opposite side of the set from the windmill, pointing towards the background and yelling, "Kill! Kill!" He'll look at the distant windmill,

which in fact sits right in front of him. Keep him stationary: if he strolls across the set he'll pass behind the model and expose the trick.

If you'd like to try a matte shot, paint on a board a simple sky and set it up where it will cover a busy background. Make sure the bottom of the board lines up with the top of a wall or some similar feature. Shoot it. The effect can be quite extraordinary.

Cardtoon Creations

Children exposed to television since birth accept everything on the screen without question, and quite often without interest. So why not give them the chance to participate as creative artists?

A cardtoon is the electronic counterpart of the puppet theater, where little figures move around on sticks. Recording the cardtoon technique on video gives youngsters the opportunity to design their own characters and write their own scripts. After the show they can sit back and view the results.

Unfortunately, video cameras don't work in the same way as the movie cameras that film Disney cartoons, so the action and movement must take place in real time. This is accomplished by cutting characters from stiff card and articulating them with tiny rivets and paper hinges.

Animation comes from fixing the various parts to hidden sticks or incorporating cardboard levers hidden behind parts of the background.

A simple example involves a picture of the sea, drawn as repeating lines of stylized ripples. Suddenly, up leaps a fish, attached to a cardboard lever and rotated between two layers of the wave pattern.

Still at sea, imagine a pirate ship sailing across, pushed or pulled from one side. Or a diver surfacing from beneath the waves.

All videography is a combination of long shots and close-ups, so we'll have to see the faces of the pirates onboard ship. You can make them speak using a simple up-and-down movement of the jaw. It's the eyes moving that give the characters the most expression.

A few versions of the same heads—left and right profile, large and small—will result in a really satisfying cardtoon.

You can usually manipulate the parts by hand, though certain creatures may have to move faster than your digits can. In these cases you can employ thin dressmaking elastic as pulling springs.

Trick of the Light

Light, like sound, is too often taken for granted. It can suggest things which aren't really there; backlit smoke that looks like fire is but one example.

Take a look at movie scenes set in the countryside. The trees and the dappled sunlight through the leaves say we're in a wood, but the effect is truly produced by shining a lamp through holes cut in thin plywood sheets.

Look at the two people in the front seat of a studio automobile. We know the vehicle is moving because the background is receding—achieved via chromakey—but the scene would look dead if it weren't for the fact that shadows continually sweep across the faces of the actors. A spotlight, some plywood, flags on broom handles and some keen staff to wave them about and we achieve the effect of an auto in motion.

For night shots sweep a hand-held lamp from front to rear.

The prison scene looks a lot more sinister if a spotlight, trained on the floor, shines through a cutout silhouette of iron bars.

Many of these effects cause the autofocus to hunt. Switch to manual whenever this occurs.

Give Them a Try

Does any of this sound like fun? It is. Just remember, you'll never know unless you get out your camcorder and do it yourself. All it takes is a little imagination.

PART IV
Post-Production Techniques

How to edit all that footage you've got "in the can" with precision and style.

45
Editing from Start to Finish

Bill Davis

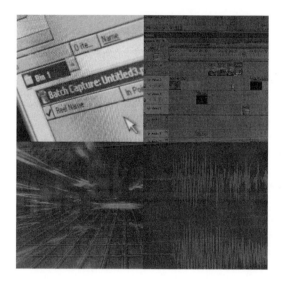

Figure 45-1

If you've been dragging your heels getting started with video editing because you think it's just too complicated, you're in the right place at the right time. This entire article breaks down a typical video project and covers a step by step explanation of the process a well-organized videographer might follow to produce a quality program.

We'll start by showing you some important steps to begin the preparation before you begin to edit, by showing you the best ways to log scenes and capture video so your editing process is smoother later on down the road. Next, we'll cover ordering clips, trimming and pacing. Then we'll tackle adding titles and graphics. And finally, we'll discuss how to add music,

special effects, editing and sweetening your sound track. When done, you should have a good overview of everything you need to know about how editing works in a modern, computer driven edit bay.

Defining the Project

The example project we will follow is a simple family history video. We'll be combining photos and live video clips with music and graphics into an easy-to-watch stroll down memory lane for family members who'll be gathering for a 30th wedding anniversary celebration. Our project goal is to create a video master that will be shown at the party and eventually used to make VHS or DVD copies for family members who can't attend.

Prep It

Step one is to do a review of the assets we need in order to create our video. For our project, our assets include a box of family photos, some old 8 mm films and some more modern home movies on Hi8 and VHS videotape. We also have home cassette recordings of Aunt Martha playing the piano. We even have some songs on CD and Mini DV tape from the very recent past. These will be easy to get on the computer, however.

Get Organized

Organization for any video project starts with the script, even for projects that rely on archival material and stock footage. Without some kind of script, it's hard to break down the shooting process into manageable steps. A clear script also helps you prepare your storyboard.

Storyboards don't have to be complicated, but they are the best way to organize your video on paper in preparation for logging and capturing. Whereas your script will indicate what you're saying to the audience, your storyboard should show where each scene or still fits into the overall flow of your project. When you review your storyboard, you can consider elements such as program themes, pacing, fonts and color pallets, and make note of where you need music and special effects.

Pre-production (as this phase is called) is also the time to organize your other program assets. Take the time to make sure you label every tape with a unique name. Open your editing software and set your preferred storage locations for clip capture, audio and render files, establish your frame rate and compression settings and preview parameters.

This is also the time to establish the structure of your project files, bins and folders with names or number codes that connect

Figure 45-2 *Log and Capture: Batch capture is where all the time you spent logging really pays off. All you need to do is load your log and hit the Batch Capture button.*

them to the project. Finally, you'll want to make sure you have enough drive space for the length of project you're planning. We'd recommend about 30 GB of space for an hour-long program, although that all depends on how efficient you are during the logging and subsequent capture phase.

Transfer It!

For our project, we'll need to scan paper photos into our computer. We'll also need to convert analog video and audio tapes to a digital format. Often, the easiest way to accomplish this is to dub analog sources, like old VHS tapes, onto digital videotape using a DV camcorder. Many DV camcorders accept analog input via S-video or RCA video (composite) and audio jacks. Although the conversion process takes as long as it takes to play back your tapes (otherwise known as "real time"), the digital conversion process is easy and high quality. As a bonus, you've just backed up your aging tape archive. (Don't throw away the originals!)

This process also works for music. Take the audio outputs of your cassette player or turntable, attach them to the audio inputs of your digital camcorder and make a digital tape copy. The result will be black video with a digital soundtrack, ready to import into your editor like any other DV source material. Film is much, much trickier and is another article entirely. Remember to allow plenty of time for transferring if you have to send your old home movie film out to a photo processor to have dubbed. Those old treasures can take weeks if you have to mail them out to a dubbing agency.

Figure 45-3 *Analog Capture: Often, the easiest way to capture analog sources to your computer is to first digitize the footage to your DV camcorder.*

Figure 45-4 *JKL: Tape logging is all about simple keyboard commands in your editor.*

Log and Batch

If you just need to capture a single clip, all video editing software allows you to manually capture a scene simply by rolling your tape and then clicking a button. This immediately initiates the capture process and writes the footage to your hard drive until you hit escape or click the Stop button. This is adequate for only the most simple of projects.

During more serious productions, you'll likely have multiple takes, duplicate shots, bits and pieces of chance happenings and surprises, all captured on your field tapes. Logging is when you get to review each shot and decide if it's the right element to contribute to your program. So insert your source tape and bring up your application's batch capture logging tool. The software will probably ask you for a reel or tape name at this point: settle on a convention and match the name you enter to the name on the label of the tape and you are set to go. Pay attention to this step, however. Labeling tapes and your projects in an orderly manner in the beginning of a project will save you many headaches later on in the process.

Tape logging is all about simple keyboard commands in your editor. Most apps follow the Avid convention of using keystrokes centered around your right hand's position on the keys J, K and L (see Figure 45-1). The spacebar lets you play your footage in order

to mark the In and Out points. This process of marking In and Out timecode points on individual clips and then collecting these individual clips into a list is what we mean by logging. The L key moves the play head downstream, much like shuttling tape forward on a deck. The J key moves the playhead upstream, like reverse shuttling or rewinding a tape. Hitting the same key multiple times typically increases the speed of the shuttle. The K key stops the playhead. Try holding down the K key while pressing either L or J to advance a frame at a time: K+L moves you forward one frame at a time, while K+J moves backward frame by frame. Some programs let you shuttle frame by frame using your arrow keys, too.

The I and O keys typically mark the In and Out points of your scenes. Finally, your software program will have a "save clip" keystroke (F2, in some programs) that will bring up the clip-naming window. Clip naming is important since if you name clips carefully, it's easier to arrange them in the proper order when you move them to the timeline. Once the I/O points are marked and the clip is named and saved, you can consider it logged.

With just a little practice, you'll reach a point when logging keystrokes become automatic as you shuttle through your footage. When you've logged your final tape, you'll likely have bins full of "offline" clips (sometimes marked by a red slash through their icon), which are merely pointers to

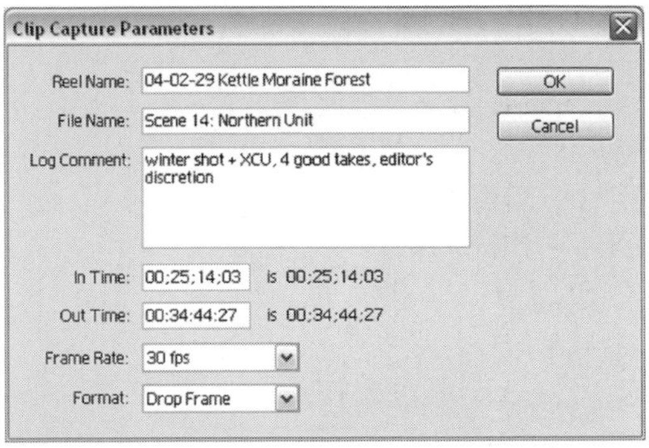

Clip Capture Parameters

Reel Name: 04-02-29 Kettle Moraine Forest

File Name: Scene 14: Northern Unit

Log Comment: winter shot + XCU, 4 good takes, editor's discretion

In Time: 00;25;14;03   is 00;25;14;03

Out Time: 00:34:44:27   is 00;34;44;27

Frame Rate: 30 fps

Format: Drop Frame

Figure 45-5 *Database: A Batch Capture log loosely mirrors your production logs and can be a sophisticated database if you use it properly.*

the original tapes that hold your digital footage. They contain the reel number and start and stop timecode of the scenes you've selected, but don't actually contain any video information. If you have labeled your tapes well and named the tape properly in your log file, you can save this tiny log file on your computer and return to capture the actual footage effortlessly, even a decade from now.

Batch Capture is where all the time you spent logging really pays off. All you need to do is load your log and hit the Batch Capture button. Your computer will work with your deck or camcorder to rewind or fast forward as necessary, cue the clip and capture all of your clips. Just sit back and watch as your trusty computer does your bidding. Or take a stretch and go walk the dog.

Our goal so far has been to organize our work, then capture and store the fundamental source media for our project. Next we'll cover moving our newly captured digital assets onto the timeline, trimming and balancing the timeline elements in a way that gives our program the proper pacing.

Get Editing! Order of Battle

Unlike narrative work such as a play or movie, the kind of family history highlights video we're planning doesn't come with a predefined story arc. Therefore, we'll need to establish our goals for ordering

our clips in some kind of sensible flow. For our program, we'll lay our clips on the timeline in a rough chronological order, with the oldest photos and clips first.

The simplest way to get our clips onto the timeline is often just to drag them from their bins onto the timeline one at a time. If you've been careful with your clip names, you can often automate some of this process by moving clips onto the timeline in batches, especially for material that is ordered chronologically.

Many editors are set up to insert batches of files onto the timeline in the order of their names. This is a powerful function since you can roughly pre-order your clips by simply naming them in groups. For example, a clip titled 01-001 will be placed on the timeline directly ahead of one titled 01-002. After the numbers, you can name the files with something more descriptive to help you remember. Most editing software also lets you add comments to the database that makes up your clip bin, so go ahead and use that if you find it useful. Most editors also have a way to pre-set the duration of a still. The result of our batch insert of the section one still shots will be a series of 6-second clips on the timeline.

Next, we'll insert the video clips for section one onto the timeline. If there are pre-built title screens, other graphics, sound effects or whatever, they get placed on our timeline next. We'll need to start paying attention to the different tracks on the timeline so that titles that will be superimposed over video will be displayed properly.

Order on the Timeline

Now that our clips are on the timeline, we can look at them and decide how to move them around into a more pleasing order. One way to time your edits is by looking at the soundtrack. The tempo of our music track can often be seen as spikes in the audio waveform. Lining up the cuts between the images and video with the spikes in the waveform gives you an automatic way to edit.

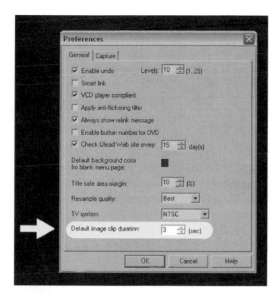

Figure 45-6 *Image Duration: Most video editors have a way to pre-set the duration of a still.*

Figure 45-7

Many beginning videographers start by doing their cuts on the beat in the soundtrack. But let's look closer at our content. The first still image here is a group shot. There are quite a few family faces in this photo compared to photo #2, which is a still of Aunt Martha playing solo. Still #3 is a closeup of her hands on the keyboard. The video is a talking head clip of Aunt Martha talking about the fun the family always had gathering around the piano at the holidays.

Rather than just marching through the photos, let's look at how a creative editor might use them to help the audience absorb the full content of the visuals and build a more effective shot progression. The opening still image covers two measures of the soundtrack, giving the audience more time to look at the multiple faces in the photo. Photo #2 has been shortened and, halfway through, it's been composited with the keyboard shot. Next, the talking head replaces the single shot of Aunt Martha, so that she can make her comments.

The result is that the same information is presented to the viewer in the same amount of time, but we've given more time to the complex shot with the multiple faces and given the audience a more interesting edit.

The video no longer simply marches to the beat of the underlying music, while it is still totally in sync. Also notice the split edit where Aunt Martha starts talking before we see her. This is a common technique that helps increase viewer interest by providing them with new information (the live audio) before seeing the clip associated with it.

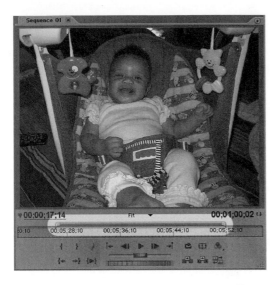

Figure 45-8 Trim It: The Trim function allows the editor to move the In and Out point of a clip in small increments. The trim bar is highlighted here.

Making the Cut

Another skill that makes many beginning editors feel uncomfortable is determining exactly where to make a cut between two scenes. In a non-linear edit system, it's easy to experiment and fine tune edit points using the trim function.

The editor sets up In and Out points and then plays that edit, plus a good chunk of the material coming into and out of the edit, again and again (i.e., loops it). The Trim function allows the editor to move the In or Out point of a clip in small increments using keyboard commands, all the time watching the resulting edit and making adjustments until it feels just right.

If you're still unsure of an edit, another helpful trick is to play the original video clip and mark your In or Out edit points on the fly. This means just playing a clip in real time and marking your edit where your instincts tell you the edit should go. One famous editor has said that when he watches the same clip three times in a row and hits the same exact Edit point three times, he knows he's found the perfect place. Remember that when you are trimming clips on the timeline, you aren't really changing the file itself. Edit points

are only relevant to the project and your source material remains unchanged.

The Order to Retreat

It's also critical to learn to see the big picture, even when you're working on the smallest edit. With the kind of precision control that editing software offers you, it's easy to get caught up in trimming a frame here or a frame there and forget to stand back and watch a complicated sequence in its entirety.

There's nothing more frustrating than working for an hour on a small sequence, tuning it up until it's nearly perfect, and then discovering that your video is too long. Then you have to face the realization that the best thing you can do for your video is to simply remove the entire section that you've just perfected. Be cruel and merciless and cut where you can.

Close Order

So, the bottom line for editing is that there is not one right way to do it. The whole object of the exercise is to arrange and trim your material in a way that keeps your audience involved in the presentation. Accomplish that, and your edit is right. No matter how you got there.

Graphic It!

Now that we've covered preparing for the edit and building the timeline, we'll look at the next step in the post-production process: spicing up your video with titles and graphics. Before videographers were empowered with the excellent titling functions built into most of today's editing software, creating good-looking titles was difficult.

Broadcast quality titlers were expensive and hard to operate. Less expensive stand-alone titlers often had severe stylistic limitations. Today, video titling is much, much easier. Any quality software is likely to have built-in graphics and titling capabilities that would have been the envy of even a network TV station only a decade ago.

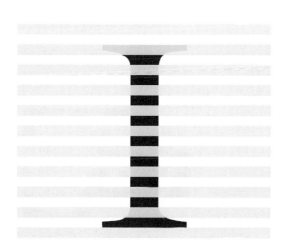

Figure 45-9 *Stripes: Using small fonts on interlaced video will result in parts of the letter blinking on and off as the screen is scanned.*

NOT a Glorified Word Processor

You may be tempted to think of your software's titling program as nothing more than a glorified word processor. Don't. The techniques necessary for putting words on a TV screen have only the most basic principles in common with the design and layout of printed documents. The video editor's goal is to get legible text to display on the comparatively rough resolution of a video raster, which is, in many ways, much harder than print on paper. It's a whole 'nother ballgame.

Raster Stuff

The term "raster" is just tech-speak for the pattern of dots organized into lines that make up a visual display of information on a computer or TV screen. Your computer typically uses a display with a progressive scan raster. In this kind of system, the display image is written as a series of lines that are generated left to right, top to bottom, one line after another until the picture is complete.

When the TV standards were set back in the 1950s, they specified that our televisions would work on an interlaced scan system. Thirty frames of video are generated each second, divided into two interlaced fields.

Each field consists of every other line of information.

In practical terms, the effective resolution of most household color TV sets typically hovers around 260 lines. So what does this all mean to someone wanting to do something simple and practical like putting a title on the video screen?

Trying to put small stuff with fine details, like text, on a TV screen can be an exercise in frustration. There simply isn't enough effective screen resolution to work with the size of type that works just fine on paper. So the first rule for video title creation is this: big and bold usually works better than small and delicate.

Color Your World

Video type designers have another challenge: movement. Unlike the print designer who has an even background once the paper type and color are selected, the video designer sometimes faces the need to layer text over moving video. This process means the type designer must work with a background that changes from moment to moment.

Imagine that you've decided to do a title over a shot of a street scene. The wall of the building opposite is dark, so you've selected a light type color. Things look great as you're building your type. Then you watch your program and, much to your surprise, after just a couple of seconds, a white truck pulls up in the frame. The light colored type that you specified to match the dark building suddenly disappears.

The experienced video type designer will understand that it's usually better to build titles in a way that they can withstand the challenge of this kind of changing background. Try adding a drop shadow to your text, preferably in a sharply contrasting color and brightness. This can help keep a title readable even when the background shifts or when the title overlaps two areas with different colors. Or you can set a background mask behind the type that dims or completely blocks the background in just the area where the type

(a)

(b)

(c)

Figure 45-10 *Shadow Land: Try adding a drop shadow to your text to keep your titles readable.*

Figure 45-11 *Title Safe: Most editing systems have a safe screen view for fonts within the center 60–80 percent of the screen.*

First, we'll generate a title screen proclaiming Grandma and Grandpa *"Saturday Night Fever*—Grand Champions!" The joke resolves itself in the next scene where we dissolve in the additional line "Wishful Thinking Division" over the gyrations of the on-screen couple.

This breaking of the invisible wall between the program and the audience isn't always appropriate, but with the family video we're discussing here, it'll be fine. Here there's no reason the videographer can't comment on the proceedings and share inside jokes with the audience, even if they're cheesy. And it's a good example of how adding type and graphics to your program gives you another way to communicate with your audience.

occupies the screen. Or you could throw a geometric colored shape behind the title. This doesn't have to be an emergency fix for a problem, either, but these ideas can and should be an intimate part of the creative design and layout of a good title.

Practical Examples

Here's an example of what we are talking about. In our scene, Grandma and Grandpa are disco dancing at a family celebration. Let's use our type generator to spice up the scene with a few humorous captions.

Keep It Safe

Not all colors in the spectrum are colors that will play out well on your TV. Wild colors can look cool on a computer, but a psychedelic green on your PC might end up looking seasick green when shown on a regular television. You also need to be aware of the safe title areas on the screen. Most editing systems have a safe screen view for fonts. It's within the center 60–80 percent of the screen, and it keeps that overly large title "Jenny's Birthday" from playing out as "enny's Birthd."

Traditional Titling

Of course titling and graphics are also at home in everything from business to wedding videos. Anyone who has ever watched a movie understands the function of an opening title sequence. In the movies, it not only displays the title of the program, but it often carries a lot of information ranging from the production company logo, to names of the stars, director and other key players. Opening titles are the first impression we get of a movie and they strongly set the tone for what is to come. And titles wind down the end of the picture as well.

Titling and graphics in your videos can do the same thing, helping orient potential viewers to what they're going to see and making sure that the people doing the hard work to create the program get the credit they deserve. If you are not the most accomplished design professional, our realistic advice is to keep it simple. Use your titles to communicate as clearly as possible and try not to make them distracting. While it's natural to concentrate on your video and audio to carry story content to your audience, don't overlook the advantages of something as simple as on-screen type. So, no matter what type of program you're working on, spending some quality time working out your program graphics and titles can be worth it.

Sweeten It!

We've made it to the home stretch. Our family tribute video example is almost finished. We've logged, captured, edited and built the video portion of our timeline, including everything from transitions to titles. So what's left? Sweetening.

Sweetening your project is like the icing on the cake. A little finesse will "wow" your fans. We do that by finalizing our audio track and getting our program ready for public viewing. We'll also talk about what you can do when you finish one project to make your next project easier. First, we'll make one final pass to add a little extra something to our project, something that can take a good program and make it great. We call this audio sweetening. We'll tweak and adjust, adding little sonic touches that can make your soundtrack stand out and really sparkle. Sweetening includes applying effects such as compression, normalization or possibly reverb to your existing soundtracks as well as the addition of sound effects and other audio enhancements. In most video projects, dialog is critically important to the story or message. So first up, let's take a look at some techniques that can help clarify dialog and speech.

Get Level

Unless all your footage comes from the same source and the same setup, the audio levels you've recorded will probably vary greatly from clip to clip. If you want the audience to hear these clips clearly, spending some time adjusting the audio levels of your clips so that they're more or less consistent is a good first step in sweetening. You can manually do this using your ears and the audio meter in your software or you can use a filter to process your entire audio stream so that it sounds more consistent.

Compression and normalization are two of the most common software processes used on spoken content and indeed much of modern popular music. Compression is a process where we lower or reduce the dynamic range of the audio, which is the difference between the softest and loudest parts of track. Essentially, it makes the softer sounds louder, while making louder sounds softer. This leaves you with a more consistent track. We'd recommend being cautious about using too much compression, however, as you'll sometimes want your actors to whisper their lines and at other times shout, but for parts like the

Figure 45-12 *Squeeze Play: A compressor stabilizes the audio of your project to prevent sudden volume changes.*

Figure 45-13 *Quest for Equality: An equalizer allows you to emphasize and de-emphasize individual frequency bands to improve the overall sound of your project.*

Figure 45-14 *Sounds Good: There are literally hundreds of sound effects libraries available online or via disc.*

voice-over narration, compression is almost a required process.

Normalization is a variant of compression, where the dynamic range is not only compressed, but after compression is applied, the volume is turned up to a maximum. Applied to a well-recorded track with a solid signal-to-noise ratio and no unwanted background sounds, normalization can yield an excellent result for helping sonic elements like narration stand out in your videos.

But ... one problem that may appear is that if your initial track isn't clean, the normalization process will take your noisy background and normalize it along with the speech you're trying to enhance. The result can be an even noisier track than one without normalization. If the recording is good, a modest amount of compression will often make it sound better. But if you discover, after applying compression, that you've managed to enhance elements of your soundtrack that are annoying, you can back off.

EQ and Reverb

There are two other digital enhancements that are commonly used by professionals to sweeten the mix. The first is equalization or EQ. This is where you bring up the bass a bit to warm the audio up or perhaps bring down the high trebles to get rid of a nasty hiss. EQ is technically easy to use, but it takes a real artist to get it right. The second tweak is reverb. This filter effect can add space to your mix and even give a sense of stereo separation to a monophonic recording. In both cases, but especially with reverb, use restraint and

concentrate on consistency first. Applying reverb to one clip and not another can make them sound as if they were recorded in two different locations.

SFX

Once you have the dialog and voice-over tracks in top shape, the next step in sweetening is to look at your program in terms of how secondary sounds can help you tell your story. Let's say our family history video has a video section where dad is teaching Junior to drive. We have silent footage transferred to videotape from old 8mm film. Why not use the sound effect of a car starting over the title slide as an audio introduction into this section? Then as dad and son drive away at a responsible and stately pace, you could add a revving engine and screeching brakes for a humorous effect.

There are literally hundreds of sound effects libraries available online or via disc. Sometimes, just browsing through the index of available sounds can spark some new creative ideas on how you can add some new interest to your program. The point is that sound is a powerful communications tool that reaches far beyond the basic processes of capturing and reproducing dialog.

Master the Moment

The timeline is complete and our program is ready to master! In this digital era, the

Figure 45-15 *Pack It Up: Include batch capture lists, project files, graphics, pictures, sounds and other media on your backups.*

whole concept of making a master videotape is actually a little out of date. Since modern editing systems simply put out a stream of digital data, making a program master is really just making a copy of your digital data in a form that someone can watch. The tape can be digitally cloned with each copy identical to another. Obviously, this makes archiving our work more flexible than ever before.

The final step in my typical production process is to do a computer backup of the data files I used in creating my program. That includes the batch capture list created by the editing software and any graphics, pictures, sounds or other media that I've created for the show.

I tend to keep the video clips on my hard drive from my last few programs just in case I need to make changes, but sooner or later, they get deleted. If I need to recreate the program later, all I have to do is reload my master files and re-Batch Capture the clip from the original tapes. Now do you see

why tape labeling, organization and a good file naming convention are important?

That's a Wrap

The video is finished. We planned carefully, logged, captured, edited, trimmed and built a dynamic and interesting timeline. We took great pains to make sure our video and our soundtrack communicated clearly. We also added some visual and sonic sparkle to our finished product. And, at the end of production, we mastered our show and took care of our system housekeeping chores in order to be ready for our next project. After all of this hard work what are you likely left with? The simple answer is a video that will delight your family and friends, but you're also left with what you've learned. And that's probably the most valuable asset in the entire production process.

Editing software programs will come and go. So will the cameras, lights, microphones and even many of the people you worked with on your productions. The one thing that will never leave you is your knowledge and understanding of the process of making a good video. The ability to tell a story in a way that can engage, inspire or delight an audience is a very valuable skill that will last you a lifetime. Show promise in this field and don't be surprised if you find yourself sought out by other people who will want you to help them harness the amazing power of video.

BIO: Bill Davis writes, shoots, edits and does voice-over work for a variety of corporate and industrial clients.

Sidebar 1

Copyright Concerns

Our fictional video features music by "Aunt Martha" performing her own compositions on the piano. This would clearly be free of copyright concerns. Copyright-protected commercial music used for family-style home video projects isn't much of a problem. All producers should be aware, however, that the use of any element protected by copyright without explicit permission of the copyright holder is a violation of the law and can make your project ineligible for entry into video judging contests. The use of commercially available "buyout" music is always a safer choice if you ever plan to use your project for any public or commercial purpose.

Sidebar 2

The Importance of Capture Settings

Modern editors don't need to render material on the timeline that remains unaltered. If you ever find yourself rendering even the simplest cuts-only sequences, you need to check your project settings. The problem is likely that your clip settings don't match the capture settings you established when you opened up your new project. In most situations, you should only have to render title sequences and transitions between clips.

Sidebar 3

Ripple Edits and Inserts

Every editing system works a bit differently in terms of specifying what kind of edit you're doing when you drop new material over old. In some modes, you'll insert the new into the old, pushing the previous material downstream (i.e., ripple edit). In another mode, the same action might simply place the new content on a new timeline layer, overwriting the old clips with the new ones. Both kinds of editing actions are valuable and as you get to know your software package, you'll learn how to switch among the various editing modes.

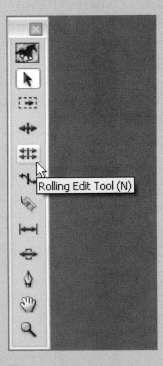

Figure 4-16

Sidebar 4

MultiSelect

There are often a number of ways to select multiple clips and move them as a group on the timeline. In the most usable software programs, the technique mirrors the behavior of your operating system. In other words: CTRL+click (OPTION+click on a Mac) to select multiple individual clips. You can also click and drag a selection area around your multiple clips in some environments or SHIFT+click to select a range on a Windows PC. Some editors have other kinds of selection tools that allow you to move clips more efficiently.

Sidebar 5

The Power of Type

The best titles give you an introduction to the tone and spirit of the film. Sit down in a theater full of rabid *Star Wars* film fans and don't be surprised if they start cheering the moment they see the hallmark tilted back yellow type against a star field opening.

It's clear that director George Lucas doesn't have any type design limitations and could have fancier titles if he wanted them. In his latest films, his modern supercomputer technology imitates what was original done with painted words on a pane of glass.

It's the same brand identification power carried by a well-known corporate logo or trademark ID. So, while you may never be lucky enough to have your works become such a pervasive brand, there's no reason you can't give the same careful thought to designing your titles and graphics.

Sidebar 6

Coming to Terms

As you explore your software's titling and graphics creation menus, you'll come upon some terms that might not be familiar to you. Here are some common graphics and titling terms and their definitions.

- Leading (pronounced "ledding" as in the metal lead) This is a typesetter's term that refers to adjusting the vertical space between lines of text.

- Kerning This is the distance between individual letters in a word. "Kerning pairs" are special cases where two letters need special spacing in order to look correct. One classic example is the letter pair "T" and "o". When enlarged as part of a title, this pair typically looks better if the "o" is slid over and partially tucked underneath the arm of the "T."

- Tracking This is adjusting the space of all the letters in a group so that they are closer or looser. One popular video type effect is to change the tracking of a short title over time so that the letters seem to float together to form a word or phrase or drift dramatically apart.

- Gradient Fill A gradient is a blended region that smoothly changes from dark to light or from one color to another. Gradient backgrounds are popular for titling.

- Slate This is typically a full-screen graphic that contains descriptive text or other program information. It may exist to communicate with engineers and programmers.

- Drop Shadow A drop shadow is a small, often partially transparent, shadow cast by a letter or graphic. It is a popular way to make a letter stand out from a background or to give the viewer the sense that a title is floating above the background.

Sidebar 7

Send in the Clones

Since going digital years ago, I've found myself developing some new archiving habits. When a program is finished, the first thing I do is make a digital clone onto a master tape for my library. Then I output another clone for delivery to my tape duplicator. I usually add one additional step that I'd like to recommend to new producers: I dub another clone of my new program onto the end of one or more of my original field tapes. Why? Why not? Since clones are identical and cost nothing more than the time to burn them, and you have extra room at the end of one of your tapes, there's no downside to having an extra copy of the master around. You can never be too safe.

46
Color Tweaking

Bill Davis

When we make video, our goal most of the time is to get lifelike images up on the screen. We chase natural skin tones, good exposure and proper white balance like racing dogs after mechanical bunnies.

But if you watch what's happening in the movies or on TV, you're probably already aware that sometimes, realistic just isn't good enough, particularly when it comes to color.

We accept daytime scenes awash in exaggerated hyper golden sunlight and nighttime sequences bathed in green or blue. And we even see the use of hybrid scenes, where some of the footage is processed in black and white while other elements retain their colors.

The Countdown of Basics

The first thing to understand about the basics of video color is that at the base level, every television signal is actually a combination of two separate signal components—one for black and white information, the other for color.

In the beginning, all TV signals were exclusively black and white. It wasn't until years after TV sets started to appear in homes that engineers added a color component to the broadcast signal.

The black and white part of the signal is referred to as luminance and given the engineering shorthand, "Y," while the color signal is known as chrominance and given the designation "C."

The standard yellow RCA video plug mixes these signals together into a composite. S-video cables, on the other hand, are sometimes referred to as Y/C cables because they keep the luminance and chrominance signals separated. If you look at the end of an S-video connector, you can see a number of separate holes or pins used to carry the signals.

This split makes it a snap to take a color TV signal from your camcorder and translate it into black and white. All that your software has to accomplish is the elimination of the color portion of the signal.

Diminishing the chrominance signal relative to the luminance yields a reduction of color intensity and creates a muted pastel look. Many editing applications have basic chrominance or saturation controls to adjust this aspect of the video.

But to dive into the more exciting aspects of colorizing your video signal, we also need to break things down further and delve into the three primary components of your signal's color: red, green and blue.

Engineering RGB Space

Color television is said to reside in the RGB color space. It is this arrangement of mixing and matching three basic colors to create the entire pallet of colors the TV can display, that makes it a snap to manipulate the color of your video footage.

Most editing software programs allow you to change the balance of the three primary colors on a global, regional or even pixel-by-pixel basis (see Figure 46-1).

Editing applications usually have some basic color manipulation tools, accessible through a panel in the main program or as a plug-in. As you manipulate the colors, you can increase or decrease parameters, such as the amount of red, green or blue applied to your selected part of a picture. You can also alter brightness and contrast,

creating a washed-out feel of pastels, or a hyper-real environment, where you deliver suppressed midrange tones and the most extreme dark and light components of your original signals to the screen.

To Boldly Go

Normally, these controls need to be handled with a light touch, since they can dramatically alter the look of your video. Remember, the beauty of working in a non-destructive video-editing environment is that a return to reality is always as close as an "undo" command.

Special-effects filters and plug-ins can often modify colors in interesting ways. Just like the filters photographers have long attached to their lenses to change the image characteristics of their shots, the video filter is simply a way of changing one or more channels of information to create a different look for your video. In most situations, it is better to apply filters in post-production, since you cannot undo on-the-lens glass filters if you don't like the results (see Figure 46-2).

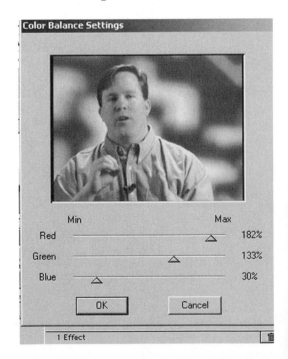

Figure 46-1 *Balance That Color—Most editing environments have basic controls that allow you to adjust the balance of red, green and blue in the video.*

Many filters have presets for popular color schemes such as sepia—a color effect that alters your footage with a yellowish-brown cast reminiscent of old-time photographs.

Beyond these kinds of simple presets are direct controls such as tint, which you can quickly apply as a global colorcast of your choosing to your footage. All those trendy colorized commercials, where the world is awash in a slightly green tint are examples of manipulating color information. You can simulate these effects with your color control tools (see Figure 46-3).

But a note of caution. Look closely at the colorization examples in broadcast work. You'll notice that while the environment around that fancy sports car often looks surreal, the people still look pretty realistic. To achieve that kind of sophisticated colorized look, you need to be careful about maintaining healthy skin highlights and other reality checks rather than just slathering everyone and everything with a greenish wash.

That's where the power of channel-specific effects comes in. Look closely at your editing interface and you may discover that you can apply color corrections to narrowly defined parts of your image.

Filters and Mattes

The real fun begins when you combine basic image manipulation with the power of masks, mattes and layers.

If you've ever watched a music video, where a brilliantly colored character danced through an otherwise black and white world, you've seen the power of multi-layer mattes and filters at work.

Shots like these stack two or more synchronized layers of the same footage on multiple video tracks. Then, a moving matte applied to the dancing character isolates it from the rest of the scene. The layer with the foreground figure remains in color while a desaturate filter, which removes

Figure 46-2 Monochrome—Some color effects require two steps: one to desaturate the image and a second to add a color tint.

Figure 46-3 Combinations—To get exactly what you want, you might need to use a number of different filters. The order of the filters can be important.

Figure 46-4 *Fancy Filters—More complex color effects may require sophisticated filters or even video mattes.*

all the color information, applies to the background footage (see Figure 46-4).

A word of warning: pulling a quality moving matte out of a single video clip without advance planning is just about impossible unless you are willing to go through and paint a matte for every frame of your video (30 of them for every second of footage). But if you have the time and patience (or a team of highly skilled animators), there's nothing to keep you from going in and isolating a character by re-shaping and moving a manually created matte to follow the character. Don't forget to tweak the softness or blur the edges of the matte to make it appear more natural.

The Adventure Begins

There's literally no limit to this other than your creativity and imagination. So, the next time you're watching TV, pay special attention to how the producers use color tinting, layers and mattes to produce eye-catching images.

Then, consider that many of those same capabilities reside right in your own editing application, awaiting your exploration.

Sidebar 1

Alpha Channel

The separate RGB portions of video are referred to as channels. Some formats also have a fourth channel, called the Alpha Channel, used to specify transparency. If your editing application allows you to view the Alpha Channel, it usually appears in grayscale with black being 100 percent transparent and white being 100 percent opaque, although it is very easy to reverse this. The flexibility of editing software even allows you to select a specific color or range of colors to set as the Alpha Channel.

Sidebar 2

TV Can't Show It All

A typical computer monitor uses over 16 million colors to draw a picture on your screen. This includes the video-preview window in your editing application. The standard color television picture in the United States is composed of only about 2 million colors. This means that the wonderful color modifications you see on your computer monitor will likely not look the same on a television. When doing any computer generated modifications to your video, you must test your adjusted video on a television before declaring your movie complete.

47
Composition 101

Kyle Cassidy

Ask a lot of people what makes good art, and they'll all have a different opinion, from an artist's use of color and paint to the subject matter or design, but one thing they'll all nearly note what separates the amateurs from the masters is composition.

The Screen Is Your Canvas

Videographers, photographers and painters are all very similar. Besides getting invited to all the best parties, they each need to tell a story within the four walls of a frame. These frames differ in dimension, but the principle remains the same: the screen is the real estate you are using to sell your vision. Use it wisely.

There are movies like *The Cell, Snow Falling on Cedars* and *Sisters* that I believe you could pause at random, print that frame, hang it on your wall, and be happy looking at it for the rest of your life. This is a worthy goal.

The Long and Short of It

Composition can vary slightly depending on what type of shot you're using. Close-ups usually fill the frame with a single object, while long shots will often include more objects.

Long shots are often establishing shots that portray characters in their environment. You may, for example, compose a shot showing the Washington Monument in the background and two tiny people sitting on a bench in the foreground. What does this tell us? That they're in Washington— they may be politicians, or spies. Or, a shot of two tiny people with the vastness of a mountain before them. What does this tell us? That people are small and frail.

One of my favorite long shots in recent history is in the climax of Ryuhei Kitamura's martial arts adventure *Azumi*: town gates open up to reveal our heroine standing alone in the distance. In between her and the man she is supposed to rescue are several hundred heavily armed pirates. A gasp of anticipation goes through the audience. What do we learn from this shot? We know that Azumi must get from point A to point B through a very dangerous expanse of pirate infested street. How well those three bits of information (heroine, villains and goal) are composed on the screen is the difference between a movie that tells a story, and one that tells a story beautifully.

(a)  (b)  (c)

Figure 47-1 *Some novices will attempt to shoot extremely close-up, and forget that a good wide shot will give the story feeling of magnitude, like this snow scene. A medium shot of a task, like the dish washing, helps set the conversation stage, and an extreme close-up gives detail lost in wider shots.*

Medium shots are often used to show interactions between characters—two people sitting at a table, a person cutting vegetables at a kitchen counter. Medium shots are how people living and working indoors usually see things. The medium shots Steven Spielberg used in the boat sequences of *Jaws* give the viewer a cramped feeling, reminding us that our heroes have very little sanctuary.

Close-ups reveal facial expressions & emotion, they take the world away and leave us alone with a character. One very effective use of close-ups was in the intro sequences of Lawrence Kasdan's *The Big Chill*—where a woman's hands are shown buttoning a man's shirt, adjusting his tie, straightening his collar. At first the audience is misled into believing that a man is being dressed for a romantic evening on the town by an attentive partner, only as the opening credits go on do we realize that the hands are that of a funeral director preparing a corpse for burial.

Compositional Vocabulary

There is a language of composition just like there's a language for football. Learning the various parts, their definitions and usage will help you immeasurably, not only in composing your own shots, but in being a critical observer of other work.

The Rule of Thirds

The "Rule of Thirds" is possibly the most crucial lesson you can learn in composition. It asks that you divide the frame into nine equal rectangles (draw a tic-tac-toe board on it) and that you place your area of interest at the intersection of two of those lines. Next time you're looking at still images or watching a movie, see how often this is used.

Leading Lines

Leading lines draw a viewer's eyes in a particular direction—railroad tracks, rivers, fallen trees, are all things that can be used to funnel the viewer's eyes across the screen to a particular object.

Juxtaposition

To "juxtapose" something is to place two things together for comparison. Sometimes this can be literal, like the millionaires in *Trading Places* juxtaposed next to Eddie Murphy playing a panhandler, or it can be symbolic, like the scene in *Star Wars*: *A New Hope*, where Obi Wan Kenobi and Darth Vader first meet. They are shown on the opposite sides of the screen, one good, and the other evil, representing the breadth of the human condition.

Headroom

Headroom is the space above a person's head. Too much or too little headroom and the image will look unbalanced or cramped.

(a)  (b)

Figure 47-2 *Imagine a tic-tac-toe grid over your viewfinder and frame your key elements in the intersections. Both of these subjects have a similar background, but the shot on the left is framed with a more interesting composition.*

(a)  (b)

Figure 47-3 *In the shot on the left, we have a good example of nose room. The man has breathing room to walk into. The woman in the shot on the right appears to bump her nose on the frame and doesn't have lead space.*

Nose Room

For some reason, it bothers us when we see someone looking into space with no room in front of them. When shooting a 3/4 or profile shot, leave space in front of the subject's nose.

Lead Room

Lead room is nose room for moving objects, like a moving horse or a car—leave space for the horse or the car to move into rather than crowding the side of the screen.

Background

Be wary of what's behind your subject. Through the viewfinder you're often very concentrated on the principal and don't realize until later that there is a telephone pole growing out of his or her head or a window sash that looks surprisingly like an arrow going in one ear and out the other. The background can also be used to add to your shot. When interviewing your grandfather about his experience in the war, for example, hanging his uniform or a map in the background, slightly out of focus, can add visual interest and useful information to the shot.

Figure 47-4 Framing your subject with good background gives your shot more interest. Try not to have him too close to the wall so he has more punch and depth.

Foreground

Likewise, the foreground can be used to add information—two people lying on a blanket in the foreground, for example, might suggest that the grassy expanse we're looking at is in a park. Put a deer in the same place, and, suddenly, it's a meadow in the woods. Place in a few well-dressed, out of focus people playing croquet, and it becomes an English manor.

Balance

Our own brain's function to keep us upright makes us seek balance in composition. An equally weighted frame appears to be at rest and makes the viewer calm. "Balanced" doesn't necessarily mean two people equal-distant apart. A person on the right-hand side of the screen might be "balanced" by a clock hanging on a wall on the left-hand side.

Tension

You don't necessarily want the viewer to feel peace and harmony all the time. One thing you often want to achieve is tension, which can be done by skewing the

balance, adding vertical or angled lines that take away from a balanced frame. Tilting the camera a few degrees to one side will keep your audience from relaxing. They might not even notice the horizon being off, but subconsciously, there is a feeling that something isn't quite right. Using a wide-angle lens that distorts a shot so that lines aren't parallel or perpendicular also creates tension.

Maintaining Your Composition

It's important to keep consistency in your composition to keep from confusing your viewer. Your actors need to look and speak in consistent directions, two characters facing one another over a dinner table, for example, shouldn't be shown in close-ups looking in the same direction.

Using Color

Color composition is a major part of many motion pictures—M. Night Shyamalan's *The Village*, for example, made good use of the color red to represent evil and cooler blues to represent good. Months before shooting begins, many directors, production designers, and directors of photography will choose a color palate for a movie, deciding what types of colors will work together to give the audience the proper "feel." For an example of hyper-color composition watch Peter Greenaway's *The Cook the Thief, His Wife & Her Lover.*

Conclusion

Don't get that cap and gown out of mothballs yet, it's not quite time for graduation.

We showed you the basics, next month; we'll show you some advanced tips on composition to take your shots from video postcards to masterpiece showcases.

48
The Art of the Edit

Janis Lonnquist

When Oliver Stone turned over the massive amount of raw footage that became *JFK*, editor Joe Hutshing knew it would be a challenge. "I wondered if it could even be watchable," Hutshing says. "It was so incredibly complicated. It was like looking at a schematic for a TV set and then imagining actually watching the TV."

From the mountain of raw footage, to the first five-hour cut, to the final three-hour-and-eight-minute editing masterpiece, Hutshing had to make decisions, consider choices and re-examine goals. This is editing.

Editing systems may range from sophisticated digital suites with all the bells and whistles to basic single-source systems consisting of a camera, TV and VCR. Still, the functions of editing remain the same:

1. to connect shots into a sequence that tells a story or records an event,

2. to correct and delete mistakes,

3. to condense or expand time and

4. to communicate an aesthetic.

Whether you're creating a Hollywood feature film or tightening a vacation video, the challenge is to take raw footage, and within the limitations of equipment and budget, transform it into something compelling and watchable.

Shooting with the Edit in Mind

Editing may be the final step of the production, but to make a truly successful video, you need to begin making editing choices in the concept stage. What will the overall look of the piece be? The mood? The pacing? Will you cut it to music? What kind of music?

There are several techniques that will help you plan. Prepare a shooting script, a storyboard or—if it is not a scripted production—an overview for your program. This will be the blueprint for your production.

A *shooting script* lists the action shot by shot, along with proposed camera angles and framing.

In a *storyboard*, actual sketches illustrate each scene. It's a good opportunity to see what will work before you shoot it.

An *overview* should include: the chronology of shots as they will appear in the video; approximate timing for each shot; and information about accompanying audio, graphics and titles for each scene.

Next, prepare a *shot sheet*. Make sure it includes every shot listed in your script or overview. Get several shots of each item on the list.

"You need a variety of shots," says Kevin Corcoran, vice president of Pacific Media Center in Santa Clara, California. "In a basketball game, for example, you get shots of the crowd, shots of the scoreboard, shots of the referee, shots of the environment. In action that's typically long and drawn out, you need to consolidate information. You need to have images to cut to in order to make it look smooth."

Even in scripted productions, Corcoran recommends getting a variety of shots.

"I always try to get a wide shot and a head and shoulders shot for each block of text," says Corcoran. "Who knows what you'll find when you go into an edit? There may be something that bothers you with continuity in the background of a wide shot. Now you have a place to go."

While Joe Hutshing had massive amounts of material to edit for *JFK*, Corcoran says the more common problem is too little material.

"Often there are large sections to be removed and no smooth way to cut," says Corcoran. "This is especially true when you're editing on a two-machine, cuts-only system. Ideally, you will have some other framing, another angle, a reaction or some other activity happening in the environment. If it's a person at a podium talking, you need an audience reaction shot or two or three. You must have cutaways to consolidate a half-hour speech without jump cuts."

You also invariably end up with footage you can't use, often due to the unexpected appearance of objects on tape that you never noticed during the shoot. Once, when editing the "dream house" segment of a TV program, I discovered a power supply right in the middle of the kitchen floor. Nobody saw it in the field and every sweeping pan—all wide shots—included the ugly box. Other than featuring a dream house with no kitchen, we had no option but to use the embarrassing piece of footage.

"There will always be things in shots you don't see when you're shooting," Corcoran says. "Things reflected in mirrors or windows, things in dark areas of the picture. It's important to change your framing to avoid having problems like this in the edit."

If you will edit your video to music, select the music in advance and time zooms and pans accordingly. If this isn't possible, shoot a slow, medium and fast version of each camera move. In general, shots should be five to 15 seconds in length. Know the pacing and shoot accordingly.

You'll enjoy a lot more options in your edit sessions if you aren't desperately "fixing it in post." Taking the appropriate technical precautions saves you from having to scrap otherwise good footage due to lighting, audio or other technical problems.

"In an event, things will only go wrong," Corcoran warns. "In weddings, for example, the light is nearly always bad. A camera light is essential, especially if you don't have gain control. And you'll need a lot of batteries for that light."

Good lighting greatly enhances the quality of your videos; invest in a lighting seminar if you need more information. As a rule, the brightest spot in your picture should be no more than 20 to 30 times brighter than the darkest spot or you'll be editing silhouettes.

You'll have trouble in your edit if you don't white balance several times during an event. This is particularly true during weddings, which may move from bright sunlight, to a dimly lit church, to fluorescent lights in a reception hall. If you don't white balance, the shots won't match—you may end up dissolving from a well-lit scene of groomsmen decorating the getaway car to a blue, blue reception.

Production Pains

Production can be exhausting, with long days of hard physical labor, but it's vital to stay alert.

On a particularly grueling corporate production a few years ago, a camera operator, who was also monitoring audio, removed his headset during a break and forgot to put it back on. Our talent, the president of the corporation, removed his lavaliere microphone to stretch, and sat down on it for the remainder of the production. Try to fix that in post.

Microphones can fall down, batteries can die, a cable can go bad. Without headphones, you may not know until it's too late.

"If you know from your headphones there's no hope for that microphone," Corcoran says, "you can unplug it and let the camera mic try. It's going to be better than what you'll get otherwise. Nothing can kill a production faster than bad audio. Wear your headphones all the time."

For most productions, steady images make the most sense. Always use a tripod. Hand-held looks, *well*, hand-held. There's a trend right now to overuse this technique, but avoid the *cinema verité*, or "shaky cam" look unless you're after a strobed look or the effect is actually motivated by something in the script.

Be sure to allow for preroll. When you switch a camera from the *stop* mode to *record*, it rolls back several seconds before it achieves "speed" and begins taping. Allow five seconds, 10 to be safe, before cuing the talent to begin speaking or executing your shot.

Unless your edit system is very precise (plus or minus two frames) you will have trouble editing to the word, so make sure that you have two seconds or more of silence before your talent begins.

This is better than saying "action" to cue the talent: if the narration begins too quickly, you may end up losing two seconds of narration in edit to cut out your cue. Instead, count "five, four, three" … and cue talent after a silent count of two and one.

With high-end systems, you can encounter a similar problem. If the tape is checked and action begins too soon, you won't be able to back up over the break in control track to execute the edit.

To allow time for a good transition, instruct your talent to fix a gaze on the camera for two seconds before and several seconds after a narration. A quick, sideways glance for approval, a swallow or a lick of the lips before or after speaking may be difficult to edit out.

If you don't have control over the talent's timing and delivery—for example, when shooting a training session or wedding—your cutaways and reaction shots will be critical to mask cuts. Remember to shoot plenty.

In the Frame

Good framing and composition are vital in achieving aesthetically pleasing video that is cohesive and makes sense. A well-composed shot provides viewers with the information needed to follow the story. It reveals, through spatial relationships, the comparative importance of individuals and objects, and the effect they have upon each other. It focuses attention on details, sometimes subtly, even subliminally. Good composition can also disturb, excite and/ or heighten tension if the script calls for it.

You can't fix poor framing and composition in post. A lack of headroom will make your subject seem suspended from the top of the TV monitor. Framing a shot to cut at the subject's ankles, chin, hands or hem line is an uncomfortable look that doesn't allow "closure," a process in which the mind fills in the missing elements.

Remember the rule of thirds: place important elements in the top or bottom third of the screen. In a closeup, place the eyes at the one-third baseline. In an extreme closeup, the eyes are at baseline of the top third, the mouth is at the baseline of the bottom third and, through closure, the chin and forehead are filled in.

Distracting or inappropriate backgrounds are nearly impossible to work around so pay attention to every detail when you shoot. In one production, a children's singing group performed a number in front of a blackboard. In the edit, I noticed one little girl standing directly in front of a large letter "M"—creating the look of two perfect, pointed ears. Again, saved by the B-roll.

Sometimes even balanced and thoughtfully composed shots don't cut together well. For example: if you're editing an interview or dialogue, cutting between head shots of the interviewer and guest, you need the heads angled slightly toward each other (to imply the interaction of the two) and off center, leaving "look space" or "nose room." Without look space, your interviewer will appear to address the edge of the TV screen. Centered, we have no sense of the spatial relationship of the two. They could be sitting back to back.

Similarly, maintain "lead room" for your subject to walk, run, bike or drive into.

Walk the Line

One production basic that can cause major consternation in the edit suite is "crossing the line."

Let's say you're shooting a parade passing in front of you, from left to right. A politician waves from a passing float, her back to you. You dash across the street and resume shooting, getting a great shot of her smiling face. When you go to edit, however, you'll find that you crossed the line: half of your parade marches left to right and the other half marches right to left. Cutting together footage from both sides of the line will create a bizarre montage where bands and floats and motorcades seem to run into one another.

Respecting the line is especially important in shots that track movement or where geography, such as movement toward a goal post, is critical to the viewer's understanding of the action.

Camera angles also play a role in the viewer's ability to interpret and believe the action. Let's say you want to show a child trying to coax a kitten from a tree. First we see the child looking up. We cut to the kitten cowering on a branch. We cut back to the child. The scene gains impact with the right camera angles. We see the child, framed left, looking up. Cut to a reverse angle shot looking down at the child, over the cat's shoulder, with the cat framed right. The camera angle duplicates the cat's line

of vision. Cut to a low angle shot of the cat from the child's point of view. The edited sequence is fluid and believable.

There are two kinds of continuity you should monitor for successful editing. First: continuity of the environment. A made-for-TV movie has a scene in which a man speaks to his doctor. He wears a shirt with the collar turned up. Cut to the doctor. Cut back to the man, and his collar is flat. Cut to a two-shot and the collar turns up again. Productions on all levels are full of goofs like this one. To avoid adding blooper footage of your own, pay close attention to detail both in production and in the edit.

For the best possible editing situation, you also need to watch continuity of action. If your talent can give you numerous takes with identical blocking, you'll have lots of editing options. Cuts-only editing is at its best when you can achieve a multicam look by cutting to different framing on action. Look for the apex of the action—the full extension of the arm, the widest part of the yawn, the clink of glasses in a toast—and use that apex as the marker to cut to a new angle of the same action.

Motivate It

Transitions should occur only when motivated by something in the story.

A *cut* is the instantaneous switch from one shot to another. The most common transition device, it duplicates the way we see. (Just try panning or zooming with your eyes.)

A *dissolve* is the gradual replacement of one image by another. Use it to show a passage of time or create a mood.

A *wipe* is a special effect of one image pushing the other image off screen. With digital technology, the options are nearly endless. A wipe can erase, burn, fold, kick or flush the first image from the screen. Wipes signify the end of a segment and the complete transition to a new time, place or concept.

A *fade* is the gradual replacement of an image with black or vice versa, used primarily to begin or end a program or video segment.

Creative editing, using a variety of transitions, is still possible on a cuts-only system. If you can't fade in or dissolve, begin your shot out of focus and gradually make the image clear. A very fast pan —15 frames or so of light, color and motion flying across the screen—is almost as effective as a dissolve. Allowing your subject to exit the shot ends a scene with the finality of a wipe. Cutting to a static shot, such as a close-up of a flower, a sign or a building, defines and separates scenes.

For greater insight, learn from the pros. Rent a well-done video and create an overview and shot sheet.

There are also seminars and many excellent books available on framing, composition and technique. For an in-depth study of media aesthetics, look for Herbert Zettl's *Sight, Sound and Motion.* Of course, editing is a practical as well as an aesthetic skill. On to the practicalities.

Editing Systems

Practically speaking, editing is simply copying selected video from the source tape to the edit master or record tape. A wide variety of systems and methods are available.

Single-Source Editing. You can perform single-source editing from your camcorder to your VCR. Your owner's manual will include complete directions; basically, you control the edit by pressing PLAY on your source deck (camera) and RECORD on the record deck (your VCR), pausing and releasing as you go. The transitions are cuts only.

This type of editing becomes frustrating quickly. As the editor you must locate edit points, manually set preroll, start the machines at the same time and react at precisely the right moment to control the edit. Frame accuracy is usually a problem. If you hit RECORD too soon, you suffer video noise between edits. Too late, and you lose frames on the edit master.

Expanded Single-Source Systems. The first investment single-source editors usually make is an edit controller. Most edit controllers allow you to shuttle to locate scenes, to mark in and out points, to read

and display frame numbers either from a pulse-count or time code system such as SMPTE or RCTC.

These editors perform the preroll function automatically and start the machines together. Many systems give you: 1) the option of insert or assemble edit, 2) the ability to "trim"—add or subtract a few frames without resetting in and out points and 3) the ability to preview your edit. Some perform audio or video only edits and interface with a computer to store an Edit Decision List (EDL).

You can also expand single-source edit systems with an audio mixer, a switcher and character generator.

Multiple-Source Systems. These give editors the capability of A/B Roll Editing. The typical system consists of two or more source VCRs (A and B), which supply material to the video switcher or computerized editing control unit. There, the material is edited, combined with effects and sent to the record VCR. Audio from the source decks is also mixed and sent to the record VCR.

Multiple-source systems allow an editor to connect two moving video sources with dissolves, wipes and other transitions.

In nonlinear systems, every frame is stored in digital form and is instantly available to the editor. Once you've designated an edit and transition on the computerized EDL or storyboard, the computer executes the edit instantly. You can grab a scene from anywhere in your source footage without waiting for a tape to cue. Experimentation becomes effortless.

As you move up to the more complex systems, do your homework. Read product reviews before you make the investment. Find out what peripherals you need for basic operations and efficient editing.

Investigate the availability of classes and user groups in your area. Is there a local production facility that rents a suite featuring the same system? You may need a back-up plan if your system goes down and you're facing a deadline.

Advanced Editing Systems. These systems feature Digital Video Effects (DVE), better compression, exciting animation, special effects, pro titles and more. They are revolutionizing editing, providing greater options, accuracy and speed.

The ramping of capabilities means a ramping of complexity; you'll need education and practice to get up to speed. The systems are relatively expensive and the technology is constantly changing. It isn't easy to know when to make the investment. Some videographers complain that editing functions have not been designed with editors in mind; they're waiting for upgrades to correct this. Others have found systems that meet their needs well, and are using them to produce amazing programs.

Again, do your homework. If you can, rent a suite and actually do an edit on a given system before you buy.

The Final Cut

It's payoff time. You planned ahead, you paid attention during production and now you can relax.

49
Title Talk

Bill Harrington

You've created the perfect video, great lighting, clean audio and beautiful editing. But be careful. All your hard work can be overshadowed if you are not careful with your titles. Titles, also called CGs (short for character generator), are the words you see on the screen. But adding titles is more than typing words onto your video. Good titles look balanced on screen and add to the message. Bad titles are like an out of tune instrument—they make the whole orchestra sound bad.

When it comes to making great titles, there are a few rules to follow. Just like making good video, it takes a certain amount of planning, knowledge and a lot of experimentation. An eye for composition doesn't hurt either. Here are some basic concepts you can use to enhance your titles.

Location! Location! Location!

Watch network television tonight and see if there is a logo in the bottom corner of the screen. It's not there by accident. The big guys understand that when it comes to the video screen, every pixel is a precious piece of real estate. In real estate, location is everything. We read from left to right, top to bottom. The bottom right corner of the screen is the last thing you will read. That logo stays imprinted on the mind, and when the friendly folks at Nielson ask you what station you watched, you can remember quite easily.

You can use that same knowledge to your advantage when you build your titles. The corners of the screen are the most powerful place for small informational graphics like logos or names. They also work well because titles placed there are less likely to interfere with the action in your video.

If you want to make a major statement, then place a title in the center of the screen, demanding your audience to take notice. This is where you would typically find the title of a program. Placed in the center of the screen, the title becomes the most important thing on the screen. More important than even the video that plays beneath it.

Play It Safe

There are some places that you really cannot put titles, though. Most CG software now has a safe title reference built in (see Figure 49-1). These lines represent recommended limits to where you place your titles within the viewing area. Any titles outside of the safe title zone risk being unreadable due to the cropping and curvature of the TV screen. Keeping your titles within a safe title area is not an absolute, but you reduce the effectiveness of your titles if they are outside of the safe title zone.

Lastly, the text on the screen has to work with everything else the audience is seeing. Your subject's name won't look good superimposed over his face. It has to balance with the video you're using. If you interview a vet about his WWII memories and he's on camera left, try putting the title on the right to balance the overall picture.

The Font Is the Message

Sometimes it's not what you say, but how you say it. This applies to the fonts you use for your titles. Graphic designers can spend years learning about font theory, but you don't need a master's degree to understand that the font—the actual shape of the letters—sends a message to the viewer. Does the text look like ancient Greek writing or is it more futuristic? There are thousands of fonts available,

and the font you choose will have a direct impact on the final product.

Let's say you videotaped a local Christmas pageant and want to add a graphic as an introduction. A font that has a cowboy feel wouldn't make any sense. Unless the name of the pageant was *Christmas on the Prairie*, such a font would just confuse the viewer. A Christmas pageant screams for something with a holiday feel. Scripted letters would look nice and would convey the holiday spirit more effectively.

Look to the video itself for clues as to what font to use. The font you use should tie into the theme of the video (see Figure 49-2). Don't overwhelm your audience with a lot of different fonts either. Stick to just one or two. If you need two separate lines of text to stand out from each other, try making one line bold or italicized rather than changing the font.

Now We're Styling

The style of a title is the sum of all the specific attributes that give it a particular look. The font plays a crucial role, but so does the color, edge, shadow and framing of the text. These characteristics, or the lack of them, also contribute to the message you

Figure 49-1 *Safety First—Remember to observe the safe area whenever you're creating titles.*

Figure 49-2

Figure 49-3 *Correct Colors—Different colors send different messages. Make sure you choose a color that communicates what you want.*

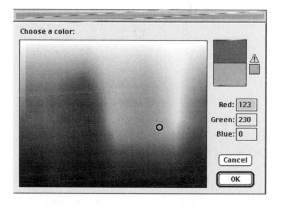

Figure 49-4 *Warning Signs—Some editing software will alert you if your color is too saturated.*

are sending. For example, lighter colors tend to be easier to read and seem happier, while darker colors can add a more urgent or even ominous tone to the title.

Color is a great tool to reinforce the theme of the project. Let's go back to the Christmas pageant title. Should you use black and orange for your text? Of course not. That would be more appropriate for a Halloween project. Christmas colors—like reds, greens and whites—would work better (see Figure 49-3).

Adding color can be a tricky task. Video tends to have problems with certain colors, particularly shades of red. The concentration of chroma/color tends to bleed across the screen. If you must use red, try adding a thick black outline to contain the bleeding. Remember, colors will look brighter on TV than they do on your computer. Make your reds and greens slightly darker than you'd like them to appear on tape. Many titling software applications have a "safe color" mode that will warn you against using a color that will over-saturate the video.

Yellow tends to be the easiest color to read (next to white) and is often used for video titles (see Figure 49-4).

What Did That Say?

After learning all of the different ways to present your title, you still need to ask the most important question, what will your title say? First, determine if you need graphics at all. Your titles should be limited to only those that advance the story in some way. Video artists often use titles extensively to add a poetic layer to their work, however, graphics with no real purpose tend to irritate the viewer more than anything else.

How long should a title stay on the screen? Rule of thumb says that a title should stay up long enough for the viewer to read it aloud three times. Any shorter is too short. Any longer and your viewers may become distracted by the presence of the title. Obviously, the longer the title the longer it must remain on the screen. A person's name may remain on the screen for as little as two or three seconds, a graphic spelling out a five-sentence quote may need to stay on the screen for thirty seconds or more. Of course, there are exceptions to every rule. If you have the quote read by a narrator, you can take it out after he has read it through just once.

Putting It All Together

Great titles don't just happen, they take knowledge, planning and a lot of experimentation. Like good video, the better you plan your project the better off you are in editing. Titles are no exception. Remember, your titles are written in video, not in stone. When you're building your titles, look at them critically. Do they make sense visually? Is your spelling correct? Do they add to the message? Don't hesitate to experiment with your titles. Try something different. If you go too far and the visuals just don't work, you can always change them before going to tape.

When it all comes together well, the titles complement the video and *vice versa*. This seamless integration of titles and video can make a word worth a thousand pictures.

Sidebar 1

Glossary of Common Titling Terms

Font. The shape and style of the letters. There are thousands of fonts available; each unique font can send a different message.

Border. The border of your font is the edge surrounding the letters. Changing the size or color of the border can have a dramatic impact.

Shadow. Separate from border, the shadow can either attach to the letters or not. Shadows can be solid or have a degree of transparency.

Justification. Where the words are in relation to the screen: left, center or right.

Kerning. The spacing between the letters of a word. Some fonts are not consistent with their spacing and may need some manual kerning.

Leading. The spacing between lines of text.

Safe Title Area. The area of a video screen where titles are easily read and without distortion: roughly the inner 60% of the screen.

Sidebar 2

Shadows and Outlines

Whether or not your text has a soft drop shadow or a hard outlined edge can add a subtle difference. Soft shadows and outlines communicate a softer message, while hard edges often imply boldness or urgency.

Sidebar 3

TV Is the Key

Want to make better titles? Watch more TV! Study the titles that you see on television, note the colors, fonts and styles that are used and try to copy them when you build your own titles.

50

Adventures in Sound Editing:
Or How Audio Post-Production Can Make Your Videos Sound Larger Than Life

Armand Ensanian

Imagine the tape you made of your kids' last campout. It's got some crickets on the sound track. At night, didn't those crickets seem to chirp louder as campers grew quieter and the sky grew darker?

When Bobby started telling Billie Jo the story of the cricket that ate sisters, didn't those chirpings seem even louder to her? With some equalization, reverb and creative mixing of your original sound track, you could let your viewers hear those monster crickets the way Billie Jo heard them.

Sound editing can turn commonplace video events into adventures that seem larger than life. With some simple electronic equipment—some of which you may already have on your stereo system—you can polish up any raw sound track. Here's how.

Know Your Sound

To make good video, you need to understand light; likewise, to make good audio, you will need to understand sound.

Webster's defines sound as "mechanical vibrations traveling through the air or other elastic medium." How many times these vibrations occur in a second is the *frequency* of the sound. A tuning fork vibrating back and forth 1,000 times per second generates sound (with a frequency of 1,000 cycles per second or Hertz (Hz). If it vibrated 200 times per second, we'd hear a frequency of 200 Hz.)

Variations and combinations of frequencies account for all the sounds we hear. At best, the human ear can recognize frequencies between 32 and 22,000 Hz. We can perceive frequencies below 32 Hz, but as vibration, not sound. This range deteriorates with age or abuse. It is not uncommon for senior adults to top out at 9,000 Hz, while losing all low-frequency sounds below about 150 Hz.

People with ear damage will adjust sound to match their deficiency. For example, a sound engineer at a rock club may set up the PA to produce ear piercing highs to compensate for such a loss of his high frequency sensitivity. So if you plan to use the services of a studio, make sure your sound engineer can hear.

The interaction of two or more frequencies creates a third sound called *harmonic*. Harmonics, also known as overtones, give sound its life, allowing the human ear to distinguish one voice from another. Poor recordings reduce or eliminate harmonics, turning sound into an unintelligible mess.

Good recordings recognize the harmonics of a sound track, and enhance them—with the help of some snazzy audio post-production devices.

The Mixer

The single most important tool for audio production is the *mixer*.

A mixer's number of input channels determines how many different signals— read sounds—you can work with simultaneously. You need at least two for mono recordings and four for stereo. More inputs allow you to control more sound sources.

Remember that the tape speed and audio recording format will determine the frequency response of the recording medium. A VHS tape recorded on the linear track at EP speed may yield a frequency response no higher than 7,000 Hz. So stick with hi-fi audio if possible.

The first step is to hook up the right cables to the proper inputs and outputs. Do not scrimp on cables, because bad connections can create a lot of buzz and noise. A good mixing console will allow an input signal to be either microphone or line level. This compensates for low-level microphone signals and high-level line inputs, such as those arriving from VCRs,

cassettes or CD players. Output will be mono or stereo, depending on your VCR.

Mixers have sliders, or *faders*, that control volume for each channel. A master fader controls overall volume. Mixers will also feature all or some of the following: attenuation, equalization, cue sends, pan pots, solo switch, monitor control, Volume Unit (VU) meters or Liquid Element Displays (LEDs) and echo/reverb.

Attenuation cuts down high input signals to prevent overloading.

Equalizers allow precise tone adjustment of selected frequency ranges.

Cue sends can send the signal to the video tape, headphone or monitor speaker.

Pan pots control the spatial position between right and left stereo channels.

The *solo switch* "listens" in on any individual channel without interfering with the recording process.

Monitor controls adjust headphone or speaker volume. We'll look at echo and reverb later.

The Equalizer

An *equalizer* (EQ) is the most common piece of signal processing equipment. It allows you to divide the entire (human) 32–22,000 Hz audio spectrum into separate bands you can adjust independently. With an EQ, you can raise or lower the levels of these bands to change the tonal characteristics of a sound, reduce noise and even create certain audio effects.

Many mixers have a simple EQ built-in, allowing you to adjust high and low frequencies independently. This is fine for broad tonal changes, but for more control, you'll need a graphic equalizer. Though a handful of mixers offer this level of tonal control, most graphic EQs are external units.

Whereas simple EQs use knobs—one for treble, one for bass—graphic equalizers have vertical sliders that show the amount of correction you applied to each band of frequencies. Thus you can tell, at a glance, what the graphic EQ is doing to the audible spectrum. Hence the term graphic.

Think of the graphic EQ as a vastly expanded bass/treble dial. The more sliders, the greater the selective control.

Say you have some music on your soundtrack that sounds flat and unexciting. Try boosting the 100 Hz and 10,000 Hz sliders, while lowering the 1,000 Hz to 500 Hz sliders. The graphic pattern on the equalizer will look like a suspension bridge–what you'll hear is rock concert sound.

If you're working with classical music, you may need to elevate the middle frequencies to bring out specific instruments. And Aunt Trudy's squeaky voice may require you to slide down the high and upper midrange frequencies.

Hooking up a stand-alone EQ is easy— simply connect it between the source output and mixer input. Or, if you want to alter your whole sound mix, place the EQ between your mixer and record deck.

On the Level

In the world of audio post-production, the strength or "level" of an audio signal is as important as the way it sounds. We have our ears to tell us that a sound is tonally correct; for clean recordings we need something to tell us about the signal's level.

VU meters and LEDs monitor the levels so you can prevent overloading and distorting the signal. VU meters use a unique scale calibrated in decibels (dB), which measure actual signal strength.

VU meters boast an ascending scale of values that start with negative numbers. Instead of being at the bottom, zero is near the top of the range. Why? Because zero dB indicates a full-strength signal. This way it's easy to remember that if a signal strays much above zero, distortion may result.

Sometimes, simply setting a record level based on the VU meter isn't enough.

Some sounds jump wildly from loud to soft, making them distorted one second and virtually inaudible the next. The difference between these very loud and soft sounds is the *dynamic range*.

Changes in dynamics, at least within reason, are good. It's the dynamic range of a recording or vocalist that conveys realism and power. Streisand's vocal style is dynamic, my grandmother's isn't.

But when recording sounds, too much dynamic range can be a problem. Thankfully, there's help available from a nifty device called a *limiter*. A limiter reduces instant signal peaks, such as a loud scream or feedback from an electric guitar. A limiter allows you to set a maximum signal level; the unit holds all sound under that limit.

A *compressor* works somewhat like a limiter, though its effects are less dramatic. Radio stations use compressors to maintain high signal levels without fearing distortion. The small sacrifice in realism may be worth it if you plan on taping loud live concerts or monster truck rallies. Good production mixers have limiters built in, for controlling sounds at the time of recording.

Reverb

Sound loses energy as it moves through the air. Sound strength drops 6 dB every time you double the distance between a mike (or ear) and the sound source. This is why good microphone technique includes moving the mike close to the sound source during live shooting or narration dubbing.

Sound waves bound off walls and hard objects. Echoes are bouncing waves that follow more than 1/20 second after the original sound; reverb is repeated reflecting waves that sound almost continuous.

Post-production electronics can simulate both these effects. Echo and reverb units can run the gamut from simple tape loops, playing back what you record immediately, to sophisticated digital reverbs simulating rooms of all shapes and sizes.

Reverb units bring fullness to sound. With a reverb you can make a three-piece band playing in the basement sound like a major concert hall event. Reverb emulates the sound of a big hall. But watch out—too much reverb will make things muddy.

Reverb also adds authority to a narrator's voice. Rock and roll's ultimate DJ, Cousin Brucie, uses a lot of reverb.

Reverb, particularly when applied to drums, can make a band sound bigger than life on tape. Now you know how rock bands maintain the ambiance of the concert hall on recorded media.

Once it's on tape, you can't eliminate reverb easily from a recording. That's why recording engineers add it later for maximum control. Use sound-absorbing dampeners—rugs, blankets, egg cartons—in small studios whenever recording to capture a clean dry sound. Then employ electronics in post-production to simulate real room resonance.

Digital delays are similar to reverbs. They electronically delay the input signal for a selected amount of time. You can produce echoes of extremely short duration. Use digital delays to double a vocal, and you can make it sound as though two people are singing together. And, if you take one output channel from the delay and run it through an EQ, you may even make it sound like two different people. The possibilities are infinite.

Phase shifters delay the incoming signal slightly, causing the delayed signal to partially cancel the original. This causes whooshing sound effects—good for planes, trains and other speedy objects.

Going for the Take

Okay, you've got your mixer and your equalizer. Now you must decide which sounds you need for the mixing session.

Much pre-recorded material is available, but you may want to experience the thrill of creating your own sound effects (SFX) like they did in the old radio shows. Crumpled cellophane, for example, makes good rain or eggs frying. But keep in mind you only have two hands to work with and will need them for the mixing board. If you can, have an assistant with you during a mix.

Say you're audio mixing a wedding tape. You can "sweeten" up all your location audio through use of both technique and equipment. You may need to clean up and equalize the live audio vocals a bit.

You'll also want to work on the sound from your outdoor segments—selectively equalizing background noises or reduce them manually during spoken passages. That waterfall, for example, near the wedding party blocked out some of the vocal interaction. An EQ can help, as well as a touch of reverb on the vocalists' voices.

When possible, record musical interludes preceding the ceremony—such as a soloist's number—on cassette rather than relying on a room mike during the shoot itself. If the bride doesn't object, the artist may have a professionally recorded tape of the same material you can use to replace the live track. After all, we are not focusing our attention on the soloist unless there are a lot of close-ups requiring lip sync.

In almost any kind of production, consider using background or "wallpaper" music track for continuity. It will fill in those silent gaps often associated with live footage. One cheap trick; try an inexpensive keyboard with built-in rhythm sounds as background. Use the individual slider on the mixer to boost the volume of the background gently during these silent periods.

If you're relying on pre-recorded music, find selections that don't clash with the theme of your video. For a wedding, don't use anything overly aggressive or dynamic; instrumentals are a safe bet. You may wish to sprinkle in some sound effects like ambience or laughter. Stock music of applause and laughter may follow special introductions at the reception.

By now you will have run out of hands. Starting the CD player just in time while cross fading from the live track to an overdub makes this a job for an octopus. Pro studios use computer sequencers and remote controls to help. It is best to try a few dry runs before actually recording onto the final tape. While practicing, send the mixer output to a cassette recorder so that you can listen later. It is very difficult to be objective while working the mixer.

With most projects, you'll find it challenging at best to audio edit the entire length in one pass. Use cuts and scene breaks in the video for audio transitions and segues. Have an assistant keep records of tape count and time passed as editing cues. Have him or her act as an audio director, coaching you through the moves.

Complicated editing may require sound recording the output to a tape recording before laying it on the videotape. A minimum of two output channels will be sent to corresponding tracks on a tape recorder. You may use the individual left and right channels of a stereo cassette recorder for two-track mono recording. This is ideal for adding narratives that may require numerous takes. You can then mix the two-track master directly onto the video. You'll have control over each individual channel.

Successive generations do add noise, but what a small price to pay for such flexibility. You can also add noise suppression or filters for the final mix-down. Four, eight, twelve, sixteen and twenty-four track audio recorders are available at recording studios for complicated mixes of numerous audio elements.

It takes a lot of practice to learn proper audio mixing technique. Even a small video switcher/audio mixer demands a lot of attention. The results, however, are light-years ahead of what you produce in-camera.

51

In the Audible Mood:
Sound Effects and Music—
Evocative, Legal and
Inexpensive

Armand Ensanian

Imagine *Popeye* without *toot toot*, *Casablanca* without *As Time Goes By*, *Jaws* without *bum BUM bum BUM bum BUM*. The soundtrack is the very lifeblood of a video, setting the mood and enlivening each scene of your work.

The trick is to find the right set of sounds to accompany your video. The options are many, from creating sound effects yourself—a la old-time radio—to buying mood music from a music library. In this chapter, we'll explore these options, and discuss the legal and financial ramifications of your choices.

The Copyright Challenge

The availability and affordability of a simple special effects generator (SEG) with built-in audio mixing has prompted many videographers to try adding music to video during editing.

It's harmless fun, attaching a favorite song to a tender moment between mother and child, a hot rock tune to fast-paced footage

at the track or some Benny Goodman to Grandma and Grandpa's 50th anniversary party tape. After all, you're not planning to make thousands of copies for distribution. What are the chances that the composer, publisher or lyricist of the songs will ever see this tape, anyway? Slim at best; no one's going to bust you for borrowing a tune or two for personal use.

The trouble begins when you turn pro or even semi-pro.

Every serious videographer will eventually land a real-world assignment: a wedding video, local commercial or contest entry video. Whatever the application, you cannot use someone else's work without permission in any video offered for sale, profit and/or distribution. Music is like photography, sculpture or any art you can hold in your hands. Yet the fact that you can't hold it in your hands makes music ripe for theft by otherwise law-abiding citizens.

You needn't stoop to theft. You can buy great sound effects and music for your videos from a number of sources. The first is the most expensive. It involves buying the rights, for one-time use, of a pop song performed by a noted artist.

Your clients will request this sort of thing often. After all, most clients can only relate to what they know and hear on the radio. You'll have to explain that you simply can't use the pop song without getting permission from the artist's representatives first.

This means the artist's publisher or licensing agency, such as the American Society of Composers, Authors and Publishers (ASCAP). You've seen the name on almost every record, cassette tape or CD you own. ASCAP operates like a big collection agency, collecting fees for the use of its artists' material. It's a fair system that keeps artists from getting ripped off—but it's an expensive one for videographers.

The price you pay for one-time use rights of a pop song depends on how you distribute the tape. Radio stations, TV stations and local bars with a jukebox pay agencies like ASCAP a blanket fee.

This fee may range from thousands of dollars for a radio station to a few hundred dollars a year for that jukebox. (For more info, call ASCAP in New York, 212-595-3050.)

Unless you expect your video to make a big profit, paying for rights to use a hit tune may be unwise. There are cheaper ways to go.

One way is to create your own music. If you've the talent and the time, this is a worthwhile option. You can use your desktop video equipment to make music; MIDI interfaces to Macs and PCs provide the musically inclined with unlimited creative potential.

Software and sound cards can produce digital sound that rivals the best CDs. Some even come with hundreds of digital sound samples, ranging from pianos to xylophones.

Despite all this automation, you'll still need to have a musical ear, something that's not included. If you don't have an ear for music, find local musicians to participate in your production. They'll have both the equipment and the ear you need.

You'll find, however, that the more people involved, the longer the process. Just make sure all parties sign an agreement transferring the rights to use the material over to you. Handshake deals don't carry the weight they once did.

The simplest solution, and perhaps the best bang for the buck, is to buy the music from a music library. The quality of the material will be as good as or better than you'd expect. You have heard music library soundtracks all your life. Commercials, opening scenes to sport events, TV news shows and presentation videos all use music made to augment video productions. In fact, most of the music is so much like what you hear on the radio that it's often easy to persuade clients to use music library tracks. Moreover, much of what's available was written and composed by award-winning musicians; the quality is first rate.

Libraries

You'd be surprised at how well music libraries categorize music—broadcast promotional; broadcast show theme; corporate imaging; corporate icon build; credit roll; documentary; events such as weddings, birthdays and anniversaries; industrial presentations; news and information; movie soundtrack; retail presentation; retail promotional; sound-alike; sports/action and underscore—to name a few.

All of us have a good sense of what these many categories sound like. Just watch some TV or look at a promo tape at the local travel agency. Still unsure?

Music libraries will gladly send you a tape or disk of material for approval for a specific tune; some even offer sample CDs.

There are many ways to buy music from music libraries. The traditional method charges per needle drop. This means you pay only for a specific selection of music used from their records, tapes or CDs. The term comes from the days of the phonograph, but applies to tapes and CDs as well. Most large music libraries will help you find exactly what you need. Computer databases allow quick searches from tens of thousands of titles.

The dollars add up quickly here, but you may obtain a very distinct tune, for a one-time production, that's not available from any other source. This is ideal for videographers who don't produce a lot of videos, but who need a unique style of music when they do.

Music library charges for needle drops depend mostly on the extent of use. For example, the charge for broadcasting the same music on the same video will vary, depending on whether it's broadcast in Smalltown, USA, or Metropolis. Determined by the number of viewers, needle-drop fees may range from $150 for a network TV broadcast opening title to only $50 for a local TV program. The only other cost: $20 for leasing the CD that contains the material. You make your choice from the CD, report the piece of music you will use and pay for it.

There are other methods of dealing with music libraries. You may buy a production-blanket where you pay only for the music for a given production. Typically you select a CD with a variety of musical themes from a library, and use as much of it as you wish, provided you restrict that use to that production. Costs depend on the size of the project and distribution, but average in the hundreds of dollars.

Annual-blanket fees allow you to buy licensing rights to a group of CDs for unlimited use during a given year. Popular with high-volume videographers, radio and TV stations, fees from reputable large firms are around $1,000 for a group of over a dozen or two different theme CDs for the year. You can also sign multi-year contracts with CD upgrades.

The best value: a buy-out library. Here you pay a one-time price for a CD, or set of CDs, that contains the music you need. You may use the CD as often as you wish, for as long as you live. You can better appreciate this deal when you know that you can purchase buy-out libraries for as little as $5 per sample tape from small independent producers advertising in the back of magazines.

But cheap can also mean poor quality. Listen to sample disks and tapes before you buy.

Sound Subscription

You may want to subscribe to a library service. Here you receive a CD every month or two, and have the option to keep it for a one-time fee. Beware, though: you may soon find yourself way overstocked, and stuck with soundtracks you'll never use.

It's like that videotape collection you started a few years back; despite the variety you always seem to stick with a few favorites. A variation on the subscription theme: lease the entire contents of a music library for a term, such as a year, and receive new CDs every month or two to add to that library.

One last note of caution: music libraries are licensed to individuals or production companies. Borrowing a library CD from a friend, and then putting your name on the finished product is a direct violation of copyright.

Stay honest. It'll pay off in the long run.

52
Seeing Sounds

Hal Robertson

Think back to high school science for a moment. Remember how we were taught that sound waves were invisible and could only be heard and felt? The humble audiometer offers a simple way for video producers to visualize audio volume as they record and post their projects. But what if I told you there are ways to look deeper into the content of your soundtrack? Would you be interested? This month, we'll explore a couple of different techniques for better understanding what's hiding inside your audio soundtracks.

Information Please

Level meters are an important tool for the video producer. During the shoot, they help identify correct sound levels, ensuring a clean, punchy soundtrack. During post, level meters keep things in check as you add audio elements to your production—too strong and the audio will distort, too weak and your viewers will lunge for the remote control. As useful as level meters are, they only tell a small part of the story—namely, volume.

Your audio editor of choice operates in a mode called "waveform view." Many NLEs have this feature as well, but you'll probably have to find and activate it. The waveform view offers a clear picture of your recorded sound from beginning to end. Tall spikes indicate loud passages while softer sections are visibly lower in volume. Using the zoom feature, it's easy to magnify various areas of the waveform for further analysis. Zooming is perfect for finding edit points in dialog and music. Learning to interpret what you see is the key professional audio editing.

Figure 52-1 is a small segment of voice-over dialog for a movie trailer. What you see is the word "starring." Closer examination shows the vowels and consonants of the word. The burst of sound at the beginning is the "S" sound followed by an intense spike for the "T" sound. As the "A" sound melds into the "R," then the "ING" you'll see a combination of waves superimposed on each other. While it would be difficult to guess the words and letters without hearing them, you can easily see the difference in the sounds. This makes it easy to identify small clicks, pops and breath sounds, simplifying your editing duties.

The next figure (Figure 52-2) is a sample of music. The goal is to extract a four-measure section to loop under a DVD menu. Waveform view makes it easy to see the beats and musical changes in the piece. After a brief listen, you find the perfect section. After setting rough cue points, zoom in tight to find the actual downbeat of the starting measure. If you zoom in close enough, you'll see exactly where the beat begins. Notice where the waveform moves from negative to positive territory. This point is called the "zero crossing" point

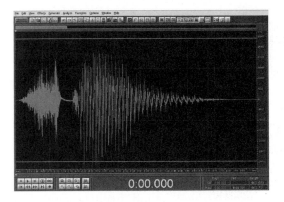

Figure 52-1 *Though this may not look like the word "starring" at first sight, it is in the language of the waveform.*

and is important in editing your perfect loop. If you do not make your edit at this intersection, you will likely hear a small click or pop at the beginning of the loop. Most popular audio editing programs automate this process or at least provide a way to easily identify the zero crossing nearest your edit point. I realize we're talking about fractions of a frame here but, if it's easy to get it right the first time, why do it any other way? After you've set the starting point, move to the end of the loop and find the exact same point and move your cue point accordingly. With a little practice, this makes it easy to identify and edit the perfect loop or cut for your video project.

The Whole Spectrum

Another useful option is spectrum or frequency analysis. You're probably familiar with the histogram view in your photo editor. Spectrum analysis is the same thing for audio, showing the intensity of specific frequencies in your soundtrack. Let's say your voice-over artist sent an audio file of his performance. You've edited the best cuts, but it sounds too boomy. You could apply a graphic equalizer and fool with the controls

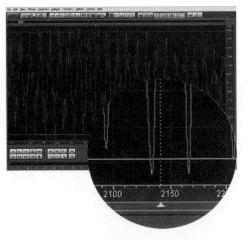

Figure 52-2 *Waveform monitors make it easier for editors to make their own looping sound bites such as this stereo four-beat piece (image left). By finding the zero crossing point at the downbeat of choice, an editor can smoothly loop a group of sounds (image right).*

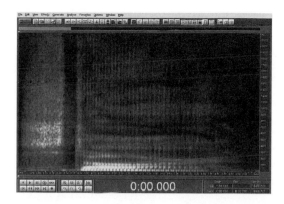

0:00.000

Figure 52-3 A spectrum analysis is very similar to a histogram view in photography, letting you see specific frequencies in your soundtrack.

until the sound improves, but there's a better way. Using spectrum analysis on a troublesome section, you can actually see the buildup of sound in the exact frequency range. This gives you the information you need to apply the proper amount of equalization or filtering to correct the problem. Spectrum analysis can be applied in several different ways. The simplest is to highlight a small segment of your audio and have the program scan the content. This produces an accurate snapshot of the audio content for that particular piece. Another method is real-time analysis. Here, you play the audio while the software shows

the peaks and valleys in real time. Watching your audio change over time is often the best way to assess the content and plan for adjustments. Some software allows you to load a WAV file for analysis—the program scans the entire file and displays frequency content for the entire piece.

The frequency analysis function in Adobe Audition offers another unique feature—pitch detection. With this option, you can actually see whether individual notes of a vocal performance are sharp or flat, and by how much. Using this information, you can apply a pitch shift to the offending note or notes, correcting the performance. Keep in mind, this only works on solo instruments and voices, but it's the type of repair that can save your project.

Scratching the Surface

This is one of those topics that require some homework on your part. Reading about visualizing sound is very different from doing it. Experience is the key. You won't want or need all these techniques all the time but, by understanding the principles, you'll know when to use them properly. Dig into your audio software, try some of the examples and you'll soon see sound in a brand new light.

Sidebar

Everyone's Different

Adobe Soundbooth (and Audition, for that matter), Apple's Sound Track Pro, Digidesign's Pro Tools and Sony Sound Forge have advanced, integrated audio analysis tools. But what if your editor doesn't have this option or you do your editing and mixing with your NLE? Google searching for "audio spectrum analysis" will reveal several options, but the king has to be Elemental Audio's InspectorXL. This amazing plugin sports every audio display you could imagine—and a couple you couldn't. Learning to interpret these displays will take time, but this level of information puts your audio productions on the leading edge.

53
Setting the Mood

Hal Robertson

The table is set with wine and roses. Candles create a soft glow as the attractive couple enters for their dinner. He holds her chair for her, then, before he finds his place at the table, he selects some mood music for their dining experience. A CD slides into the player … he punches the play button, and … we hear the screaming sounds of a heavy metal guitar solo shredding through the speakers.

Now, I like a good head-bang from time to time, but it just doesn't suit this scene. Music has the power to make or break your project and selecting the proper piece is crucial for any job you tackle. Let's take a few minutes to consider how music sets the mood in a video and how to find just the right cut for your project.

Choose Wisely

There are obvious and not-so-obvious elements to selecting music for your video project. I always like to start at the end of the process—the viewer. Who will see your finished video and what do they expect. Will they watch it on television, DVD or the Internet? Is there a stereotypical

music genre associated with the content of your project? If you're not sure of the answers to these questions, look for examples of similar videos at your local video store, library or even online. While watching the samples, pay attention to the style, tempo and mix of the music—you'll find plenty of hints and maybe even a bad example or two. Dramatic stories often have orchestral music or a blend of pop and orchestra. Tender, thoughtful moments will likely be accented with a solo instrument like a piano or guitar. Action scenes have a fast-paced music track that is full and aggressive, complete with pounding drums. Of course, there are other options, but this is a good start.

Let's get back to our viewer for a moment. How do you want him or her to feel during your video? Music is perfect for creating moods and enhancing emotions. The right selection can make your viewer feel sympathetic, angry or upbeat. In advertising and product videos, proper music selection can help your viewer feel good about the product purchased or the number he or she is about to dial. In a training video, music can move the content

Figure 53-1 *The correct music, whether a full score or used as background, helps set the mood you want your viewer to feel. A battle scene might call for a full orchestra, but a romantic interlude might require only a simple piano tickling. Drum solos or crashes make a strong beat for hip action shots.*

along, keeping the viewer's attention focused on the information and not the clock on the wall. Maybe you don't like country music, but a video about farming or bull riding should probably have a country flavor to create a familiar feel for your audience. Regardless of the video topic or genre, keep the viewer in mind.

Music from Where?

Today's video producer has many musical options to choose from. There have never been more choices in style, cost or variety. In fact, the hardest part may be narrowing the field to the right music for your project. In any case, you can buy it, create

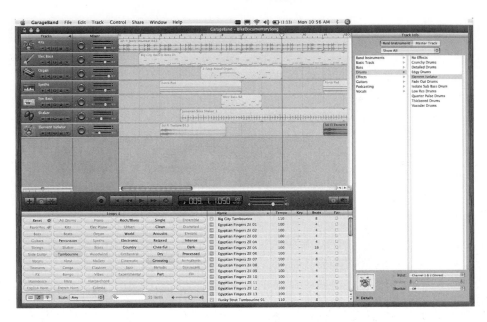

Figure 53-2 *Garage Band is an easy to use yet sophisticated looping music production program that ships free with new Apple computers.*

it or shape it. Buyout music is a huge category for the video producer. A quick Google search for the phrase "buyout music" will yield over 2,000,000 pages! Alternatively, you may want to start by leafing through the advertisements in this magazine. You'll find several vendors supplying buyout or royalty-free music. Buyout music is what the name implies—buy once and it's yours to use as many times as you want, in any number of projects. Buyout music comes in many forms—from MP3 downloads to variety CDs and even entire libraries. Most vendors allow you to sample each song online to help find the perfect mood-setting track for your project. Once you've found the song or songs you need, you can download and use them immediately or order the CD and wait a few days. If you can afford it, buying a variety of songs is a great way to go. This offers flexibility in both current and future projects.

If you're a musically creative type, you may want to build your own custom music with a program like Acid, Garage Band or even Adobe Audition. This type of loop-based music creation software lets you combine short loops of sounds—drums, bass, keyboards, guitars, you name it—on a timeline to create an original song. The advantage here is the level of control you leverage over the musical elements. Need a hole for dialog? You can either leave some loops out in that section or draw a volume envelope to bring things down. Want to create a suspenseful moment? Change the key of the music or create a whole new section from a different set of loops—you are in complete control of the mood and style of the music. If you're new to loop-based music, drop by AcidPlanet.com and download its free version of Acid Xpress. It has everything you need to decide if this is the musical path to take.

If buyout music is too rigid for your taste and loop-based creation is more than you wanted to tackle, consider shaping your music with these tools. Digital Juice has created a unique option with its Juicer software and the Stack Traxx libraries. Stack Traxx volumes contain 40 songs in a certain genre. By loading a song into the Juicer, you can create new versions by removing certain instruments or tracks. Is that guitar solo a mood-killer? Just eliminate it and output a new mix minus the offending instrument. Or better yet, use the multi-track

Figure 53-3 *The intuitive SonicFire Pro 4 from SmartSound lets the producer define the emotion with its Mood Mapping solution.*

output option and load individual tracks into your audio editor or NLE. Using keyframes and volume envelopes, you can shape the song as you like—emphasizing certain parts and moving others to the back of the mix. It takes some experimentation, but this may be just what you need to create the right mood for your video.

Alternatively, SmartSound and Sony have each introduced products that do something they call "mood mapping." Both programs work with your finished video, allowing you to set markers at scenes where you want the musical mood to change. By selecting specific moods from a list, the software will create a soundtrack that synchronizes musical changes to your markers. Each product works in a different

way, but both have similar goals. This may be the perfect option for small producers who need specific moods but don't have the time or budget to hire musicians.

In the Mood

This article has just touched the surface of creating moods with music. You'll have to decide which method is best for your production. Maybe you'll use a different one every time, who knows? Just remember the power of music to create a mood and evoke a response from your viewer. Picking the right music for the right moment is a compelling way to enhance the quality and impact of your video.

PART V

Television Distribution

Broadcasting your programs through cable and over-the-air TV.

54
Commercial Distribution: Mapping Your Way to Financial Success

William Ronat

Making video means working with motion, sound, color, words, composition, light— all combined in a maximum creative effort. That's fun.

Many have produced enough video to get good at it. This means putting in long hours planning, shooting and editing programs. That's work.

When you work for a company, you expect a paycheck when you finish your work. That's reasonable.

When you work for yourself, however, you can expect to work just as hard to sell your product as you did to make it. That's life.

Fun and Profit

To sell your product, several things have to happen. People have to know your product exists. They have to decide that the product is something they want. Then they have to pull their money out of their pockets and hand it to you.

This exchange can take the form of tickets at a theater, credit card information over the phone, money from the advertisers running commercials on your show or checks from all those networks buying your product. It all boils down to this: you get paid.

That's what you want. You may travel many paths to this destination. You can sell directly to the consumer through magazine ads or direct mail; you can work through a distributor; you can sell your program to broadcast TV; or you can buy airtime from a cable company, and then sell commercials during your show.

The path you choose (Figure 54-1) depends on your product and, to some extent, how deep your pockets are. Being in business involves taking risks, which means you sometimes have to shell out some cash before it starts to flow back to you.

Figure 54-1

Is It Good?

The first step in the process is to take a long, very critical look at your product.

Is this a show that other people will want to watch? Would they pay money to watch it? Would you? Ask your friends to watch it and tell you what they think. Now do the same with your enemies. That should give you a nice range of viewpoints.

Is the target audience large enough to justify the production costs? You can produce the greatest video ever on *Growing Beans in Sandy Soil*, but if this subject doesn't appeal to enough people, then you may not get your investment back—even if every potential member of your target audience buys your product. You have to believe strongly in your product—just make sure you can justify that belief.

Your next consideration: production value. Producing on consumer-level equipment will work for some uses, but if you plan to sell your show to a broadcast or major cable network, you may want to work with professional gear. Also, use the best crew and talent that you can afford. If your show is perfect, *except* for the lighting, *or* the audio, *or* the on-camera spokesperson's delivery, you could be in trouble; one of these flaws alone could flag your project for rejection.

Let's say that (based on your long and successful track record) your product is intellectually compelling and technically flawless (congratulations). Now you're ready to distribute that perfect video. Let's start with the cheapest way to do it—by yourself.

Birth of a Salesman

This method seems fair and natural to most people. You worked hard on your video; it's only right that you should enjoy all the profit from this effort. Remember, however, that this also means assuming all the risk and fronting all the money for the advertising, postage, dubbing costs, shipping and so on. Also figure in time and effort for answering inquiries about your product, as well as packaging and addressing these packages when you do make a sale.

Let's say your glorious video details the proper maintenance of inboard marine engines. Is this program any good? You think so. Your friends think so. Even your enemies admit to liking it. But these opinions won't do you much good when it comes time to sell. What you need is a review.

Check all the magazines covering your subject (*Inboard Boating Illustrated*, *Marine Engine World* and so on) and read them. Do they review books or videos of interest to their readers? If they do, write a professional cover letter to the editor of each, describing your show in a straightforward manner. (If they don't, send out letters (Figure 54-2) anyway; your product may be good enough to set a few precedents.) Don't hype your product at this point; journalists don't like that approach. Also send along VHS dubs of your program for the editors to pass on to their reviewers.

Don't expect replies, unless you also enclose an SASE (Self-Addressed Stamped Envelope) in each letter. If you want your dub back, then send an SASE with enough postage to cover its weight.

Getting a review is not a quick process. The reviewer has to view your show, write up the review and get the review to the magazine. Depending on the publication, it may be two to three months from the

Figure 54-2

point the review reaches the editor's desk until it actually gets into print.

If the review is favorable, your show has just taken a big step toward legitimacy. A major publication (*Inboard Boating Illustrated,* no less) has complimented your show in print. This tells your potential buyers that your program is for real, that you did not just fall off of a turnip truck and that the video is worth spending their money to see.

Another way to lend legitimacy to your tape is to have an expert introduce the material. You can also put the expert's picture on the cover of the tape's package. Potential buyers see their favorite inboard engine expert on the tape and say to themselves, "Hey, I trust Joe Inboard. This tape must be good." Of course, Joe Inboard will probably ask you to pay for his image, or he may even ask for a piece of the action (such as a percentage of the profits).

If *Inboard Boating Illustrated* uses a rating system (four little boats equal excellent, and three little boats equal good), then you have a perfect element for your next step in selling your product—advertising in the magazine. In your display ads, you'll feature "FOUR BOATS—*Inboard Boating Illustrated*" as prominently as possible.

The cost of your ad will vary according to the number of people who read the magazine, how much space your ad takes up and how many colors appear in the ad. As you might expect, the price goes up as readers, colors and space requirements go up. If you run an ad more than once (which you almost always have to do to have any

impact), the amount per issue goes down. Magazines often offer breaks for running an ad three times (3×) or six times (6×).

Fulfillment

Once the ad runs, the orders start to pour in.

But how do you get them? Do customers order by credit card over the phone (any time of the day or night)? Or do they send you a check? Do you wait for checks to clear before you send customers their tapes? What if the check bounces? Which—if any—credit cards will you accept? What about a money-back guarantee?

You can avoid some of these headaches by working out a deal with a fulfillment house. I once used a service from a company that made dubs of my show and kept them on hand. The company provided me with its 800 number, which I used in my ads. My customers placed their orders with this company. The company performed a number of services for me:

- recording the pertinent customer information,

- accepting credit cards,

- waiting for checks to clear and

- sending out the videos, using a pre-printed slip sleeve that I provided.

At the end of each month, the company sent me a statement telling me how many units sold during that time, along with a check—minus the fees they charged for their fulfillment services.

This is a good, convenient service; but it does mean additional expense. Also, fulfillment services typically require the assurance that they make a minimum amount of money per month, which means selling a minimum number of your videos each month. If the total falls below this, you may pay a penalty.

Direct Mail

Another method of reaching potential customers is direct mail. You get direct mail from advertisers at home all the time; you probably think of it as junk mail. But it's only junk if the ad is trying to sell you something you don't want. That's why you must make sure that the people you mail your ad to are the people who want your product.

There are companies that sell lists of business names, preformatted on sticky labels for easy use. These lists break down according to type of business, number of employees, region of operation and so on. Be selective, and you can buy the right list for your target market.

Also, *Inboard Boating Illustrated* probably sells its subscriber list to advertisers. Consider buying subscriber lists from appropriate publications.

Once you buy the right list, find a local company that handles large mailings. This way, you won't have to stuff any envelopes. If you've ever licked more than twenty stamps at a sitting, you'll know this service is worth the expense.

When you determine the price of your program, remember to figure in the advertising costs. For example, if you buy a list of 10,000 names from a magazine, print up 10,000 ads and stuff 10,000 stamped envelopes for your direct mailing, you've shelled out some serious money. The direct mail industry considers a one percent response rate "good"; that's 100 orders from a mailing of 10,000. So you could lose money if you don't charge enough for your product.

Libraries and Video Rental Stores

After you've fully exploited the inboard boating market, exploit libraries.

There are public libraries, college libraries, high school libraries and more. Most have videotape departments stocked with a variety of videos; especially popular are how-to programs.

Check out the magazines covering this market: *Booklist* (you won't find it at the newsstand, it goes out directly to librarians); *School Library Journal*; *Library Journal* and *Wilson Library Bulletin*. Each

Figure 54-3

of these publications reviews videotapes, so getting a review is a good place to start.

The local video rental store (Figure 54-3) is another option. One method would be to walk in, ask to see the owner and try to sell the show then and there. But this would be much like trying to teach a pig to sing. It wastes your time and annoys the pig.

Rental stores buy their programs almost exclusively from major distributors that publish catalogs every week. One is the Major Video Concept catalog (800-365-0150), which boasts lots of four-color ads for Hollywood features. One page advertises foreign films and other videos.

Distributors

When you distribute a product, such as a videotape, there is a certain amount of infrastructure that has to be in place. You must let the customer know that the product is available, you must be able to take orders and fulfill them. This is true whether you have one product in your line or a thousand. Obviously, this infrastructure is less expensive per product if you have a thousand products. This is why there are companies called distributors.

In the early years of the motion picture industry, there were no major film studios.

The people who owned the theaters needed product. Viewers didn't ask for much, they would watch a man petting a dog or a horse running down a road and be happy. But they always wanted more.

Finally, the people who owned lots of theaters and thus needed the most product decided to make their own movies. That's how the major studios were born. Distribution was the key.

For video, there are hundreds of small specialty distributors. One distributor might serve a market of gardeners. Every few months the distributor sends a catalog to these gardeners featuring all the books and videos on pruning and planting. The gardener can pick out several and order all of them at the same time. Convenient.

You can usually find a list of distributors at your local library. Books listing all the video products available for the current year often include a list of distributors for ordering purposes.

The names may not tell you much about the distributors. So before you send out copies of your program to distributors, call the companies and chat with the owners about your product. Even if these people show no interest in your video, they may recommend distributors who might.

When a distributor decides to handle your show, you'll negotiate a contract. You won't sell the show, but rather license it. This means that while you still own the material, the distributor will receive a percentage of the retail price of product sold. This could be a healthy percentage, like 75 percent. Or it could be less, depending on how good a negotiator you are and how much the distributor wants the product.

When negotiating remember that the distributor is paying for advertising, fulfillment, storage and so on; you assume none of the risk. These services are worth something.

The Big Screen

You've always dreamed of seeing your work on the big screen. This means selling your work to film distributors—not an easy sell.

Major film festivals are a good place to show off your work to distributors. Events such as the Berlin Film Festival and the Sundance Film Festival are places to see and be seen by "the players." Before you can enter your show, however, check the entrance requirements. Pay particular attention to format. If you shot on video, you will have to transfer the master to 16 mm or 35 mm. Expect to pay a couple of thousand dollars for this process.

There are many video festivals as well. Entering and winning prizes for quality and great content can't hurt your chances of interesting a distributor in your show. And the price of a dub for your entry will be less expensive than a 35 mm film print.

Seeing your work "on the air," either on a broadcast or a cable station, is always a thrill. Again, there are many avenues you can take to reach this goal.

Vid News Is Good News

Many local news shows encourage videographers to be on the lookout for newsworthy events (Figure 54-4). Even in large markets, a news director has only a limited number of crews to cover the station's area. Given the improved quality of consumer gear, stations are more likely to get footage of dramatic events as they happen if a quick-thinking videographer happens to be on the scene.

The value of the footage depends on its newsworthiness; most stations pay $50 to $100 for short news pieces. You can expect a lot more if you get the Loch Ness monster, Bigfoot or some natural or man-made disaster on tape.

If you live in an area which has a low-power television (LPTV) station or a small cable company, you might be able to get on the air by forging a partnership. If the station or company doesn't have a production arm, make yourself useful to them by offering to: 1) cover city council meetings, 2) produce promotional spots and 3) shoot public service work.

Could you do this out of the goodness of your heart? You could, or you could offer

Figure 54-4

to do all this work in exchange for airtime on the channel, say an hour a week.

On the Air

Now you own an hour of airtime; how do you profit by it? There are a number of ways to boost your bottom line. If you live in an area that attracts lots of tourists, create a show that reviews restaurants, profiles interesting people and recommends local hot spots. Sell 30-second spots on the show to some of these same businesses. Then produce the 30-second spots for them, charging for production services.

Or take your hour of airtime and sell it to a syndicator. The syndicator will then fill the time with an infomercial or an entertainment program, commercials included.

Or you could run a telethon and ask for donations from viewers in order to keep your telethon on the air. (If you succeed at this one, be sure to tell me about it.)

Leased Access and Satellite Time

If you have a great programming idea and live in an area where the cable company carries more than 36 channels, you

Figure 54-5

may be able to lease your own time. The Cable Act of 1992 requires cable operators to set aside a certain percentage of their channels for lease by independent programmers.

This sounds good; but some cable companies hesitate to sell time to independents, and others charge too much when they do. Contact your local cable operator (Figure 54-5) and ask about its leased access policy; be ready to fight for the time that is legally yours.

Destination Distribution

Distribution paths are many. Some involve risking your money; some involve spending your time and others involve sharing your profits with others.

The key is to find the ones that work for you and your video. Persevere and you can sell your show.

All it takes is a little effort and a little luck ... and a great product.

55
Public Access:
Produce Your Own TV Show

Sofia Davis

You can have your own TV show. It's easier than you might think and best of all, it's absolutely free! How, you ask? The answer is public access.

Public access television is noncommercial airtime made available to the public, free of charge. The only requirement to utilize public access, is that you live in the community where the show will be produced. Most public access facilities offer training in shooting, audio and editing, and provide all the equipment you'll need.

While the law no longer requires that cable companies air public access programs, a certain percentage of cable revenue in any market must go to the host city or municipality. A portion of this money goes towards public access television, so most markets (even small ones) have a public access channel and a modest studio.

Does producing and broadcasting your own public access TV show sound enticing to you? This article will tell you how to get started.

Getting Started

The first step is to contact your local public access station and sign up for an orientation class. Most facilities have ongoing seminars and continuing education to help you increase your production knowledge. If you have questions during a shoot, a staff person is usually available to help you (see Figure 55-1).

Once you finish the orientation and get tested on the equipment, you're ready to produce your show. Usually, you must submit a finished program to the public access facility before it airs so someone can view your tape and make sure it fits the station's guidelines. Once approved, you will receive a time slot for your show to air.

Remember, your program has to be noncommercial; that means you cannot say or show phone numbers, dates of events, prices or store names within the show itself. You can put phone numbers at the end of the show, typically for no longer than 10 seconds. Anything longer than that is considered advertising.

Figure 55-1 *Teach Me—You often need to bc trained to use the equipment. This is a greut opportunity to learn.*

Figure 55-2 *Equip Me—The gear at the station might be ancient or it might be the latest and the greatest.*

Everything You Need

If you have no experience with video or TV production, public access can be a great place for you to start. At most public access stations everything is provided for you—a studio for shooting, editing facilities, digital video cameras for location shooting, computer editing systems, microphones and audio cables, dressing rooms and more. This is a big help for a beginner or a person that does not have equipment (see Figure 55-2).

Although most studios now have well-maintained digital equipment, this is public access, so don't necessarily expect cutting-edge equipment. They will, however, provide everything you need to shoot and edit a program.

Other producers are usually available to crew for you, and in turn, it is expected that you will crew for them. Most facilities have a book that lists people who are certified and available to work on a production crew.

Different Time, Same Channel

Depending on your city, you may have to wait for a time slot before your program can air. And, you don't always have the option of choosing the time slot you like.

Typically, you will not have a time slot for more than 13 weeks, so it can be hard to build an audience to follow your program. You may be on Saturday at 8 p.m. and then moved to Wednesday at 7 a.m. Your 8 p.m. audience will wonder where you went. You cannot advertise the move in advance, because you won't know where you're going until the move has been made. There is typically nothing you can do about this. The facility has to make space for new producers.

If you are in a facility that has a lot of producers, you may be asked to go off the air (if your show has been airing for a period of time), to give new producers a chance.

The Golden Rule

Each station will have its own rules and regulations about the use of equipment, crew and time slots. Check with your local access station for specifics. However, there is one guideline to which all public access programs must adhere: You cannot make any money from the show.

The station staff will watch your show carefully. If they find that you've produced a commercial show, you can be banned from having a show, or using the facilities and editing equipment.

You've Got Access

The opportunity is there for you to take your own program to the airwaves. Despite some restrictions and scheduling irregularities, managing your own public access time slot is a wonderful opportunity.

Sidebar 1

Insurance?

Since your show is non-commercial, insurance is not required. You do not have to have Errors & Omission Insurance to produce a show.

Sidebar 2

Public Access Hints

- Take as many educational classes as possible.

- Crew for everyone you can. If there are people that are particularly experienced, crew for them; you will learn a lot.

- Volunteer to help edit someone else's show. Sit in with them to learn how they edit and why.

- Follow the rules of the facility. Most provide these services free; if you had to pay for it, it could really cost you. Therefore, be respectful of the rules.

56
PBS and ITVS:
Fertile Soil for Independent Videographers

Alessia Cowee

If you've ever dreamed of seeing your video production on television or bringing your vision to a broader audience than friends and family, now is the time and PBS is the place. PBS—both independently and through its liaison with ITVS—offers unparalleled opportunities for videographers with unique vision and a compelling story. You'll find a surprising number of opportunities with ongoing series (such as *Frontline, American Masters, POV* and *American Experience*), limited jointly curated series (like *Digital Divide* and *Independent Lens*) and one-offs (stand-alone, independent films). This chapter will help you evaluate whether your project is PBS/ITVS material and show you how to break into this ever-expanding market.

PBS, ITVS and You: The Time Is Now

PBS has a strong tradition of working with independent producers. It's a common misconception, but PBS is not a television network. Instead, it is a membership organization made up of independent public television stations around the country, funded, in part, by the Corporation for Public Broadcasting, a private corporation created by the US Congress in 1967. PBS is available to 99% of US households and strives to reach all portions of the population with quality, accessible, relevant programming. Pat Mitchell, PBS President and CEO, says key components of the PBS mission are "to inform, to inspire and to educate."

Independent producers frequently challenge convention and provide in-depth analyses of complex topics. PBS makes available programming designed to spur discussion and active community involvement in social issues. Its goal is to provide thorough examination of a story, theme or issue, including all conflicting points of view.

The Independent Television Service (ITVS) was created in 1991 in response to

Figure 56-1 *Acting as guide and gateway into the public television arena, ITVS links independent producers with public television programming opportunities.*

demand from independent media producers and community activists for programming by and for diverse, underrepresented audiences (such as minorities and children) not adequately served by the networks or by PBS.

Acting as guide and gateway into the public television arena, ITVS links independent producers with public television programming opportunities (see Figure 56-1). ITVS offers producers feedback during the creative process (including programs which apply, but are rejected for financial aid), content development assistance, funding options and an extensive marketing and publicity package in conjunction with Community Connections Project (CCP—a network of community organizers).

Content Confab: Programming Possibilities

What are PBS and ITVS looking for and how do you know if your program is right for them? The most obvious question is often the most overlooked: Do you want to produce a program or a series? If your long-range goal is theatrical release, PBS is probably not the proper venue for your project. Some films, however, do get additional play after a public TV release, for example, in educational distribution, at festivals and in home video and foreign broadcast markets.

Though the guidelines and needs vary for each program and funding initiative, it can be said that PBS and ITVS seek innovative, adventurous, compelling stories told in distinctive, contemporary and engaging formats. Of special interest are projects that provide interactive opportunities for community participation. No subject is taboo, though projects too narrow in scope may not have many market options. Wide-market appeal creates more programming possibilities, but success is not strictly about raw ratings in public broadcasting. You should also avoid controversy for controversy's sake. Journalistic integrity

Figure 56-2 *An excellent way to keep abreast of developments is to subscribe to the* Beyond the Box *newsletter.*

in research, documentation and development is expected.

Is it easier for emerging or established videographers to break in with a one-off or with a series segment? ITVS Executive Director, Sally Jo Fifer, explains, "It's always difficult to get funding because the competition is so fierce. The one essential is to have a great idea and tell it in a creative, thorough, smart proposal. Tell a great story in a unique, 'the viewer can't stop watching' way."

Funding

ITVS offers several initiatives for producers seeking financial support for completion of a film, although it actually funds less than five percent of proposed projects. Open Call accepts proposals in any genre and funding rounds occur twice yearly (in February and August). LinCS (Local Independents Collaborating with Stations) provides matching ITVS funds

for producers who pair up with a specific public television station and is perfect for programs with a more local appeal.

PBS is currently implementing a program, called *In The Works*, to support production on a limited number of projects for use with its series *POV* as funding becomes available. An excellent way to keep abreast of developments is to subscribe to the *Beyond the Box* newsletter (see Figure 56-2). Available funding and application procedures vary for each program and initiative.

Public television is commercial-free, but other outside opportunities exist for acquiring financial assistance. Corporate and minority consortia funds are available for resourceful producers, as are grants from state and national arts councils.

Getting the Green Light

ITVS uses a peer-reviewed process to screen applicants for funding. ITVS selects juries based on diversity of ethnicity, vocation, religion, geographic region and other demographic criteria. The jury considers each application on its own merits, individually evaluated and scored. The screening process has three levels, with weaker proposals eliminated at each stage. The panels often request additional application materials from producers who advance to the next level during the review process. At the full panel meetings, members advocate for their favorite projects until they can arrive at a consensus on which proposals to fund for that round.

Criteria the panel may consider when reviewing your project:

- Is the project accessible, relevant, formatted in the most effective manner?

- Is the treatment thorough, concise, written with passion? Does it clearly show the project trajectory and structure?

- Is the audience easily identifiable? Is it broad enough? Does it represent ITVS and PBS mission statements?

- Is the producer or the team experienced enough to complete the project on budget and on deadline?

Ms. Fifer warns that producers frequently do not read the application guidelines carefully enough. She also suggests that producers weigh the appeal of their projects, "Programmers tell us repeatedly that they don't need six shows on one subject. They especially don't need six okay shows on one subject. What they need is one great show on that subject."

Sample materials and written treatments must outshine their competitors. There are not nearly enough programming hours available for the number of submissions received by PBS and ITVS, of course, and top-notch productions often do not make the cut the first time around. You may find the keys to the public programming kingdom in the feedback you get even if your proposal is rejected. But remember, not all venues are suited to all programs. Keep reevaluating your project to determine where it fits best.

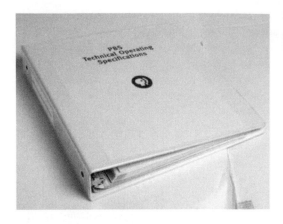

Figure 56-3 *Your video must meet all of the very rigorous PBS technical requirements, as set forth in the Technical Operating Specifications (TOS).*

Technical Specifications

Almost any shooting format is viable for PBS/ITVS programming. Choose the format that most effectively showcases your subject matter or the one that is most readily available. In the end, however, the final video must be digitally mastered and must meet all of the very rigorous PBS technical requirements, as set forth in the Technical Operating Specifications (TOS) (see Figure 56-3). This handbook and the ITVS production manual are available for purchase online. Standard program lengths for PBS/ITVS are 26:40 and 56:40. Feature films of non-standard length are considered on a case-by-case basis.

Ready, Set, Video

You've set your sights on PBS and chosen the appropriate funding initiative. You've studied existing series strands and talked with producers who have worked with PBS. Your sample and treatment are flawlessly prepared and you can meet all of the technical specifications. The story you've chosen to tell is unique, passion-filled and appeals to a broad audience while remaining interesting and diverse. Now what?

Once you mail your application, the review process may take up to six months. If your proposal is selected, you must typically complete the project within one year of acceptance. Should ITVS license your film, it may offer it to stations directly, without benefit of a time slot or an air date. The film could be distributed over PBS Plus or on a soft-feed, which allows member stations to fit the program into available airtime. It might even earn a spot on the National Program Service (hard-feed) or other subscription services such as *Independent Lens* or *POV*.

It takes perseverance, persistence, resourcefulness and a dedication to vision, voice and mission, but dozens of independent video producers share compelling stories and unique perspectives via PBS every year. This could be the year the spotlight shines on your work.

Sidebar 1

Electric Shadows

ITVS is breaking ground with digital technology. If interactive media and Web release are what you crave, check out *Electric Shadows*, an extraordinary blend of digital audio, video, interviews and still photography, enhanced with feedback forums and lesson plan suggestions.

Sidebar 2

PBS.org

Stay current with the needs of PBS. PBS updates its Web site frequently with content priorities. Preview the strands you are interested in producing for before submitting your film or applying for funding. Does your format, vision, style and subject matter fit within the program's parameters? If not, consider another strand or funding source.

Sidebar 3

ITVS Information
Independent Television Service
501 York Street
San Francisco, CA 94110
Phone: (415) 356-8383
email: itvs@itvs.org

Sidebar 4

Online Resources for Producers
Producing for PBS
http://www.pbs.org/producers/

Online Version of PBS Redbook
http://www.pbs.org/insidepbs/redbook/index.html

PBS Production Guidelines
http://www.pbs.org/insidepbs/guidelines/index.html

Beyond the Box Online Content:
http://www.beyondthebox.org/

ITVS Funding Applications and Guidelines
http://www.itvs.org/producers/funding.html

57
Paths to Broadcast Television

Mark Bosko

Let me relate to you the story of a fellow videographer who "made good." John started like most of us, goofing around with his parents' film equipment. Though just a child, the creative art of cinematography really clicked for him. He created one film after another to the delight of his family and friends.

Though the passion for this "art" festered inside John, he became frustrated with what seemed like a wasting of his time. The whole purpose of producing a movie was for an audience's enjoyment. After five years of basement screenings, family and friends hardly qualified as a legitimate audience anymore. John knew there just had to be a better way, but didn't latch onto it quite yet. Much later, in college, John enrolled in the school's teleproduction class. He knew a little bit about TV production, but was still mainly a "film" guy. It was here that he discovered what would later "rule" his world—videotape.

Even with excellent marks, John still yearned for that elusive "audience." Luckily, he was outspoken about this need, and a professor took notice. The professor, as it happens, was on the board of the local public television station. He was primarily responsible for development of new local programming.

Thinking of John's desires, and some of the super productions the students were showing, the teacher came up with a "Young Filmmaker's" showcase program. The show would give aspiring film and videographers (now John's medium of choice due to cost and time considerations) a place to present their programming to a potentially large viewership.

Happy ending: John got his audience, the station got quality programming, and viewers got some alternative shows to watch.

Not all stories involving broadcast TV are so inspiring, and sometimes PBS networks are the hardest nuts to crack. But the example above does point out the many opportunities that exist for videographers looking for distribution of their productions within these "hallowed halls." For some reason or another, broadcast television stations have the image of an "insider's club." You've got to know someone or already work there in a lower capacity to get an in. If you weren't a part of the community's filmmaking "elite," your chances for broadcast were nil. Maybe ten or so years ago that was true, but today, this is simply not the case. Especially for dedicated, experienced videographers.

One of the reasons for this "opening" may be attributable to the increase in number and types of broadcast outlets on the map. Before everyone in America had cable, there existed a strong distinction between broadcast and cable fare. Broadcast programming was free, contained some locally produced programming (created at the station, not by independents), and carried the network shows as they "came down the line." Cable, on the other hand, carried new movies and other, non-traditional television material. It was also perceived (rightly so) as being very costly.

As the years passed and more media moguls developed, the number of cable stations quadrupled, the cost for the service plummeted and the demand by consumers who "wanted their MTV" skyrocketed. This led to the confusing mix of cable and broadcast stations that currently exists on your channel selector. This influx of new entertainment choices spurred a huge void in the supply of programming able to fulfill the scheduling needs of the stations.

Another reason broadcast stations unlocked their doors to outsiders was the fact that now they wanted to compete with the trendy and popular cable networks. The old, stodgy rules of operation were changing, and any new face that had something to add to the party was welcome.

And, in recent years, a new broadcast outlet, Low Power Television (LPTV) became popular. The limited signal put out by these stations reaches a relatively small, geographically close audience. The LPTV stations tend to be carriers of downloadable national satellite programming, mixed with an unusually high amount (for broadcast) of local fare.

While all of this is certainly encouraging (if not educational) for the future of aspiring videographers, what real opportunities exist now, in the present, for those of you who can't wait a lifetime for your dreams to be fulfilled? What does broadcast television offer you in the form of distribution?

VHF

You've got a job (that you like) and possess some fine-tuned production abilities. You own a little equipment, no Industrial Light and Magic, but a respectable "studio" on your own right. You've made some industrials, a whole slew of weddings, even an instructional tape on gardening for your spouse. You got some good ideas for programming that you think will go over big with the locals, but how do you get it on the tube?

Time saving tip number one: skip the VHF channels in your broadcasting area. VHF slots, usually reserved for network affiliates, offer the independent videographer little in the form of finding an audience. The stations are network controlled, meaning they have mega-bucks at their resources. They're not rude, but why would they want to mess with your $1.98 Talent Show when they can program a re-rerun of *Who's the Boss*? It just doesn't make sense for the big boys to play with you.

About the only exposure you may achieve through a VHF outlet is sale of news-type footage. And this comes from personal experience. My town was literally burning down. A huge fire started in the historical district, and I happened to be at the right place at the right time with my camcorder. I got some great shots before any of the large news crews showed up. They were aware of my presence and asked to buy the footage for inclusion in the coverage of the story. I was only too glad to succumb to their wishes. But don't plan on getting rich from selling news footage. These deep-pocketed network guys could only scrape together $50 for the whole 30-minute tape. And then I didn't even get an on-air credit!

UHF

If you've seen the Weird Al movie of the same name, then you are aware of the possibilities available for independent programming to air on these channels. While it's not quite as zany as the Weird Al film, opportunities do exist (especially in smaller markets) for videographers to find an audience.

Many UHF stations are becoming network affiliates (FOX has conquered quite a few), so the chances with these stations are slimming. If you live in a large TV city (one with more than four or five UHF channels), then you should be able to locate a willing outlet. In the Cleveland-area, a late-night television host on a UHF channel hosts a viewer's film's series. It's a great show comprised of shorts (one shot-on-video feature has played) broken up with interviews of the videographers. There is no pay involved, but the audience is pretty big, and loyal. The program is also popular with local advertisers who recognize the local customer base tuning in.

If there is a late-night gig in your city, why not hit up the host with this idea? It makes his or her job infinitely easier, and becomes attractive to sales personnel at the station.

Sunday morning talk and "city" shows also seem popular with UHF channels. Easily produced, these programs focus on community events and personalities. Often, the production may center on one specific area, and the show is a submission from a freelance videographer.

Fairly new to the broadcast arena, Low Power Television stations are basically UFH stations, only with less signal amplification. These stations function much like their big cousins, only with a greater concentration of the local goods.

Cashing In

Knowing that there's some distribution avenues available in UHF and LPTV is good news, but, you'd like some compensation for your efforts, right? Well, just like the VHF networks, these stations pull in the reins when it comes time to pay. In fact, you may be the one paying them to show your program.

WAI-TV, part of a three-channel LPTV network in Cleveland and Akron, offers air-time for sale. Going for $250 and up per half-hour (depending what day and time you buy) the channel is a natural for independents. "We have space for sale just like every other television network. It just happens that ours is available to the independent," says Bill Klaus, owner of the station. Klaus makes it clear that the reason an independent can buy time from his network is because it is affordable. "Sure, someone with a home-grown production could go to their local VHF station and buy a half-hour of time to broadcast the show, but they'd probably have to mortgage their house to do it. My network makes it affordable, and we often barter time as well so the videographer can actually make a buck."

Bartering, as Klaus mentioned, is another favored option of UHF and LPTV programmers. What this means is that you retain some of the commercial time allotted within your programming block. As an example, let's say you buy a half-hour of air time for $200. That's the flat rate. With that price, you are the owner of all 8 minutes of commercial space. You can deal with the station, letting them keep 4 minutes of ad time, dropping your payment to $100. And, it also works in reverse. If they want to buy your show (yes—that actually happens sometimes), they may offer you the commercial time in exchange for any payment. This way they don't have a cash outlay, but fill their schedule. You, on the other hand, have found a profitable distribution outlet.

The large, network-affiliated stations will not likely be interested in your bargain broadcasting, but many independent stations will take a look. Local interest, interview shows, documentaries, community affairs and sporting events are all good ideas to present to any small broadcaster in your neighborhood.

When you go door knocking, bring an attractive demo and a professional presentation package outlining your programming ideas. This packet should present your work in its best possible light. While you may think you are the only indie out there (or at least the only one in the neighborhood), the fact is that programming managers deal with many proposals from many people. "It's probably hard to believe, but I get at least a proposal a week from independent video producers," states Klaus. "Most of the production ideas have no substance. If I got one backed by a demo, or put together in a professional manner, I might pay more attention to them. But too many of them look like a half-hearted effort to get a show on the air.

"I don't mind working with independents," Klaus continues. "In fact I like it, but they just have to be more professional in their approach. If a videographer wants to make some money by getting his programming on the air, instead of spending it to buy time, he should prepare the idea as completely as possible. That would be the type of producer I would look to work with."

There are no set rules here. Just remember that it's the fact that people are able to view your production through their television sets for free that's important, not the amount of bills you have wadded in your pocket.

The multitude of small and low-power broadcasting outlets has created a void of original, low-cost scheduling alternatives. There are only so many stations that can broadcast *The Andy Griffith Show* at any one time, and it's that fact that opens up the audiences to you.

58
Promotion Strategies: Fame and Fortune on a Budget

Mark Steven Bosko

If you don't tell people about your video, they won't even know it exists. The more aware the public is of your work, the greater fame and fortune you'll eventually achieve.

You can promote your work in many ways—from buying expensive full-color magazine advertising to sending out a simple press release. Full-blown promotional plans practically guarantee increased video sales, but they're often too expensive for the first-time videographer.

But there are less expensive ways to promote your work. In this chapter, we'll survey a selection of promotion strategies that will cost you little more than the price of pen and paper—and some hard work.

The Press Release

The press release is the most widely used and abused promotional technique. This one-page synopsis tells the media what you want them to know about your video. Media outlets such as newspapers, magazines and broadcasters receive hundreds of these daily; to make sure yours receives proper attention you need to a) submit it in regulation form and b) make it stand out from all the others.

Press releases follow a standard format. Deviate from this format and no one will read it. This sounds harsh but it's true. If you want the press to read it:

- *Keep it short.* You don't need 10 pages to communicate your message. One page is best, two is the maximum. If it is longer, re-write it; include just the basics.

- *Title it.* Without a headline, they won't know what the release is about. Trust me: they won't take the time to read it to find out. The best headlines are short and to the point.

- *Say who sent it.* The upper left-hand corner of the page should set out the following information: your company's name, address, telephone number and—most important—a contact to call for further information. You're the best contact; if you can't do it make sure you choose a contact well versed in all aspects of your video.

- *Provide a release date.* Write "For Immediate Release" on the press release; this tells the press that they can use the information revealed in your release right now. If you don't want the information released until a specific date, then provide this "embargo date" in place of the usual "For Immediate Release" (i.e., "For Release October 10, 2003").

- *Use the standard form.* Type the release, double-spaced with ample margin areas. Check for any errors in spelling, punctuation, grammar or content; this kind of mistake screams amateurism.

Now you think your press release is going to look like all the others—and if the format is correct, it probably will. But Joe Reporter down at the *Daily Globe* doesn't care about fancy formats; he's looking for interesting content. Write your release so it not only answers the stock journalism questions—who, what, where, when, how and why—but also leaves the reader wanting to know more. Appeal to the natural curiosity of the reporter—without getting cute—and no doubt your video will see some press.

Mail, fax, transmit electronically or hand deliver your release to every possible media outlet. The wider the distribution, the better your chances of getting press.

Radio and TV Interviews

Turn on the radio. Flip through the stations. Listen. You hear a lot of talk, don't you? Radio stations live on music and talk; they have plenty of music, but they need the talk. That's where you come in.

More than 80 percent of the 11,000 radio stations in the United States air some sort of interview program; getting on one of these interview shows is easier than you might think. Best of all, it's free.

Call the stations you know that air interview programs and ask how they book their guests. Send the person in charge of booking a press release, some data sheets naming the subject, cast, crew, locations and length of your video and a cover letter. The cover letter is important; think of it as a sales letter selling you and your video. This letter should persuade the booking manager that your video is an ideal choice for the program—due to its exploitative elements, controversial theme, local interest or whatever "hook" will prove irresistible to the station.

With any luck, someone will give you a call to find out more about your project and determine if you would make a suitable guest for the show. When you get the call, be sure to answer all queries with confidence and grace; you want to prove you're a coherent, interesting individual who won't freeze up during the program.

Interviews are a great promotional vehicle, but they do offer one distinct disadvantage: lack of control. You don't have the benefit of complete pre-planning. You can't predict what the interviewer will ask you or what part or parts of the interview will air. With live, call-in formats, you face the additional challenge of fielding questions from the listening public, who may or may not approve of you and your video. Two suggestions for handling radio interviews:

1. Restrict contact with the media to yourself or one or two other people associated with your production. You should coach these people–talent, director, producer–on appropriate responses to possible questions. You certainly don't want to hear your cameraman giving out details that contradict your press release.

2. Listen to the radio program before appearing on the show. Observe how the DJ deals with guests. By listening, you'll discover if the host and callers are friendly or abusive, the show is live or taped and whether the focus is straight news or fluff. Prepare your answers based on your observations.

Now that you've successfully conquered radio, turn your attention to the other half of the broadcast spectrum: television.

Compared with radio, the market for TV guests is small; the chances of landing an interview are smaller still. To boost those chances, approach the TV station about an interview in the same way you approach the radio stations, but do more follow up. Don't wait for someone to call you; make those return calls yourself. TV people are always busy, and they believe that if you want to book yourself on a show you should do all the work.

You do have one advantage: you're promoting a video. Videos are visual and naturally lend themselves to the medium of television. Include a trailer of your best scenes—those most visually compelling—with your press release. This way the person in charge will know you have something unique to offer.

Most local television interview programs are not overwhelmed by low-budget video producers trying to land spots as guests on a regular basis. You're one of a kind; play up the glitz and glamour you bring to your hometown.

Tell the show's producers about any publicity stunts you plan and ask that they cover it to air with your interview. Keep the subject exciting and visual, and you shouldn't have any problems.

Screeners/Trailers

"We want to see the video."

That's what you can expect to hear hundreds of times while promoting your project. The press wants to see a *screener*. A screener is a full-length, promotional copy of your tape, provided free of charge to media personnel upon request.

They need to see first-hand what your video is all about. Screeners allow reporters to check out such considerations as budget, acting, effects and production values. Now your video must live up to the expectations you've created for it. Did you exaggerate too much in your press releases?

The press uses screeners most often for reviewing purposes; media outlets occasionally request them as well, primarily to check out authenticity. Nobody wants to devote space to a "phantom" video, especially national magazines.

Providing these screeners for everyone who asks becomes an expensive proposition. There is, however, a low-cost alternative: the *trailer*.

Short compilations of your best scenes, trailers can accomplish all a full-length screener can—at less than a third of the cost.

A general rule of thumb: use screeners for press outlets that want to review your program and trailers for those who just want to "take a look." Some suggestions:

• Use a disclaimer on screeners. When duplicating screeners to send to media outlets, superimpose or key the words "For Promotional Use Only" over the video during its entire duration. Not that the press is dishonest, but if your video lands in the wrong hands, nothing will stop those hands from selling the video as their own. The practice of using a disclaimer offends no one; it's always better to be safe than sorry. This tip comes from a video newsletter in California investigating a small cable station making illegal dupes to sell in Mexico. So protect your property!

• Duplicate screeners and trailers on B-grade tape. Most of these videos will be viewed only once or twice, making a high-grade tape unnecessary. The press outlets can handle a little dropout.

• Use a copyright. Place a copyright notice prominently on all screeners and trailers. Put a notice physically on the tape and within the program itself.

• Limit trailers to 5 minutes or less. This is adequate time to show your tape's highlights. Keep it "lean and mean."

• Make your trailer available in broadcast formats. Some broadcast press outlets may want to include your trailer as part of the story on your project. Don't miss out on this free advertising by not having the proper tape available. Most stations can work with three-quarter-inch format. It's cheap and widely available.

• Include any televised press on distributors' screeners. Tag a mini-trailer of any televised news stories about your project onto the beginning of the screener. How impressed will that distributor be when he sees your story as it appeared on *Entertainment Tonight*? A lot more impressed than he'll be when you just tell him about it. Be sure to check with news agencies concerning legalities of duplicating such stories.

Press Kit

It's now time to compile all of the press you've received thanks to your promotion strategies and organize it into a *press kit*.

The most useful weapon in your promotional arsenal, a press kit represents the culmination of all your efforts. Its purpose: to show the attention your project has received, proving that your video is worthy of further coverage such as newspaper space and TV airtime.

Some people say to include only the big "headline" stories. I say include everything—from that one-paragraph blurb in your local newspaper to the full-page story in *Variety*.

Press is press. The more you can show a media outlet, the easier it is to get more coverage.

Some tips on putting together a decent press kit:

1. Use a high-quality bond for reproduction of the originals. The heavier weight paper lends a classy look.

2. Check the clarity of copies, especially when articles include photographs.

3. Place articles in descending order of importance, starting with the most prestigious—usually national media.

4. Articles buried in the editorial section should be shown with the cover or masthead of the publication; copy it and place it on the reproduction with the article.

5. Allow for only one article per page, unless the articles are extremely short and from the same publication.

6. Use the proper tape formats when including televised or radio coverage.

7. Put all the print elements along with a cover letter into a slick folder.

The press release (P.R.) strategy alone should garner enough press for a substantial press kit. And if you've employed the other promotional strategies as well, you may find you cannot include everything—your kit would be so thick, you'd go broke on postage. So choose only the best of your material for your press kit.

Publicity Stunts

Publicity stunts can be a great low-cost promotional technique, attracting both media and public attention to your video project.

Used with great success by the film industry, publicity stunts have traditionally accompanied the release of new movies. The "golden age" of publicity stunts was the 1950s, when the following tactics drew big crowds:

• Nurses in theater lobbies, placed there by smart promotional men asking viewers to sign medical releases, in the case of heart attacks brought on by the shocking subject matter they were about to see. A particular favorite of science fiction and horror film promoters.

• Bogus pickets, carried by "protesters" hired by a film company's publicity department to demonstrate against a film's sex and violence quotients.

• Film "banning," which implied that a movie's subject matter was so offensive it should not be shown in certain areas.

Your own publicity stunts don't have to be so melodramatic, however. Try setting up a live magic act in the video stores stocking your *Magic Made Simple* video. Or, celebrate the release of your *Keep Our Town Clean* video with a litter collection contest for local school kids; offer the winners some free production time. Any stunt you can think of that involves the public and creates interest in your video makes for good publicity.

To ensure success: keep the press informed and keep it legal. Check out all local laws that may apply to your particular stunt.

9 Ways to Cut Promotion Costs

Mailing and distributing press kits and screeners can prove expensive. Still, there are ways to economize:

1. Don't use envelopes when mailing press releases. Tri-fold the paper and staple the bottom.

2. For big mailings use pre-printed postcards—they're cheaper to mail and cheaper to produce.

3. Order return address stickers bearing your company name from one of the many mail-order catalogs that offer such merchandise. They look good and cost substantially less than printed versions.

4. Shop for supplies and copy services at a large office supply store. Many of these places duplicate the same document for as little as two cents a page.

5. Mail screeners fourth class. Fourth class costs less than half the first-class rate and takes only two to four more days to deliver.

6. Save on postage by using air bubble envelopes instead of cardboard VHS tape mailers for screeners.

7. Put together a trailer instead of mailing out full-length screeners; this reduces postage and duplication costs.

8. Save big on phone bills by using toll-free phone numbers when calling distributors, TV/radio stations and publications. You'll find them listed in the toll-free directory at your local library.

9. When making long-distance toll calls, place them when it's most cost effective; keep time zone changes in mind. Contact your long-distance carrier for specifics.

The Bitter Fruits of Publicity

Execute a proper and thorough low-budget video promotional campaign, and your life will drastically change.

The good news is people will see your work. The bad news is more complicated.

First, you're apt to lose much of your leisure time to your publicity efforts. Sure, it is great to come home, pop open a beer and settle in to watch *Divorce Court*. But you're not going to get on any magazine covers that way. Not that you must devote every waking minute to the promotion of your video—we all need some time to relax—it's just that sooner or later the marketing machine you create will take on a life of its own. Instead of playing cards with the guys or hitting the mall, you will probably find yourself fielding phone calls and writing letters. If the process threatens to consume you, write "free time" right into your work schedule.

Promoting your video does not have to alienate you from friends and family, though this often proves the case. So go shoot hoops with friends or spend some quiet time with your spouse when you can.

The second source of grief that accompanies promotion efforts: reviews. Reviews are a necessary part of the marketing process; you'll need to develop a "thick skin" to survive the nastier negative criticism. Remember, you are sending out your video to literally hundreds of outlets, hoping to generate publicity and resources for a press kit. Among all these people watching your tape there will undoubtedly be some who don't like your work, for whatever reasons.

Who cares? What do critics do, anyway? They sit in front of a monitor all day, pointing out faults in something they never had the guts to try to do themselves. These people make their living by proclaiming what—in their own minds—is good and what is bad.

At least this is what you must tell yourself when bad reviews come in. You will, on the other hand, admire the intelligence and good taste of the reviewer who raves about your show.

There's one sort of criticism to which you should pay special attention—that of your fellow videographers. Send your video around to other producers who have "made it" in your field. Suggestions and insight from such individuals are very valuable, often saving you time and money on your next production.

A final thought: prepare yourself for the fame that will haunt you after your name begins to appear in the media. No longer will you be able to venture out into the world a nobody. You'll become a local celebrity and if your video is a big hit, national fame will follow. Standing in the limelight is fun, but it can be dangerous.

If you're flitting around like some self-important media butterfly and your project takes an unexpected turn for the worse, your fall from grace will hurt all the more.

Promoting your video should be a fun and exciting experience. Be sure it stays that way!

Tell 'Em and Sell 'Em Again

With the right promotion strategies, fame and fortune can be yours. The key is persistence. It takes time to create and execute a promotion plan, but it's worth it.

If you believe in your video's success, as you surely do, nothing can stop you.

59
The Demo Tape

Mark Steven Bosko

With so many of today's videographers relying on their video skills and equipment for income, marketplace competition is keener than ever. To succeed, these courageous entrepreneurs (or hopefuls) need all the help they can get.

A good demo tape should be your number one marketing tool. There's nothing like it to showcase (and sell) your videography talent. A well-done demo attracts new clients, creates good public relations, and can even lure competent employees.

Unfortunately, a good demo is not that easy to make. In this chapter we explore elements of the demo tape—its reason for being, its creation, its uses. Once you see what a demo can do, you'll wonder why you never got around to making one before.

Why You Need One

Say Uncle Bob, the dentist, needs a marketing video. He wants to feature basic information on his facility—friendly staff, low prices, after-work appointment hours.

He'll show the tape around to factories and large corporations. The vast numbers of employees within these companies permit him to offer attractive discount plans.

In production terms, the video sounds easy. Some interior shooting. A couple of staff interviews. You'll finish it off with narration and graphics. You're a member of the family, so getting the job's no problem, right?

But during your meeting with Bob, he asks to see something you've done. A representation of past work. Some evidence you're competent to make a video to his liking.

Uncle Bob Wants a *Demo*. You Have One, Don't You?

If you're like many small video companies and independent producers, the answer is probably no. But it takes more than smooth talk to convince clients—even Uncle Bob—that they can trust you with their money. Videos aren't tangible things. Until a camera comes out of the bag, they're just talk and writing. Investing in someone's videography skills without having viewed his work is like buying a car based on nothing but a sales pitch.

Videos often record those once-in-a-lifetime events. A potential client must be certain you'll get it right the first time. He can't stage his daughter's wedding again because you forgot a microphone. He needs a good look at your "credentials."

The demo also is a simple way to attract new business. It shows off the power of the medium. It gets your foot in the door.

As a fund-raising tool, a demo can't be beat. Whether you hope to make a low-budget feature, a social issues documentary or an instructional tape, it takes more than expendable income to pay for a vision.

To paraphrase, "Demos talk. Bragging walks." Investors must see proof of your abilities. No amount of pipe-dream description will get you the cash you need.

Low-budget producers often shoot a couple of scenes of the planned work, and present this "demo" to potential investors.

J.R. Bookwalter of Akron, Ohio, is the definitive real-life example. He admired the work of Hollywood producer Sam Raimi (*Darkman*, *The Evil Dead*), and pegged him as a possible backer. Raimi screened the novice filmmaker's previous efforts. He was so impressed by the badly exposed Super 8 "demos" he agreed to finance a low-budget film.

To the Tune of $125,000

"Raimi told me that of all the proposals he'd received at that point, only mine was accompanied by a representation of my experience," Bookwalter says. "I'm sure if I hadn't screened my films, the deal would never have gone through."

This isn't a common scenario, but it proves the demo's potential.

Just remember: No demo has more impact than a bad demo, while a great demo pays the bills.

Creating a truly effective demo tape takes more than some assemble edits and a blank tape. Careful planning is the first step.

Consider the Content

You want to show off only your very best work in your demo tape. Scan all your videos, noting outstanding shots, imaginative camera-work and good production values. You want to show a broad spectrum of abilities.

If a particular vacation video looks good, include it. Earmark for use any wedding footage that came out better than normal. Sporting events, community functions and film-to-video transfers all provide raw material for a demo.

Don't be impatient. Getting the best possible footage may mean scanning three entire weddings to find that gorgeous sunset kiss sequence. Any extra effort invested at this point will only make the demo that much more powerful.

Let's say your video services have just become available. Let's also say that you really haven't had any legitimate (paying) jobs yet. Sure, you've goofed around with camcorders for a couple of years. But until now, videography wasn't something you'd considered a career choice. How can you put a demo together without footage?

By Creating What You Need

For example, to target the wedding and event video market, you'll need footage of a wedding or two. Check nuptial schedules of area churches and get permission from some couples-to-be to shoot some footage. You don't have to cover the entire wedding. Just get a few shots good enough to convince a prospective client you can handle the job.

Nobody wants to be your first client. If you include wedding footage in your demo you'll appear to have experience in this area.

One caveat. Be certain you really can adequately produce a wedding video. Acquiring a few stray shots and actually shooting and editing a cohesive and attractive ceremony are two very different things. You don't want to misrepresent yourself.

Which leads us to another option for acquiring demo footage: Shoot it for free.

Don't cringe. I realize making money is the whole point. But we all should pay a few dues. Free production work is one way to do this.

Hundreds of organizations gladly accept the donation of video work. Any nonprofit entity (your local food bank? SPCA?) is a good place to start. Call. Explain your situation. Make your offer of free service. Beyond getting demo material, this philanthropic practice increases your working experience. And it's not bad for your reputation, either.

Inform local press of your charitable video "donations." This is great free advertising. Doesn't it feel good to help out others?

A Manual of Style

How you edit your demo can have as much impact as its contents.

First, set an appropriate length for your tape. Your projected audience pretty much determines this. A 3-minute demo isn't really long enough to warrant an award of cash.

Nor would you want to solicit a commercial account with a half-hour production. The client wants a 30-second spot, not a TV series.

Rule of thumb: Keep it short. For the general production market, 5 to 10 minutes is about right. It's not so long the viewer gets bored but not so short a potential client will question your experience. There's ample time to display your best work, professionally and courteously.

Applying the term "courteous" to a demo tape may seem odd, but your customers lead busy lives. They have better things to do than sit through your 30-minute extravaganza. Like anyone else, they want to get their information as quickly as possible. (You can always include supplemental materials with tapes you send to major funders.)

You've decided on a 5-minute demo. Now you're ready to edit footage, right?

Wrong. We're not done planning: Determine the order and style for presenting your experience before you start cutting. And it's a good idea to create a detailed script. Map out the order of each segment of footage.

Now consider style. Who's your target market? How can you reach them most effectively?

If they're serious business people, try a straightforward presentation—interspersing your footage with defining graphics and augment it with a clean voiceover. The key here is quick-paced editing with a clear demonstration of your abilities.

Perhaps you plan to approach several markets using a single demo tape. Intersperse interviews shot expressly for the demo—remarks from enthusiastic past clients—with cuts of your footage.

Taping these interviews means a little extra work, but it's well worth it. The boast of a satisfied customer impresses potential clients more than any claim you can make.

The testimonial is popular for all facets of advertising—just check out the commercials during network prime time. Using this technique in a small-town framework pays off especially well.

Business people and ordinary citizens see neighbors and friends—familiar faces—on the tape. If a prospect's competition or friend up the street is using you, chances are good you've found a new client.

The truly motivated may want to host their demos. The hosted demo is an innovative approach most smaller production companies seldom take advantage of.

If you're not a smooth talker, find someone who is. Create a script and have the emcee introduce each clip or segment. You can structure this many ways, for a serious, comedic or down-home feel.

Take care, though, if you're going for laughs. Your sense of humor might not be that of the general public. It's less risky to be serious.

Consider your host's setting, wardrobe and narrative. All these play a big part in the presentation's effectiveness.

Experiment. You may want to combine styles. Try a hosted demo that includes interviews with satisfied clients. Voiceover client comments while rolling footage from a particular job. Incorporate shots of your equipment in the demo.

Interview yourself—talk about customer satisfaction, your state-of-the-art gear, your sincere goal of creating the best possible product.

Shameless self-promotion adds a personal touch, and it's as popular as the testimonial. Again, just take a look at any network TV program for abundant proof.

Show It Around

There are a surprising number of additional ways to get your tape to roll where it counts most:

• Event videographers should keep a tape available for loan at photography studios. Drop a couple at local bridal and tux businesses.

• Film-to-tape transfer specialists might leave a copy at film shops.

• Attend county fairs, business expos or video industry trade shows with demo in hand. These functions are tailor-made to sell your business. You'll meet business owners and potential clients face to face.

• Present your demo to church, school and community groups. These organizations always have some sort of function in the works. Allow them to witness the advantages of having videotape recording of their event.

Following Up

People can be lazy. Your demo may pique their interest, but you're dreaming if you think it's enough to inspire every viewer to make the call. It often takes some additional sales effort to get the job.

Back to tooth-man Bob. As he considers a marketing plan, he gets your demo tape in the mail. Until now, direct mail, print ads and weekly shoppers had seemed the way to go. They require little effort on his part, pricing is reasonable, and audience delivery is good.

But now he's struck by the impact of live, talking images. Potential patients can "tour" his high-tech facility. Nurses and staff can show their friendly faces. Bob himself can make an earnest plea for healthy teeth. Done well, the demo may intrigue Bob enough to give you a call.

Or you could call him. Dispel the high-cost myth associated with video production. Explain how the video will attract clients just as it attracted him to your work. Let Bob know he can be as involved as he wants in making the tape.

Putting together an effective, professional-quality demo is not something you do one afternoon out of boredom. It takes patience, planning, creativity and hard work. You want to show yourself at your best.

To do just that, keep a few key ideas in mind.

• Include only your best work. Don't be impatient when scanning your videos for footage. You want to show a broad spectrum of ability. If necessary, create the footage you need.

• Set an appropriate length. Rule of thumb: Keep it short. Five to 10 minutes is about right.

• Plan order and style before editing your footage. Keep in mind your target market. When possible, create a detailed script. Try incorporating testimonials and self-promotion. You may even want to host your demo.

- If you need funding, shoot a couple of scenes of your planned work. Present this "demo" to potential investors.

- Follow up your demo presentations with a personal sales effort. Dispel the high-cost myth. Explain how your videos will benefit your client.

Rely on these key ideas and you'll create a demo impressive enough to convince even Uncle Bob.

PART VI
Internet Distribution

Getting your videos seen on screens all over the World Wide Web.

60
Producing Your Own Vidcast

Brian Peterson

With the explosion of the Podcast comes a new way of sharing videos, vidcasting. Now, you, too, can be a broadcaster and launch your own vidcast.

Perhaps 10 years ago you had a techno-savvy friend who asked you for your email address; chagrinned, you admitted you didn't have one yet. Five years ago, you still hadn't gotten around to putting up a personal webpage. And now your e-trendy friend is cajoling you for not having a vidcast espousing all the cool stuff you do. Whether you call them vidcasts, video podcasts, vlogs or something else, episodic video shows are quickly becoming an important form of content delivery.

And while they are not quite as ubiquitous as personal websites, individuals and small businesses have found that a vidcast can help them develop a dedicated community by providing specialized content.

We are going to review everything you need to know to plan, produce, edit, and distribute your own vidcast. First, let's tackle the critically important planning phase covering five key areas; assessment, format, quality, frequency, length and cost. In each of these areas we'll prompt you to ask yourself important questions, so have a pen and paper handy (yes, a computer works too) to jot down your answers. At the end of this chapter, you should have a working outline for your vidcast.

Assessment: Is a Vidcast Right for You?

If you simply have a few thoughts you'd like to share with the world, then just set up a webcam, don a silly hat, and fire off a soliloquy or two and be done with it. If, on the other hand, you have special skills, products or information that would be best delivered in small chunks over the course of many weeks, months or even years, then maybe a vidcast is just what you need. Do you have a hobby, sport or interest that you have trained your camcorder on that warrants methodic unveiling? Are you an educator that would like to share your knowledge with a wider audience? Do you think there is a group of people that are interested in what you have to offer? And how important is it for you to develop a community of regular viewers?

Ask yourself these questions and don't be daunted by thinking small. In fact, you should. Developing and distributing niche content is precisely what a vidcast can do for you better than just about any other form of content distribution. Unless you're banking on an early retirement from selling lots of advertising, you don't necessarily need thousands of people to make your vidcast successful.

So is a vidcast right for you? Well, if there's even a little, "maybe" in your response, then read on!

Format

Your audience, delivery environment and content largely determine the format of your vidcast.

Who is your audience? Will they be about your age or will they be much younger or older? Do they have, or are they aspiring to acquire the same level of knowledge you have about your subject? You may not know right away, but you should have in mind a very particular audience. This awareness is critical to shaping the look and feel of your vidcast.

If you've poked around the net much, you've no doubt noticed that the general look of most vidcasts is markedly less formal than the 6:00 news. In fact, they can be everything from pseudo-slick to downright grungy. And don't think grunge can't work. Diggnation has been one of the most popular vidcasts to date with little more than a dumpy couch in a living room and clothes that have never seen an iron ... and perhaps even a washing machine. This underscores how having compelling information presented by knowledgeable and witty talent can overcome even the most pedestrian settings.

How will you prepare your content? Will you be providing mostly information or will there be a dash of entertainment? Will it require research or are you already able to talk for a sustained period of time on your topic? Will you memorize, refer to notes on paper, or use a teleprompter? While not really a classic teleprompter that allows you to look directly into the lens, software such as that used by Adobe's recently acquired Vlog It, allows users a very intuitive and reasonably priced method of reading a scrolling script.

How will you deliver your message? Will you do this through the classic, "talking head" or will you also use demonstrations, additional video and still images or even illustrations? Will you be the host or will there be others to serve as "on-camera

Figure 60-1 *If you're using a teleprompter, try to make the script easy to comfortably read. If using notes, keep them in outline form, so the talent doesn't read verbatim with his head buried in script.*

talent?" What about interviews on your set, in the field, or over the phone?

Quality

There are three main areas you could invest time and money to increase the quality of your vidcast. In approximate order of importance they are: content development, lighting and set-design and equipment.

Fortunately, for the success of your vidcast, the most important area is also the least expensive. Just about everybody's

got a camcorder; many have pretty decent ones. What they often lack is a compelling reason to turn it on. Spend the majority of your time gathering information and your thoughts, and you'll already be well ahead of a large number of current vidcast "producers." Good preparation and an outline should not stifle your delivery or make your vidcast stiff; just the opposite. It should provide you with the freedom to be casual and informative with a structure that will prevent you from rambling.

If you need to invest in anything it's likely your lighting. If you've been using hardware store lighting fixtures until now, this might be the time to replace them with real lighting instruments. A large softbox or fluoropan for your main light, a focusable rim light or two, and some spotlights with barndoors for the background, positioned correctly, will give your vidcast a professional feel.

Your set is probably the biggest factor in determining the "look" of your vidcast. It can also be one of the most time-consuming and costly. Is a battered couch all you need or are you conjuring up blueprints that require planning commission approval? Starting simply is always a good idea, but if you want to start with some pizzazz on a budget, consider a virtual set. If your shot will be static and not too wide, a simple chromakey set may be just right.

For now, if you have a camcorder you are happy with for general videography, there's no need to upgrade just for your vidcast. If, on the other hand, you're looking for a feeble rationalization ... sure, a better camcorder will translate into better images online.

Frequency and Length

How often you produce your vidcast has a lot to do with its popularity. Not only will your viewers come to look forward to your next installment, but it seems evident that several of the leading RSS aggregators, like iTunes and FireAnt, use frequency as a factor in ranking. We have found that a

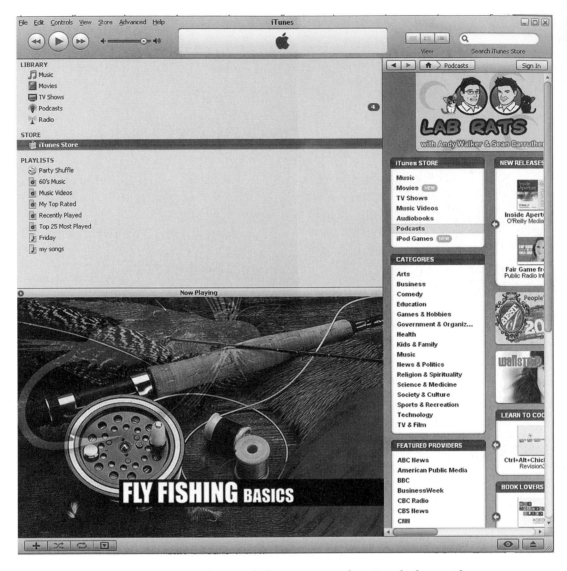

Figure 60-2 *Although every episode may differ, try to "envelope" each show with a common video and/or graphic open, clean graphic bylines, and a closer that stays the same show to show.*

weekly show will rank higher than one that is less frequent. Releasing on the same day each week, while not critical, may also have an impact on ranking.

Length is certainly determined by your subject matter, your capacity to sustain its delivery and your intended audience's attention span. However, there is another factor that you need to account for in this planning stage; web server bandwidth. A few of the early vidcasts got quickly swamped with viewers that rung up hefty bandwidth fees. We're talking many thousands of dollars.

So while it may be a welcome "problem," it's a good idea to check with your current web host provider what charges may apply if you go over your included monthly bandwidth allocation.

Cost

The last step in planning is to estimate how much your new vidcast will end up costing you. Review all of your answers to the questions above and tally everything

Figure 60-3 *Learning simple "hand signals" and techniques will keep your show tight and help the talent stay informed of segment durations.*

you'll likely need to get started. Don't forget to allow for purchase of props and perhaps some extra hard drive or optical media storage.

If you've been trying to answer these questions as you read along, you're probably beginning to see how much there is to consider in planning for your first vidcast. But don't let this dissuade you from learning first-hand what works for you. It still can be as simple as turning a camcorder on yourself and talking about your passion.

Production

We laid the foundation of planning the production of your own, now let's dig into the details of set design, talent and crew and equipment. There's a lot to cover, so let's get right to it.

Set Design

Don't let the term "set design" scare you. It can mean anything from creating plans and using power tools to dragging a beat-up

couch into position. One of the first things to consider is if there is a way to include the theme of your subject matter into the set. Let's say you are developing a show on the small world of scale trains; integrating a train motif into your set design would make sense. This might include rustic old train signal lanterns or railroad crossing signs. If you are putting together a set for a genealogy show, you could populate tables and walls with a large assortment of family photos to create a sense of hominess. You get the picture.

How much room will you have for your set? If you are going to turn your garage or living room into a makeshift studio, will you be able to leave it in place or will it need to be set up for each show? If you are handy at woodworking, create set pieces out of easily collapsible components that stack or fold. Also, try to estimate how many people will be on your set at one time and design for that size. Will you be using props or displaying odd-sized objects? If so, how many and how large with they be? Give it your best guess and have a table or flat area that will provide enough room.

A virtual set might be a good solution if you're in a small apartment or cleaning the garage would take too long. It does require a little more technical finessing, especially in post, but a simple chromakey background and some pre-built virtual sets will make the most of your limited space. Remember that while the mini DV format may not produce results as pleasing as professional formats such as Betacam, if you light well, it can be very acceptable.

If you survey current vidcasts, you'll see some very Spartan sets; so don't get bogged down here. Simply set up your camcorder on a tripod and hook up the output to a TV or monitor so you can easily adjust the placement of your set elements the way they look the best in relation to the framing of your main camcorder. Note these locations and, if you do need to break down after each episode, place gaffer's tape on the floor marking table, chair and other set object positions for quick placement next time.

(a)

(b)

Figure 60-4 *Set design can be as simple as filling up a corner with thematic gizmos and gadgets. This can be practically any place you decide to make your stage.*

Talent and Crew

Who is going to be in front of and behind the camera? It is certainly possible to do it all yourself by locking down your cameras, but you'll be able to include higher production value elements, like camera and even talent movement, if you have at least one camera operator. As you get more people to serve as crew members, you may want to add the following positions in roughly this order:

Camera B operator—this will be the close-up camera on talent and props. Camera A is your main shot and is locked down.

Audio—having a separate person concentrating on just audio can save you a great deal of pain in post.

Camera A operator—two cameras that can move gives you much greater flexibility, however, it also requires more coordination and planning.

Director/Floor director—if you have a second camera operator, a floor director will coordinate camera movement and provide cues to your talent.

A refreshing difference between vidcasts and broadcast television is that the people in front of the camera don't need to be professionally trained "talent." In fact, it's more important that they (or you) are

Figure 60-5 *(a) Camera angle "A" is your main camera, which your talent will address. When the crew is small, an operator can lock it off and attend to Camera "B." (b) Camera angle "B" is your b-roll or cutaway camera angle. This angle gives the audience a closer look while also giving you some room for sneaky editing.*

passionate about the subject and that this passion comes across in your show. How you do this will be up to you and the time you want to put into your production. Depending on the target length of your show and the expertise of your talent, ad libbing may be perfectly fine. If, however, you have several key subject areas to cover, you should at least create a one-page outline that they can rest in their lap or on the table. This type of casual approach is the norm for current vidcasts, but some producers are finding low-cost teleprompters add another level of professionalism to their show.

Equipment

There's a good chance you already have all the equipment you need to shoot your vidcast. The bare bones include just a camcorder, a sturdy tripod, a microphone and probably a few lights. But let's look at each in more detail.

- Your camcorder should have, at a minimum, the following three features:

- A mic input (preferably an XLR connection).

- Manual exposure control. If you light your set dramatically (hard light sources throwing dramatic shadowing), or if your background is mostly dark, automatic exposure control will likely overexpose your subject.

- Manual focus. You'll be supremely frustrated if you must rely on your camcorder's auto focus, particularly if you will be using props.

Not as critical, but still very helpful, other camcorder features include: manual control of audio levels, phantom power for external mics and smooth zooming capability. Also, having a second camcorder available for close-ups and cut-aways will give you much more flexibility when editing. Position this camcorder about 45 degrees to either side of your main camcorder.

If space permits, set up your camcorder just a little above the height of your talent's head and far enough away so that you are not on your camcorder's widest focal setting. This will help prevent subject distortion near the frame edges. If this is your only camcorder, keep any movement to a minimum. If you must get closer at some point, it is better to stop that take, zoom in, focus, and begin a new take. Cutting to the close-up will provide a much cleaner transition than trying to unlock your tripod head, take control of the camcorder and zoom in all in the same take.

Your tripod legs and head should be stable and smooth enough to tilt and pan without any jerkiness. Try to avoid operating the tripod at its full extension, as this is usually less stable.

The decision to use a wired or wireless microphone is less important than ensuring

Figure 60-6 *You don't need much gear to make it happen. Even this line-up could be reduced by taking the audio mixer out of the mix.*

Figure 60-7 *Placing a lapel mic up high is good. However, be aware if your talent turns his head dramatically, it may not pick up as well.*

that you have good cables and batteries always at the ready. That means backups too! A lapel-type mic is easiest to use as it doesn't require a boom operator. Just be sure not to position it up too high as you may experience dramatic volume changes if your talent turns his head away from the camera. If you will have two or more people on the set at one time, an audio mixer also becomes necessary.

The only equipment category you may find you are a little short of is lighting. Traditional three-point lighting is by no means the norm or even necessary for all vidcasts, but it still provides you with the most flexibility. Start by setting up your main, or key light a little left or right of and above your main camera position. Try using a medium-sized softbox or umbrella to soften the shadows. Your fill light should be closer to your main camcorder but positioned on the opposite side. This light should be larger than your key to avoid introducing secondary shadows. If you decide to use a third light, use it as a rim or hair light above and to the rear of your talent. You can use additional lights to throw patterns on your background or to highlight set features.

Quiet on the Set

You've now got your set in place, your crew in their positions and your equipment checked and ready. Are you ready to roll? Well, almost. As the producer, it will be your job to not to fall into the "it's-good-enough-for-the-Internet" syndrome. With the proliferation of video sharing sites, we all have become somewhat numb to the quality gap between "Internet" video and broadcast television. So even though you will be distributing in a reduced resolution online, keep in mind that good set design, camerawork, audio and lighting will be all the more important to help your production rise above the rest.

Editing and Distribution

We talked about key production elements like set design, talent and crew and equipment, now, wrapping it up with editing and preparing your vidcast for the web.

For Openers

Having a short catchy open that visually summarizes what your vidcast is all about is important. Since it's the first thing new viewers will see, it has the awesome task of compelling them to continue watching. It can be as simple as cutting together a few clips from your first show or as complex as a high-energy array of shots highlighting unique aspects of your subject matter complete with custom graphics and logo. In either case, keep it short, say five to 15 seconds, and be sure to at least include your show's title and possibly the episode number.

The Edit

Unless you have chosen to use special hardware to encode and upload your vidcast live to a streaming server, then you have two types of editing ahead of you. The first we could call "best takes" and the other, "live from tape."

Best takes editing is probably very familiar to you; after transferring footage to your edit computer, you simply select the best takes from one or more camcorders and create a rough cut of your main or "coverage" camcorder. Next, insert second or third camera angles, tweak your in and out points, add your open, appropriate transitions, music, graphics and credits and you have your final cut.

With two or more camcorders, you have the option of editing live from tape that resembles a live studio production. This requires a little more preparation prior to shooting along with software and a computer capable of handling multiple streams of video, but it can result in significant time-savings in post. With this method the whole vidcast, or contiguous segment, is shot as if it were live ... with the exception that if you make a mistake you can start all over (of course, this greatly slows down the edit process and somewhat defeats the purpose).

After transferring all of your footage to your edit computer, you sync each of your video streams at the beginning and roll all simultaneously. Your computer is now effectively a live switcher and you are the technical director, "cutting" from wide-angle to close-up shots on the fly. In the

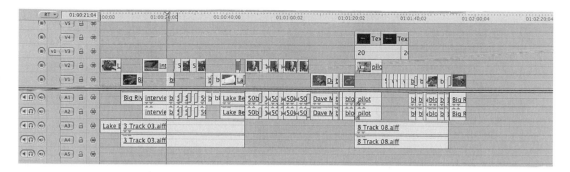

Figure 60-8 *Editing a "live" style show can get a little messy on your timeline. Keeping common elements on separate tracks can help make sense of it all.*

Figure 60-9 *NLE applications that have a multi-cam editing mode (e.g., Canopus Edius Pro v4) can simplify an editing session when there are multiple "live" camera angles.*

end, you should have a finished product, less possibly some graphics and music.

While there are not many unique aspects of editing a vidcast, there are several work-flow habits that will make your job easier when editing episodic shows. First, be sure to establish a consistent filing system. Have video assets you will reuse on each show, like your open, graphics, music, credits and any other transitional elements all in one directory. This will greatly speed up your edit session. Next, create and stick to a consistent project naming sys-tem. There's no need to get creative here; clarity is far more important. The episode number and date work well if used like this—"2007_Episode_45_5-01." This way when you go to sort your project files in the same folder, they will be in order even across multiple years.

Preparing for the Internet

There are three general areas you'll need to keep in mind when preparing your video for online distribution; the media player your audience will use; the file size and quality and, if you choose to also provide your show by RSS, the requirements of specific video aggregators like the heavy-weight iTunes and others like FireAnt.

There are many media players and related file types out there and it is no small challenge to decide which one or several will be right for your audience. But determining this is the first step. If you have a large email list of people that are likely viewers, such as a club or social group, simply send an email asking which media player they prefer. Another infor-mal survey would be to post the same question on a user group site dealing with your vidcast's subject matter.

Some of the currently popular media players include Quicktime/iTunes, Win-dows Media Player, Flash and RealPlayer. Others, such as DivX, Theora and Xvid have their followers as well. Some of these players use proprietary codecs that you will need to use to create file types that

will play back correctly in a given player. Again, the most important question to answer is which media player you believe your audience will be using. Once you know the player, you will know the file type(s) you will need to prepare. If your vidcast has lots of good information that does not rely on just visuals, you may also consider adding an MP3 version to your list.

The next question you'll want to address is how big should you make your frame size and at what quality settings should you use to encode? As more people are now connected with high-speed connec-tions, larger frame sizes are becoming possible. Don't be afraid to try full-frame 720 × 480 at medium quality settings. This usually means video bitrates around 600–700 kbps. But it is still common prac-tice to offer multiple media player formats and in at least a high and low quality/size offering. So, pick the top two or three media players and encode with those file types. Once your show has been running for a while and you are getting some traffic, you can analyze which files types are the most popular and possibly drop the least accessed.

RSS requires doing an additional step of creating an XML file that allows aggrega-tors to recognize, and people to subscribe to, your vidcast feed. An easy way to get going is to visit www.feedburner.com and follow its instructions on how to proceed.

Upload

You've now got your vidcast edited and encoded into a popular file type(s), now where will your new show live? Do you already have a website or blog dedicated to your show's topic? Perhaps you've opted to deliver your shows exclusively via RSS. And what about those free video sharing sites?

With the obvious exception of free hosting sites, be sure to check into a few details from your provider. The first is your monthly bandwidth allocation. If your show is lengthy, or if you've encoded

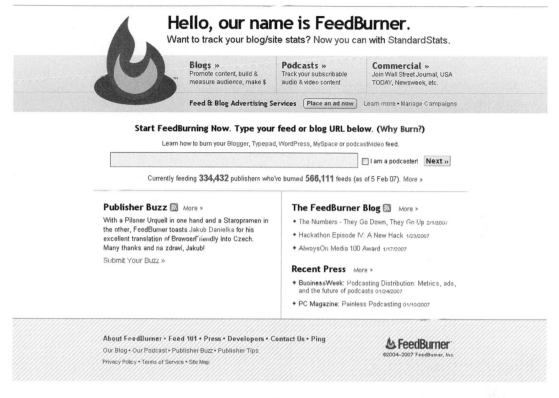

Figure 60-10 *If manually creating your own RSS Feed sounds like brain surgery, consider using an automated feed generator, such as FeedBurner (http://www.feedburner.com). It's free.*

using a high quality setting, you will likely have a large file that people will be downloading. And if your show becomes popular, you could easily exceed a modest monthly bandwidth limit. Early popular vidcasts like Diggnation found their initial bandwidth projections were way off ... and excess bandwidth can cost a lot. The second detail is to confirm with your web host that you'll have enough server storage space for all of your future vidcasts. You may find you'll need to increase this, but it is usually something you can do as it becomes needed.

What about uploading to popular free video sharing sites, like YouTube? While it won't hurt to use these additional free sites, they probably should not form the core of your distribution plan for episodic shows like a vidcast. This may change, but they are currently most popular for one-time videos rather than reoccurring shows.

It's Up. But Now What?

Congratulations! You've got your first vidcast up. But we're not done quite yet. While the incredible popularity of online video may provide opportunities for us as video producers, it also provides challenges as we shift our role to distributor and marketer. Because so many people are readily consuming video online there is a whole new level of access to potential audiences. But the widespread delivery of online video makes cutting through the clutter that much more difficult. We'll conclude our series with five tips that will help get your new vidcast seen by as many people as possible.

- Create an easily recognizable small icon (AKA, chicklet or avatar). This effectively becomes the logo for your show that aggregators use in their listings.

- Add your RSS feed to popular aggregators and directories like iTunes and FeedBurner.

- Send an email with a link announcing your new show to everyone you know.

- Link with other vidcasters, forums and user groups with complementary or similar interests.

- If you've housed your vidcast on your website, include a link to your current show on your homepage.

Figure 60-11 *These "chicklets" are small thumbnails that graphically represent your vidcast on feed aggregators (e.g., iTunes, Feedburner, etc.). Due to their small size, it's best to keep the info simple and easy to read to establish a clean icon.*

Sidebar 1

Virtual Sets

Getting a good clean key is critical to making a virtual set look believable. To do this, make sure you have very even lighting on your chromakey background. Video generally uses a green background, but it is more important to use a color that is not in your subject. And, depending on the software you use to knock out the background, you may not even need to use a large backdrop. Various companies make small to large paper and fabric backgrounds ranging in prices from about $40 to $400. If you can spare a wall, special chromakey paint is even available.

Figure 60-12a and b

Sidebar 2

Direct to Disk Recorders

If you shoot with more than one camcorder and find that you are spending more time than you'd like transferring your footage from tape, check out the latest generation of direct to disk recorders now on the market. Since ingesting footage from tape is a real-time process, you automatically gain one-to-one timesavings by having your material already on disk. And, as most recorders allow you to edit directly from the portable disk, you don't even have to transfer (at least immediately) to your edit computer. Depending on the size of your camcorder and options for external brackets, the only tricky part can be finding an appropriate mounting surface.

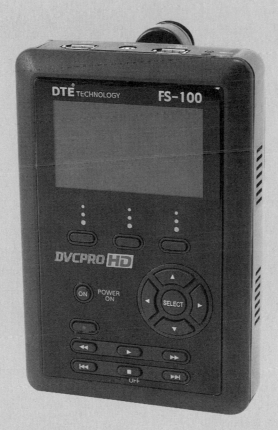

Figure 60-13

61
The 4th Codec

Joe McCleskey

How MPEG-4 will Revolutionize Digital Media

If you are at all familiar with digital video and audio technology, you've probably heard or read the term MPEG (emm-peg) by now. This acronym, which stands for Moving Picture Experts Group, refers to a set of standards agreed upon by an international group of top-notch audio/video technicians for creating and playing digital video and sound. The MPEG set of standards has worked its way into our everyday lives: DVD, digital satellite television, digital cable and Internet music all make use of the MPEG standards.

In this article, we'll take a look at one of the newest and most promising of these standards: MPEG-4. We'll examine what makes MPEG-4 so interesting and how you can expect to make use of MPEG-4 in your future video creations. By the time you're finished with the chapter, we hope you'll be as excited as we are about the possibilities that this technology presents to videographers, audio specialists and digital content creators of all stripes.

What It Is

All of the members of the MPEG family of standards are codecs or COmpression-DECompression schemes. The primary task of a codec is to reduce the size of a digital media file and thus reduce the bandwidth, or data rate, necessary to play the file. If you find this confusing, don't worry; we're going to break it down a bit more.

The first issue, file size, is especially important for video storage. Uncompressed video takes a huge amount of storage space, regardless of whether you're storing it on a hard drive, DVD or digital tape. To imagine how much space is required, consider that a typical uncompressed still frame of video, at the quality most of us are used to viewing, requires just under one megabyte to store. Video in the United States typically plays at 30 frames per second. This means that your typical uncompressed video might occupy 27 megabytes per second to store. Do a little more math, and you'll soon discover that the new 80 gigabyte hard drive that came with your computer will only store about

50 minutes of raw, uncompressed video—and that's before you add the audio into the equation. Do one more calculation and you'll see that a DVD disc (at 4.5 GB) can hold less than three minutes. Clearly, we need some form of digital compression to reduce that file size.

The second issue is so closely related to the first that it's really the same problem viewed from another angle. Imagine you have an uncompressed VHS-quality video file sitting on a hard drive, ready to play. In order to provide smooth playback, your hard drive would have to dump data to your computer at a sustained 27 megabytes per second (or, as an engineer would think: 216 megabits per second [27 * 8 bits/byte]). Storage systems are available that can hit these speeds, but they're very expensive. Now consider that you want to deliver that same video to the masses, via the Internet. Whatever technology you use, the speed of that technology (bandwidth) would have to match that 27 megabytes per second, without fail.

MPEG 1, 2, 3

Enter the MPEG family of codecs, which compresses the file size down to a manageable level, then decompresses the moving images and sound as you watch them on the fly. MPEG-1, the first standard agreed upon by the group, is widely used for small Web video, CD-ROM video and VCDs, which were popular in Asia. It's also the most (in)famous format for compressing songs on the Internet, swapped using file-sharing services. MP3 is not MPEG-3 and actually stands for MPEG-1, Layer 3. MPEG-1 video and audio are fairly highly compressed, but the more compression you use, the worse the image appears. It's possible to achieve a compression ratio of 200:1 with MPEG-1, thus reducing the file size to about one megabyte per six seconds of full-sized video, but the resulting image is very difficult to watch at that point. Most MPEG videos use 50:1 or less.

MPEG-2 has gained widespread use in home DVDs and digital television broadcasts. Much more advanced and efficient than MPEG-1, MPEG-2 video achieves a very stable and watchable picture at around a 40:1 compression ratio. "More advanced" also means "more computationally intensive" and MPEG-2 video requires a faster computer than MPEG-1 video.

MPEG-3 was originally developed for use in HDTV broadcasts, but the advances made under the MPEG-3 name were eventually incorporated into MPEG-2. For this reason, MPEG-3 is a dead codec, one that served its purpose and is now no longer a separate standard.

This brings us to MPEG-4. MPEG-4 takes advantage of the experience gained by the development of MPEG-1 and MPEG-2 and goes one step further by adding in elements such as 3D objects, interactive sprites, text, digital photos and other media types. In other words, you can watch a video program, press a button to bring up some text navigation buttons, scroll through options, make a selection to move to another scene or even make a purchase. "But I can do this already," you say. Sure, you can, however, when you do this now, the interactivity usually comes from the television or the DVD player or some other proprietary set-top box. With MPEG-4, the interactivity is embedded within the video itself. This means content creators will have total control over how that interactivity appears and plays out for the viewer, regardless of the device or medium used to play the MPEG-4 file.

This sounds interesting, doesn't it? It's even a little intimidating for the home videographer. But even if you never intend to bring this kind of interactivity to your videos, MPEG-4 still represents one of the most advanced codecs available for simple digital video and audio capture, storage and delivery.

Why It Matters

MPEG-4 really shines in the areas of efficiency, scalability and industry support.

- Efficiency—Because it represents a refinement of earlier advances in MPEG compression and decompression technology, MPEG-4 promises to deliver higher quality video and audio at smaller data rates and file sizes. Yes, you heard that right: better video, smaller files and thus lower bandwidth (data rate). Of course this means you'll also need a faster computer.

- Scalability—Scalability just means that MPEG-4 is designed to deliver video and audio content at nearly any data rate, over any network, whether it's connected by high-speed fiber optics or dial-up modems. This is an advance over MPEG-2, which is limited primarily to DVD-quality video.

- Industry support—MPEG-4 is currently supported by just about every major player in the media world, including Apple, Microsoft, Sun, Dolby, AOL Time-Warner, Lucent and Sony (among others). MPEG-4 content is already in use in a huge number of media and communications devices, from televisions and home video players to mobile phones and, yes, camcorders.

So how can you make MPEG-4 work for you? Pretty simple, really. Because Apple's QuickTime technology has already fully embraced the MPEG-4 standard, any product that currently supports the latest version of QuickTime will allow you to export your videos using MPEG-4 compression. These products include, but are not limited to, Final Cut Pro, Adobe Premiere, Discreet Cleaner and many others. Microsoft, too, has embraced MPEG-4 as a standard, and all Microsoft products (including XP's free Movie Maker 2 software) support it via the Windows Media 9 Series technology. It's worth noting, however, that the ISO (International Standards Organization) has chosen QuickTime as the standard for MPEG-4 delivery.

See for Yourself

Don't take our word for it: investigate the MPEG-4 phenomenon for yourself. Apple's MPEG-4 pages (www.apple.com/mpeg4/) are loaded with information about how QuickTime has embraced the standard and numerous sample MPEG-4 files are available for viewing. Tech-heads will find a wealth of information at the MPEG-4 industry forum (www.mp4if.com). Of course, this research is only necessary if you explicitly want to watch MPEG-4 video for the sake of watching MPEG-4. The technology is so pervasive at this time that just by browsing around the Web for video, perhaps to watch the latest movie trailer, you'll eventually run into a QT or a WMV file that uses MPEG-4.

At the time of this writing, MPEG-4 is primarily used for small, easily transportable Web videos and, unfortunately, pirating Hollywood feature films. Keep your eye on this standard, however: it's mainly interesting not for how it's being used today, but for how it could potentially be used in the future. Within MPEG-4 lies the ability to create a whole new generation of devices, delivery systems, educational titles, corporate training objects, games, higher-quality music files, better disc-based interactivity and higher-quality video. All it takes is for people to dream about the possibilities.

62
Peer to Peer File Sharing

Kyle Cassidy

Peer to Peer could be the answer to your video distribution questions.

Asked to describe radio, Albert Einstein answered: "The wireless telegraph is not difficult to understand. The ordinary telegraph is like a very long cat. You pull the tail in New York, and it meows in Los Angeles. The wireless is the same, only without the cat." To paraphrase Einstein, Peer to Peer (P2P) video file sharing is just like sharing videotapes, only without the videotape.

One Big Server

So you have a collection of brilliant videos and you want to share them and your directorial genius with the world. You can go about distributing them in two ways. One is to store them at central locations frequented by people who look at videos, like your local video store. In the computer world, we call this the "client/server" model. The video store is a "server" and the people who patronize it are "clients." There are advantages to this model: people know where to go to look for a video, the stock is consistent, easily predictable and you can ask a friendly store employee for help finding what you want. The downside of this is the limited hours of operation, their fees, and their selection of videos. For example, they might not want to carry the video of your trip to the zoo.

Sharing Servers

A second model for video distribution is to make copies and hand them out to your friends and family. They may reciprocate with videos of their own. Or one friend may loan your video to another. This is "Peer to Peer" sharing. Everybody in the distribution chain is equal with every other person, there's no corporate headquarters, no brick and mortar store and no limited hours of operation. There are many advantages to this model beyond not needing a store or employees, nobody decides what videos you can share and what ones you can't.

Most people who use the Internet are already familiar with the client/server

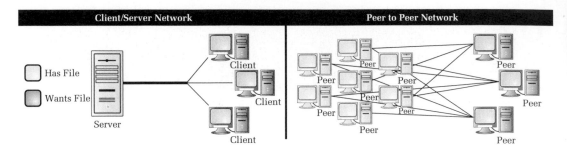

Figure 62-1 *A traditional client/server model serves the data from a file from only one computer, while a Peer to Peer network can serve the same file from several different computers to several other computers.*

model of distributing video online. You go to cnn.com or some other site, click on a link and video begins to play in a window. This is fine for consumers of video, but not always great for the producers of video. Chances are, CNN isn't going to put up the video of your zoo trip or even the really funny eight minute clip of your nephews Moe and Elvis.

Figure 62-2 *The first version of Napster was one of the first Peer to Peer networks. It has since become a place to purchase music, which is no longer distributed to end users on a Peer to Peer basis.*

The Rise of P2P

In 1999, Shawn Fanning realized that the problem with sharing files over the Internet was that the process required large, centralized servers. Why not, he reasoned, have thousands, or even millions, of less powerful computers act as mini-servers? A few sleepless Jolt Cola nights later, he'd written the software which would become Napster. Sean was interested in swapping music files, and that became the backbone (and the bane) of his company. Each Napster user became a mini-server. Though primarily used to trade music, Peer to Peer software could be used to share any types of files, images, sounds and even computer programs. For a while at least, millions of people traded music files with abandon. Some colleges and universities reported that students trading music files occupied 90% of their bandwidth. In February of 2001, Temple University Vice President Arthur C. Papacostas stated: "[T]he Office of Computer and Information Services commenced an investigation and found that

the University's bandwidth was insufficient to permit both the use of Napster and the delivery of educational materials and services."

It wasn't just a bandwidth concern, however. The Recording Industry Association of America (RIAA) had a fit. Artists like Metallica complained bitterly about lost royalties and legal action killed off the original Napster software three years later. The P2P sharing genie was out of the bottle, however, and there are a bunch of other applications that fill the gap today, including (but not limited to) Grokster, Kazaa, LimeWire and Bearshare.

Try It Out

So I decided to try P2P sharing one of my creations. I chose a short video and made a compressed 320 × 200, 15 frame per second. AVI version of it suitable for transmission over the Internet. There are more Peer to Peer file sharing programs than you can shake a stick at, but here's my experience with one.

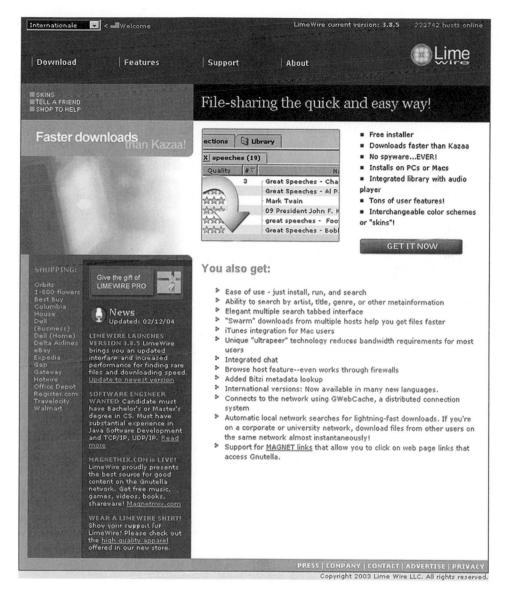

Figure 62-3 *LimeWire is a Peer to Peer service that allows sharing of any file on your hard drive.*

LimeWire (http://www.limewire.com) is available for Windows, Mac and Linux platforms. The layout is simple and user friendly and the installation is very straightforward. LimeWire also has a nice search feature that makes it easy to run multiple searches at the same time. On top of all this, the Apple version has iTunes support built-in, which allows you to buy music a song at a time.

As soon as the software is running (and you're on the Internet), you have a default shared directory (which you can change). Putting your files online is as easy as dragging and dropping files into this directory. Now, as long as your computer is online, it acts as a server, sharing everything in this directory, including your Magnum Opus. Using the search feature in LimeWire, anyone can find your movie, as long as they know what to look for.

Share It

Your first problem is that your audience can only get to your file while you are online. When a viewer downloads your video using LimeWire, it's automatically shared on the viewer's computer. Load balancing means sharing the server duties between multiple servers and this speeds propagation. The more popular a file is, the faster it downloads, because it can be downloaded from everyone who has previously viewed and downloaded your video. Of course, only people who are online can share your video with others, but with more high-bandwidth always-on connections, the technology is becoming more practical by the day. The more people who watch your video, the more available it will become. If you were in marketing, you might say that this is a scalable distribution model that automatically grows with demand. But that's sort of a Catch-22 at first, if no one knows about your movie.

Figure 62-4 *MagnetMix is a Web site that indexes some of the best content available on LimeWire.*

Publicizing Your File

So nobody knows the title of your swank indie short even though you've made it readily available. A database with a subject or keyword search would be great, but that just hasn't been implemented in the LimeWire interface yet. Traditional electronic Internet marketing, on a Web site, message board or by e-mail, will certainly work, but that's not the P2P way. The best solution is using the Website Magnet-Mix (http://www.magnetmix.com), which is designed to integrate with LimeWire. MagnetMix is a far-minded endeavor meant to showcase independent creative output (music, video, still images and computer software) over P2P. MagnetMix is a greatest hits content archive and LimeWire has a button that connects to MagnetMix.

Once on MagnetMix, there are convenient links for submitting content. I clicked on the "Submit Content" button and added information for my file. Two days later, I got an e-mail from MagnetMix telling me that my file was being carried in their Video section. Now, folks who are interested in the state of indie film on the Internet can find my movie with ease.

The Future of P2P and Video File Sharing

It's easy to see how P2P can transform the accessibility of media on the Internet. Granted, the bulk of most of the current usage is still for commercial MP3 music files and commercial movies, but the technology works just as well for legitimate content providers. P2P could start a flurry of people watching other people's indie videos and begin a distribution revolution by sharing their videos. What are you waiting for? Let's see what you've been shooting lately.

Sidebar 1

Is P2P Legal?

Peer to Peer file sharing is legal. Stealing copyrighted material is not. It is illegal, for example, to duplicate a VHS tape that you don't own the copyright to and give it to a friend. The same is true for P2P file sharing. For video that you do own the copyright to, and that would include any and all original creations, you can share all you want. And P2P is a good way to do this.

Sidebar 2

Success!

Several days later, a vanity search for my name on LimeWire shows that several people are sharing my video! Looking for like-minded individuals? Right clicking on the filename gives you the option to "Browse host" and you can see all the files that user is sharing. If he's sharing your indie video, he may be film fans sharing other indie videos. Looking for feedback? A smiley face icon next to the file name means that user has enabled "chat" and you can send him instant messages (right click on the filename, select "Chat with host"). Maybe you've found a fan.

PART VII
Authoring DVDs

Burning video onto discs that will play in DVD players and computers.

63
Jacks of All Trades

Charles Fulton

Disc authoring suites are versatile and reasonably powerful one-stop solutions for a wide variety of media management tasks.

Way back in 1999, CD-burning drives were just beginning to cross into practical price ranges. A video-editing computer was still an expensive and tricky beast to configure and no one thought DVD burners would be inexpensive and widely available anytime soon. The typical software bundled with a typical circa 1999 CD-R drive was barely enough to burn a data CD or audio CD. Even today, the software packages that come in the box with most CD and DVD burners are not the same as the full-featured premium suites a number of companies offer. The core of this software is still burning discs and the software is usually very good at this. As these packages have gone from simple data burning to also include audio CDs, MP3 ripping and video DVDs, most companies have built more comprehensive packages of applications, or suites. These suites handle all of your needs as far as basic disc authoring is concerned. Let's investigate some of the features found in a typical disc authoring suite.

Video Editing

Frequently, the video editing features found in a suite tend to be rather basic, but functional. They're great if you need to throw a simple, quick project together. They're no replacement for your beloved copy of Avid, Premiere Pro or Vegas if you're embarking on a more involved project, but if you're just cutting up a single-track project and audio needs are simple, you'll find what you need.

Disc Authoring

Most disc authoring suites support a wide array of disc formats. Most packages burn DVD-video projects and audio CDs to a broad variety of discs, which can include CD-R and DVD-R data discs and burning MP3 discs for use in mobile digital audio players.

When it comes to burning DVD-video projects, most of the packages include templates for menus, which will help you create your project quickly. Interestingly, Dolby Digital audio encoding has found its way into a large number of these packages, which we applaud. Dolby Digital audio is widely considered to be the ideal format for audio on DVD, since it's defined as one of the mandatory formats in the DVD standard, yet it doesn't take excessive amounts of data to encode.

Audio Management

Music management has become an increasingly common feature in disc authoring suites. Most suites now handle a staggering array of formats. MP3 is by far the most common audio format, but a number of other formats have become popular with Internet audio fans. These include the open-source Ogg Vorbis format, Microsoft's WMA, as well as AAC, which was co-developed with Dolby Laboratories and popularized by Apple.

Almost all of the packages can also rip (extract) CD audio tracks from discs that conform to the CD Digital Audio standard. This allows you to copy the tracks to the format of your choice for your own personal use, such as cataloging music on your hard drive for use with jukebox applications or using your music with portable personal audio players.

Other Features

A number of suites offer data backup and restore features. Like many functions performed by suites, data backup capabilities tend to be on the light side when compared to other dedicated backup utilities. You can create and print basic labels and inserts using the included layout software, but, again, the features are limited compared with a dedicated labeling application.

A disc authoring suite is a software upgrade that is always worth considering. They're inexpensive, very useful and often surprisingly powerful. If you're ready to proceed deeper into the world of media creation than that which your basic burning software can handle, it's time to give a disc authoring suite a careful look.

64

To DVD or Not to DVD?
(There is no question.)

Bill Davis

Okay, we're now officially smack dab in the middle of the era of the "homemade" DVD.

DVD burners are included with most modern computers and the ubiquitous shiny discs are rapidly pushing aside VHS tape as the "home recording" format of choice. So if you haven't made the switch to your own home DVD authoring environment, now's the time.

I use the term "environment" rather than "program" because quite a few people who want to create their own DVDs are turning to stand-alone DVD burners, rather than authoring their DVDs in a software application on a computer. Both approaches yield similar results—take your pick. This article focuses on computer-based DVD burning, but if you're considering a stand-alone recorder, see the sidebar, The Appliance Path.

building a navigation "front end" so that the end-user can find and play the content on the disc.

Most DVD authoring software typically comes with pre-packaged templates, so if you just want to get the job done fast and easy, look for these templates to give you a head start. More robust software provides customization options, including control over the "look and feel" of your interface. The best software programs allow you to start with a professionally built template but essentially "deconstruct" them in order to customize them for your particular use.

For example, if the original template designer specified 4 animated picons (picture icons) for scene selection, but you have 5 scenes, you can often copy and paste another picon link and, with a few clicks and some simple drag-and-drop screen re-arrangement, be ready to go.

Getting Started

All DVD authoring requires at least basic menu creation. This is the process of

Going Outside to Play

Power users will typically do their menu design outside the DVD creation process,

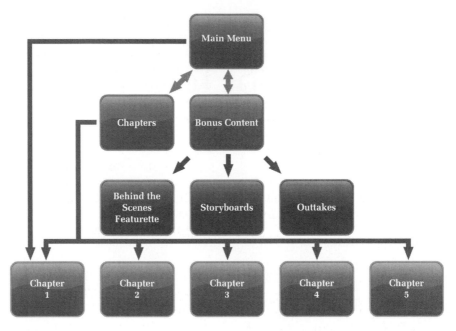

Figure 64-1 *A complete DVD workflow may include several different links between menus.*

using tools like Photoshop or similar high-end design software to precisely specify every background, button, nuance and shading of the interface. After you have your menu design developed, you need to link it to the actual actions the buttons or hot zones should invoke. (A hot zone is basically a place on a DVD menu where a change occurs in the look of the area when the cursor reaches it—often used for highlighting buttons or other interface elements.) DVD programs have various ways of accomplishing this linking process.

Some use a table-like interface, where you link actions on one side to button titles on the other. Other programs provide robust graphical linking environments, where you drag connecting lines between the button itself and the action you want that button to invoke. Each software implementation might be different, but there MUST be a way—either automated or manual—to link buttons to actions, or your DVD won't do anything.

Simplicity—Its Own Reward

The challenge with linking is that, if you have a lot of menu actions, the navigation

Figure 64-2 *A simple menu generally provides your audience the easiest way to access your content.*

can get complex. And there are lots of stories of beginners forgetting, for example, to link the END of a block of content to a "return to menu" function. So essentially someone will play a part of your DVD and get stuck in a blind alley, unable to do anything but eject and re-install the disc. Bummer.

Clear navigation that makes sense to the user and always provides clues to "what to do next" is an art. Studying the templates in good software can give you clues such as placing "home" buttons on all screens and making sure your user choices are clear.

DVD Is NOT Videotape!

Finally, all of us trained to make videos are conditioned to thinking in a beginning-middle-end linear process. The magic of the DVD is that it's non-linear in nature. As a DVD designer, you need to think differently. Are there parts of your project that your audience would enjoy being able to skip directly to? What about "special content" like outtakes and bloopers? The very non-linear nature of DVD makes it a perfect vehicle for providing your viewers with extras like these.

The flexibility of the DVD format makes it a much more robust way to store and play back video, but that same flexibility makes it more complicated to burn even a simple DVD than it was, for example, to record to VHS tape.

As with any complex endeavor, the key is to dive in, experiment and learn. Before too long you should be burning DVDs like a pro. And taking comfort in the fact that your creations should look better and be much more durable than the tape-based copies of yesterday.

Happy Authoring!

Sidebar

Standing Alone

For a lot of occasional users, complex computer-based DVD authoring is just too much trouble. So consider the "stand-alone" DVD burner's "all in one" approach.

Gone is the computer. In its place is a dedicated box that contains the burner, the MPEG-2 encoder needed to make DVD player-compliant files and in many cases a hard drive that stores the video footage during the encoding and burning process. These units make DVD creation about as easy as it can be. But not as easy as the "one button" VHS recording you're likely accustomed to.

That's because at least some basic titling, chapter marking and navigation are required for any DVD. In the stand-alone recorder, the typical process is a guided series of menus where you enter your text for titles and mark your chapter breaks by pushing control buttons on a handheld remote control. It's a little like text messaging on a cell phone. Still, the resulting DVDs work just like those authored on computer-based systems. And while the menus might not be as fancy, at least your computer is free for other work while your stand-alone DVD recorder is burning your latest video project to disc.

Figure 64-3 *Lite-On's LVW-5045 DVD recorder includes a hard drive for recording programming, a progressive-scan output and a FireWire port for capturing footage from DV camcorders.*

65

From Video to Disc: A DVD Software Buyer's Guide

Pat Bailey

Understanding the Basics of DVD Authoring Software and Hardware

Nowadays, it seems like all videographers want to make DVDs. But this means more than just burning video straight onto a blank DVD. You want your video's packaging to match the first-rate look and features of the pros.

Well, you're in luck. Fortunately, manufacturers are aware of this demand and have created a broad range of hardware and software products to meet the needs of nearly every budget.

Getting Authorized

Authoring great looking DVDs is now a rather simple process, thanks to the continued improvements and wealth of features offered by manufacturers' products. Even if you've never authored a DVD, there are great start-up tools offered in many software packages to help you quickly and easily make DVDs like the pros.

"Great, so what's all this talk about authoring DVDs?" Glad you asked. Authoring simply refers to the process of organizing and presenting all of your media production assets (video, audio, titles, etc.) in an interactive format. The result of this process is what viewers experience when they play a DVD—menus, graphics, and setup options, which create a visually enhanced presentation.

Knowledge Is Power

Before you bald your tires in a frenzied race to be first in line at the local software stores, it's best to know what you'd like to get out of your DVD authoring software. With a broad price range and dozens of titles available, a little bit of forethought pays off before heading to the checkout counter.

Some of the aspects to consider before purchasing DVD authoring software are price, features, ease-of-use, and compatibility. We'll take a quick look at these aspects by breaking down the discussion into three main user categories—consumer/ hobbyist, prosumer and professional.

Software: More Bang for the Buck

Regarding price, we'll define the consumer/ hobbyist products as those between $50 and $250. Prosumer's wallets is a bit larger, so they get to spend between $250 and $1,000. Professionals have access to company credit cards and corporate mega-budgets. As such, we'll define their financial prowess as purchasing anything over $1,000.

The biggest factor determining software price tends to be features. Generally, the rule of thumb is more features equal a bigger price tag. The consumer-level software includes titles such as Apple's iDVD, Sonic Solutions' MyDVD Studio, Studio Delux and Studio Delux Suite, Pinnacle Systems' Studio Plus, Mediachance's DVD-lab Standard, DVD-lab Studio and DVD-lab Pro and Nero Ultra.

Consumer software offers basic functionality and features. At this level, the trade-off is between features and ease-of-use. Inexperienced DVD authoring users get the advantage of automated features and template designs. These tools help create your DVD menus and chapters, and allow you to include static background images or, in some cases at this price range, animated backgrounds. Customization is very limited compared to prosumer and professional software.

The limitations imposed at the consumer level are generally safeguards to make DVD authoring as error-free as possible. The brute-force approach limits user creativity, but helps ensure everyone goes from start to finish as painlessly as possible.

Even with the limitations, there's good news. Fortunately, competition for market share causes software developers to keep adding more and more features. What you get from a basic software title now is much more than just a year ago. One of the more helpful tools, available in even some of the basic titles, is DVD proofing. Proofing

your work before burning DVDs can't be overemphasized. You don't want to wind up wasting countless hours and dozens of discs before getting the desired result.

Prosumer software titles include Sonic Solutions' DVDit! and DVDit Pro, Apple's DVD Studio Pro, Adobe's Encore DVD, Sony's Vegas+DVD, and Ulead's DVD Workshop. The prosumer software throws in more customization and some more advanced features. Additional features included at this price range are support for animated menu backgrounds, 16:9 wide-screen video, high-definition support and surround sound audio systems. Real-time proofing and compatibility options are also common in prosumer products.

While the learning curve for some features is comparable to consumer-level software, the more advanced features take some getting used to (customization always comes with a price). When you're making decisions about custom layouts, compression, audio formats and player compatibility, things are trickier than the user-friendly drag-and-drop interfaces of consumer titles.

If you're completely new to DVD authoring, have little interest in advanced design options, or don't want to be bothered with the technical aspects such as compression and formatting, then selecting software with more automated features is your best choice. At the professional level, DVD authoring software gives most users the most customizable control. These software titles enable you to configure region coding, copyright protection, surround sound, advanced sub-titling and closed-captioning options, multiple camera-angle support and formatting engine controls for the widest possible compatibility range. Although beyond what most of our readers may use, Scenarist (from $4,999 to $35,000) is one example of software in this product range.

Hardware: Duplicators and Burners

OK, having tackled the basics and given an overview of the DVD authoring software world, now let's look at authoring-related hardware. To begin, understand that the hardware is divided into two main categories: duplicators and burners.

Let's start with DVD burners, since they tend to be the more popular of the two categories. Why so popular? These devices are the quickest, least expensive method for creating a DVD. Referred to as DVD recorders or burners, these drives appear and operate identically to their CD counterparts, and are available as both internal and external devices. If you know how to burn CDs, then you already know how to use one of these types of DVD burners—it's the same concept. Additionally, some of these devices are bundled with user-friendly burning software packages.

Internal burners are relatively cheap nowadays, although professional burners are still rather expensive, comparatively speaking. You can find consumer-level internal burners as low as $40, but most are between $50 and $150. For the more professional models, expect to pay anywhere from $350 to $700. For external burners, expect to pay $100 to $300 over a comparable internal drive—typically between $120 and $700. Some of the standard manufacturers of internal and external DVD burners include TEAC, Sony, HP, Pioneer, Phillips, and Toshiba (the developers of DVD technology).

DVD burners are fine for producing small quantities of discs, but if you frequently need to produce dozens or hundreds of discs, you want a better, more efficient solution. Enter DVD duplicators. Duplicators are similar to DVD burners, although they're designed to record multiple discs simultaneously—many even do so unattended. You can find single-disc duplicators for about $300, and a multi-disc tower device costs between $500 and $6,000. DVD duplicator manufacturers include R-Quest, NEC, Pioneer, Kanguru, Disc Makers, Primera, Rimage, Vinpower and Plextor.

Other Considerations: Layers and Formats

Some final things to consider when thinking about DVD authoring hardware are single-layer and dual-layer recorders, as well as authoring format (SD, HD-DVD and Blu-Ray). Single-sided, single-layer DVD records enable you to record upto 4.7GB of information per disc (DVD-5) on single-sided, single-layer DVDs, where single-sided, double-layer holds up to 8.5GB. Dual-layer recorders are slightly more expensive, but well worth the money if you're recording longer format videos.

Although HD-DVD (15GB single, 30GB dual-layer capacity) and Blu-Ray (roughly 25GB single, 50GB dual-layer capacity) formats offer considerable video image quality, it may not be too wise to invest in either of these formats just yet. Why? Two reasons: 1) neither format is the victor of the next format-standard war; 2) the original SD-DVD format remains the most commonly used format.

As far as economics is concerned, SD-DVD is cheaper and covers the largest market share. Hi-Def digital video, in general, remains to be too expensive for most people. The move to Hi-Def digital video is analogous to the transition from dial-up to broadband Internet service and, as such, it's wiser to aim your video projects at the widest target audience.

Sidebar 1

Stand alone or PC?

Stand-alone or turnkey DVD recorders provide the convenience of one-stop DVD production, but don't offer the creative flexibility found in PC-based authoring software and hardware. Also, if something breaks on a stand-alone recorder, you'll have to return the entire unit for repair, unlike repairing individual PC parts.

Sidebar 2

Sticky Situation

It gets a bit tricky when it comes to labeling DVDs as a paper sticker such as the type used on CDs will often throw these faster spinning optical discs off balance while being read. This can damage the disc or even the reader. Handwriting with permanent markers are a favorite method but not very professional looking. Some HP burners use LightScribe technology that uses a laser to etch a good looking monotone image onto specially coated blank media. Another option is a special ink jet printer with an optical tray for printing multi-color designs onto DVDs. Professional dup and replication houses silk screen images onto optical media and we even know of a guy who hand silk screens onto his DVDs with glow in the dark ink.

66
Burner Basics: An Introduction to DVD Burners

Charles Fulton

When the first CD burners hit the market, the equipment was very expensive, but prices fell rapidly and, today, most entry-level computers come with a CD burner. One could safely expect that this will soon be the situation with DVD burners.

Times were simpler back when the first CD burners came out, though. There was really only one standard with two types of discs: the write once discs (CD-R) and the rewritable discs (CD-RW). DVD is a little more complex. The first recordable DVD formats developed by the DVD Forum were DVD-R, DVD-RW and DVD-RAM. The DVD+RW Alliance, led by Philips and Sony, created a different format: DVD+RW and DVD+R. Both the DVD Forum (−R) and DVD+RW Alliance (+R) claim better compatibility. For the consumer, this can seem confusing. Rest assured, this format war shouldn't cause the end user to lose too much sleep.

Will It Play in Peoria?

Naturally, both the proponents of the DVD+R/+RW and those of the DVD−R/−RW formats claim that *their* discs are the most compatible with the installed base of living room DVD players.

Who's Right?

Many factors contribute to whether a given disc will play in a given player. For the home DVD author, the hardware burner, the authoring software and type of blank media are all part of the equation. In the end, however, we've found that the bulk of compatibility problems are with the player. In our tests, living room DVD players that play DVD-R discs also tend to play DVD+R discs, and vice versa. This is a broad generalization and is not 100% true across the board.

That said, it is our responsibility as content creators to do everything we can to make the most compatible discs possible and the material on the disc itself is sometimes the problem. Many complex projects must be tweaked and re-built before the project can be widely distributed. We've experienced this firsthand when building our own *Basics of Videography* DVD. It can take a lot of patience (as well as a tall rack of DVD players and an intern to do some quality assurance tests) to find all of the problems that might crop up in a disc.

Who Makes 'Em?

The big players to watch are the manufacturers of the drive mechanisms, primarily Pioneer for DVD-R/RW mechanisms and Ricoh for DVD+R/RW mechanisms (and Panasonic for DVD-RAM mechanisms). There is a wide cross-section of computer peripheral manufacturers that are offering branded-DVD burners, including Verbatim, TDK, Memorex, Pioneer, Panasonic, Toshiba, HP, Sony and LG. (See the *DVD Burner Manufacturer Listing* sidebar for the entire gamut.) There are also companies who repackage drives in their own enclosures, and bundle them with software and cables to create a convenient and consumer-friendly single-box DVD authoring solution (such as Pacific Digital, QPS, EZQuest, Fantom Drives and LaCie). Shop around and you're sure to find something that meets all of your needs, whether it's a complete kit or a bare drive.

Speed Demons

Need that disc yesterday? Drives get faster every day, with the fastest Pioneer drive currently burning at 4×. (This drive initially had a firmware problem that has since been corrected. If you have an older drive with a Pioneer mechanism, be sure to visit Pioneer's Web site at www .pioneerelectronics.com/hs/.)Confusingly,

1× for DVD (1,321 KB/s) is not the same as 1× for CD (150 KB/s). In other words, 1 × DVD = 9× CD. DVD burners, whether +R/RW or −R/RW will burn CDs also, although they can't burn CDs as fast as some of the newer CD burners on the market.

A Bigger Buffer Is Better

A feature to watch for when buying a DVD burner is the size of the internal buffer. The buffer is a bit of RAM on the drive that temporarily stores data before it is burned onto the disc. The disc-mastering program that you use will try to keep the buffer as full as possible. There is an important reason for this: DVD burners (and CD burners, for that matter) need a steady flow of data. The buffer on the burner compensates for a certain amount of variability in the data stream, with larger buffers able to handle more difficulties. Most DVD+R/RW drives have a 2MB buffer, while newer DVD-R/RW drives generally have a more generous 8MB buffer (we'd expect this to change very rapidly). Buffer underruns were a common cause of CD-coasters a few short years ago, but modern technologies can easily deal with interruptions in the data flow, using such tactics as throttling down the drive to a lower speed when the buffer level falls below a specific point.

Interfaces

Among internally mounted drives, IDE (ATAPI) drives are by far the most common. Only a handful of SCSI drives exist anymore, although they once were common. Externally, FireWire is the interface of choice, but a number of drives using the fast USB 2.0 standard also look very promising. Several companies that market off-the-shelf drives in custom enclosures offer external drives with both FireWire and USB 2.0 connections.

Laptop DVD burners are not common at this point. If the trailblazing CD-R drives have taught us anything, it's that DVD drives will become faster, smaller, less expensive and more available. Currently, Toshiba and Apple offer recordable DVD drives on laptops, but we fully expect that other manufacturers will have this feature in the near future.

The War Is Over

At the beginning of this article, we told you not to worry about the DVD Forum vs. DVD+RW Alliance format war too much. In a very real sense, the war is over for consumers, although a winner has not been declared. TDK and Sony now offer writers that burn both DVD-R/RW and DVD+R/RW discs. We'd expect more manufacturers to offer more format agnostic burners over the coming year. These drives are a little more expensive, but if you are concerned about compatibility, this is the way to go. You'll still have to decide on the media you use, but at a dollar or so a disc, the cost of burning incompatible discs is not high.

The Future

Recordable DVD is still a young technology, although second and third generation devices are making it to market as we write. We expect the combination of future drives and future software to yield discs that are even more compatible than discs authored with today's drives and software. Prices will also continue to fall somewhat, although not as rapidly as they did over the last year. Of course, better living room players are also coming out, and that should help home authors as well.

Witnessing the rapid rollout (and rapid price drop) of recordable DVD technology makes us wonder what will happen when the recordable version of the next high-capacity optical format comes around. We're brimming with excitement to see what the future will bring, but we are also very happy with the state of today's technology (see Figures 66-1 through 66-4).

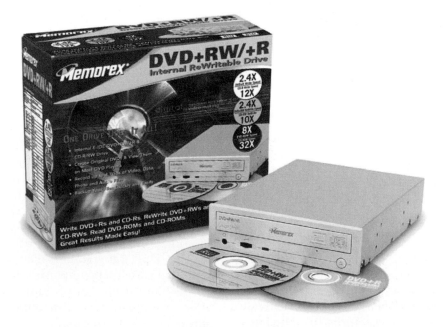

Figure 66-1 *Memorex: DVD+RW/+R Internal Rewritable Drive, $380.*

Figure 66-2 *Sony: DRU-500A, $349.*

Figure 66-3 *TDK: Indi DVD AID+420N, $349.*

Figure 66-4 *Pioneer DVR-A05, $299.*

Sidebar 1

No Computer? No Problem!

One of the latest consumer electronic products to hit the shelves is the stand-alone living room DVD burner. Externally, these devices look exactly like the DVD player already connected to your TV. Functionally, they work more like your VCR: just press Record. All have inputs for analog video, but we are especially excited about the recorders that have FireWire input. While prices may be a bit high this year, with so many products from so many manufacturers, we expect stand-alone DVD recorders to be the next must-have product for the living room, and a neat extra for videographers who want simple DVD-recording functionality. Would-be DVD authors should note that while these stand alones will record video to disc, they do not offer a means of creating custom menus or fancy navigational structures.

Sidebar 2

General vs. Authoring Media

If you've ever shopped for blank DVD-R discs, you've undoubtedly seen references to authoring discs (as opposed to general purpose discs). These discs are written with a different laser wavelength (635 nm, as compared to 650 nm for general discs). Authoring discs can't be burned in drives meant for general media, and vice versa.

So why in the world are there authoring DVDs, anyway? Authoring DVDs were originally designed for professional use, and can hold information that general discs can't. For example, an authoring DVD with standardized Cutting Master Format (CMF) data can be submitted to a duplication house instead of a DLT (digital linear tape). Authoring burners are, of course, significantly more expensive than the general burners discussed in this chapter.

Sidebar 3

Don't Call It "Minus"!

When the burnable DVD world consisted solely of DVD-R drives, everyone just called them "Dee Vee Dee Arr." When the first DVD+RW drives came out, a distinction had to be made. Many people instinctively said "Dee Vee Dee Plus Arr Double-You." And, logically, the opposite of "plus" is "minus" and many people began talking about DVD-R as "Dee Vee Dee Minus Arr." The DVD Forum folks in charge of marketing DVD-R are not terribly fond of the negative connotation of "minus" and would respectfully request that you call it "Dee Vee Dee Dash Arr" instead. We suppose you could refer to it as "Dee Vee Dee Hyphen Arr," but, officially, it's a dash.

67

DVD Flavors: What's the Deal with DVD Compatibility?

Roger B. Wyatt

Good-bye, stretched tapes and dropouts—hello, pristine digital images, generation after generation. With the right hardware and software you can simply burn an edited project to DVD with the click of a mouse. Sound like a dream? It's not. The first affordable DVD recording devices are already in stores, in mail-order catalogs and on the Net. While first generation units were in the $5,000 range, today's recorders list for under $1,000, with street prices below $800.

Unfortunately, there is more to DVD than meets the eye. When DVD manufacturers told us that the initials "DVD" stood for "digital versatile disc," they weren't kidding. The recordable standards vying for your dollars are DVD-RAM, DVD-R, DVD-RW, DVD+R and DVD+RW. The good news is these are all very exciting technologies, some excelling at high capacity data storage and some offering convenient distribution. The bad news is they aren't all compatible with each other, and most won't play in the

DVD player you have in your living room. Before you commit to a DVD format, you'd better know the difference. To help you understand these emerging formats, we've developed this handy guide to bring you up to speed on all of the issues.

DVD-Video

The standard that started it all was DVD-Video (and DVD-Audio, too), those discs you pop in your DVD Player to watch feature films and interactive productions. The standard supports a capacity extension up to 8.5GB per side, but this is not available at this time. DVD-Video is a playback-only format.

DVD standards (including DVD-Video) have been developed over the years by the DVD Forum (dvdforum.org), which is composed of over 220 companies including Hitachi, JVC, Matsushita, Mitsubishi, Philips, Pioneer, Sony, Thomson, Time

Warner, IBM, Intel, NEC, Samsung, Sharp and Toshiba, among others. It's a veritable who's who of consumer electronics. When it came to DVD-Video, this broad consortium spoke with one voice, and an industry standard was born.

Somehow, that group unity on the playback-only standard fractured when recordable DVD standards were developed.

DVD-RAM

DVD-RAM is a recordable and rewritable standard that the DVD Forum supports (see Figure 67-1). The current second-generation discs store 4.7GB per side (for a total of 9.4GB) and cost as low as $20, although other sizes and capacities are available. DVD-RAM discs come in a plastic cartridge or housing that makes them physically incompatible with non-DVD-RAM drives and therefore can only be played back in DVD-RAM drives.

An interesting variation on DVD-RAM is the small 80mm (8-centimeter) disc. Those little discs hold 1.46GB per side and are used in the new MPEG-2 digital camcorders, such as the ones from Hitachi, and in some digital still cameras

from Sony. With this feature, you can shoot and edit without the tedious step of capturing; assuming you had a DVD-RAM drive or hybrid DVD drive on your computer. (However, see the *MPEG-2 Cams—Not the Ultimate* sidebar for an important caveat.)

DVD-R and DVD-RW

DVD-R is a write-once format, fully supported by the DVD Forum (see Figure 67-2). It is single-sided, has a top capacity of 4.7GB and is rapidly extending into the emerging DVD-RW format. Like DVD-R, DVD-RW (the format formerly known as DVD-R/W) is optimized for video, but can be written to numerous times. Clearly, this format is very significant to videographers. These formats strive to be analogous to the now standard CD-R and CD-RW formats. DVD-R discs are rapidly falling in price, approaching the $6 per disc range, while DVD-RW disc prices are also falling, but remain more expensive at about $16 per disc. The first DVD-R/DVD-RW drive, the Pioneer DVR-A03, is very reasonably priced. Expect to see a number of competitors and a corresponding drop

Figure 67-1 DVD-RAM; a) best for multiple rewrites, b) good for data and files, c) often needs a cartridge, d) DVD-RAM: $12. DVD-RAM discs act similar to a hard disk, allowing you to write and rewrite with random access.

Figure 67-2 DVD-R and DVD-RW; a) best for sequential writes, b) good for large files, such as movies, c) claimed compatible with DVD video players, d) DVD-R: $4, e) DVD-RW: $13. The DVD-R/RW format is touted as the logical extension of CD-R/RW technology we are all used to.

in price soon. DVD-R and DVD-RW discs are designed to work with DVD-ROM drives as well as stand-alone DVD players, provided the disc is correctly formatted. There are, however, occasional compatibility problems mostly associated with older devices. These issues will disappear as the format matures. The DVD-R and DVD-RW format is good for creating standard DVD-Video formatted discs as well as long format data such as video files.

DVD+RW and DVD+R

DVD+RW is the rewritable standard that Sony, Philips and Hewlett-Packard originally developed to compete with DVD-RAM (confusingly, not with DVD-RW, although it is now a competitor of that format as well) (see Figure 67-3). Note the use of the plus sign (+) instead of the hyphen (-). Philips and Sony (both members of the DVD Forum) argue that their non-DVD Forum-sanctioned DVD+RW format is more compatible than DVD-RAM, largely because DVD+RW discs do not use a physically incompatible cartridge.

Figure 67-3 *DVD+RW and DVD+R; a) best for sequential writes, b) good for large files, such as movies, c) qclaimed compatible with DVD video players, d) DVD1RW: $14, d) DVD1R: unavailable. The DVD1RW format is the newest format and claims to be more compatible than others. DVD1R has not yet been rolled out.*

They are right, but the compatibility argument was largely rendered moot by the DVD-RW format, which also uses no cartridge. At press time, we couldn't find any DVD+RW discs for sale, but we expect the price to be competitive with DVD-RW. DVD+RW is designed for greater compatibility with existing stand-alone DVD-Video players, but this claim is impossible to test at this time.

The DVD+RW camp has also announced, a bit backwards chronologically perhaps, that it will support a DVD+R format that will allow write-once capabilities. The DVD+R and DVD+RW formats are theoretically good for creating standard DVD-Video formatted discs (although, at press time, there were no DVD+RW units on the market to be tested) as well as long format data such as video files.

RAM vs. RW

The RAM in DVD-RAM stands for random access memory. DVD-RAM discs read and write much the same way as your hard disks. This is an important aspect of this format and differs from the other read/write DVD formats (-RW and +RW), which are optimized for sequential recording. In other words, DVD-RAM is a data storage format that is perfectly happy scattering thousands of tiny files (and parts of files) here and there across the entire disc. This allows for faster access times and yields a more robust rewriting and erasing format. DVD-RW and DVD+RW, in contrast, do not offer random access in the same way, are not as robust as rewriters and are not designed to act like a hard disk. They are, however, optimized for long, sequential reads/writes and occasional rewrites of large chunks of data, which is exactly what videographers need.

Standards Shmandards

Do multiple standards guarantee trouble? Not really. The DVD Forum came up with a plan to prevent conflicts among DVD formats and assure compatibility between

DVD products. They call it DVD Multi, a set of hardware specifications that enables disc and manufacturer compatibility for virtually all DVD Forum consumer electronics and personal computer formats. Look for a logo identifying DVD Multi products. The specification covers many formats including DVD-Video, DVD-ROM, DVD-Audio, DVD-RAM, DVD-R and DVD-RW.

You can measure these discs' capacities in two ways. First, for finished productions, MPEG-2 DVD-Video can have a duration as long as two hours. MPEG-2 video is compressed, often resulting in compression artifacts, which can range from unnoticeable to debilitating, depending on the quality of the encoding. Compressed video is not suitable for editing, mastering or storage purposes. Second, capacity can be measured in terms of data storage and expressed in gigabytes. At S-VHS quality, each minute of video data might occupy 120 MB of storage (although it could be much more). So, 4.7 GB works out to almost 40 minutes of recording capacity, per side. DV data occupies roughly 216 MB of space for a minute of video, or approximately 22 minutes per side, per DVD disc.

New hardware devices are hitting the market almost every day. The first DVD-R, DVD-RW drives, such as the Pioneer DVR-A03 or the Panasonic LF-D311, are widely available at less than $500. Also, watch for hybrid DVD-R, DVD-RW, DVD-RAM combo drives (called DVD Multi) that can read and write the three DVD Forum formats. One model from Panasonic (LF-D311) sells for just under $500. This drive allows you to avoid much of the format war controversy, writing and rewriting to DVD-RAM for your personal use and writing DVD-R discs to play on your television. We are extremely excited about this technology and hope that it does not suffer from the compatibility problems that plagued the first CD-R drives.

The DVD+RW camp, on the other hand, is aggressively marketing recordable and rewritable DVD+RW drives. Other computer manufacturers, like Apple and Compaq, are shipping boxes with DVD-R drives built-in.

Early Adopters Only?

Is it time to move to DVD optical recording? For data purposes, permanently saving your video projects, media and all, has become a distinct possibility for the first time. And burning your productions to DVD for playback on stand-alone DVD players gives you a very high quality way to conveniently distribute your work. At $500 for a recorder and $6 per disc, DVD recording is at a very tempting price point for the home video enthusiast, although we certainly expect prices to fall over the next year. With the right purchase, you can enjoy recordable DVD products that will play on all your gear.

Sidebar 1

MPEG-2 Cams—Not the Ultimate

Are they the best things since sliced bread? Probably not. While the quality of DVD-Video is very high, it is nonetheless MPEG-2 compressed video. As such, it is very problematic to edit and you should not consider it for mastering, archiving or editing purposes. A good digital strategy is to shoot and capture at the highest quality (e.g., DV or MJPEG), edit at highest quality, master at highest quality and finally, distribute MPEG-2 on DVD.

Sidebar 2

Yes, Master

One undeniably exciting aspect of the latest multi-format hybrid DVD recorders is the possibility of burning DVD-Video discs to send high-quality versions of your movies to your friends and then burning a DVD-RAM disc (two-sided 9.4GB) of the project as a master. How many times have you watched a movie you created two years ago and cringed, wishing you could fix it up? Although burn speeds and transfer rates mean taking some time to back up and restore a project, it is undoubtedly faster than recapturing and recreating a project from scratch.

Sidebar 3

The Media

Format	DV	DVD	VCD	SVCD	Mini DVD
Resolution	720 × 480	720 × 480	352 × 240	480 × 480	720 × 480
Recording Time	60 mins tape	2 hrs	74 mins	35 mins	15 mins
Video Compression	DV	MPEG-2	MPEG-1	MPEG-2	MPEG-2
Audio Compression	PCM	MPEG-2, AC3	MPEG-1	MPEG-1	MPEG-2, AC3
Size/min	216 MB/min	30–70 MB/min	10 MB/min	10–20 MB/min	30–70 MB/min
DVD Player Compatibility	None	Excellent	Great (2/3)	Good (1/3)	Poor
Quality	Excellent	Great	Fair	Good	Great

*Table by Scott Anderson.

68
Step by Step Guide to Making DVDs

D. Eric Franks

More and more of this magazine is being devoted to DVD each month. DVD gear, DVD media, DVD software, but we're afraid we are missing the forest for the trees. If you've been reading the magazine and have a good grip on what you need, here is a path through the trees: our Step by Step Guide to Making DVDs.

Overview

First, a little encouragement: DVD creation on a computer is considerably easier than editing video. The entire process can be summed up in four steps (but see the sidebar for a One-Step Solution).

- Capture—You need to get video onto your computer. How you edit it is entirely up to you and is not what this article is about, so we are going to assume that you have a tape with video on it that you want on DVD.

- Encode—Once your video is on your computer, it needs to be transformed and encoded into DVD-friendly MPEG-2

video. This process can be one-click easy or hardcore technical and tedious.

- Author—Authoring is what we call the process of actually designing and creating the DVD menus. This is the fun part.

- Burn—Yawn. This process should definitely be one-click easy.

Capture

So you have a video tape that you'd love to distribute on DVD. What is the easiest way? We have two answers for you, one for digital video and one for analog tapes.

First, for those of you with digital video (DV) source material, you should use your FireWire port on your computer to dump your digital data to your computer. You don't need a fancy computer or expensive editing software, but you will need a ton of hard disk space, about 20GB for an hour of video for a complete DVD project. On a Windows XP or Mac, the capture tools you need are included with your computer.

DV is so easy because the video is already in a format your computer can handle. If you have analog video tapes (such as VHS), you need to convert that video into digital data for your computer. To do this, you'll need some kind of capture card, otherwise known as a digitizer. Some computers come with analog capture cards (e.g., an Ati All-In-Wonder card), but most do not. If you are not interested in hacking about inside of your computer to install a new card (and who is?), there are a few devices that digitize your video and then send the data to your Windows computer via a USB 2.0 connection. ADS Tech's Instant DVD 2.0, Adaptec's VideOh! DVD and Pinnacle's Dazzle Digital Video Creator 150 are three competitive products (all less than $200) worth researching. The most convenient aspect of these boxes is that they digitize straight to MPEG-2 video.

Encode

If the video on your computer is not DVD ready, you will need to encode it to the MPEG-2 format. This is what you will need to do with FireWire-transferred DV video and DV video projects from your editing software. The encoding process (also called compression or transcoding) can happen immediately when you finish editing, although most DVD authoring programs now automatically encode any video of any format that you use on your DVD. In your editing software, you'll usually be able to find an Export or Render As option that will open an encoding dialog. In this dialog, select a DVD MPEG-2 encoding template and render away. Encoding is very computationally intensive, so get ready to wait a long time for the process to finish, typically twice as long as your video's duration. We usually start encoding before we go to bed at night.

Of course encoding can be much more complicated. There are entire applications dedicated to the task (e.g., cleaner, ProCoder, Squeeze), books explaining the technology (like the ones from Ben Waggoner) and experts in Hollywood who are Career Compressionists. For this chapter, it is only important that you know that all of your media (video, audio and stills) needs to be in DVD-compatible MPEG-2 format before it can be put on a disc. Hopefully, your authoring software will take care of it for you.

Author

Authoring is the fun part of creating a DVD. The process requires some organizational skills, a little design talent and a dollop of artistry, but you can usually get by even if you aren't particularly gifted in these areas.

The first step is to start a new project and collect your media together. This will of course include your video, but also might involve stills for a slide show and music for menu backgrounds. Again, everything, even stills and audio, will end up in a DVD-compatible format, but for now you only have to organize the pieces and parts.

The next step involves designing the navigation of your disc. Like the Web, DVD discs have buttons that you can highlight and click, although you use your DVD player's remote control to make the click. DVDs are much simpler than Web pages, however, and you basically need only a Play button to allow folks to watch your movie and maybe a Scenes button to allow them to jump to the various parts of your movie that they want to skip to. You can have more complex navigation schemes and special features, but work conservatively and cautiously so that you don't overwhelm and confuse your viewers. The dozens of Hollywood discs you've rented can serve as examples, both good and bad, for you to emulate or at least learn from.

The final part of authoring is the best part: designing attractive menus. From backgrounds to buttons, the DVD menu is going to be the first impression your viewers will get of your project. Most DVD authoring programs come with a bunch of templates that can be used as-is or that can be used as jumping off points for your own unique discs. In our reviews of DVD authoring programs, pay careful attention to what the writer says about the templates and how much they can be customized. If you only need a quick disc and aren't very interested in authoring, templates may be all you need. If you are a production house with a talented design professional onboard, make sure your software lets her do her thing.

Burn

We call the actual process of writing a DVD "burning" and it is just about as boring as can be. Usually, it involves inserting a blank disc into your DVD drive and clicking a button or, at most, selecting a menu item. It either works or it is broken. Fortunately, it almost always works nowadays.

Compatibility with stand-alone, living room DVD players is a serious issue. In almost every case, compatibility problems are not caused by the burning process. In fact, almost all compatibility problems are caused by the DVD player and not by the DVD authoring process outlined here. It doesn't much matter whether you are using an HP 300i or a Pioneer DVR-105, or whether you are using DVD-R or DVD+R (don't use rewritable discs for distribution). The discs are designed to play back in the same players. Once you find a DVD player that plays one kind of disc, you'll find that it plays back most kinds. Of course we are skimming over many issues here that are covered in much more depth

in other articles in this magazine (such as the Winter 2003 issue).

As far as media goes, there are two approaches. You can play it safe and go with a branded media, like Verbatim or TDK (or even Ritek) or you can get a spindle of generic discs. The advantage of going with a branded disc is that you get a guarantee from the company and can be assured that there was some quality control during the manufacturing process. Generic discs are cheaper, of course, and can be of very high quality, but the problem is that you just don't know until you have some experience. Some blank media companies offer sampler packs of various kinds that you can test. As of this writing, we look for 4× certified media, which is required for newer burners. Ultimately, you shouldn't sweat the media too much: if it is going to fail, it'll fail during the burn process.

Best Thing Since Sliced Bread

Capture, encode, author and burn. That's all there is to it. Sure, each step warrants its own article and that's part of *Videomaker*'s goal each month, but we hope this chapter has encouraged you to give DVD a shot. It's not nearly as hard as other computer video tasks. Durable blank discs cost less than a dollar, postage costs less than a dollar and nearly everyone you know has a DVD player in their living room. Home DVD authoring is the best thing to happen to us since the advent of digital video.

Sidebar

One-Step DVD Solutions

OK, we hear you: four steps are too many, especially the part about capturing video. If you can operate a VCR, we have a one-step solution for you. If you haven't already seen them, go down to your local electronics store and check out the stand-alone living room DVD burners on sale. Prices have dropped significantly below $600 on many models and they work just like a VCR. Pop in a blank disc, hook up your camcorder and press Record. The menus usually aren't very attractive, but they get your video onto a disc and you don't even have to think about capture/encode/author/burn.

69
What Makes DVDs Go 'Round and 'Round

Marshal M. Rosenthal

When it comes to making your own DVD, the only thing more important than the movie is how the viewer gets to see it: will you start with an animated splash screen? Or will it go directly to the main menu? Will you have all sorts of buttons to select from? Or will you use just a few straightforward panels with text? These are the decisions to consider before you make your DVD. Let's look at some commercial DVDs and how they handle the menus.

Using Animation: Lion King 1 1/2

Most discs start with some type of start up animations, previews or warning screens, and Disney's *Lion King 1 1/2* is no exception. After the Disney logo and a spate of video previews (which you can skip), the screen goes black and then changes into a frenzy of activity. The main menu is quite active and busy. Our old friend Timon the merekat looks on as various animals move all of the scenery into position on a movie stage. Once all the action

is complete, the title appears on a static screen, accompanied by music and random animation of Timon popping up from the tall grass.

Animation can add a lot to a menu. In this case, the opening is so entertaining and goes by so fast that it only enthralls the viewer. And, since the main audience for this disc is children, a little bit of craziness is probably appropriate. For most adults, the animation is cute once, but could quickly become quite annoying to watch over and over again. When you select a feature from the main menu, there's another brief animation featuring Timon that takes you to a new screen. The new screen features its own animation and music and quickly shows you the choices you can now select.

These animations require you to watch until they finish, but they move very fast. Since DVD menus are just MPEG-2 movies, anything you can encode for a DVD you can use as a menu. Basically, this means you have unlimited creative possibilities. An important consideration is whether the viewer must wait for the

Figure 69-1 *The* Lion King 1 1/2 *DVD.*

animation to finish before pressing a button to continue.

Theme music from the movie is constantly playing in the background of the menus, but it changes depending upon which menu you are on. It's fairly long, so it doesn't become too repetitive. Music clips can be short or long, but the only reason for having a lengthy audio track is if you have a lot to look at on a particular menu screen. If you do not have an animated or video background, music can increase the amount of space the menu takes up on the disc.

Using Photos: *The Maltese Falcon*

Children's discs are colorful, loud and fun, but a classic movie, such as *The Maltese Falcon*, would take a very different approach. Humphrey Bogart stars in this classic tough guy detective film and the opening splash screen is as subtle as our detective ain't: it's just a simple, static photo of Bogey at a desk with the Maltese Falcon perched before him. The black and white image has been colorized and the menu buttons highlight when pressed.

This is a good example of a straightforward main menu page. Taking this as an example, you have all of the choices presented right there in front of you without any distractions.

Pressing one of the buttons takes you immediately to other screens which also use photos. There's a consistency that keeps you in the era and mood of the movie. It's important to maintain a consistent feel throughout your DVD's various menus, whether using artwork, video clips or photography. Theme music from the movie plays during the opening menu, but disappears once you go to the other menus. The menus are also a part of the content of the disc, as a series of menus superimposed over photos serve as a history about detectives. The photo here is very stylized and simple, which keeps the text from being lost and so remains easy to read. When you place text over a photo, strive to make sure the photo isn't competing with the text.

Motion Video: *Indiana Jones and the Raiders of the Lost Ark*

The *Raiders of the Lost Ark* DVD jumps right in (after the obligatory Paramount logo) and hits the ground running. The action-packed splash screen goes on for quite a while, but what's really cool about it is that the text seen at the bottom is active: you can navigate to any part of the disc during the splashy introduction. Once the main menu appears, you'll still have access to the same choices, of course. This disc really has two menus that serve the same purpose as far as navigation is concerned. This is not a bad idea at all and allows the producers to present some exciting footage without interfering with disc navigation.

When the main menu finally comes up, it continues the theme of motion video by having a moving map rotate in the background. And after about 30 seconds, if you don't touch anything, the splash video starts up again. If you select a feature, animations appear as a transition between menu screens (a plane flying you from one screen to another, for example). The new screen also features different music to suit the mood.

Suddenly going back to the splash screen can be annoying and the transition gets old quickly as well. If you have a cycling screen, it's a good idea to make sure that there's enough time for the viewer to digest everything before it starts

Figure 69-2 Indiana Jones and the Raiders of the Lost Ark *DVD*.

Figure 69-3 National Lampoon's Animal House *DVD*.

up again and the viewer can get out of it quickly. Still, *Raiders* is a fun action film, so there's really no reason the DVD can't be fun as well. If your movie falls into a genre where this sort of excitement is appropriate, menus like this can be quite fun.

Video: *National Lampoon's Animal House*

Comedy flicks are another genre that often has unusual menus that are more than just navigational aids and *National Lampoon's Animal House* (*Double-secret Probation Edition*) is a good example. Following the Universal logo and a series of previews that you can't skip, the *Animal House* splash screen begins. It's a riotous blending of video and text and music that really sets the mood for what this comedy is all about.

You might not need to run previews on your DVD for marketing purposes, but if you have any splash screens that come up before your main menu, you should seriously consider whether you want to prevent viewers from skipping them. Advanced DVD authoring software allows you to disable remote control button presses like stop, fast forward, next and menu. Be very cautious about doing this, however. If you do want to force your viewers to watch something (e.g., an FBI warning screen), keep it short and make sure it really is vital.

Once on the *Animal House* main menu, the music cycles through selections from the film, as do the video clips on one side

of the screen. The right side is static and changes only when making a selection. Then the text flies off the screen as everything blurs and becomes a new screen with new selections to make. Having motion video on one side and text and the selection buttons on the other can be very effective. It lets you show something while at the same time the viewer can decide to move on to something else. Sometimes, however, all a menu screen needs to work is plain text, accompanied by a plain background or a simple photograph.

Animation and Photos: *24—Season 2*

The television show *24 Season 2* DVD also has a sharp menu. Similar to the fast paced action of the show, a high-tech surveillance map of the world unveils itself at breakneck speed as a set of moving cross-hairs track back and forth before dissolving into the main menu. Background music begins and ends with this splash video.

A quick moving splash opening can intrigue the viewer, especially if there's a sense of urgency involved. The main menu itself is static and features a photo of the main character, Jack Bauer, tinted in blue. When you select an episode, the menu immediately switches to a sub-menu which features a new photo interwoven with chapters of the episode.

At this point, it's up to the viewer to decide what to watch. Sometimes it's good to let people feel they're the ones in control. The viewer can watch deleted scenes

Figure 69-4 24 Season 2 *DVD.*

in content within each episode. While the disc gives you access to a lot of content, moving from a menu to a sub-menu and then playing the episode might be too much clicking for some people. The faster

you can get the play button on the screen the better, in our opinion.

Before You Burn

Unlike VHS, DVD isn't linear and you can create links between how a video plays, and that changes the viewing experience. Creating the way your DVD starts and how it's going to let the viewer move through the selections does require thought, but don't forget that a menu system isn't just pragmatic. Don't be afraid to mix it up. The movie may be your primary concern, but the menu is the first impression folks will get.

Jargon:
A Glossary of Videography Terms

.asf Active Streaming Format

.avi Short for Audio Video Interleave, the file format for Microsoft's Video for Windows standard.

.gif Graphics Interchange Format—a bit-mapped graphics file format used by the World Wide Web, CompuServe and many BBSs. GIF supports color and various resolutions. It also includes data compression, making it especially effective for scanned photos.

.jpeg Joint Photographic Experts Group image format. A popular Internet compression format for color images.

.mov File extension used with Quick-Time movies.

.mov File extension used with Quick-Time, a popular file format for video on a computer developed by Apple.

.rm Most common file extension used with RealMedia files.

.wav A sound format for storing sound in files developed jointly by Microsoft and IBM. Support for WAV files was built into Windows 95 making it the de facto standard for sound on PCs. WAV sound files end with a .wav extension.

8 mm Compact videocassette format, popularized by camcorders, employing 8-millimeter-wide videotape. [See Hi8]

720 p An ATSC high definition video standard size of 1,280 × 720 pixels, progressive scan at various frame rates.

1080i An ATSC high definition video standard size of 1,920 × 1,080 pixels, interlace scan at various frame rates.

A/B roll editing Two video sources played simultaneously, to be mixed or cut between.

A/V (Audio/Video) A common shorthand for multimedia audio and video.

action axis An imaginary line drawn between two subjects or along a line of motion to maintain continuity of screen direction. Crossing it from one shot to the next creates an error in continuity. It is also referred to as the "180-degree rule."

ad-lib Unrehearsed, spontaneous act of speaking, performing or otherwise improvising on-camera activity without preparation.

aDSL Asymmetric (or Asynchronous) Digital Subscriber Line. A "fat pipe."

New technology to carry high-speed data over typical twisted-pair copper telephone lines. ADSL promises be up to 70 times as fast as a 28.8 modem.

AFM (audio frequency modulation) The analog soundtrack of the 8 mm and Hi8 video format. [See PCM]

AGC (automatic gain control) A circuit on most camcorders that automatically adjusts a microphone's gain (volume) to match environmental sound levels.

ambient sound (ambience) Natural background audio representative of a given recording environment. On-camera dialog might be primary sound; traffic noise and refrigerator hum would be ambient.

amplify To magnify an audio signal for mixing, distribution and transducing purposes.

analog An electrical signal is referred to as either analog or digital. Analog signals are those signals directly generated from a stimulus such as a light striking a camera picture tube. You can convert an analog signal to a digital signal by using an analog to digital converter.

animation Visual special effect whereby progressive still images displayed in rapid succession create the illusion of movement.

aperture/exposure A setting that manipulates the amount of light falling onto the camera's CCD(s). This control adjusts the size of the camcorder's iris.

apps (application) Software that performs a specific function.

artifacting The occurrence of unwanted visual distortions that appear in a video image, such as cross-color artifacts, cross-luminance artifacts, jitter, blocking, ghosts, etc. Artifacting is a common side effect of compression, especially at lower bit rates.

artifacts Unwanted visual distortions that appear in a video image, such as cross-color artifacts, cross-luminance artifacts, jitter, blocking, ghosts, etc.

artificial light Human-made illumination not limited to the "indoor" variety: fluorescent bulbs, jack-o'-lanterns and a car's headlights all qualify. Typically,

it has lower color temperature than natural light, and thus more reddish qualities. [See color temperature, natural light]

aspect ratio Proportional width and height of on-screen picture. Current standard for a conventional monitor is 4:3 (four-by-three); 16:9 for HDTV.

assemble edit Recording video and/or audio clips in sequence immediately following previous material; does not break control track. Consecutive edits form complete program. [See edit, insert edit]

ATSC Advanced Television Systems Committee. A new TV broadcast standard (replacing NTSC) for high definition televison. It is composed of several frame rates and sizes, including standard definition formats, as well as 720 p and 1080 i video.

ATV (amateur television) Specialized domain of ham radio, transmits standard TV signals on UHF radio bands.

audio dub Result of recording over prerecorded videotape soundtrack, or a portion thereof, without affecting prerecorded images.

audio frequency modulation (AFM) Method of recording hi-fi audio on videotape along with video signals. Used in VHS Hi-Fi Audio, and also the analog soundtrack of the 8 mm and Hi8 video formats.

audio mixer The piece of equipment used to gather, mix and amplify sounds from multiple microphones and send the signal on to its destination.

automatic exposure Circuitry that monitors light levels and adjusts camcorder iris accordingly, compensating for changing light conditions.

automatic gain control (AGC) Circuitry found on most camcorders that adjusts incoming audio levels automatically to match environmental sound levels.

available light Amount of illumination present in a particular environment: natural light, artificial light or a combination of the two.

AVCHD Advanced Video Codec High Definition: An MPEG-4-based codec used to record High Definition video to camcorders using hard drives, DVD discs, or flash memory cards.

AVI (Audio Video Interleave) One of the oldest file formats for digital video on PCs.

backlight Lamp providing illumination from behind. Creates sense of depth by separating foreground subject from background area. Applied erroneously, causes severe silhouetting. [See fill light, key light, three-point lighting]

balanced line Audio cables that have three wires: one for positive, one for negative and one for ground.

bandwidth A measure of the capacity of a user's data line. Video looks its best on a high-bandwidth connection, like DSL, cable modems or satellite modems. Conversely, trying to download or stream video on a low-bandwidth connection like a dial-up modem can be a frustrating experience.

bandwidth compression Reducing the bandwidth that is required for transmission of a given digital data rate.

barndoors Accessories for video lights; adjustable folding flaps that control light distribution.

batch capture The ability of certain computer-based editing systems to automatically capture whole lists or "batches" of clips from source videotapes.

Betamax More commonly known as "Beta," half-inch videotape format developed by Sony, eclipsed by VHS in home video market popularity. [See ED Beta]

bidirectional Microphone pickup pattern whereby sound is absorbed equally from two sides only. [See omnidirectional, unidirectional]

black box Generic term for wide variety of video image manipulation devices with perceived mysterious or "magical" capabilities, including proc amps, enhancers, SEGs and TBCs.

bleeding Video image imperfection characterized by blurring of color borders; colors spill over defined boundaries, "run" into neighboring areas.

Blu-Ray A high definition optical disc format, using a blue laser. It has a capacity of 50 GB for dual-layer discs. Hoping to be the successor to the popular DVD format.

BNC (Bayonet Fitting Connector aka British Naval Connector) A durable "professional" cable connector, attaches to VCRs for transfer of high-frequency composite video in/out signals. Connects with a push and a twist.

boom Any device for suspending a microphone above and in front of a performer.

booming Camera move above or below subject with aid of a balanced "boom arm," creating sense of floating into or out of a scene. Can combine effects of panning, tilting and pedding in one fluid movement.

C See chrominance.

cable/community access Channel(s) of a local cable television system dedicated to community-based programming. Access centers provide free or low-cost training and use of video production equipment and facilities.

cameo lighting Foreground subjects illuminated by highly directional light, appearing before a completely black background.

Cannon See XLR.

capacitor The part of the condenser mike that stores electrical energy and permits the flow of alternating current.

capture card A piece of computer hardware that captures digital video and audio to a hard drive, typically through a FireWire (IEEE 1394) port.

cardioid A microphone that picks up sound in a heart-shaped pattern.

CCD (charge coupled device) Light-sensitive integrated circuit in video cameras that converts images into electrical signals. Sometimes referred to as a "chip."

character generator A device that electronically builds text which can be combined with a video signal. The text is created with a keyboard and program that has a selection of font and backgrounds.

chroma Characteristics of color a videotape absorbs with recorded signal, divided into two categories: AM (amplitude modulation) indicates color intensity; PM (phase modulation) indicates color purity.

chromakey Method of electronically inserting an image from one video source into the image of another through areas designated as its "key color." It is frequently used on news programs to display weather graphics behind talent.

chrominance Portion of video signal that carries color information (hue and saturation, but not brightness); frequently abbreviated as "C," as in "Y/C" for luminance/chrominance. [See luminance]

clapstick Identification slate with hinged, striped top that smacks together for on-camera scene initiation. Originally used to synchronize movie sound with picture. [See lip-sync]

closeup (CU) A tightly framed camera shot in which the principal subject is viewed at close range, appearing large and dominant on screen. Pulled back slightly is a "medium closeup" while zoomed in very close is an "extreme closeup (ECU or XCU)."

CODEC (compressor/decompressor) A piece of software that converts a raw stream of uncompressed video to a compressed form. The same piece of software can also play the compressed video on-screen.

color bars Standard test signal containing samples of primary and secondary colors, used as reference in aligning color video equipment. Generated electronically by a "color bar generator," often viewed on broadcast television in off-air hours. [See test pattern]

color corrector Electronic device that dissects the colors of a video signal, allowing them to be adjusted individually.

color temperature Relative amount of "white" light's reddish or bluish qualities, measured in degrees Kelvin. Desirable readings for video are 3,200 K indoors, 5,600 K outdoors. [See artificial, natural light]

comet tailing Smear of light resulting from inability of camera's pickup to process bright objects—especially in darker settings. Object or camera in motion creates appearance of flying fireball. [See lag]

component video Signal transmission system, resembling S-video concept, employed with professional videotape formats. Separates one luminance and two chrominance channels to avoid quality loss from NTSC or PAL encoding.

composite video Single video signal combining luminance and chrominance signals through an encoding process, including RGB (red, green, blue) elements and sync information.

compositing Superimposing multiple layers of video or images. Each layer may move independently. Titles are a simple and common example of compositing.

composition Visual make-up of a video picture, including such variables as balance, framing, field of view and texture—all aesthetic considerations. Combined qualities form an image that's pleasing to view.

compression An encoding process that reduces the digital data in a video frame, typically from nearly one megabyte to 300 kilobytes or less. This is accomplished by throwing away information the eye can't see and/or redundant information in areas of the video frame that do not change. JPEG, Motion-JPEG, MPEG, DV, Indeo, Fractal and Wavelet are all compression schemes.

condenser mike A high-quality mike whose transducer consists of a diaphragm, backplate and capacitor.

continuity [1: visual] Logical succession of recorded or edited events, necessitating consistent placement of props, positioning of characters, and progression of time.

contrast Difference between a picture's brightest and darkest areas. When high, image contains sharp blacks and whites; when low, image limited to variations in gray tones.

control track A portion of the videotape containing information to synchronize playback and linear videotape editing operations.

Control-L A two-way communication system used to coordinate tape transport commands for linear editing. Primarily found in Mini DV, Digital8, Hi8 and 8 mm camcorders and VCRs. [See Control-S, synchro edit]

Control-S A one-way communication system that treats a VCR or camcorder as a slave unit, with edit commands emanating from an external edit controller or compatible deck. Primarily found on 8 mm VCRs and camcorders. [See Control-L, synchro edit]

cookie (cucalorus) Lighting accessory consisting of random cutout shapes that cast patterned shadows when light passes through. Used to imitate shadows of natural lighting.

crawl Text or graphics, usually special announcements that move across the screen horizontally, typically from right to left across the bottom of the screen.

cross-fade Simultaneous fade-in of one audio or video source as another fades out so that they overlap temporarily. Also called a dissolve.

cucalorus (cookie) Lighting accessory consisting of random pattern of cutouts that forms shadows when light passes through it. Used to imitate shadows of natural lighting.

cue [1] Signal to begin, end, or otherwise influence on-camera activity while recording. [2] Presetting specific starting points of audio or video material so it's available for immediate and precise playback when required.

cut Instantaneous change from one shot to another.

cutaway Shot of something other than principal action (but peripherally related), frequently used as transitional footage or to avoid a jump cut.

cuts-only editing Editing limited to immediate shifts from one scene to another, without smoother image transition capabilities such as dissolving or wiping. [See cut, edit]

D1, D2, D3, D5, Digital-S, DVCPRO, DVCAM, Digital Betacam Entirely digital "professional" videotape recording formats.

decibel (dB) A unit of measurement of sound that compares the relative intensity of different sound sources.

decompression The decoding of a compressed video data stream to allow playback.

deinterlace To convert interlaced video into progressively scanned video, for use with computers.

depth of field Range in front of a camera's lens in which objects appear in focus. Varies with subject-to-camera distance, focal length of a camera lens and a camera's aperture setting.

desktop video (DTV) Fusion of personal computers and home video components for elaborate videomaking capabilities rivaling those of broadcast facilities.

diaphragm The vibrating element in a microphone that responds to the compressed air molecules of sound waves.

diffused light Indistinctly illuminates a relatively large area. Produces soft light quality with soft shadows.

diffuser Gauzy or translucent material that alters the quality of light passing through it to produce less intense, flatter lighting with softer, less noticeable shadows.

diffusion filter Mounted at front of camcorder lens, gives videotaped images a foggy, fuzzy, dreamy look. [See filter]

digital audio Sounds that have been converted to digital information.

digital video effects (DVE) Electronic analog-to-digital picture modification yielding specialty image patterns and maneuvers: tumbling, strobing, page turning, mosaic, posterization, solarization, etc.

digitization The process of converting a continuous analog video or audio signal to digital data for computer storage and manipulation.

digitizer Device that imports and converts analog video images into digital information for hard drive-based editing.

directional light Light that illuminates in a relatively small area with distinct light beam; usually created with spotlight, yields harsh, defined shadows.

dissolve Image transition effect of one picture gradually disappearing as another appears. Analogous to audio and lighting cross-fade. [See cross-fade]

distribution amp (distribution amplifier) Divides single video or audio signals, while boosting their strength, for delivery to multiple audio/video acceptors. Allows simultaneous recording on multiple VCR's from the same source, especially useful for tape duplication.

DivX ;-) A recent codec for MPEG-4 video, developed on the Internet.

dolly Camera movement toward or away from a subject. The effect may seem to be the same as zooming, but dollying in or out results in a more dramatic change in perspective than using the zoom.

dollying Camera movement toward or away from a subject. Effect may appear same as zooming, which reduces and magnifies the image, but dollying in or out maintains perspective while changing picture size.

dongle A device that prevents the unauthorized use of hardware or software. A dongle usually consists of a small cord attached to a device or key that secures the hardware. The term is also used to signify a generic adapter for peripherals.

download and play A way of viewing Web video that requires a user to download a video before playing it. Download and play files are usually higher quality than streamed video.

dropout Videotape signal voids, viewed as fleeting white specks or streaks. Usually result of minute "bare spots" on a tape's magnetic particle coating, or tape debris covering particles and blocking signals.

DTV Desktop video.

dub [1] Process or result of duplicating a videotape in its entirety. [2] Editing

technique whereby new audio or video replaces a portion(s) of existing recording.

DV (Digital Video) With a capital "D" and a capital "V," DV is a specific video format; both a tape format (like Hi8) and a data format specification.

DVE (Digital Video Effect) Electronic special effects and picture modification yielding specialty image patterns and maneuvers, such as tumbling, strobing, page turning, mosaic, posterization, solarization, etc. [See F/X]

dynamic mike A rugged microphone whose transducer consists of a diaphragm connected to a moveable coil.

ED Beta (extended definition Beta) Improved version of the original half-inch Betamax video format, yielding sharper pictures with 500-line resolution. [See Betamax]

edit Process or result of selectively recording video and/or audio on finished videotape. Typically involves reviewing raw footage and transferring desired segments from a master tape(s) onto a new tape in a predetermined sequence. [See assemble edit, in-camera editing]

edit control protocols Types of signals designed to communicate between editing components, including computers, tape decks and camcorders. Allows components to transmit instructions for various operations such as play, stop, fast forward, rewind, record, pause, etc.

edit controller Electronic programmer used in conjunction with VCRs/camcorders to facilitate automated linear videotape editing with speed, precision and convenience.

edit decision list (EDL) Handwritten or computer-generated compilation of all edits (marked by their time code in points and out points) to be executed in a video production.

edited master Original recorded videotape footage; "edited master" implies original copy of tape in its edited form. Duplications constitute generational differences.

editing appliance A self-contained machine, essentially a small computer, which only edits video. Editing appliances usually contain most features found in standard computer-based editing systems.

EDL (edit decision list) Handwritten or computer-generated compilation of all edits (marked by their time code in points and out points) planned for execution in a video production.

EFP (electronic field production) Film-style production approach using a single camera to record on location. Typically shot for post-production application, non-live feed.

EIS (electronic image stabilization) A process of limiting shaky camera shots with digital processing within a camcorder. [See OIS]

electret condenser Microphone type incorporating a pre-charged element, eliminating need for bulky power sources. [See condenser]

electronic image stabilization (EIS) A process that limits shaky camera shots with digital processing found within a camcorder. [See OIS]

encoder Device that translates a video signal into a different format—RGB to composite, DV to MPEG, etc.

encoding The actual process of compressing video for streaming or for downloading.

ENG (electronic news gathering) Use of portable video cameras, lighting and sound equipment to record news events in the field quickly, conveniently and efficiently.

enhancer (image enhancer) Video signal processor that compensates for picture detail losses and distortion occurring in recording and playback. Exaggerates transitions between light and dark areas by enhancing high frequency region of video spectrum.

EP (extended play) Slowest tape speed of a VHS VCR, accommodating six-hour recordings. [See LP, SP]

equalization Emphasizing specific audio or video frequencies and eliminating others as signal control measure, usually to produce particular sonic qualities. Achieved with equalizer.

equalize To emphasize, lessen or eliminate certain audio frequencies.

essential area Boundaries within which contents of a television picture are sure to be seen, regardless of masking differences in receiver displays. Also called the "critical area" or "safe action area," it encompasses the inner 80 percent of the screen.

establishing shot Opening image of a program or scene. Usually, it's a wide and/or distant perspective that orients viewers to the overall setting and surroundings.

extra Accessory talent not essential to a production, assuming some peripheral on-camera role. In movie work, performers with fewer than five lines are called "under fives."

f-stop Numbers corresponding to variable size of a camera's iris opening, and thus the amount of light passing through the lens. The higher the number, the smaller the iris diameter, which means less light enters the camcorder.

F/X Special effects. Visual tricks and illusions—electronic or on camera—employed in film and video to define, distort or defy reality.

fade Gradual diminishing or heightening of visual and/or audio intensity. "Fade out" or "fade to black," "fade in" or "up from black" are common terms.

feed Act or result of transmitting a video signal from one point to another.

feedback [1: video] Infinite loop of visual patterns from signal output being fed back as input; achieved by aiming live camera at receiving monitor. [2: audio] Echo effect at low levels, howl or piercing squeal at extremes, from audio signal being fed back to itself.

field Half a scanning cycle. Two fields comprise a complete video frame. Composed of either all odd lines or all even lines.

field of view Extent of a shot that is visible through a particular lens; its vista.

fill light Supplementary illumination, usually from a soft light positioned to the side of the subject, which lightens shadows created by the key light.

[See backlight, key light, three-point lighting]

film-style Out-of-sequence shooting approach, to be edited in appropriate order at post-production stage. Advantageous for concentrating on and completing recording at one location at a time, continuity and convenience assured.

filter Transparent or semi-transparent material, typically glass, mounted at the front of a camcorder's lens to change light passing through. Manipulates colors and image patterns, often for special effect purposes.

filter effect Digital effect added to colorize or otherwise alter a clip in post-production.

FireWire (IEEE 1394 or i.LINK) A high-speed bus that was developed by Apple Computer. It is used, among other things, to connect digital camcorders to computers.

fishpole A small, lightweight arm to which a microphone is attached, hand-held by an audio assistant outside of the picture frame.

flare Bright flashes evident in video. Caused by excessive light beaming into a camera's lens and reflecting off its internal glass elements.

flat lighting Illumination characterized by even, diffused light without shadows, highlights or contrast. May impede viewer's sense of depth, dimension.

floodlight Radiates a diffused, scattered blanket of light with soft, indistinct shadows. Best used to spread illumination on broad areas, whereas spotlights focus on individual subjects.

fluid head Tripod mount type containing viscous fluid which lubricates moving parts, dampens friction. Design facilitates smooth camera moves, alleviates jerkiness. [See friction head]

flying erase head Accessory video head mounted on spinning head drum, incorporated in many camcorders and VCRs to eliminate glitches and rainbow noise between scenes recorded or edited. By design, all 8mm-family and DV-family equipment has flying erase heads.

focal length Distance from a camcorder's lens to a focused image with the lens focused on infinity. Short focal lengths offer a broad field of view (wide angle); long focal lengths offer a narrow field of view (telephoto). Zoom lenses have a variable focal length.

follow focus Controlling lens focus so that an image maintains sharpness and clarity despite camcorder and/or subject movement.

foot-candle A unit of illumination equal to the light emitted by a candle at the distance of one foot. One foot-candle equals 10.764 lux. [See lux]

format Videotape and video equipment design differences—physical and technical—dictating compatibility and quality. In the most basic sense, refers to standardized tape widths, videocassette sizes. [See Betamax, D1/D2, 8mm, three-quarter-inch, VHS]

FPS (frames per second) Measures the rate or speed of video or film. Film is typically shot and played back at 24 FPS. Video is recorded and played back at 30 FPS.

frame [1] One complete image. In NTSC video a frame is composed of two fields. One 30th of a second. [2] The viewable area or composition of an image.

framing Act of composing a shot in a camcorder's viewfinder for desired content, angle and field of view.

freeze frame Single frame paused and displayed for an extended period during video playback; suspended motion perceived as still snapshot.

frequency Number of vibrations produced by a signal or sound, usually expressed as cycles per second, or hertz (Hz).

frequency response Measure of the range of frequencies a medium can respond to and reproduce. Good video response maintains picture detail; good audio response accommodates the broadest range, most exacting sound.

friction head Tripod mount type with strong spring that counterbalances camera weight, relying on friction to hold its position. More appropriate for still photography than movement-oriented videomaking. [See fluid head]

full-motion video A standard for video playback on a computer; refers to smooth-flowing, full-color video at 30 frames per second, regardless of the screen resolution.

gaffer Production crew technician responsible for placement and rigging of all lighting instruments.

gain Video amplification, signal strength. "Riding gain" means varying controls to achieve desired contrast levels.

GB (Gigabyte) Giga- is a prefix that means one billion, so a Gigabyte is 1,000,000,000 bytes. Most commonly used to measure hard disk space.

gel Colored material placed in front of a light source to alter its hue. Useful for special effects and correcting mismatches in lighting, as in scenes lit by both daylight and artificial light.

generation Relationship between a master video recording and a given copy of that master. A copy of a copy of the original master constitutes a second-generation duplication.

generation loss Degradation in picture and sound quality resulting from an analog duplication of original master video recording. Copying a copy and all successive duplication compounds generation loss. Digital transfers are free of generation loss.

genlock (generator locking device) Synchronizes two video sources, allowing part or all of their signals to be displayed together. Necessary for overlaying computer graphics with video, for example.

ghosting Undesirable faint double screen image caused by signal reflection or improperly balanced video circuitry. "Ringing" appears as repeated image edges.

giraffe A small boom that consists of a counterweighted arm supported by a tripod, usually on casters.

glitch Momentary picture disturbance.

grain Blanketed signal noise viewed as fuzziness, unsmooth images—attributable to lumination inadequacies.

grip Production crew stagehand responsible for handling equipment, props and scenery before, during and after production.

group master fader A volume control on an audio board that handles a subgroup of input channels before they are sent to the master fader.

handheld mike A microphone that a person holds to speak or sing into.

hard disk Common digital storage component in a computer.

HDMI High Definition Multimedia Interface. A connection type that combines high-definition video and multi-channel audio into a single cable.

HDTV (high-definition television) a television system standard affording greater resolution for sharper pictures and wide-screen viewing via specially designed TV equipment.

HDV High Definition Video. A videotape format that records 1080i or 720p using MPEG-2 compression video on DV tape.

head Electromagnetic component within camcorders and VCRs that records, receives and erases video and audio signals on magnetic tape.

headroom Space between the top of a subject's head and a monitor's upper-screen edge. Too much headroom makes the subject appear to fall out of the frame.

hi-fi (high fidelity) Generalized term defining audio quality approaching the limits of human hearing, pertinent to high-quality sound reproduction systems.

Hi8 (high-band 8 mm) Improved version of 8 mm videotape format characterized by higher luminance resolution for a sharper picture. Compact "conceptual equivalent" of Super-VHS. [See 8 mm]

high impedance A characteristic of microphones that have a great deal of opposition to the flow of alternating current through them and therefore must have short cables; they are less likely to be used in professional situations than low impedance microphones.

hiss Primary background signal interference in audio recording, result of circuit noise from a playback recorder's amplifiers or from a tape's residual magnetism.

horizontal resolution Specification denoting amount of discernable detail across a screen's width. Measured in pixels, the higher the number, the better the picture quality.

IEEE 1394 (Institute of Electrical and Electronics Engineers) Pronounced "eye-triple-E thirteen-ninety-four" the institute establishes standards and protocols for a wide range of computer and communications technologies, including IEEE 1394, which is a specification FireWire data transmission widely used in DV. Sony refers to the ports on its products with the proprietary term "i.LINK."

image enhancer Video signal processor that compensates for picture detail losses and distortion occurring in recording and playback. Exaggerates transitions between light and dark areas by enhancing high frequency region of video spectrum.

image sensor A video camera's image sensing element, either CCD (charge coupled device) or MOS (metal oxide semiconductor); converts light to electrical energy. [See CCD]

impedance Opposition to the flow of an audio signal in a microphone and its cable.

in-camera editing Assembling finished program "on the fly" as you videotape simply by activating and pausing camcorder's record function.

incident light That which emanates directly from a light source. Measured from the object it strikes to the source. [See reflected light]

indexing Ability of some VCRs to electronically mark specific points on videotape for future access, either during the recording process (VISS: VHS index search system) or as scenes are played back (VASS: VHS address search system).

input channel On an audio board, the control into which a microphone, tape recorder or other source is plugged.

insert edit Recording video and/or audio on tape over a portion of existing footage without disturbing what precedes and follows. Must replace recording of same length.

interlace To split a TV picture into two fields of odd and even lines. Under the interlaced method, every other line is scanned during the first pass, then the remaining lines are scanned in the second pass. All analog TV formats (NTSC, PAL and SECAM) use interlaced video.

interlaced video Process of scanning frames in two passes, each painting every other line on the screen, with scan lines alternately displayed in even and odd fields. NTSC video is interlaced; most computers produce a noninterlaced video signal. [See noninterlaced video]

iris Camcorder's lens opening or aperture, regulates amount of light entering camera. Diameter is measured in f-stops. [See f-stop]

jack Any female socket or receptacle, usually on the backside of video and audio equipment; accepts plug for circuit connection.

jitter Video image aberration seen as slight, fast, vertical or horizontal shifting of a picture or portion of one.

jog/shuttle Manual control on some VCRs, facilitates viewing and editing precision and convenience. Jog ring moves tape short distances to show a frame at a time; shuttle dial transports tape forward or reverse more rapidly for faster scanning.

jump cut Unnatural, abrupt switch between shots identical in subject but slightly different in screen location, so the subject appears to jump from one screen location to another. Can be remedied with a cutaway or shot from a different angle.

Kelvin Temperature scale used to define the color of a light source; abbreviated as "K." [See color temperature]

key light Principal illumination source on a subject or scene. Normally positioned slightly off-center and angled to provide shadow detail. (See backlight, fill light, three-point lighting)

keyframe A complete image, used as a reference for subsequent images. To keep the data rate low, other frames only have data for the parts of the picture that change.

keystoning Perspective distortion from a flat object being shot by a camera at other than a perpendicular angle. Nearer portion of object appears larger than farther apart.

Killer app An application of such technological importance and wide acceptance that it surpasses (i.e., kills) its competitors.

lag Camera pickup's retention of an image after the camera has been moved, most common under low light levels. Comet tailing is a form of lag.

lapel mike A small mike often clipped inside clothing or on a tie or lapel.

lavalier A small mike that can be worn around the neck on a cord.

LCD (Liquid Crystal Display) Commonly used in digital watches, camcorder viewscreens and laptop computer screens, LCD panels are light-weight and low-power display devices.

LiIon (Lithium Ion) The most common battery type among new camcorders. More expensive, but has a higher capacity and fewer memory rechanging problems.

linear editing Tape-based VCR-to-VCR editing. Called linear because scenes are recorded in chronological order on the tape.

lip sync Proper synchronization of video with audio—lip movement with audible speech.

long shot (LS) Camera view of a subject or scene from a distance, showing a broad perspective.

LP (long play) Middle tape speed of a VHS VCR, accommodating four-hour recordings. [See EP, SP]

LTC (longitudinal time code) Frame identification numbers encoded as audio signals and recorded lengthwise on the edge of a tape, typically on a linear audio track of VHS or S-VHS tape. [See time code, VITC]

luminance Black-and-white portion of video signal, carries brightness information representing picture contrast, light and dark qualities; frequently abbreviated as "Y."

lux A metric unit of illumination equal to the light of a candle falling on a surface of one square meter. One lux equals 0.0929 foot-candle.

macro Lens capable of extreme closeup focusing, useful for intimate views of small subjects.

master Original recorded videotape footage; "edited master" implies original tape in its edited form.

master fader The audio volume control that is located after all the input channel controls and after the submaster controls.

matched dissolve Dissolve from one image to another that's similar in appearance or shot size.

media player A program that plays back audio or video. Examples include Microsoft Windows Media Player, Apple's QuickTime Player and RealPlayer.

medium shot (MS) Defines any camera perspective between long shot and closeup, viewing the subjects from a medium distance.

memory effect Power-loss phenomenon alleged of NiCad—camcorder batteries, attributed to precisely repetitive partial discharge followed by complete recharge, or long-term overcharge. Considered a misnomer for "voltage depression" and "cell imbalance."

MIDI (musical instrument digital interface) System of communication between digital electronic instruments allowing synchronization and distribution of musical information.

mike (also "mic") short for microphone.

mix [1: audio] Combining sound sources to achieve a desired program balance. Finished output may be mono, stereo or surround. [2: video] Combining video signals from two or more sources.

model release Agreement to be signed by anyone appearing in a video work, protecting videomaker from right of privacy lawsuit. Specifies event, date, compensation provisions, and rights being waived.

monitor [1: video] Television set without receiving circuitry, wired to camcorder or VCR for display of live or recorded video signals. Most standard TVs have dual-function capability as monitor and receiver. [See receiver] [2: audio] Synonymous with speaker.

monopod One-legged camera support. [See tripod]

montage A sequence of shots assembled in juxtaposition to each other to communicate a particular idea or mood. Often bridged with cross-fades and set to music.

mosaic Electronic special effect whereby individual pixels comprising an image are blown up into larger blocks—a kind of checkerboard effect.

MPEG (MPEG-1) A video compression standard set by the Moving Picture Experts Group. It involves changing only those elements of a video image that actually change from frame to frame and leaving everything else in the image the same.

MPEG-2 The highest quality digital video compression currently available. MPEG-2 is less blocky than MPEG-1 and is used in DVDs and DBS satellite TV systems.

MPEG-4 A recent data compression format that can get better quality out of a given amount of bandwidth. MPEG-4 can compress a feature film onto a CD-ROM disc with VHS quality.

natural light Planetary illumination—from the sun, the moon, stars—whether indoors or out. Has higher color temperature than artificial light, and thus more bluish qualities. [See artificial light, color temperature]

neutral-density filter (ND) Mounted at front of camcorder lens, reduces light intensity without affecting its color qualities. [See filter]

NiCad (nickel cadmium) Abbreviation coined and popularized by SAFT America for lightweight camcorder battery type designed to maintain power longer than traditional lead-acid batteries. Rare among new camcorders, supplanted by Li-Ion and NiMH.

NiMH (nickel metal hydride) Battery technology similar to NiCad, but more environmentally friendly, with higher capacity and fewer memory recharging problems.

NLE (nonlinear editor/editing) Hard drive-based editing system defined by its ability to randomly access and insert video in any order at any time. This is in contrast to linear, tape-to-tape editing which requires rewinding and fast forwarding to access material.

noise Unwanted sound or static in an audio signal or unwanted electronic disturbance of snow in the video signal.

noninterlaced video Process of scanning complete frames in one pass, painting every line on the screen, yielding higher picture quality than that of interlaced video. Most computers produce a noninterlaced video signal; NTSC is interlaced. AKA progressive scan.

nonlinear editing Digital random access editing that uses a hard drive instead of tape to store video. Random access allows easy arrangement of scenes in any order. It also eliminates the need for rewinding and allows for multiple dubs without generation loss.

nonsynchronous sound Audio without precisely matching visuals. Usually recorded separately, includes wild sound, sound effects, or music incorporated in post-production. [See synchronous sound]

nose room The distance between the subject and the edge of the frame in the direction the subject is looking. Also called "look room."

NTSC (National Television Standards Committee) U.S. television broadcasting specifications. NTSC refers to all video systems conforming to this 525-line 59.94-field-per-second signal standard. [See PAL, SECAM]

off-line Until recently, the low quality of computer video images limits the DTV computer to "off-line" work. That is, making the edit-point decisions (EDL) for use in a later "on-line" session, using the original tapes to assemble the edit master. Today's editing systems are capable of on-line quality output by themsleves, relegating this term to history.

OIS (optical image stabilization) A process of limiting shaky camera shots with mechanical movement of the optical system within a camcorder. [See EIS]

omnidirectional A microphone that picks up sound from all directions.

outtake Footage not to be included in final production.

over-the-shoulder shot View of the primary subject with the back of another person's shoulder and head in the foreground. Often used in interview situations.

PAL (phase alternate line) 625-linc 50-field-per-second television signal standard used in Europe and South America. Incompatible with NTSC. [See NTSC, SECAM]

pan Horizontal camera pivot, right to left or left to right, from a stationary position.

PCM (pulse code modulation) A popular method of encoding digital audio. [See AFM]

pedestal A camera move vertically lowering or raising the camcorder, approaching either the floor or ceiling, while keeping the camera level.

phone plug Sturdy male connector compatible with audio accessories, particularly for insertion of microphone and headphone cables. Frequently referred to by its sizes, usually 1/4-inch and 1/8-inch. Not to be confused with phono plug.

phono plug (RCA) Shrouded male connector used for audio and video connections. Frequently referred to as RCA plugs, they only come in one size. Not to be confused with phone plugs.

pickup [1] A video camera's image sensing element, either CCD (charge coupled device) or MOS (metal oxide semiconductor); converts light to electrical energy. [See CCD] [2] A microphone's sound reception.

pickup pattern Defines a microphone's response to sounds arriving from various directions or angles. [See omnidirectional, unidirectional]

PiP (picture in picture, p-in-p, pix in pix) Image from a second video source inset on a screen's main picture, the big and small pictures usually being interchangeable.

playback Videotaped material viewed and heard as recorded, facilitated by camcorder or VCR.

playback VCR Playback source of raw video footage (master or workprint) in basic player/recorder editing setup. [See recording VCR]

point-of-view shot (POV) Shot perspective whereby the video camera assumes a subject's view and thus viewers see what the subject sees.

polarizing filter Mounted at the front of the camcorder lens, thwarts undesirable glare and reflections. [See filter]

post-production (post) Any video production activity following initial recording. Typically involves editing, addition of background music, voiceover, sound effects, titles and/or various electronic visual effects. Results in completed production.

posterization Electronic special effect transforming a normal video image into a collage of flattened single-colored areas, without gradations of color and brightness.

POV (point of view) The apparent position of the observer in a shoot that defines the camera's position.

pre-roll [1] Slight backing-up function of camcorders and VCRs when preparing for linear tape-to-tape editing; ensures smooth, uninterrupted transitions between scenes.

preamp An electronic device that magnifies the low signal output of microphones and other transducers before the signal is sent to a mixing board or to other amplifiers.

proc amp (processing amplifier) Video image processor that boosts video signal's luminance, chroma, and sync components to correct such problems as low light, weak color or wrong tint.

progressive scan A method of displaying the horizontal video lines in computer displays and digital TV broadcasts. Each horizontal line is displayed in sequence (1, 2, 3, etc.), until the screen is filled; as opposed to interlaced (e.g., first fields of odd-numbered lines, then fields of even-numbered lines).

props Short for "properties," objects used either in decorating a set (set props) or by talent (hand props).

PZM (pressure zone microphone) Small, sensitive condenser mike, usually attached to a metal backing plate. Senses air pressure changes in the tiny gap between mike element and plate. Trademark of Crown International. Generically, "boundary microphone" is preferred.

QuickTime Computer system software that defines a format for video and audio data, so different applications can open and play synchronized sound and movie files.

rack focus Shifting focus between subjects in the background and foreground so a viewer's attention moves from subject to subject as the focus shifts.

RAID Acronym for Redundant Array of Independent Disks. Hard drives installed in multiples that are accessed as a single volume. RAID 0 systems (stripe sets) are common in higher-end video editing systems, as they allow for faster access to video. Other RAID configurations are used in some servers to keep important data accessible and protected, allowing access to data even after one of the hard drives crash.

RAM (Random Access Memory) The short-term memory of a computer which temporarily holds information while your computer is on. Distinct from storage, which is more permanent and is held on hard disks or some other media, such as CD-ROM.

raw footage Pre-edited footage, usually direct from the camcorder.

RCA plug (Recording Corporation of America) A popular cable connector for home audio as well as video components. The standard connection for direct audio/video inputs and outputs.

RCTC (rewritable consumer time code) The time-code format used with 8 mm and Hi8 formats.

reaction shot A cutaway to someone showing his or her facial response to the primary action or subject.

real time Occurring immediately, without delay for rendering. If a transition occurs in real time, there is no waiting; the computer creates the effect or transition on the fly, showing it immediately. Real-time previewing is different from real-time rendering.

real-time counter Tallying device that accounts for videotape playing/recording by measure of hours, minutes and seconds.

RealNetworks Developed the leading streaming technology for transmitting live video over the Internet using a variety of data compression techniques and works with IP and IP Multicast connections.

RealPlayer A program developed by RealNetworks to play live and on-demand RealAudio and RealVideo files.

RealVideo A streaming technology developed by RealNetworks for transmitting live video over the Internet. RealVideo uses a variety of data compression algorithms.

recording VCR Recipient of raw video feed (master or workprint) and recorder of edited videotape in basic player/recorder editing setup. [See playback VCR]

reflected light That which bounces off the illuminated subject. Light redirected by a reflector. [See incident light]

reflector Lighting accessory helpful for bouncing light onto a subject. Often made of lightweight reflective material.

remote Video shoot performed on location, outside of a controlled studio environment.

render The processing a computer undertakes when creating an applied effect, transition or composite.

render time The time it takes an editing computer to composite source elements and commands into a single video file so the sequence, including titles and transition effects, can play in full motion.

resolution Amount of picture detail reproduced by a video system, influenced by a camera's pickup, lens, internal optics, recording medium and playback monitor. The more detail, the sharper and better defined the picture. [See horizontal resolution]

Rewritable Consumer (RC) Time code sent through Control-L interface permitting extremely accurate edits. Each frame is assigned a unique address expressed in hours:minutes:seconds:frames.

RF (radio frequency) Combination of audio and video signals coded as a channel number, necessary for television broadcasts as well as some closed-circuit distribution.

RF converter Device that converts audio and video signals into a combined RF signal suitable for reception by a standard TV.

RGB (red, green, blue) Video signal transmission system that differentiates and processes all color information in separate red, green and blue components—the primary color of light—for optimum image quality. Also defines type of color monitor.

ringing Undesirable faint double screen image caused by signal reflection or improperly balanced video circuitry. "Ringing" appears as repeated image edges.

RM (Real Media) A popular file format used for streaming video over the Internet.

roll Text or graphics, usually credits, that move up or down the screen, typically from bottom to top.

rough cut Preliminary edit of footage in the approximate sequence, length and content of a finished program.

rule of thirds Composition theory based on dividing the screen into thirds vertically and horizontally and the placement of the main subject along those lines.

S-video Also known as Y/C video, signal type employed with Hi8 and S-VHS video formats. Transmits luminance (Y) and chrominance (C) portions separately via multiple wires (pins), thereby avoiding the NTSC encoding process and its inevitable picture-quality degradation.

S/N Ratio Relationship between signal strength and a medium's inherent noise. Video S/N indicates how grainy or snowy a picture will be, plus color accuracy; audio S/N specifies amount of background tape hiss present with low- or no-volume recordings.

safe title area The recommended area that will produce legible titles on most TV screens; 80 percent of the visible area, measured from the center.

scan converter Device that changes scan rate of a video signal, possibly converting it from noninterlaced to interlaced mode. Allows computer graphics to be displayed on a standard video screen.

scan line Result of television's swift scanning process which sweeps out a series of horizontal lines from left to right, then down a bit and left to right again. Complete NTSC picture consists of 525 scan lines per frame.

scan rate Number of times a screen is "redrawn" per second. Computer displays operate at different scan rates than standard video.

scene In the language of moving images, a sequence of related shots usually constituting action in one particular location. [See shot]

scrim Lighting accessory made of wire mesh. Lessens intensity of light source without softening it. Half scrims and graduated scrims reduce illumination in more specific areas.

script Text specifying content of a production or performance, used as a guide. May include character and setting profiles, production directives (audio, lighting, scenery, camera moves), as well as dialogue to be recited by talent. [See storyboard]

SECAM (sequential color and memory) 625-line 25-frame-per-second television signal standard used in France and the Soviet Republic. Incompatible with NTSC; PAL and SECAM are partially compatible. [See NTSC, PAL]

SEG (special effects generator) Permits video signal mixing from two or more sources—cameras, time-base correctors and character generators—for dissolves, wipes and other transition effects.

selective focus Adjusting focus to emphasize desired subject(s) in a shot. Selected area maintains clarity, image sharpness while remainder of image blurs. Useful for directing viewers' attention.

sepia Brassy antique color effect characteristic of old photographs.

shooting ratio Amount of raw footage recorded relative to the amount used in edited, finished program.

shot Intentional, isolated camera views, which collectively comprise a scene. [See scene]

shotgun A highly directional microphone used for picking up sounds from a distance.

signal-to-noise ratio (S/N) Relationship between signal strength and a medium's inherent noise. Video S/N indicates how grainy or snowy a picture will be, plus its color accuracy; audio S/N specifies amount of background tape hiss present with low- or no-volume recordings. Higher figures represent a cleaner signal. Usually cited in decibels (dB).

Skylight (1A) or haze (UV) filter Mounted at front of camcorder lens, virtually clear glass absorbs ultraviolet light. Also excellent as constant lens protector. [See filter]

SMPTE Time-code standard which addresses every frame on a videotape with a unique number (in hours, minutes, seconds, frames) to aid logging and editing. Format used for film, video and audio. Named for the Society of Motion Picture and Television Engineers, which sanctions standards for recording systems in North America.

snake A connector box that contains a large number of microphone input receptacles.

snoot Open-ended cylindrical funnel mounted on a light source to project a narrow, concentrated circle of illumination.

snow Electronic picture interference; resembles scattered snow on the television screen. Synonymous with chroma and luma noise.

solarization Electronic special effect distorting a video image's original colors, emphasizing some and de-emphasizing others for a "paint brush" effect. [See DVE]

sound bite Any short recorded audio segment for use in an edited program—usually a highlight taken from an interview.

sound effects Contrived audio, usually prerecorded, incorporated with a video soundtrack to resemble a real occurrence. Blowing on a microphone, for example, might simulate wind to accompany hurricane images.

soundtrack The audio portion of a video recording, often multifaceted with natural sound, voiceovers, background music, sound effects, etc.

SP (standard play) Fastest tape speed of a VHS VCR, accommodating two-hour recordings. [See EP, LP]

special effects F/X. Tricks and illusions—electronic or on camera—employed in film and video to define, distort, or defy reality.

special effects generator (SEG) Video signal processor with vast, but varying, image manipulation capabilities involving patterns and placement as well as color and texture: mixing, multiplying, shrinking, strobing, wiping, dissolving, flipping, colorizing, etc.

spotlight Radiates a well-defined directional beam of light, casting hard, distinct shadows. Best used to focus illumination on individual subjects, whereas floodlights blanket broader areas.

stabilizer Video signal processor used primarily for tape dubbing to eliminate picture jump and jitter, maintain stability.

star Filter mounted at front of camcorder lens, gives videotaped light sources a starburst effect. Generally available in four-, six-, and eight-point patterns. [See filter]

stereo Sound emanating from two isolated sources, intended to simulate pattern of natural human hearing.

stock shot Common footage—city traffic, a rainbow—conveniently accessed as needed. Similar to a "photo file" in the photography profession.

storyboard Series of cartoon-like sketches illustrating key visual stages (shots, scenes) of planned production, accompanied by corresponding audio information. [See script]

Streaming Playing sound or video in real time as it is downloaded over the Internet as opposed to storing it in a local file first. Avoids download delay.

strobe Digital variation of fixed-speed slow motion, with image action broken down into a series of still frames updated and replaced with new ones at rapid speed.

Super VHS (S-VHS, S-VHS-C) Improved version of VHS and VHS-C videotape formats, characterized by separate carriers of chrominance and luminance information, yielding a sharper picture. [See VHS, VHS-C]

superimposition (super) Titles, video or graphics appearing over an existing video picture, partially or completely hiding areas they cover.

sweetening Post-production process of adding music and sound effects or otherwise enhancing the existing audio with filters and effects.

swish pan Extremely rapid camera movement from left to right or right to left, appearing as image blur. Two such pans in the same direction—one moving from, the other moving to, a stationary shot—edited together can effectively convey passage of time or change of location.

switcher Simplified SEG, permits video signal mixing from two or more sources—cameras, time base correctors, character generators—for dissolves, wipes and other clean transition effects.

sync (synchronization) Horizontal and vertical timing signals or electronic pulses—component of composite signal, supplied separately in RGB systems. Aligns video origination (live camera, videotape) and reproduction (monitor or receiver) sources.

synchronous sound Audio recorded with images. When the mouth moves, the words come out.

talent Generic term for the people assuming on-screen roles in a videotaping.

tally light Automatic indicators (usually red) on a camera's front and within its viewfinder that signal recording in progress—seen by both camera subject(s) and operator.

telecine converter Imaging device used in conjunction with a movie projector and camcorder to transfer film images to videotape.

telephoto Camera lens with long focal length and narrow horizontal field of view. Opposite of wide-angle, captures magnified, close-up images from a considerable distance.

teleprompter (prompter) Mechanical device that projects and advances text on mirror directly in front of camera's lens, allowing talent to read their lines while appearing to maintain eye contact with viewers.

test pattern Any of various combinations of converging lines, alignment marks, and gray scales appearing on screen to aid in video equipment adjustment for picture alignment, registration, and contrast. Often viewed on broadcast television in off-air hours. [See color bars]

three-point lighting Basic lighting approach employing key, fill and backlights to illuminate subject with sense of depth and texture. Strategic placement imitates natural outdoor lighting environment, avoids flat lighting. [See backlight, fill light, key light]

three-quarter-inch (U-matic) An analog video format utilizing 3/4" tape. Very popular in professional, industrial and broadcast environments in the past, though beginning to be supplanted by digital formats.

three-shot Camera view including three subjects, generally applicable to interview situations.

three-to-one rule A microphone placement principle that states if two mikes must be side by side, there should be three times the distance between them that there is between the mikes and the people using them.

tilt Vertical camcorder rotation (up and down) from a single axis, as on a tripod.

time base corrector (TBC) Electronic device that corrects timing inconsistencies in a videotape recorder's playback, stabilizing the image for optimum quality. Also synchronizes video sources, allowing image mixing. [See sync]

time code Synchronization system, like a clock recorded on your videotape, assigning a corresponding hours, minutes, seconds and frame-number designation to each frame. Expedites indexing convenience and editing precision. [See SMPTE]

time-lapse recording Periodically videotaping a minimal number of frames over long durations of actual time. Upon playback, slow processes such as a flower blooming may be viewed in rapid motion.

timeline editing A computer-based method of editing, in which bars proportional to the length of the clip represent video and audio clips are represented on a computer screen.

titling Process or result of incorporating on-screen text as credits, captions or any other alphanumeric communication to video viewers.

tracking Lateral camcorder movement that travels with a moving subject. The camcorder should maintain a regulated distance from the subject.

transcode To convert analog video to a digital format, or vice versa.

tripod Three-legged camera mount offering stability and camera placement/movement consistency. Most are lightweight, used for remote recording. [See monopod]

turnkey DVD authoring system Any computer system designed to author (and usually burn) DVDs right out of the box, needing only trivial changes in its configuration.

turnkey nonlinear editing system Any computer system designed to edit video right out of the box, needing only trivial changes in its configuration.

turnkey system Any computer system which is considered ready-to-use right out of the box, needing only trivial changes in its configuration.

two-shot A camera view including two subjects, generally applicable to interview situations.

U-matic An analog video format utilizing 3/4" tape. Very popular in professional, industrial and broadcast environments in the past, though beginning to be supplanted by digital formats.

umbrella Lighting accessory available in various sizes usually made of textured gold or silver fabric. Facilitates soft, shadowless illumination by reflecting light onto a scene.

unbalanced line Audio cables that have two wires: one for positive and one for both negative and ground.

unidirectional Highly selective microphone pickup pattern, rejects sound coming from behind while absorbing that from in front. [See bidirectional, omnidirectional]

variable bit rate (VBR) A way of coding video to maximize image quality over a connection's available bandwidth, usually provided by more recent codecs.

VCR (videocassette recorder) Multi-function machine intended primarily for recording and playback of videotape stored in cassettes.

vectorscope Electronic testing device that measures a video signal's chrominance performance, plotting qualities in a compass-like graphic display.

vertical interval time code (VITC) Synchronization signals recorded as an invisible component of the video signal, accessed for editing precision. [See time code]

VHS (video home system) Predominant half-inch videotape format developed by Matsushita and licensed by JVC.

VHS-C (VHS compact) Scaled-down version of VHS using miniature cassettes compatible with full-size VHS equipment through use of adapter. [See Super VHS]

video card The PC card that controls the computer's monitor display. Don't confuse the computer's video (VGA, SVGA, Mac monitor and so on) which is non interlaced, with NTSC video. PC cards for DTV are also called capture, overlay or compression cards. Most do not generate NTSC video output.

video prompter A mechanical device that projects and advances text on a mirror directly in front of a camera lens, allowing talent to read lines while appearing to maintain eye contact with viewers.

videocassette recorder (VCR) Multi-function machine intended primarily for recording and playback of videotape stored in cassettes.

vignette Visual special effect whereby viewers see images through a perceived keyhole, heart shape, diamond, etc. In low-budget form, vignettes are achieved by aiming a camera through a cutout of a desired vignette.

vignetting Undesirable darkening at the corners of a picture, as if viewer's peering through a telescope, due to improper matching of lens to camera—pickup's scope exceeds lens size.

VITC (vertical interval time code) Synchronization signal recorded as an invisible component of the video signal, accessed for editing precision. [See LTC]

VOD Abbreviation for Video on Demand. Usually only heard in the context of delivering full-frame, full-motion video to a television; since most video on the Internet is provided on-demand.

voiceover (VO) Audio from an unseen narrator accompanying video, heard above background sound or music. Typically applied to edited visuals during post-production.

waveform monitor Specialized oscilloscope testing device providing a graphic display of a video signal's strength. Plus, like a sophisticated light meter, aids in precise setting of picture's maximum brightness level for optimum contrast.

WebCam Abbreviation for Web Camera. A small camera connected to a computer, usually through a USB port. WebCams usually produce small, progressive-scanned images.

whip pan (swish pan) Extremely rapid camera movement from left to right or right to left, appearing as an image blur. Two such pans in the same direction, edited together—one moving from, the other moving to, a stationary shot—can effectively convey the passage of time or a change of location.

white balance Electronic adjustment of camcorder to retain truest colors of recorded image. Activated in camcorder prior to recording, proper setting established by aiming at white object.

wide-angle Camcorder lens with short focal length and broad horizontal field of view. Opposite of telephoto, supports viewer perspective and tends to reinforce perception of depth.

wild sound Nonsynchronous audio recorded independent of picture i.e., rain on roof, five o'clock whistle—often captured with separate audio recorder. [See nonsynchronous sound]

windscreen Sponge-like microphone shield, thwarts undesirable noise from wind and rapid mike movement.

wipe Transition from one shot to another, where a moving line or pattern reveals the new shot. In it's simplest form it simulates a window shade being drawn.

wireless mike A microphone with a self-contained, built-in miniature FM transmitter that can send the audio signal several hundred feet, eliminating the need for mike cables.

workprint Copy of a master videotape used for edit planning and rough cut without excessively wearing or otherwise jeopardizing safekeeping of original material. Also called "working master."

wow and flutter Sound distortions consisting of a slow rise and fall of pitch, caused by speed variations in audio/video playback system.

XLR (ground-left-right) Three-pin plug for three-conductor "balanced" audio cable, employed with high-quality microphones, mixers and other audio equipment.

Y Symbol for luminance, or brightness, portion of a video signal; the complete color video signal consists of R, G, B and Y.

Y/C Video signal type (also known as S-video) employed with Hi8 and S-VHS video formats and analog output-on digital camcorders. Transmits luminance (Y) and chrominance (C) portions separately via multiple wires, thereby avoiding picture quality degradation.

YUV (y = luminance, u = B − Y or blue and v = R − Y or red) Video signal used to compose a component NTSC or PAL signal. [See RGB]

zoom Variance of focal length, bringing subject into and out of close-up range. Lens capability permits change from wide-angle to telephoto, or vice versa, in one continuous move. "Zoom in" and "zoom out" are common terms.

zoom ratio Range of a lens' focal length, from most "zoomed in" field of view to most "zoomed out." Expressed as ratio: 6:1, for example, implies that the same lens from the same distance can make the same image appear six-times closer. [See focal length, zoom]

Contributing Authors

Loren Alldrin is a freelance video and music producer.

Scott Anderson is the author of animation software and a book about digital special effects.

Pat Bailey is a digital video technical support analyst and freelance writer.

Gene Bjerke is a professional scriptwriter and author of the book *Writing for Video*.

Mark Steven Bosko is a freelance writer and an independent video and film producer.

Kyle Cassidy is a visual artist who writes extensively about technology.

Alessia Cowee is a freelance writer, editor and mother of three.

Bill Davis writes, shoots, edits and does voiceover work for a variety of corporate and industrial clients.

Sofia Davis is a leased access and public access producer.

Edward B. Driscoll, Jr. is a freelance journalist covering home theater and the media.

Armand Ensanian is a professional video producer, photographer and former columnist for *Video Review*.

Bill Fisher is a documentary video producer.

Michael Fitzer is an Emmy award-winning commercial and documentary writer/producer.

D. Eric Franks is a technical writer and video podcast personality.

Charles Fulton is *Videomaker*'s Associate Editor.

Michael Hammond is a 25-year communications veteran, teaching electronic media and producing independent video.

Bill Harrington is a former production manager at a television station.

Michael J. Kelley is a freelance media production consultant.

Robert J. Kerr is a consultant, teacher and writer in the video industry.

Larry Lemm is a long-time technology writer.

Michael Loehr is a foreign documentarian.

Janis Lonnquist is a writer and producer.

Garret C. Maynard is a video and film-maker and guest lecturer.

Joe McCleskey is a multimedia producer and freelance writer.

Carolyn Miller is a scriptwriter and journalist specializing in new media projects.

Robert G. Nulph, Ph.D. is an Assistant Professor of Communication Studies and an independent video/film producer/director.

Jennifer O'Rourke is *Videomaker*'s Managing Editor.

Brian Peterson is a video production consultant, trainer and lecturer.

Brian Pogue is a news photographer/editor at a television station.

Stray Wynn Ponder is a writer and producer of television commercials and industrial training videos.

Hal Robertson is a digital media producer and technology consultant.

William Ronat is the owner of a video production company.

Bill Rood is an engineer at a television station.

Tad Rose is a writer and independent producer.

Marshal M. Rosenthal is a technology/entertainment writer whose experience in the industry spans 20+ years.

Jim Stinson is the author of *Video: Digital Communication and Production*.

Paul M. J. Suchecki writes for network TV and shoots and produces documentaries.

John K. Waters is a freelance scriptwriter and editor.

Dave Welton is a community college instructor and freelance writer.

Randal K. West is the Vice President/Creative Director for a DRTV full service advertising agency.

Bernard Wilkie designed special effects for the BBC for over 25 years.

James Williams is an independent film-maker and video journalist.

Roger B. Wyatt is a partner in a new media company.

Index